D0498126

RENEWALS 691-4574
DATE DUE

APR 07			

WITHDRAWN
UTSA Libraries

THE
CENTENARY EDITION
OF THE WORKS OF
NATHANIEL HAWTHORNE

Volume II

THE HOUSE OF THE
SEVEN GABLES

EDITORS

WILLIAM CHARVAT
ROY HARVEY PEARCE   *General Editors*
CLAUDE M. SIMPSON

FREDSON BOWERS   *Textual Editor*
MATTHEW J. BRUCCOLI   *Associate Textual Editor*
L. NEAL SMITH   *Assistant Textual Editor*

A PUBLICATION OF
THE OHIO STATE CENTER FOR TEXTUAL STUDIES

NATHANIEL HAWTHORNE

THE HOUSE OF THE SEVEN GABLES

Ohio State University Press

CENTER FOR EDITIONS OF
AMERICAN AUTHORS

AN APPROVED TEXT

MODERN LANGUAGE
ASSOCIATION OF AMERICA

®

Standard Book Number: 8142–0060–5
Copyright © 1965 by the Ohio State University Press
All Rights Reserved
Printed in the United States of America
Second Printing, 1971

LIBRARY
University of Texas
At San Antonio

ACKNOWLEDGMENTS

THE EDITORS of the Centenary Hawthorne are grateful for the generous assistance given by librarians, scholars, and bibliophiles. We are indebted to the late William A. Jackson, William H. Bond, and Miss Carolyn Jakeman, Houghton Library, Harvard University; John Cook Wyllie, William H. Runge, and the late Louise Savage, Alderman Library, University of Virginia; Herbert Cahoon, Pierpont Morgan Library; John D. Gordan, Berg Collection, and Robert W. Hill, Manuscript Division, New York Public Library; Marcus A. McCorison, American Antiquarian Society; Roger E. Stoddard, Brown University Library; Charles Mann, Pennsylvania State University Library; Donald Gallup, Yale University Library; Kermit Cudd and Miss Jane W. Gatliff, Ohio State University Libraries; Rollo Silver, Simmons College; W. S. Tryon, Boston University; Norman Holmes Pearson, Yale University; John S. Van E. Kohn, Seven Gables Bookshop; Robert Metzdorf, New York City; Peter Keisogloff, Cleveland; and C. Waller Barrett, Charlottesville, Virginia. Special acknowledgment is made for the work of Mrs. F. Russell Hart, Charlottesville, and Edward Pfeffer, Columbus. We are particularly indebted to Hyman W. Kritzer, Ohio State University Libraries, and C. E. Frazer Clark, Jr., Detroit.

We thank the Houghton Library, Harvard University, for permission to transcribe and edit from the manuscript of *The House of the Seven Gables*.

THE EDITORS

CONTENTS

• ix •

CONTENTS

ILLUSTRATIONS

Portrait of Nathaniel Hawthorne, painted in 1852 by George P. A. Healey, now in possession of the New Hampshire Historical Society, Concord.
(facing page xv)

Folio 65 of the printer's-copy holograph manuscript of *The House of the Seven Gables* in the Houghton Library of Harvard University (MS Am 121.26).
(facing page xxix)

THE HOUSE OF THE
SEVEN GABLES

— Bettmann Archive

NATHANIEL HAWTHORNE

FROM A PORTRAIT PAINTED IN 1852 BY GEORGE P. A. HEALEY,
NOW IN POSSESSION OF THE NEW HAMPSHIRE HISTORICAL SOCIETY

INTRODUCTION TO
THE HOUSE OF THE SEVEN GABLES

B Y SEPTEMBER, 1850, less than six months after the publication of *The Scarlet Letter,* Hawthorne had begun writing *The House of the Seven Gables.* The prospect for a career as a novelist seemed promising: five thousand copies of *The Scarlet Letter* had been printed, and the first stereotyped edition was on the way. His reputation was so solidly established that he could write with a sense of security, and he was developing the professional attitude which enabled him to say, about a year later, "As long as people will buy, I shall keep at work, and I find that my facility for labor increases with the demand for it."[1] His publishers had national prestige, and were ready to put their imprint on anything he wrote and to reprint his earlier works. " . . . I intend this fall," James T. Fields wrote him that summer, "to sell a good many thousand for you of whatever you choose to give the public."[2] He had moved permanently away from

[1] July 22, 1851, to Horatio Bridge, in the latter's *Personal Recollections of Nathaniel Hawthorne* (New York, 1893), p. 127. Compare his statement to Bridge after he had finished *The Scarlet Letter*: "The fact is, I have a natural abhorrence of pen and ink, and nothing short of absolute necessity ever drives me to them" (February 4, 1850. *Ibid.,* p. 111).

[2] August 20, 1850, MS, Berg Collection, New York Public Library. As Fields's confidence in Hawthorne's future increased, he resorted to machine imagery to express it: "We intend to push yr. books a-la-Steam Engine . . . " (January 14, 1851, MS, Berg Collection, New York Public Library). "We shall apply the publishing steam to this new volume with the confident assurance that it will run like a locomotive" (January 30, 1851, MS, Berg Collection, New York Public Library).

Salem, and his bitter memories of it faded after he settled in Lenox in western Massachusetts, where he enjoyed the summer visits of writers, editors, and publishers. On August 5 he met Melville, who was writing *Moby-Dick* in a house not far away, and who was soon to express his faith in Hawthorne's genius in a series of famous letters to him. In short, he was pursuing what he defined as the "only sensible ends of literature . . . first, the pleasurable toil of writing; second, the gratification of one's family and friends; and, lastly, the solid cash."[3]

Yet his problems as a professional writer were to continue. The cash he was receiving was solid enough, but insufficient: he must keep on producing. The modest success of *The Scarlet Letter* was gratifying, but he had been troubled by the lack of "cheering light" in the story, and was sure that its popularity was due in large part to the Custom-House sketch. He and his critics were aware that two of his talents had been separated in that work. All his humor and charm and sense of the contemporary were in the sketch; all his gloomy power and his sense of the tragic in history were in the story. This split had been evident in his tales, most of which tended to be either light and intimate sketches, or dark and brooding dramas. Those, like "My Kinsman, Major Molineux," in which he had been able to combine comedy and power, were few.

For his new book he conceived a subject and found a tone, which, he thought, suited his talents far better than *The Scarlet Letter*. It was, he confided to E. A. Duyckinck, "a more natural and healthy product of my mind, and [I] felt less reluctance in publishing it."[4] It was also a work "more characteristic of my mind, and more proper and natural for me to write, than 'The Scarlet Letter'. . . . "[5]

[3] March 15, 1851, to Bridge. Bridge, *op. cit.*, p. 125.
[4] April 27, 1851, MS, Duyckinck Collection, New York Public Library.
[5] July 22, 1851, to Bridge. Bridge, *op. cit.*, p. 126.

His confidence and his financial need were reflected in the speed with which he wrote most of the book. He must have been well along with it by August 20, for on that date Fields asked when Hawthorne would let him begin printing "the new story."[6] Hawthorne replied, " . . . I religiously seclude myself, every morning. . . . But the summer is not my natural season for work. . . . However, I make some little progress; and . . . I should not much wonder if I were to be ready by November. If not, it can't be helped. I must not pull up my cabbage by the roots, by way of hastening its growth."[7] Fields again pressed for permission to set up "the 1st part of it & to proceed to the other when it is ready," and hoped for completion by December 1.[8] Hawthorne allowed him to announce the book,[9] but he did not want a repetition of his experience with *The Scarlet Letter*: no part of *The House of the Seven Gables* was sent to the printer until the whole was completed. By October 1, however, he was so far along with it that he was able to estimate (fairly closely, it turned out) the number of pages that would be devoted to the historical parts of the story. Hawthorne calculated that only "thirty or forty pages" would deal with the past; in the first edition about forty-seven pages may be so described.[10] A month later he had slowed down, and confessed to Fields that "the book requires more care and thought than the 'Scarlet Letter';—also, I have to wait oftener for a

[6] MS, Berg Collection, New York Public Library.

[7] August 23, 1850, MS, Columbia University Library.

[8] October 3, 1850, MS, Berg Collection, New York Public Library. The firm advertised "A new Romance by the author of 'The Scarlet Letter'" in the *Literary World*, October 5, 12, 19, and 26.

[9] The book was not advertised by title in the *Literary World* until January 18, 1851. Fields had begun advertising it as "in press" before he received the manuscript: "We are having daily orders in answer to our advertisement of it as in Press" (Fields to Hawthorne, January 14, 1851, MS, Berg Collection, New York Public Library).

[10] To Fields, Hawthorne-Fields Letter Book, Houghton Library, Harvard University. Another copy of this letter at the Houghton Library is dated October 6.

mood. The Scarlet Letter being all in one tone, I had only to get my pitch, and could then go on interminably."[11]

On November 29 he was hoping to complete it in "two or three or four weeks,"[12] but ten days later he was floundering: "My desire and prayer is, to get through with the business already in hand—after which, it will be time enough to think of other things. I have been in a Slough of Despond, for some days past—having written so fiercely that I came to a stand still. There are points where a writer gets bewildered, and cannot form any judgment of what he has done, nor tell what to do next."[13] Not until January 12 could he report to Fields that it "is, so to speak, finished; only I am hammering away a little on the roof, and doing up a few odd jobs that were left incomplete. Then I must read it to my wife. . . . "[14]

Even after that date, Hawthorne refused to let Fields rush the work into print. The publisher wrote him on January 22 that he wanted to issue the book before March,[15] but it was not until January 27 that Hawthorne sent off the manuscript.[16] He must have worked on it until the last moment, for the Preface bears the same date. The book that he had thought was near completion after three months had taken five.

Fields read it at once, pronounced it a "great Book," and was pushing it through the press by February 2.[17] He now hoped to publish it the second week in March, but an old New England book-trade custom caused a delay of another

[11] November 3, 1850, MS, Houghton Library, Harvard University.

[12] To Fields, MS, Collection of Norman Holmes Pearson.

[13] December 9, 1850, to Fields, MS, Hawthorne-Fields Letter Book, Houghton Library, Harvard University.

[14] MS, Hawthorne-Fields Letter Book, Houghton Library, Harvard University.

[15] MS, Berg Collection, New York Public Library.

[16] To Fields, MS, Hawthorne-Fields Letter Book, Houghton Library, Harvard University.

[17] February 2, 1851, Fields to E. A. Duyckinck, MS, Duyckinck Collection, New York Public Library.

month: Fields waited until three or four thousand bound copies were available for his store so that he could monopolize the retail sale in Boston.[18] Meanwhile, Hawthorne read the proofs,[19] and Fields was busy with advance publicity. The first part of the work seen in print by the public was six pages of the first chapter, in Duyckinck's *Literary World*, March 29, under the heading, THE FOUNDER OF THE "HOUSE OF THE SEVEN GABLES." Duyckinck's long and favorable review appeared on April 26.

The book was officially published April 9, 1851. Two printings were issued on that day, a third in May, and a fourth in September—a total of 6,710 copies.[20] The book sold for a dollar, and Hawthorne's royalty was fifteen per cent.

[18] March 12 and 26, 1851, Fields to Hawthorne, MSS, Berg Collection, New York Public Library. This procedure bears significantly on the matter of the location of Hawthorne's audience.

[19] February 22, 1851, to Fields. "The book reads very well in the proofs. . . . " Printed from the MS in the Library of Congress by Nancy L. Eagle, "An Unpublished Hawthorne Letter," *American Literature*, XXIII (November, 1951), 360–62. This letter contains Hawthorne's list of complimentary copies.

[20] For data on these and other printings to 1858, see W. S. Tryon and William Charvat (eds.), *The Cost Books of Ticknor and Fields, 1832–1858* (New York, 1949). There were two English editions in 1851, although none was authorized. Fields dispatched the "early sheets" to England (March 26, 1851, Fields to Hawthorne, MS, Berg Collection, New York Public Library), but, failing to effect a sale of the English rights, sent over a supply of American copies (April 8, 1851, Fields to Hawthorne, MS, Berg Collection, New York Public Library). This letter also establishes the publication date of the first edition: "To-morrow, Wednesday, we issue the book. . . . " "The Trade are quarrelling among themselves and will not buy the Mss. or early sheets of an American Book" (August 14, 1851, Fields to Hawthorne, MS, Berg Collection, New York Public Library).

In the letter of March 26 cited above, Fields wrote Hawthorne that he had begun negotiations for a German edition (in English) by Tauchnitz of Leipzig, and in the April 8 letter he was still hoping that Tauchnitz would pay for editions of all Hawthorne's works. On September 30 he sent Hawthorne a letter from Tauchnitz, and urged him to write the latter direct "accepting his offer to reprint, but would suggest The Scarlet Letter to begin with. . . . Let him pay you if they are successful just what he pays other Transatlantic authors" (MS, Berg Collection, New York Public Library). On May 21, 1852, he wrote Hawthorne that *The House of the Seven Gables* was going through an edition in French (MS, Berg Collection, New York Public Library). The editors know of no French edition published before 1865.

There were 190 review copies, compared to 100 of *The Scarlet Letter*. In spite of active promotion, sales lagged after the fourth printing. Fields tried to give the impression that the work was as popular as *The Scarlet Letter* by advertising in May, 1852,[21] that each book was in its sixth thousand. Actually, by that date, printings of *The House of the Seven Gables* totaled 6,710, of *The Scarlet Letter*, 7,800. From then on, the latter was always ahead. The record of printings for the first thirteen years of each book before Hawthorne's death is as follows:

	The Scarlet Letter	The House of the Seven Gables
First year	6,000	6,710
First three years	8,800	8,710
First thirteen years	13,500	11,550
Average per year	1,038	888

These figures are interesting when we consider that *The House of the Seven Gables* was generally believed to be more attractive to the general reader than *The Scarlet Letter*. In writing it Hawthorne was, for the most part, doing what he wanted to do, but he did not ignore the professional or commercial aspects of his project. One such aspect was reflected in his efforts to decide on a title, which he began thinking about as early as October 1. The first title he mentioned on that date turned out to be definitive, but he also thought that "The Seven Gables" had the "great advantage that it would puzzle the devil to tell what it means."[22] On November 3 he was tending toward emphasis on the Pyncheons: "The Old Pyncheon House; a Romance"; "The Old Pyncheon Family; or the House of the Seven Gables; a Romance."[23] The

[21] Randall Stewart, *Nathaniel Hawthorne* (New Haven, 1948), p. 114.
[22] October 1, 1850, to Fields. See note 10.
[23] November 3, 1850, to Fields. See note 11.

publishers had chosen the present title by November 18,[24] but two months later Hawthorne was still uncertain. "What do you think of 'Maule's Well'—? and we might add 'or the House of the Seven Gables.' This well has not a very strong connection with the story, though quite sufficient, in my opinion to justify the title, which, in itself, and for the glibness with which it rolls out of the mouth, is preferable to the other."[25] The last sentence need not be taken too seriously. In a similar mood he had referred to the House as "the old shanty."[26]

The denouement of the story must also be considered a professional problem. We cannot ignore the possibility that Hawthorne, in concluding his book as he did, was yielding to the world's wish that in stories everything should turn out well. Judge Pyncheon's death follows naturally what has happened previously, but it is especially "satisfactory" that he should die while plotting a final monstrous injustice for his feeble victim. In all Hawthorne's work there is no other such unmitigated villain.[27] The opportune death of the Judge's only child makes all the "good" people in the story wealthy heirs. Phoebe and Holgrave, the Montague-Capulet pair, become engaged—but not until love turns the radical individualist Holgrave into a conservative. As an observer of the happy exodus from the House remarks, "Pretty good business."

24 November 18, 1850, Hawthorne to John H. Francis, Jr., MS, Houghton Library, Harvard University. In various letters Fields cited support of this title by E. P. Whipple, Charles Sumner, H. W. Longfellow, and G. S. Hillard.

25 January 12, 1851, to Fields. See note 14.

26 October 1, 1850, to Fields. See note 10.

27 Yet Hawthorne's subtle analysis of Pyncheon's villainy takes this character out of the realm of melodrama. He may have been referring to Pyncheon when he wrote, " . . . I should not wonder if I had refined upon the principal character a little too much for popular appreciation . . . " (March 15, 1851, to Bridge. Bridge, *op. cit.*, p. 125).

Two or three weeks after the book was published Hawthorne made the rather hazy statement that "in writing it,
I suppose I was illuminated by my purpose to bring it to a
prosperous close; while the gloom of the past threw its
shadow along the reader's pathway."[28] Rather more con-
vincing is a sentence in a letter of November 29, when he
was struggling with the problem of a conclusion: "It darkens
damnably towards the close, but I shall try hard to pour
some setting sunshine over it."[29] It thus appears that after
more than three months of writing and "within two or three
or four weeks" of completion, Hawthorne perceived that the
logic of his story was leading to a somber ending. What he
poured over it may be called sunshine, perhaps, but it was
no part of his original plan, if, indeed, he had planned his
conclusion at all.

It was as professional novelist as well as craftsman that
Hawthorne had been troubled not only by the gloom of his
"hell-fired" *Scarlet Letter*, but by its lack of relief and variety.
That was why he had argued against its separate publication:
"diversified no otherwise than by turning different sides of
the same dark idea to the reader's eye, it will weary very
many people. . . . "[30] In *The House of the Seven Gables*
he corrected that defect: his plan permitted him to mingle
humor and pathos, present and past, sunshine and shadow—
combinations universally approved by critics and readers. In
addition to having a plot which included three deaths that

[28] April 27, 1851, to Duyckinck. See note 4.

[29] November 29, 1850, to Fields. See note 12. Significantly, Fields
quoted this statement verbatim to the critic, E. A. Duyckinck, but asked
him not to print it (December 10, 1850, MS, Duyckinck Collection,
New York Public Library). Fields himself thought that "the closing
scenes" were "full of pathos and beauty & a power quite equal to anything
I remember in the history of romance writing" (January 30, 1851, to
Hawthorne, MS, Berg Collection, New York Public Library).

[30] January 20, 1850, to Fields, Hawthorne-Fields Letter Book, Houghton
Library, Harvard University.

looked like murders, and a lost land-deed, discovered at last by a touch on a secret spring, the work ranged over a variety of subjects and styles—ancient witchcraft, modern witchcraft (mesmerism), contemporary machines (the railroad and the daguerreotype), satire, sentiment, descriptions of nature, little generalizing essays, and quantities of easy symbolism. Something of this abundance, and also some of the tones of the book, derive from Dickens, whose works he often read aloud to his wife during the months of composition.

Hawthorne's notebooks[31] yielded up more diverse materials for the new work than they had for *The Scarlet Letter*. Ready to hand were jottings that went into the passages on the Pyncheon hens,[32] the organ grinder's monkey,[33] Holgrave's ideas on the influence of the dead on the present,[34] the railroad station where Hepzibah and Clifford alighted,[35] and Judge Pyncheon's corpse in the chair.[36]

History provided some raw materials. There are analogies between the Pyncheon and Hawthorne ancestors as persecutors of witches. The Hawthornes, like the Pyncheons, had once laid claim to extensive lands in Maine,[37] but for this theme Hawthorne also drew upon the well-known story of General Knox's land patent in that state.[38] There are parallels between Clifford's supposed murder of his uncle and the sensational murder in Salem in 1830 of Captain Joseph White by hirelings of a person who wanted to destroy White's will.[39]

[31] Randall Stewart (ed.), *The American Notebooks by Nathaniel Hawthorne* (New Haven, 1932).

[32] Chapter 10, HSG. *Notebooks*, p. 130.

[33] Chapter 11, HSG. *Notebooks*, p. 117.

[34] Chapter 12, HSG. *Notebooks*, p. xxxix (parallel passages).

[35] Chapter 17, HSG. *Notebooks*, p. 245.

[36] Chapter 18, HSG. *Notebooks*, p. 130.

[37] Vernon Loggins, *The Hawthornes* (New York, 1951), pp. 109, 155, 169–70.

[38] Thomas Griffiths, *Maine Sources in The House of the Seven Gables* (Waterville, Maine, 1945).

[39] *Notebooks*, pp. 121, 279, 302; Loggins, *op. cit.*, pp. 242–54.

Allusions to mesmerism and daguerreotypy[40] reflect extensive discussions of these phenomena in the periodicals of the 1840's.

Hawthorne's choice of the name "Pyncheon" resulted in some unanticipated vexations. Hawthorne wrote Fields on May 23:

> Peter Oliver, Esq. of Boston has written to me, complaining that I have made his grandfather infamous! It seems there was actually a Pyncheon (or Pynchon, as he spells it) family resident in Salem, and that their representative, at the period of the Revolution, was a certain Judge Pynchon, a tory and a Refugee. This was Mr. Oliver's grandfather, and (at least, so he dutifully describes him) the most exemplary old gentleman in the world.

Oliver went on to complain that Hawthorne probably had "this actual family" in his eye and considered "himself infinitely wronged and aggrieved." Hawthorne was particularly unhappy over this "joke" because, so he wrote, he had never heard of any such Pyncheons and "took the name because it suited the tone of my book, and was as much my property, for fictitious purposes, as that of Smith." He had written Oliver a "very polite and gentlemanly letter." And he asked that Fields let him write an appropriate preface for future editions, should there be any.[41] Fields replied, May 24, that the Oliver joke was "most excellent" and promised Hawthorne "a chance in the next issue to assert your innocence in a brief preface."[42]

Then, on June 3, the Reverend Thomas R. Pynchon of Stockbridge accused Hawthorne of implying that his account of the Pyncheons in his book was a history of the Pynchon family, and of "holding up . . . the good name of our An-

[40] Alfred H. Marks, "Hawthorne's Daguerreotypist: Scientist, Artist, Reformer," *Ball State Teachers College Forum*, III (Spring, 1962), 61–74.
[41] MS, Huntington Library.
[42] MS, Berg Collection, New York Public Library.

cestors to the derision and contempt of our countrymen." His indignation reached a climax in a bitter—and interesting—compliment to Hawthorne's "realism":

> The difficulty arises from the fact that your work though called a Romance is written in such a way as to make it difficult for the reader to rid himself of the impression that it is a real Family History, some of the members of which are still living [some twenty, he said earlier in the letter]. The life-like naturalness of the Book is the very thing we complain of: It is that which makes this a case, wholly different from the ordinary use of Historical names by writers of Fiction: Every man possessed of a spark of the ordinary self respect of a man, can appreciate it, by putting his own name in the place of ours: and so making the House of the Seven Gables: the history of his own Family as you have made the public believe it is of ours.

Hawthorne wrote grimly to Fields on June 5 that he would probably get protests from all twenty of "these Pyncheon jackasses. . . . After exchanging shots with all of them, I shall get you to publish the whole correspondence, in a style corresponding with that of my other works; and I anticipate a great run for the volume." In a postscript he added that the Stockbridge Pynchon "demands that another name be substituted instead of that of the family;—to which I assent, in case the publishers can be prevailed on to cancel the Stereotype-plates. Of course, you will consent! Pray do!"[43]

On August 18 he sent Fields a disclaimer about the Pyncheons:

> You are going to publish another thousand of the Seven Gables. I promised those Pyncheons a brief preface. What if you insert the following?

[43] For fuller details, see Norman Holmes Pearson, "The Pynchons and Judge Pynchon," *Essex Institute Historical Collections*, C (October, 1964), 235-55. The Pynchon letter is dated "June 4th 1851," but Hawthorne's reply refers to "your communication of the 3ᵈ inst." Both the Pynchon and Hawthorne letters are in the Essex Institute. Hawthorne to Fields, June 5, is in the Buffalo and Erie County Public Library.

The author is pained to learn, that, in selecting a name for the fictitious inhabitants of a castle in the air, he has wounded the feelings of more than one respectable descendent of an old Pynchon family. He begs leave to say, that he intended no reference to any individual of the name, now or heretofore extant; and further, that, at the time of writing his book, he was wholly unaware of the existence of such a family in New England, for two hundred years back—and that what ever he may have since learned of them is altogether to their credit.[44]

Fields reported to Hawthorne that this note arrived too late for the fourth printing, but promised that it would be inserted in "the *next* thousand."[45] It was never added to the Preface.

In the writing of *The House of the Seven Gables*, Hawthorne's major problem was the combining of disparate materials. This difficulty not only made severe demands on his craftsmanship but rendered him uncertain about the acceptability of his book. From the beginning to the end of writing, Hawthorne thought of his story as a "romance." Several of his proposed titles contained the word, and his Preface ends with the plea that the work "be read strictly as a Romance." Yet, very early in the writing process he could state that "all but thirty or forty pages of it refer to the present time,"[46] or to "our own broad daylight," as he phrases it in the Preface. The Preface also defines a novel as (unlike a romance) aiming at "a very minute fidelity . . . to the probable and ordinary course of man's experience." Though there is a great deal of such fidelity in this book, and though the "narrative" is of "humble . . . texture," he refused to think of the work as a novel because his "attempt to connect a by-gone time with the very Present" put it in the category of the romance.

If the problem had been strictly a private one—a matter of finding a way to write a story—it would have no place in

[44] MS, St. Lawrence University Library.
[45] August 21, 1851, MS, Berg Collection, New York Public Library.
[46] October 1, 1850, to Fields. See note 10.

a factual history of the book. But he made it a professional and a public problem in letters to his publisher, in the Preface, and in direct and indirect addresses to the reader within the story itself. "Many passages of this book," he wrote Fields, "ought to be finished with the minuteness of a Dutch picture"[47]—that is, with the "minute fidelity" appropriate to a novel. But he insists that he is writing Romance, which is always "on the utmost verge of a precipitous absurdity." Again, "It has undoubtedly one disadvantage, in being brought so close to the present time; whereby its romantic improbabilities become more glaring."[48] And again, he would not wonder if "the romance of the book should be found somewhat at odds with the humble and familiar scenery in which I invest it."[49]

In the story Hawthorne is consistently self-conscious about the conflict, and repeatedly apologizes for it. Hepzibah has a "deeply tragic character that contrasted irreconcilably with the ludicrous pettiness of her employment" (page 37). He confesses that "It is a heavy annoyance to a writer . . . that so much of the mean and ludicrous should be hopelessly mixed up with the purest pathos" (pages 40–41). He appeals directly to his audience: "The author needs great faith in his reader's sympathy; else he must hesitate to give details so minute, and incidents apparently so trifling" (page 150). He justifies himself by declaring that "This contrast, or intermingling of tragedy with mirth, happens daily, hourly, momently" (page 295). In short, he and the reader must accept the fact that "Life is made up of marble and mud" (page 41).

Perhaps it was both the difficulty and the necessity of reconciling marble and mud, and his unspoken belief that he had succeeded, which made him say often that *The House of*

[47] November 3, 1850. See note 11.
[48] January 27, 1851, to Fields. See note 16.
[49] March 15, 1851, to Bridge. Bridge, *op. cit.*, p. 125.

the Seven Gables was a better book than *The Scarlet Letter.*
On the other hand, he confessed to Horatio Bridge that "for
that very reason [it is] less likely to interest the public." In the
same letter is a statement that turned out to be wrong, but
which in the merely logical terms of literary history should
have been right: " . . . I think [it] is more sure of retaining
the ground it acquires."[50] Was he foreseeing the developing
taste for realism which was to dominate the next era in
fiction, when Twain and Howells tended to ignore or disguise
the marble and emphasize the mud of common and humble
life? In this work and in the next one, *The Blithedale
Romance,* Hawthorne was at least on the edge of what was
to become the main stream of American fiction.

W. C.

---

[50] July 22, 1851, to Bridge. Bridge, *op. cit.,* pp. 126–27.

cloth of the richest damask, looked worthy to be the scene and centre of one of the cheerfullest of parties. The vapor of the broiled fish arose like incense from the shrine of a barbarian idol, while the fragrance of the Mocha might have gratified the nostrils of a tutelary Lar, or whatever power has scope over a modern breakfast-table. Phoebe's Indian cakes were the sweetest offering of all — in their hue, befitting the rustic altars of the innocent and golden age — or, so brightly yellow were they, resembling some of the bread which was changed to glistening gold, when Midas tried to eat it. The butter must not be forgotten — butter which Phoebe herself had churned, in her own rural home, and brought it to her cousin as a propitiatory gift — smelling of clover-blossoms, and diffusing the charm of pastoral scenery through the dark-panelled parlor. All this, with the quaint gorgeousness of the old China cups and saucers, and the crested spoons, and a silver cream-jug (Hepzibah's only other article of plate, and shaped like the rudest porringer) set out a board, at which the stateliest of old Colonel Pyncheon's guests need not have scorned to take his place. But the Puritan's face scowled down out of the picture, as if nothing on the table pleased his appetite.

By way of contributing what grace she could, Phoebe gathered some roses and a few other flowers, possessing either scent or beauty, and arranged them in a glass-pitcher, which, having long ago lost its handle, was so much the fitter for a flower-vase. The early sunshine — as fresh as that which peeped into Eve's bower, while she and Adam sat at breakfast there — came twinkling through the branches of the pear-tree, and fell quite across the table. All was now ready. There were chairs and plates for three. A chair and plate for Hepzibah — the same for Phoebe; — but what other guest did her cousin look for?

Throughout this preparation, there had been a constant tremor in Hepzibah's frame; an agitation so powerful, that Phoebe could see the quivering of her gaunt shadow, as thrown by the firelight on the kitchen-wall, or by the sunshine on the parlor-floor. Its manifestations were so various, and agreed so little with one another, that the girl knew not what to make of it. Sometimes it seemed an ecstasy of delight and happiness. At such moments, Hepzibah would fling out her arms, and enfold Phoebe in them, and kiss her cheek, as tenderly as ever her mother had; she appeared to do so by an inevitable impulse, and as if her bosom were oppressed with tenderness, of which she must needs pour them out a little, in order to gain breathing-room. The next moment, without any visible cause for the change, her unwonted joy shrank back, appalled, as it were, and clothed itself in mourning; or it ran and hid itself, so to speak, in the dungeon of her heart, where it had long lain chained; while

FOLIO 65 OF THE PRINTER'S-COPY HOLOGRAPH MANUSCRIPT OF
"THE HOUSE OF THE SEVEN GABLES" IN THE
HOUGHTON LIBRARY OF HARVARD UNIVERSITY
(MS AM 121.26)

TEXTUAL INTRODUCTION:
THE HOUSE OF THE SEVEN GABLES

PRINTED by Metcalf and Company from type-pages set and stereotyped by Hobart and Robbins, of Boston, *The House of the Seven Gables* was published on April 9, 1851, by Ticknor, Reed, and Fields.* The book collates, 8⁰: [1]⁸ 2–21⁸ 22⁴, 172 leaves, pages [i–iii] iv–vi [vii–viii] [9] 10–344. The title page is on page i, the copyright and stereotyper's notice on page ii, the Preface on pages iii–vi, and the Contents on page vii. Page viii is blank. The text begins with Chapter I on page 9. Variously dated advertisement inserts are found. According to the *Bibliography of American Literature* five states of the stamping appear in the binding.

Six pages from the first chapter were printed in Duyckinck's *Literary World* for March 29. Substantive variants do not occur except for a cut corresponding to Centenary 16.1–6; hence this early appearance contains no evidence (except negative) bearing on the transmission of the text prior to publication of the first edition.

Initial publication on April 9 consisted of two printings, the first of 1,690 copies, and the second of 1,969. *The Cost Books of Ticknor and Fields* record a third impression of

---

* For a consideration of the evidence that seems to bear on such a division of typesetting and presswork, see the Note on the Typesetting.

2,051 copies in May, and a fourth of 1,000 copies in September. No textual variants occur in these printings, but they may be distinguished by the condition of the plates. The first three lines of page 149 are battered in the right-hand margin in the first-printing plate but reset for the second printing. Some type batter during the course of the second printing from the plates produces within this impression the variant "apparent-apparen" in 50.25 and "or-o" in 278.25.[1] For the third printing page 58 was completely reset. In the original plate the question mark in line 17 is to the left of the "y" in "lady", but in the reset plate the question mark is directly beneath the "y". In the fourth printing the plate for page 57 has its last three lines reset. In line 33 of the original plate the "c" of "child" is slightly to the right of the "f" in "for", but in the reset lines the "c" is directly beneath the "f".

The Cost Books list an 1852 printing ordered in September, but no example with this date has been observed. Instead, it is almost certain that the date 1851 was not changed in the imprint, and hence that an observed fifth printing falsely dated 1851 must represent this 1852 impression. The fifth printing has the characteristics of the fourth but may be differentiated by gutter measurements. For example, in the fourth impression the gutter between pages 120 and 121 measures 3.3 cm., as does that between pages 216 and 217. However, in the fifth (1852) impression the gutters measure 3.8 and 3.7 cm. respectively.[2]

[1] In 1865 this "o" was incorrectly altered in the plate to read "of".

[2] For these five impressions, see Matthew J. Bruccoli, "Concealed Printings in Hawthorne," Papers of the Bibliographical Society of America, LVII (1963), 42–45.

The following Ohio State University Libraries copies were completely machined: (1) PS 1861.A1; (2) PS 1861.A1.1853a; (3) PS 1861.A1.1851e.copy 2; (4) PS 1861.A1.copy 5. The following University of Virginia copies were completely machined: (1) PS 1861.A1.1851.526362, (2) PS 1861.A1.1851.254983. The following Library of Congress copies were spot-checked: (1) PS 1861.A1.1851 [deposit copy]; (2) PS 1861.A1.1851 copy 2 [deposit copy]; (3) PS 1861.A1.1851.copy 3; (4) PS 1861.A1.1851.copy 4. The following Ohio State copies were spot-checked: (1) PS 1861.A1.copy 2;

All printings from first-edition plates exist in two states distinguished by the presence or absence of a comma after "solitude" in 343.31 (Centenary 319.3). Since this variant is constant in all impressions, including the first, it must have resulted from the use of duplicate plates to print half-sheet gathering 22, and thus the variant would appear in each impression evenly divided between the two states of the page. (The Hinman Machine demonstrates that only one type-setting exists for the page, though in the two states.) The comma after "solitude" is present in the manuscript; hence it is a normal supposition that it appeared in the original typesetting that was to be plated. Moreover, no dislocation is seen as between the two states such as would have resulted from the mortising-in of a comma. From these two pieces of evidence the inference follows naturally that the comma must have been removed in error and was not inserted to repair a hypothetical original mistake, even granting that such a minor error would have been detected in the course of plating. The most likely explanation is that the comma sort was jerked out when the flong was removed from the type-page to make the cast for the first plate. Presumably the resulting hole was not noticed (or, if noticed, was plugged with a space) so that no comma appeared in the second plate cast from the next flong applied to the type-page. The manuscript comma appears, of course, in the Centenary text since it is authorized by the manuscript.

The explanation for this error does not run contrary to the *Cost Books* evidence cited by Professor Bruccoli in his study of the printings (see footnote 2 above) that the first printing

(2) PS 1861.A1.copy 3; (3) PS 1861.A1.copy 4; (4) PS 1861.A1.1851e; (5) PS 1861.A1.1851c; (6) PS 1861.A1.1851d; (7) PS 1861.A1.copy 6; (8) PS 1861.A1.1852; (9) PS 1861.A1.1851c.copy 2; (10) PS 1861.A1.1851c. copy 3. The following University of Virginia copies were spot-checked: (1) Barrett PS 1861.A1.1851c.566024.copy 2; (2) Barrett PS 1861.A1.1851c. 566026.copy 3; (3) Barrett PS 1861.A1.1851c.566023; (4) Taylor 1851.H38 H6.506620; (5) Barrett PS 1861.A1.1851b.451059; (6) Barrett PS 1861.A1. 1851e.566025; (7) PS 1861.A1.1851a.409766.

was machined with 22 formes. Since the regular gatherings are in 8's, it would seem that the plates for the 16 pages comprising the inner and outer formes of each gathering were imposed together in one forme, and quires 1–21 were printed by the work-and-turn method that would provide two copies of each gathering when the whole sheet was cut apart after perfecting. This 16-page forme explains the reason for the duplicate plates for gathering 22 in 4's, since one set of plates would comprise only eight pages and the gathering normally could not be printed from an 8-page forme except by cutting the sheets before machining. With the duplicate plates of gathering 22 imposed in a 16-page forme, each full sheet would be cut apart, after perfecting, into four copies of the gathering, of which two would be in each state. When, starting with the second printing, double sheets of paper were used and the 16 pages of two consecutive gatherings would be imposed together in one 32-page forme for work-and-turn printing, the sixteen pages of gathering 21 would have been imposed with the sixteen pages for gathering 22 in duplicate.

The original plates (I) served for further impressions of 1,000 copies in 1853, 500 copies each in 1855, 1857, and 1860, 280 each in 1861, 1863, and 1864, another 500 in 1864, and so on. The latest identified use of these plates is in the New Fireside Edition, first issued in 1886 and reprinted four times. Machine collation establishes that throughout the printings eleven changes occurred in the plates, all in 1865: apparen [apparent (50.25; Centenary 43.28), ith [with (150.22; Centenary 138.17), clues [clews (165.34; Centenary 152.25), criticize [criticise (205.34; Centenary 190.30), inordinate [mordinate (225.4; Centenary 208.29), visiter [visitor (242.8 and 309.23; Centenary 226.4 and 288.14), visiters [visitors (246.23; Centenary 230.8), clue [clew (277.33; Centenary 259.15), or [of (278.25;

Centenary 260.4), political [poliitcal (291.17; Centenary 272.9).[3]

The Little Classics Edition of 1876, published by James R. Osgood and Company, introduced a new typesetting (II) derived from (I), the first-edition plates (in their 1865 form), with no infusion of fresh authority but with some corruption as is to be expected in a reprint. Various "editions" (i.e., impressions) were manufactured from these plates, including the Popular Edition (1891), the Salem (1894), and the Concord (1899).

The famed Riverside Edition of 1883 (III), published by Houghton, Mifflin and Company, was set from the Little Classics text in a late state of the plates and was issued originally both in trade and in large-paper form.[4] The text of this edition is notoriously corrupt. In addition to the normal line of reprints from the Riverside plates, for *Seven Gables* there are text-book reprints: Riverside Paper Series (1892), Riverside Literature Series (1896), Riverside School Library (1896). These printings have not been examined.

In 1899 a new typesetting of *Seven Gables* (IV) with illustrations by Maude and Genevieve Cowles was published by Houghton, Mifflin and Company in two volumes. The text of this edition (derived from III) has not been collated beyond the 1899 printings: the presumed first printing in large-paper format limited to 250 copies and the trade printing. Machine collation shows no variants between these.

[3] The attempt to regularize "clue" and "visiter" in these plates was not thorough—see first-edition 92.29, 251.22, 318.10, 139.27, and 139.28 where the spellings remain unrevised.

[4] Evidence from *The Scarlet Letter* (Centenary Edition, 1962, pp. lix–lx) suggests that the plates for the trade edition were made from the typesetting before printing and were thereupon corrected in a few details before reimpression in a second trade printing, followed by printing of the large-paper copies from type metal. These details have not been investigated in *The House of the Seven Gables*.

The last of the collected editions collated for the Centenary text is the Autograph Edition of 1900 (V) set from the Riverside text (III) in a late state of the plates and published by Houghton, Mifflin and Company in a white binding with tipped-in signed illustrations, and in a blue binding with unsigned illustrations. Both appear to have been bound from sheets of the same impression.[5] The further history of these Autograph plates has not been investigated for the purposes of the Centenary text, although one may note an Old Manse impression printed from them in 1904.

Two English editions were published in 1851. The first was printed for Henry G. Bohn and the second for George Routledge and Company. The Bohn text appears to have been set from the first- or second-impression sheets of I, and the Routledge independently from the same source. The lack of common error unique to these two texts seems to show that one is not dependent upon the other. Since both editions were piratical, no opportunity for authorial changes can exist and hence their variants have not been recorded in the Historical Collation although they were collated for the information of the editors.

Fields took possession of the printer's-copy holograph manuscript of *The House of the Seven Gables*, which was bequeathed to Harvard University in December, 1915, by Mrs. James T. Fields and is now deposited in the Houghton Library as MS Am 121.26. This manuscript is bound in marbled boards with black leather spine and corners. Inside the front cover is inscribed: "Manuscript of Hawthorne's | 'House of the Seven Gables'. | Copy sent by the author to | the printer. J. T. F." Two portraits of the author are bound in ahead of the title page. On the verso of the rear endpaper is the inscription: "opposite is Longfellow's poem on the | Death of Hawthorne, in the poet's | hand-

[5] The Historical Collation has been prepared from a copy with the blue binding in the Ohio State University Libraries.

writing. | J. T. F." Then pasted in is a two-leaf manuscript headed "Concord | May 23.1864" followed by the poem beginning "How beautiful it was, that one bright day", subscribed "Henry W. Longfellow | June 23.1864."

The manuscript is composed of 241 leaves, all written on the recto only, except for page 2 of the Preface, the direction for an insertion on folio 15 verso, "Insert—They were called Alice's Posies", and a deleted false start of folio 17 inverted on folio 18 verso. The paper (identical with that used the following year for *The Blithedale Romance*) is a light-blue wove, measuring 9 5/8 by 7 3/4 inches, with a seal consisting of three plumes above the initials "B & G". Folios 11–16 are either bound in closer or are 1/4 inch narrower. The writing is in a black ink now somewhat faded. Beginning with a new paragraph at the sixth line of folio 127 a different ink was used that is now much browner. The leaves have been folded horizontally one or more times, in batches, and, often, vertically as well. These packets, sometimes of as many as twenty or more leaves, may possibly represent copy returned with proof to Hawthorne, although there is no external evidence that he received copy along with the proof sheets sent him.

The first four leaves of the manuscript are preliminary. The recto of the first is occupied by the title, which reads "The House | of | The Seven Gables, | a | Romance. | By Nathaniel Hawthorne." The verso is blank. The recto of the second leaf (verso blank) contains the Contents with chapter numbers and titles. The printer has added the page numbers of the first edition. The Preface starts on the recto of the third leaf and is continued on its verso (page 2), concluding with page 3 on the recto of the fourth leaf. The text begins, numbered 1, on the fifth leaf and continues to the end on folio 237.

The numerous examples of false starts and corrected eye-skip in the inscription of the manuscript (recorded in the appendix Alterations in the Manuscript) would in themselves be sufficient to suggest that the Harvard manuscript does not represent the papers of the original composition. Indeed, the textual evidence is precisely similar to that in the manuscript of *The Blithedale Romance,* where we are so fortunate as to have preserved a single leaf of another form to demonstrate that Hawthorne made a fair copy of an earlier manuscript to send to the printer.[6] This *Blithedale* leaf is clean enough to have been used for printer's copy, and the fair transcript Hawthorne made from it exhibits no far-reaching changes but only stylistic polishing, plus general expansion of the same kind as the lesser alterations within the printer's-copy manuscript, similar to that found in the printer's copy for *The House of the Seven Gables.* We find a reference to an earlier state of *Seven Gables,* however, in a letter from Hawthorne to Fields of January 27, 1851:

> I intend to put the House of the Seven Gables into the express-man's hands to-day; so that, if you do not soon receive it, you may conclude that it has been miscarried—in which case, I shall not consent to the Universe existing a moment longer. I have no copy of it, except the wildest scribble of a first draught, so that it could never be restored.[7]

This quotation indicates that the preserved manuscript is a fair copy made from the first draft. Whether the draft was as wildly scribbled as Hawthorne intimates may be in question on the evidence of the *Blithedale* leaf, which could well be a first draft also. However, so much rewriting must have gone into the fair copy that Hawthorne could well be forgiven for despairing of reconstructing his second version of *Seven Gables* in any stylistically similar manner.

[6] See *The Blithedale Romance* (Centenary Edition, 1964), pp. xxxi–xxxii.

[7] Hawthorne-Fields Letter Book, MS, Houghton Library, Harvard University.

The Harvard manuscript holds, on an average, about forty lines per page. Very few pages fail to show alteration of some variety made during the course of the inscription or as part of a general review. Much of the alteration was made *currente calamo*, ordinarily by wiping out with a finger while the ink was still wet and writing over the same space. In the appendix Alterations in the Manuscript these changes are distinguished from the interlineations, which presumably were made at a later time, at least after the ink had dried. The most prominent of the additions or alterations made at the end as part of a general review are the chapter numbers and titles, which Hawthorne wrote in, using a different ink, and hence after completion of the manuscript. The thoroughgoing alteration of the references to Hepzibah as "the Old Maid" and the substitution of her name or of a whole series of locutions were also made after initial inscription had been completed.

The alterations over wiped-out letters and words offer the most serious difficulty to recovering the readings of the initial inscription, especially as no more than a letter or two, often, may have been written before the error was detected or a change decided on. Whenever anything of the original can be recovered, it is listed in the appendix, since sometimes even a single letter, in context, can suggest the probable word that was started. Less commonly, substitute words were written over the discarded original when little or no erasure had been attempted. The manuscript displays hundreds of cases of apparent alteration which, on examination, prove to be no more than the tracing-over of an identical original word, or some letters in a word, in order to increase the legibility. Occasionally, the same word is interlined for clarity to this end. No attempt has been made in the appendix to record these tracings or interlined duplications, whether of words or of letters, when legibility alone was their purpose.

Some hand other than Hawthorne's has interlined a few words when the original did not seem clear.

That the Harvard manuscript was the printer's copy is demonstrated by the regular marking of the compositorial stints on its pages. Nine compositors sign the pages: Emery, Fox, Henderson, Jackman, King, Letts, Loring, Whittle, and Willis.[8] Of these, Emery, Fox, and Henderson were to work on the composition of *The Blithedale Romance* the following year.

Emery set only the three and a quarter pages of the first-edition Preface (pages iii-vi), page 9—the start of the text—and the upper part of page 10, for a total of 117 lines in one stint. Thereafter he disappears. For the rest, working in some sort of rough groupings for simultaneous composition, Fox set 2,244 lines of type in 23 stints, Letts 1,742 lines in 18 stints, King 1,696 lines in 18 stints, Jackman 1,403 lines in 14 stints, Henderson 1,212 lines in 13 stints, Willis 1,124 lines in 12 stints, Loring 1,010 lines in 11 stints, and Whittle 344 lines in 3 stints. Whittle went off the job after page 42. Loring entered on page 58, Jackman on page 74, and Henderson on page 130. The usual "take" (number of manuscript folios assigned) was two leaves, but there were six takes of three leaves, and three takes of four leaves. The compositors signed the first leaf of each of their takes (usually in ink but sometimes in pencil) in the left margin in the space provided by the indention of the first paragraph on that leaf.[9]

---

[8] In *The Boston Directory, For the Year 1851*, James W. Emery, printer, is listed at 3 Pleasant Street; Frederick E. Fox, engraver, at 6 School; Abraham King, printer, at rear 51 Prince; William Letts, printer, at 56 Chambers; and Henry A. Willis, printer, at 3 Fruit. In the 1852 *Directory*, James Henderson, printer, is listed at 8 Fayette, and Willis' address has been changed to 25 Vine. The others are unlisted in either directory, although it is interesting to notice that there is a Charles Fox, publisher, at 11 Marion Street; and a Benjamin Loring & Co., stationers, with a shop at 120 and 122 State Street.

[9] That this position was specified in their instructions may be indicated by manuscript folio 31, where Loring first wrote his name in the indention

The purpose of this signing was to establish the point at which the compositor of each take had started to set type. Since a group of simultaneously setting workmen do not set manuscript directly into pages, and these must be made up later, the start of the initial paragraph provided the first place in each take where a compositor could begin to set into galleys with a full line.[10] This was a necessity, since only when a compositor began his stint with a chapter heading could he know, at that time, that he was starting a fresh page.

Two general methods were in use to assign the text above the compositor's signature on the first folio of a take. The first appears to have been employed in *The Blithedale Romance,* set in the same shop in 1852. Here when the first compositor in a group toward the end of his take had either paged his galleys himself or had had a maker-up mark his copy as the pages were determined, he could decide to continue to set type from the remaining text on the last manuscript leaf of his take and to keep on until he had completed another page from the unset material above the compositor's signature on the first leaf of the succeeding take. Or, on the

for the second paragraph, six lines down, and then crossed it out and rewrote his name in the initial paragraph indention, which was much shallower, two lines from the top. Similarly, Whittle on folio 27 had mistaken the place for his signature and rubbed out his name from the second paragraph indention in order to insert it correctly in the first. On folio 119 Henderson in error signed the second paragraph, not the first, but did not repair his mistake. These are the only exceptions, save for the end of Emery's stint and the beginning of Letts's. The distinction between these particular stints is marked on folio 1, line 25, by a left-hand square bracket drawn in ink between the two "m" letters of "commence", and Letts signed his name over the second syllable. It seems clear that Letts took over from Emery at this point despite the fact that in the first edition the unbroken word "commence", not the second syllable, begins line 15 of page 10. It would seem to be no accident that Emery set 34 lines of text, a normal type-page. That his stint ended with line 14 of page 10 is accounted for by the fact that only 20 lines appear on page 9 owing to the space occupied by the head-title and chapter heading.

[10] The account of the method of typesetting *The House of the Seven Gables* and *The Blithedale Romance* is based essentially on remarks about different practices contained in Thomas MacKellar, *The American Printer* (Philadelphia, 1872 ed.), pp. 202–5, and Theodore L. De Vinne, *Modern Methods of Book Composition* (New York, 1914 ed.), pp. 77–83.

contrary, he could turn over his final leaf, and its remaining text below the marked page ending, to the next compositor. The latter would then know where his first page could begin and would set from the lower part of this leaf and continue from the top of the first leaf of his own take until he came to the paragraph opening where he had, earlier, started to set. He could then page, or turn his galleys over to a maker-up for paging, and when he came to the final leaf of his take he could treat the next compositor, in turn, according to the material on his final leaf. The manuscript of *The Blithedale Romance* contains pencil markings (in a non-compositorial hand) which consist of a bracket, the next page number, and the name of the compositor who was to begin that page. Such notations usually occur on the last leaf of a take and in their reference to the compositor who had signed the next manuscript leaf seem to represent the foreman's assignment of the material at the juncture of the stints of simultaneously composing workmen. In this manuscript the markings show that on relatively few occasions would a compositor continue to set an incomplete page from the text on his final leaf and then finish the page from material above the next workman's signature on the first leaf of the succeeding take. Ordinarily, on completion of the final full page, the last leaf of a take was handed over to the next workman, who would then set type until he had reached the type already composed from the first paragraph on the initial leaf of his own take. And so on, through the group of simultaneously composing workmen.

The manuscript of *The House of the Seven Gables* is like *The Blithedale Romance* in that it was set simultaneously by compositors working in groups who signed the first paragraph opening of their take, where they had begun typesetting. However, except for only two instances,[11] the fore-

11 Within the first line of folio 129 a pencil left-hand bracket followed by the page number 201 and Henderson's name (not in his hand) appear

man's markings are absent, and the compositors' signatures are the sole indication of their stints. It follows that a different procedure must have been adopted from that used in setting *The Blithedale Romance.* In *Seven Gables,* it seems evident that each compositor automatically continued typesetting over onto the first leaf of the next one's take until he came to the end of the paragraph above where the compositor of the take had begun his typesetting with the next line, as indicated by his signature. The number of type-lines would be entered in the foreman's book so that credit could be given each compositor for the linage set. One may speculate that the difference in the systems between the two books was, at least in some part, governed by the length of the takes, which agree roughly with De Vinne's distinction between "short" and "long." Since the usual take for *Seven Gables* was only two manuscript leaves, as against the three and four leaves common in *Blithedale,* it would have proved inconvenient for rapid paging to have compositors backtracking in their typesetting. (Possibly some difference in the personnel who made up pages, whether the compositors or a maker-up, could have influenced the choice.) Although any stint would vary considerably according to the position of the initial paragraph on the first leaf of a take, a perfectly respectable equalizing took place over the course of composition. The markedly longer stints were always due to a larger assigned take. The longest was Jackman's first take of 200 type-lines, the next King's seventh take of 170 lines, and the next Fox's ninth take of 160 lines. The shortest

above Henderson's signature, which is in the paragraph indention in line 4. It seems clear that this is an official notation that Henderson had here moved back from the start of his stint in the manner found in *Blithedale.* Secondly, on the verso of folio 82 is written vertically in pencil the running-title and page number "The Pyncheon of To-day 136", a notation of the kind found in *Blithedale* to aid in the making-up of pages. Here it refers to the start of Jackman's stint (actually on page 134) below his signature on folio 82 recto. One or two other markings may have been made by the foreman (see below, page xlv).

was Henderson's eleventh take of 59 lines, followed by Willis' twelfth of 62 lines, and then Henderson's third of 64 lines. Jackman, in part owing to a long take or two, averages 100 lines of type in each of his stints, followed by Fox with 97.6 lines, Letts with 96.8 lines, King with 94.2 lines, Willis with 93.7 lines, Henderson with 93.2 lines, and Loring with 91.8 lines. Whittle had averaged 115 lines, but his three stints gave little opportunity for long-term equalization. In general, each stint produced somewhat under three type-pages.

Various printer's markings in ink appear to indicate in the manuscript the division or the numbering of certain type-pages. The marks have nothing to do with the compositorial stints or with casting-off copy but instead appear to relate in some manner to the making-up of pages. The step brackets are the same as occur later in *The Blithedale Romance* manuscript and hence are systematic, like the compositorial signings. Their exact function is not altogether clear. They are found irregularly and at highly variable intervals. What is consistent in both manuscripts, however, is that the intervals between them are multiples of three type-pages, such as three, six, nine, twelve, fifteen, and so on. Whether the type was made up into pages in three-page galleys, or whether these marks and their page numbers have to do with the process of imposition is uncertain. The most likely guess is that they are written by no more than one or two hands, that they mark some series of made-up pages, and that the notation is made in the manuscript as a record.

In a few cases the step brackets are in error. On folio 21 the step bracket actually marks the start of the thirty-second type-line on page 42 and it is numbered "42" in error for "43", whereas an ink square bracket, unnumbered, correctly starts page 43. Interestingly, the cycle of intervals of three calls for page 42 to be marked, not page 43. The correctness of the square bracket here would seem to indicate that it was drawn after the step mark. On the other hand, on folio

37 an unnumbered step bracket correctly marks off the start of page 68 whereas an unnumbered square bracket marks the end of the second line on the page. This error is inexplicable. Chapter IV had begun on page 64, and page 65 is 33 lines (instead of the normal 34) in order to prevent a "widow" (i.e., initial part-line) on page 66; but pages 66-68 are all the normal 34 lines.

The error in marking folio 1 as if it had ended Emery's stint with a 34-line page has been noticed above. But a further error was engendered in Chapter I. The step bracket and number 15 on folio 4 actually mark off the start of the seventh line on page 15. This mistake is readily explained because page 15 would have started at that line if the first page of Chapter I had been the normal 27 lines of text, plus the chapter heading. But the maker-up forgot, evidently, to set the necessary head-title "THE HOUSE | OF | THE SEVEN GABLES.", which occupies the space of seven lines. That the mistake is of only six lines on page 15 results from the present making-up of page 14 with 35 lines in order to avoid a widow on page 15. The next step mark appears with 24, which marks off the start of the seventh line on page 24. However, as now made up, the intervening page 17 is only 33 lines in order to prevent a widow on page 18. Ordinarily, therefore, the step bracket should have marked off the eighth line on the page, not the seventh. But in making-up pages according to the original error, a widow would have occurred on page 20, and presumably, then, page 19 was reduced originally to 33 lines, which would make the step mark on page 27 correct. This illustration demonstrates neatly that the step brackets deal with pages correctly made up with due regard for widows. On page 27 another step mark correctly marks off the original start of the page, although placed before the seventh line. The next step bracket marks page 33 eight lines down, but this is one line in error without apparent reason. Presumably, before Chapter

II was imposed on page 36 the mistake was discovered and the pages correctly made up to take account of the added head-title, for though the next step bracket, on page 42, is wrongly placed, its error seems to have no relation to the wrong original series in Chapter I.

On folio 144 the step bracket and its page number 223 are correct. On folio 162 the next one, marking page 247, originally referred to the tenth line; but this has been deleted and an unnumbered step drawn in after the eighth line. This error is explained by the change in layout that takes place with the start of Chapter XV on page 239 whereby the type-page is reduced regularly by one line to the end of the volume. From page 239, then, the chapter-heading pages hold 26 lines and the normal text page 33 lines. Thus the substituted step bracket marks, correctly, what would have been the beginning of page 247 if the original layout had been maintained. From this point the errors in marking increase mathematically until, finally, on folio 230 the ink step bracket for page 334 instead refers to the third line of page 337. Normal making-up would have ended the volume with three lines of text on page 341, which would have been the fifth page of gathering 22. The printer could have reduced these five pages to four and machined this final gathering as a quarter-sheet by adding a thirty-fifth line to the final pages in order to end on page 340, setting (or plating) the last four pages in duplicate, and printing these two quarter-sheets together as a half-sheet. On the evidence, however, he chose to adjust the make-up of his type-pages and to re-impose the pages back to page 239 in order to stretch the originally composed text out to eight pages for gathering 22, which he then plated in duplicate and machined as a full sheet. It is clear that stereotypes had not been made for page 239 (the thirteenth page of gathering 15) and its successors at the time the final page of the book was set, else this readjustment of the type requiring new plates would have proved too expensive to contemplate.

In addition to these step brackets, a few miscellaneous printer's markings also appear. The square brackets in pencil setting off the start of Letts's stint on what is now page 10, and the ink correction of the step marking for page 43 have been mentioned. Another occurs, in error, on folio 37 where the step had been correct for page 68. A pencil square bracket and a large "131" correctly indicate the beginning of this page on folio 79. On the verso of folio 37 a pencil "70" reflects the start of page 70 on folio 38 recto, although a step and 70 are marked in ink on folio 38 correctly. On the verso of folio 87 appears the pencil figure "141", although page 141 had started on folio 86. It is possible that these last three markings were made by the foreman.

The purpose of a few other notations is obscure. On folio 35 the figure "36½" is pencilled below King's signature in the first paragraph opening, and the figure is repeated above the same line in the right margin. On the verso of folio 157 several computations are pencilled. First, 27 is multiplied by 7 for the result 189. Then, 800 and 100 are added to form 900. Finally, 189 and 23 are added to total 212. Usually such sums estimate the length of copy, and it is probable that these figures have something to do with the rearrangement of the make-up after page 239, which had begun with Chapter XV starting on folio 156.[12] At the foot of folio 199 is written in pencil what seems to be "rim in".

The only authorial marking on a verso is Hawthorne's brief insert on folio 15 verso, and his deleted false start of folio 17 on what became the verso of folio 18.

The textual theory adopted for the Centenary Edition establishes the Harvard manuscript as the copy-text, that is,

[12] For example, beginning with Chapter XV, seven chapter-heading pages, each normally of 27 lines, remain in the volume. The other figures are not readily to be explained.

as the major basis for the edited text. Since this manuscript is a fair-copy holograph, it is clear that its "accidentals," or the forms of its spelling, punctuation, capitalization, and word-division, must be more authoritative than the house style imposed on this same copy by the compositors. On the other hand, if Hawthorne can be conjectured to have corrected or revised any of the "substantives" (i.e., the words themselves) in the course of reading proof, such variant first-edition substantives would represent his final intentions and would become more authoritative than the corresponding manuscript readings.

Since indisputable evidence exists for Hawthorne's revisions in proof, the present edition adheres to Sir Walter Greg's classic exposition of the theory of copy-text [13] and has utilized, with only a few specific exceptions, the manuscript accidentals in preference to those of the first edition.[14] In this general texture of authoritative accidentals from the manuscript, all such variant substantive readings of the first edition have been incorporated that may be thought to represent Hawthorne's proof-alterations in the original typesetting from the manuscript or are necessary corrections that might have been made as readily by the compositor as by the author.

All in all, perhaps as many as three to four thousand differences exist in the accidentals between the manuscript and the print of *The House of the Seven Gables*. That any great part of these should be taken as stemming from Hawthorne's proofreading is fantastic. Authors then as now were accustomed to accepting the printer's house style. Moreover, the characteristics of the print, in contrast to the manuscript, are just about the same in *The Blithedale Romance* set in the

[13] "The Rationale of Copy-Text," *Studies in Bibliography*, III (1950–51), 19–36.

[14] Evidence indicating that Hawthorne could not have been responsible for the majority, at least, of the differences in the accidentals between manuscript and print is discussed in the Textual Introduction to *The Blithedale Romance* (Centenary Edition, 1964), pp. xxxvii–xxxix.

same shop the following year. One would scarcely wish to argue that Hawthorne made hundreds and hundreds of proof-alterations in the *Seven Gables* sheets contrary to the style of his manuscript, and then ignored the new system he had embraced and returned to his former ways in the manuscript of *The Blithedale Romance*—only to alter them once more in proof.

The matter comes down to the point, then, that whereas a critic can on literary grounds (aided by whatever bibliographical evidence is available) make some attempt to judge whether substantive alterations are authorial or not, no one can thus adjudicate the authority of most of the accidentals altered from the manuscript in the print. With comparatively few exceptions, therefore, a definitive edition must follow the forms of the manuscript and not of the print. In doing so, the editor will perhaps lose a small number of Hawthorne alterations in the accidentals; but in the unknown and undeterminable cases he will at least preserve an authorial reading, even if not the final one, and he will protect himself from reproducing many hundreds of printer's house-style variants as if they were the author's.

Hence the Centenary text transcribes Hawthorne's own accidentals in all their flavor and with all the literary intent that ordinarily governed his usage. An author's accidentals are an important part of his total style by which he conveys meaning; indeed, on the evidence of the manuscripts, Hawthorne took some care to adjust the weight of his punctuation to the desired nuance of the content,[15] and thus his desires

[15] After surveying the difference between reading Hawthorne in the manuscript and in the first-edition versions, Professor William Charvat was moved to write to the textual editor: "It comes to me now, for the first time, that Hawthorne's style is essentially parenthetical, and that this characteristic reflects the basically essayistic, generalizing, and speculative quality of his fiction. His parentheses give him the latitude and flexibility that this quality requires. He modulates the degree of isolation of a unit by selecting (usually) just the right pair of separators: parentheses, or dashes, or commas. I don't think he did this selecting consciously, and

have been scrupulously preserved save where mechanical correctness required alteration.

The view that Hawthorne was a rapid and careless proofreader originates chiefly in his treatment of material which was not creative (like the biography of Pierce) or which was being reprinted in collections, like the tales, from copy that had already seen print. Yet what evidence there is indicates that Hawthorne's main object in insisting on reading proofs for *The House of the Seven Gables* was not so much to incorporate second thoughts and improvements suggested by a resurvey in type as it was to insure the substantive correctness of what he had written in the manuscript. Thus on January 15, 1850, he wrote to Fields about *The Scarlet Letter* proofs: "The proof-sheets will need to be revised by the author. I write such an infernal hand that this is absolutely indispensable." [16] When on January 27, 1851, he notified Fields that the manuscript of *The House of the Seven Gables* had been sent by express, he insisted: "I deem it indispensable that the proof-sheets should be sent me for correction. . . . My autography is sometimes villainously blind; and it is odd enough that wherever the printers do mistake a word, it is just the very jewel of a word, worth all the rest of the Dictionary." [17]

On February 3, 1851, Fields wrote: "In a few days I shall send the first proofs. The arrangement which will secure

---

probably the restoration of his own punctuation, after the compositors mangled it, looked like too much drudgery. Certainly, the compositors show very little sensitivity about his modulations." To this perceptive statement one can add only that the various examples of change exhibited in the manuscript in which Hawthorne usually weighs more heavily, but occasionally lightens, the parenthetical punctuation might lead one to suppose that sometimes, at least, he had a quite clear idea of what he was doing and was consciously altering his original sense of the modulations. The list of Alterations in the Manuscript records a number of examples.

[16] Hawthorne-Fields Letter Book, MS, Houghton Library, Harvard University.

[17] Hawthorne-Fields Letter Book, MS, Houghton Library, Harvard University.

the most rapid returns will be to mail each package & ask you to send back by return of mail. When we begin to send, a package will come every day to Lenox. . . ." [18] Under this arrangement only a sheet or two could reach Hawthorne at a time,[19] and he complained bitterly (as he usually did about reading proof) on February 22, 1851, to Fields: "Good-by. I must now trudge two miles to the village, through rain and mud, knee-deep, after that accursed proof-sheet." [20]

Under these circumstances, Hawthorne seems to have made fewer improvements than he did the following year in the proofs of *The Blithedale Romance,* and to have contented himself generally with an attempt at securing correctness. That he was not uniformly successful even in this modest aim may be indicated by the somewhat lengthy Centenary list of Rejected First-Edition Substantive Readings. Not all of these are obvious misprints that escaped attention: a number like "throe" for "term" (37.30), "Wiggins" for "Higgins" (81.17), "barn-yard" for "barn-door" (90.27), "stop" for

[18] Fields to Hawthorne, MS, Berg Collection, New York Public Library.

[19] A little earlier than his February 3 letter, Fields had written to Hawthorne on January 30, 1851: "We shall begin to stereotype immediately & shall wait untill we get considerable matter in type before we begin to send you proofs—" (MS, Berg Collection, New York Public Library). The meaning of this sentence is obscure. The printer could not make a stereotype plate until all proof-correction of the page had been completed. Possibly Fields meant that stereotyping would begin before the volume was completely in corrected type, sheet by sheet as it was corrected; but more likely he meant that the first edition would be printed from plates, not from type. At any rate, his subsequent letter seems to indicate the actual sheet-by-sheet dispatch of proof. That this was customary may be indicated by a letter from Hawthorne to Fields on July 15, 1851, about the *Wonder-Book:* "I must see the proof-sheets of this book. . . . Can't you manage it so that two or three, or more sheets may be sent at once, on stated days; and so my journeys to the village be fewer?" (Hawthorne-Fields Letter Book, MS, Houghton Library, Harvard University).

[20] Hawthorne to Fields, MS, Library of Congress. On February 12, 1851, Sophia Hawthorne wrote her mother: " . . . Mr Hawthorne goes to the village for his proofs. They began to come last Saturday, & when he finds one or more, he remains at the post-office, & corrects them & puts them directly back into the mail" (MS, Berg Collection, New York Public Library).

"step" (103.23), "class" for "chaos" (149.25), "thrilled" for
"trilled" (192.24), or "drop" for "droop" (307.12), represent some indeterminate blend of compositorial misreading,
memorial failure, and sophistication that made sense but not
the right sense of the manuscript and went undetected, even
to the wrong name for one of the characters.

Correspondingly, the substantive variants that seem to have
been made in proof by the author constitute only relatively
minor improvements or corrections and are therefore more
than ordinarily difficult to identify as authorial instead of
compositorial. If we isolate nine variants as such obvious or
necessary corrections of manuscript errors that they could
have been altered by the compositor in the process of typesetting,[21] we are left with sixteen substantive variants between manuscript and print that may be accepted as probable
authorial proof-changes, although only eight of these can be
regarded as definitely authoritative. Of the remaining, two
may be thought of as doubtfully authoritative since some
evidence may be adduced in their favor, and six as almost
completely indifferent as between author or compositor.

Of the eight alterations assumed positively to be authorial
proof-alterations, "infinitely" is changed to "far" at 7.24;
at 24.31 Hawthorne excised "In fine," beginning a sentence;
at 80.32 he substituted "old maid" for "Hepzibah" in order
to avoid a repetition caused by an alteration within the
manuscript; at 102.24 to indicate a moment of stress "dear"
is intensified to "dearest"; at 214.27–28 "light of a ruddy,
cheerful fire" becomes the "ruddy light of a cheerful fire";
at 299.22 "inside" becomes "within"; the "social and political

[21] These nine substantive variants may be found in the list of Editorial
Emendations in the Copy-Text at 48.29, 93.33, 161.30, 181.2–3, 182.26,
196.35, 221.33, 278.30 (see Textual Note), and 282.1. In addition, the
following twenty-five manuscript errors and slips were even more of a
nature to be corrected by the compositor automatically: 29.18, 35.31, 43.1,
45.14, 48.34, 58.21, 81.1, 105.27, 141.21, 145.20, 152.24, 153.13, 170.23,
178.26, 181.5–6, 181.8, 186.1, 213.4, 242.16, 244.12, 281.25, 283.2, 285.26,
299.19, and 310.24.

world" at 309.2 is altered to the "social world"; and at 310.26 "indicating" is substituted for "showing".

These relatively clearcut proof-alterations appear respectively in sheets 1, 2, 6, 7, 15 (one change in each) and 21 (three changes). The compositors represented are, in order, Letts, Letts, Fox, King, Jackman, King, Letts, and Letts.

More doubtful readings are discussed in the Textual Notes for 169.31 and 276.8. These two readings appear in sheets 12 and 19 in pages set by King and Henderson. Neither of these sheets is represented in the list of firmly accepted authorial alterations.

The six relatively indifferent readings occur at 111.16, 186.24, 234.3, 266.17, 287.31, and 291.31. Less plausible explanations account for these variants than for the doubtful group, but they have not been considered as absolutely indifferent although each could almost as well be a compositor's memorial error or sophistication as an authorial change. Their sheets are, respectively, 8, 13, 16, 18, 20 (twice), and the compositors are King, Henderson, King, Fox, Fox, and King. Even though King is in some respects the third most reliable compositor, the three variants in his pages are perhaps the most doubtful of the lot, especially since two produce a mirror-image of the same kind of change.

Fifty-two substantive variants between manuscript and print have been rejected as non-authorial. Classification of such variants is sometimes difficult, as at 171.22 where "on" becomes first-edition "or" and the question is whether this is a mechanical error by Loring or some obscure memorial lapse or misreading. Again, it is impossible to decide whether Henderson's change of manuscript singular to plural at 306.35 is a real misprint or a memorial error. Some sense is made, although markedly inferior to that of the manuscript.

Of these fifty-two variants, three may be set aside as presumptive misprints, i.e., as inadvertent mechanical errors that are plainly wrong on any grounds of meaning. These are 79.19, 129.14, and 171.22 in sheets 6, 9, and 12; the compositors were King, Henderson, and Loring.

Twenty-one variants appear to have resulted from simple misreading of the manuscript where the letter formation was not entirely clear. These are 32.4 King, page 38, sheet 3; 37.30 King 44(3); 45.33 Whittle 53(4); 52.4 Loring 59(4); 64.25 Loring 73(5); 65.8 Loring 73(5); 81.17 Fox 91(6); 88.20 Letts 98(7); 89.34 Jackman 100(7); 103.23 Fox 113(8); 106.26 Jackman 117(8); 106.31 Jackman 117(8); 127.14 Willis 139(9); 144.20 Willis 156(10); 149.25 Willis 162(11); 171.2 Loring 185(12); 179.19 Jackman 193(13); 185.5 Fox 199(13); 192.24 Letts 207(13); 209.15 King 225(15); and 224.8 Henderson 240(15).

The foregoing variants seem to have an ascertainable physical cause that may serve to remove any doubt about the actual authority of the changes. The remaining twenty-eight differences are less certain in their origin. Jackman's change of "barn-door fowl" at 90.27 to the more familiar "barnyard fowl" could have been memorial confusion as readily as deliberate "improvement" of a fancied mistake. Moreover, this group differs considerably in its various degrees of demonstrable error. That "bolt" at 69.6 is right and Jackman's setting of "door" is wrong is reasonably clear from the context, whether the error arose from a simple misunderstanding of the sense or from memorial contamination with "door" in the preceding sentence. Correspondingly, Henderson's "impulses" in the print at 306.35 can scarcely, on grounds of sense, be an authorial correction of the singular; and the same compositor's "drop" is manifestly contrary to Hawthorne's idiomatic manuscript use of "droop" (307.12) here and elsewhere. But that it was not Hawthorne, but the compositor, who altered manuscript "such depth" at 137.23 in King's stint to "such a depth", the subjunctive "were" in Henderson's stint to "was" at 255.31, or "this" to "the" in a

Willis page at 280.26, cannot be affirmed with absolute certainty.

These twenty-eight rejected readings,[22] therefore, seem to represent varying combinations of simple mistake, memorial lapse, and real sophistication. What they share in common, as also with the twenty-one inferred pure misreadings, is acceptable sense: never superior sense but sometimes indifferent and sometimes inferior. No reason seems to exist to impute them to Hawthorne, and they may safely be regarded as compositorial corruptions not recognized in the proofreading. The compositors responsible are Willis (6), Henderson (6), Jackman (6), King (5), Fox (2), Loring (2), and Letts (1).

If we consolidate all fifty-two of the rejected first-edition substantive readings, the score by compositors is Jackman (10), Willis (9), Henderson (8), King (9), Loring (7), Fox (5), Letts (3), and Whittle (1). Given such small evidence, statistics have little meaning perhaps,[23] but, for what the information is worth, Willis made one uncorrected error for every 125 lines set, or .80 errors per 100 lines; Jackman one error every 143 lines, or .71 per 100; Loring one error every 144 lines, or .69 per 100; Henderson one error every

[22] The readings are 31.33 King 37(3); 44.7 Willis 51(4); 62.26 Letts 71(5); 64.10 Loring 72(5); 69.6 Jackman 77(5); 84.1 Loring 93(6); 90.27 Jackman 100(7); 113.4 King 124(8); 127.11 Willis 139(9); 127.32 Willis 139(9); 137.23 King 149(10); 170.9 King 183(12); 174.34–35 Henderson 188(12); 214.14 Jackman 230(15); 228.12 Jackman 244(16); 228.18 Fox 244(16); 254.5 Jackman 272(17); 255.31 Henderson 273(18); 266.27–28 Fox 286(18); 275.3 Jackman 294(19); 278.30 King 298(19); 280.26 Willis 300(19); 303.20 Willis 326(21); 304.11 Willis 327(21); 306.35 Henderson 330(21); 307.11 Henderson 330(21); 307.12 Henderson 330(21); and 308.27 Henderson 332(21).

[23] For instance, if we arrange the compositors in the order of the number of lines of type that they set, we have Fox (2,244), Letts (1,733), King (1,696), Jackman (1,403), Henderson (1,212), Willis (1,124), and Loring (1,010). This bears a rough inverse approximation to the over-all accuracy of the compositors, but whether the general correlation results from the printer's having assigned takes on such a basis or from the unbalanced statistical leverage exerted by error in the work of compositors with fewer stints, is moot. However, Letts, Fox, and King still seem to merit attention as the superior workmen, although one may have reservations about certain features of King's work.

152 lines, or .61 per 100; King one error every 188 lines, or .53 per 100; Fox one error every 449 lines, or .22 per 100; and Letts one error every 578 lines, or .17 per 100. On the other hand, if we disregard the errors for which ascertainable reasons may be assigned, like misreading and mechanical slips, and confine ourselves to the textually more debatable group where memorial failure or sophistication predominates, we find that Willis made one undetected error for every 187 lines set, or .53 errors per 100 lines; Henderson one error every 202 lines, or .50 per 100 lines; Jackman one error every 234 lines, or .43 per 100 lines; King one error every 339 lines, or .29 per 100 lines; Loring one error every 504 lines, or .20 per 100 lines; Fox one error every 1,123 lines, or .09 per 100 lines; and Letts one error every 1,733 lines, or .06 per 100 lines. Under either system Willis is the worst and Letts and Fox are the best compositors. Henderson and Jackman are in the upper range of error; King in the middle range. Loring is in the upper range for total errors, but his percentage decreases when memorial error or sophistication is in question.

In this framework it is at least interesting to observe that of the eight alterations accepted as Hawthorne's and thus not to be imputed to compositorial error, four come in Letts's pages, two in King's, and one each in Fox's and Jackman's, but none in Henderson's, Loring's, or Willis'. The concentration in Letts's stints is unusual but fortuitous, like the absence of change in Loring's and Willis' pages. Of the two changes doubtfully attributed to Hawthorne, one each appears in the work of King and Henderson. Three of the relatively indifferent variants are in King's pages, against two in Fox's and one in Henderson's. The fact that four of the eight doubtful or indifferent variants appear in King's work is not a point in their favor, as it would be, for example, if Letts had set them (Fox has two of these variants, also, and Henderson two); but at least statistics show that King is a generally more trustworthy workman than Loring, Jackman, and Willis, who, fortunately, are not represented at all in this category.[24]

To summarize, wanting the lost proof sheets of *The House of the Seven Gables* any reconstruction of the full extent of Hawthorne's proof-alteration must always remain hypothetical. Such alterations could have been in four categories. First, the printer's errors that Hawthorne recognized and corrected. Since for these the manuscript and the print would agree after correction, no evidence as to their extent can be recovered from the preserved documents. Second, the alterations in proof that Hawthorne may have made of any readings in the accidentals. Some three or four thousand such differences exist between the manuscript and the first edition. Of these, certain categories can be positively identified as house-styling by the compositors and not as any possible Hawthorne proof-alteration. Even though other categories containing large numbers cannot be identified with confidence as one or the other, the presumption is that any variant between the first edition and the manuscript in the accidentals must ordinarily be laid to the printer. In these circumstances, therefore, except for unusual cases it is folly to attempt to distinguish authorial proof-alterations in the accidentals from compositorial variants except in such special cases as described in the Textual Note for 30.13.

In the third category come variant substantive readings that an editor may fairly believe to be compositorial errors overlooked by Hawthorne in reading the proofs. In the

[24] Henderson was responsible for an astonishing six of the eleven inferred compositorial errors in *The Blithedale Romance,* and Fox for two. Henderson would have come off much better in *Seven Gables* were it not for his mistakes in sheet 21; yet each of his four variants there seems to be a clearcut compositorial error. It is also an oddity that three of the eight accepted authorial proof changes cluster in sheet 21 and that this same sheet also contains six supposed uncorrected compositorial errors, of which four are Henderson's and two are Willis'. In sheet 21 Fox set 132 lines, Henderson 109, Willis 95, King 79, and Letts 75.

fourth, the remaining substantive differences between manuscript and print must be taken to represent words that had originally been set by the compositors in accord with the manuscript but that were altered by Hawthorne to other words in the proofreading process.

If we put aside the first-edition correction (almost surely compositorial) of thirty-four obvious slips in the manuscript (see footnote 21 above), collation discloses that seventy-eight substantive variants exist between the manuscript and the print. Of these, the Centenary editors believe that sixteen may be taken to represent Hawthorne's revisions in the proof sheets of authoritative and satisfactory readings in the manuscript, ten may represent his correction in proof of his own manuscript errors (at least, such as escaped compositorial correction), and fifty-two represent printer's errors that he overlooked and that an editor must reject.

If we compare these figures with the estimates for *The Blithedale Romance* set in the same shop the following year, at least one significant difference may be observed: the proportion of assumed printer's errors is considerably smaller in the later volume, in proportion to author's corrections. In *The Blithedale Romance* twenty-eight variants are assigned as Hawthorne's revisions of satisfactory manuscript readings, and only eleven as printer's errors that should be rejected. Author's corrections, thus, are about two and one-half times as frequent as overlooked compositorial errors. On the other hand, in *The House of the Seven Gables* the situation is exactly reversed in that substantive printer's errors to be rejected outnumber authorial alterations (even most liberally construed to include up to ten of his own manuscript errors) by two or three to one.

The evidence points inescapably to Hawthorne's having proofread *The Blithedale Romance* with greater care than he gave to *The House of the Seven Gables*. Despite the relative shortness of the book, the actual number of author's alterations in *Blithedale* is higher than in *Seven Gables*. Moreover, the nature of the variants differs in that the authorial changes in *Seven Gables* are small in number and essentially trivial in nature, whereas in *Blithedale* some occasional effort was made to improve the style in a significant manner by substitution of more meaningful words, the authority of which cannot be questioned. The number of variants approaching the indifferent status is considerably higher in *Seven Gables*, and it may be that the Centenary editors have been insufficiently conservative in admitting from the first edition as many as eight doubtful variants beyond the basic eight that seem to be quite certain.

The causes for this discrepancy in the trustworthiness of the first-edition text in the two volumes are obscure. It may be that Emery and Munn were superior workmen to King, Jackman, Loring, and Willis, and that the effects of typesetting a shorter book with longer takes by four selected compositors (if they were indeed more careful workmen) proved superior to the composition of a longer book by using seven major compositors and shorter takes. The extra workmen may well not have been so competent as Emery and Munn, to whom only one and two corrected errors, respectively, are assigned in *The Blithedale Romance* as against two for Fox (one of the most careful workmen on the *Seven Gables* job), and six for Henderson (who is in the lower half of competency among the *Seven Gables* compositors). It may be, also, as the evidence suggests, that Hawthorne found the proofreading less burdensome in relatively convenient West Newton than in Lenox, where he had a two-mile trudge almost every day to the post office. Under more agreeable conditions he seems to have devoted closer attention to the proofreading and to the improvements of the text.[25]

The Centenary text is essentially an exact transcript of the Harvard manuscript in its finally revised state. Substituted for manuscript readings are sixteen substantives from the first edition believed to be Hawthorne's revisory proof-corrections, and ten additional readings from the first edition thought to be Hawthorne's corrections of manuscript errors (in case these escaped the compositors' correction), excluding twenty-five obvious manuscript slips doubtless corrected by the compositors in the setting. Excluded are fifty-two first-edition substantive variants thought to represent unauthoritative printer's errors not corrected in the proofreading. For these the manuscript readings have been preferred.

A very few normalizations of spelling forms have been attempted when Hawthorne's own practice was generally different, or when though invariable (as in "cieling") it was well out of step with approved usage of his time. The editors have had to use their discretion in the transcription of a few words with -*ise* or -*ize* endings, since Hawthorne's inscription of *s* and of *z* does not always differentiate the two letters clearly. Moreover, his minuscule *a* is sometimes left open and cannot always be distinguished firmly from his *u*. Thus the forms to reproduce must sometimes be determined from other occurrences in the manuscript or in similar documents. The editors have carefully considered each case on its merits and transcribed the form that seemed to be intended in the inscrip-

[25] The inferentially corrected errors in proof are evenly spaced save for the cluster in sheet 21: 1(1), 2(1), 6(1), 7(1), 8(1), 12(1), 13(1), 15(1), 16(1), 18(1), 19(1), 20(2), 21(3). These represent the sixteen confirmed, doubtful, and indifferent variants. If one adds the nine manuscript errors that could as easily have been corrected by the compositors in setting type as by Hawthorne in proof, then a correction will also appear in sheets 4, 11, and 14. On the scanty evidence, therefore, it would seem that Hawthorne looked over every sheet, although no evidence exists about the possible correction of sheets 3, 5, 9, 10, 17, and 22. Uncorrected inferential errors appear in the following sheets: 3(3), 4(3), 5(5), 6(3), 7(3), 8(4), 9(4), 10(2), 11(1), 12(4), 13(3), 15(3), 16(2), 17(1), 18(2), 19(3), 21(6).

tion and that was consistent with Hawthorne's established custom.

Critical emendation of the word-division has been undertaken to normalize anomalies according to the forms customarily favored by Hawthorne.

Some punctuation emendations have proved necessary (a) to normalize anomalies, as above; (b) less often, to substitute necessary or manifestly superior first-edition punctuation which in a very few cases may be (though not necessarily) the result of proof-alteration; and (c) to correct a few manuscript errors reproduced in the print. All the foregoing have been recorded.

The usual silent alterations, in the categories listed in the general discussion of textual procedures appended to this volume, have been made. Also, the differences in the manuscript between such forms as "M^r" and "Mr." have not been reproduced or recorded, and Hawthorne's superior "o" without apostrophe (as in his "^{o}clock") has been transcribed silently as "o'" as in the first edition. Missing manuscript periods have been supplied silently. Manuscript and first-edition spacing, like "I 'll" or "had n't", not always consistent in the manuscript, has been silently modernized. Dashes that Hawthorne inserted to fill out the manuscript line to the right margin have been ignored unless ambiguous.

In the apparatus, non-substantive variants are ignored when they are not the point of variance that is being recorded; in these circumstances the form of the variant in the MS copy-text is the only one noted. For example, the item in the list of Editorial Emendations at 43.30 reads: Daguerreotypist] CENTENARY; daguerreotypist MS, I-V. Here the only pertinent information is that certain editions agree with the manuscript in reproducing "daguerreotypist" with a lower-case "d". That the manuscript follows the word with a dash and the first edition with a comma and a dash is not recorded, since it is not the variant that is being listed as an emendation.

Apart from the divergences noted above and in the appendix discussion of general textual procedures, the text of *The House of the Seven Gables* is established here for the first time in the relative purity of its manuscript form.[26]

F. B.

---

[26] When this Introduction was in proof, a paperback Riverside Edition of *The House of the Seven Gables* (Boston, 1964) appeared, edited by Hyatt H. Waggoner, and based on a manuscript-first edition collation. The above statement, therefore, is no longer true. However, the Riverside text will be found to differ considerably from the Centenary text in its transcript of the manuscript and its estimate of the amount of authorial proof-correction.

NOTE ON THE TYPESETTING

SOME misunderstanding of the relation between typesetting and stereotyping may arise from the fact that in
the Ticknor and Fields *Cost Books* the only firms mentioned (other than engravers, paper dealers, and binders)
are stereotypers and *printers*. What were printers? Usually
they both set type and did presswork. What were stereotypers?
Did they cast plates only, or did they also set type for their
plates? On the surface, the entries leave open the possibility
that type for a book was set *for* the stereotyper by another
firm.

However, this editor has never seen an instance, in or out
of the *Cost Books*, from the beginning of general use of
stereotype plates in the 1830's, in which a typesetter is mentioned in conjunction with a stereotyper. His evidence in-
cludes cost books of firms in Philadelphia, the letters and
other records of publishers in the large coastal cities, and the
business records and correspondence of the authors of the
period 1830–70. Moreover, the papers of authors who owned
some or all of their own plates (Longfellow, Lowell, and
Cooper, among others) contain bills from their stereotypers
which always lump the total cost of producing plates without
ever a mention of a separate typesetter. The figures in all
these documents, and in the *Cost Books*, leave no doubt

about the considerable difference between the cost of setting type and the combined cost of setting and plating. One can tell, whenever the cost per "em" or "m" is given, whether a book was plated or not.

Generally typical of the entries in the *Cost Books* for unplated and plated books are the following.

For the unplated first edition of *The Scarlet Letter*, entry A 173a, page 156:

```
1850.  2500   The Scarlet Letter        2500
              By Nathl Hawthorne
              16 Mo. 324 pps. Metcalf & Co
              57 4/20 Reams.
                    18½ x 29. 33.  4.75        268 30
              302.586 ms.       @ 43¢.         130 11
              115 Tokens.            75.        86 75
              Ext Corrections                    9 50
              Copt. on 2400— @. 15%            270 00
              Binding               10         250 00  1014 66
              Cost Sheets 32.    clo 42.
              Trade 75   ¼ [discount]
              Published Mar. 1850.
```

The book itself does not identify the printer. The charge for "ms" indicates that Metcalf set the type; the charge for "Tokens", that Metcalf also did the presswork.

For the plated first edition of *The House of the Seven Gables,* entry A 214a, page 188:

```
1851   1690   House of the Seven
                   Gables. Hawthorne     1690
              Steo. 1st Edn. 344 pps.
              Metcalf & CO
Mar 6         40 Rms. 18½ x 29. 36. 4.50       180 00
     24       72½ Tokens.            80         58 00
```

Binding   10   169 oc
Copt 1500 Cops 15 ¢
  on 1500   225 oc 632
_____

(Eds Cops. 190)   632
Cost. on 1500 Cops. to manf.   42.
  "   "   "   inclu'g. Plates. —60—
Sells   @ 1.00
Published Apl 1851.

The book itself, on the copyright page, names Hobart & Robbins as the stereotypers. The difference between the cost to manufacture (42 cents per copy) and the cost including plates (60 cents per copy) is 18 cents, which means that Hobart & Robbins charged about $270 for the plates. As no separate charge for "ms" is given, the cost of typesetting was part of the cost of the plates. For this book Metcalf did the presswork only, the charge for which is given in the "Tokens" line.

In the *Cost Books*, therefore, when the name of a "printer" is given in addition to and other than that of the stereotyper, it is to be assumed that he did the presswork only. Once the plates had been cast, they could be, and usually were, shipped to some other shop for the presswork. Before the 1850's few firms had the equipment to perform all three operations— typesetting, plating, and presswork. But after 1855, when capitalization in the printing industry was generally improving, the *Cost Books* entries indicate that several large firms were able to do the whole job of producing stereotyped books.

For books printed from type metal, the assumption must be, in the absence of evidence to the contrary, that the printer named in the *Cost Books*, and/or in the book itself, did both the typesetting and the presswork.

W. C.

THE HOUSE OF THE
SEVEN GABLES

PREFACE

WHEN a writer calls his work a Romance, it need
hardly be observed that he wishes to claim a certain
latitude, both as to its fashion and material, which
he would not have felt himself entitled to assume, had he
professed to be writing a Novel. The latter form of composition is presumed to aim at a very minute fidelity, not merely
to the possible, but to the probable and ordinary course of
man's experience. The former—while, as a work of art, it
must rigidly subject itself to laws, and while it sins unpardonably, so far as it may swerve aside from the truth of the human
heart—has fairly a right to present that truth under circumstances, to a great extent, of the writer's own choosing or
creation. If he think fit, also, he may so manage his atmos-
pherical medium as to bring out or mellow the lights and
deepen and enrich the shadows of the picture. He will be
wise, no doubt, to make a very moderate use of the privileges
here stated, and, especially, to mingle the Marvellous rather
as a slight, delicate, and evanescent flavor, than as any portion
of the actual substance of the dish offered to the Public. He
can hardly be said, however, to commit a literary crime, even
if he disregard this caution.

In the present work, the Author has proposed to himself
(but with what success, fortunately, it is not for him to

judge) to keep undeviatingly within his immunities. The point of view in which this Tale comes under the Romantic definition, lies in the attempt to connect a by-gone time with the very Present that is flitting away from us. It is a Legend, prolonging itself, from an epoch now gray in the distance, down into our own broad daylight, and bringing along with it some of its legendary mist, which the Reader, according to his pleasure, may either disregard, or allow it to float almost imperceptibly about the characters and events, for the sake of a picturesque effect. The narrative, it may be, is woven of so humble a texture as to require this advantage, and, at the same time, to render it the more difficult of attainment.

Many writers lay very great stress upon some definite moral purpose, at which they profess to aim their works. Not to be deficient, in this particular, the Author has provided himself with a moral;—the truth, namely, that the wrong-doing of one generation lives into the successive ones, and, divesting itself of every temporary advantage, becomes a pure and uncontrollable mischief;—and he would feel it a singular gratification, if this Romance might effectually convince mankind (or, indeed, any one man) of the folly of tumbling down an avalanche of ill-gotten gold, or real estate, on the heads of an unfortunate posterity, thereby to maim and crush them, until the accumulated mass shall be scattered abroad in its original atoms. In good faith, however, he is not sufficiently imaginative to flatter himself with the slightest hope of this kind. When romances do really teach anything, or produce any effective operation, it is usually through a far more subtile process than the ostensible one. The Author has considered it hardly worth his while, therefore, relentlessly to impale the story with its moral, as with an iron rod—or rather, as by sticking a pin through a butterfly—thus at once depriving it of life, and causing it to stiffen in an ungainly and unnatural attitude. A high truth, indeed, fairly, finely, and skilfully wrought out, brightening at every step, and crowning the final developement of a work of fiction, may add an artistic glory, but is never any truer, and seldom any more evident, at the last page than at the first.

The Reader may perhaps choose to assign an actual locality to the imaginary events of this narrative. If permitted by the historical connection, (which, though slight, was essential to his plan,) the Author would very willingly have avoided anything of this nature. Not to speak of other objections, it exposes the Romance to an inflexible and exceedingly danger-ous species of criticism, by bringing his fancy-pictures almost into positive contact with the realities of the moment. It has been no part of his object, however, to describe local manners, nor in any way to meddle with the characteristics of a com-munity for whom he cherishes a proper respect and a natural regard. He trusts not to be considered as unpardonably of-fending, by laying out a street that infringes upon nobody's private rights, and appropriating a lot of land which had no visible owner, and building a house, of materials long in use for constructing castles in the air. The personages of the Tale—though they give themselves out to be of ancient stabil-ity and considerable prominence—are really of the Author's own making, or, at all events, of his own mixing; their virtues can shed no lustre, nor their defects redound, in the remotest degree, to the discredit of the venerable town of which they profess to be inhabitants. He would be glad, therefore, if— especially in the quarter to which he alludes—the book may be read strictly as a Romance, having a great deal more to do with the clouds overhead, than with any portion of the actual soil of the County of Essex.

Lenox, January 27, 1851.

THE HOUSE OF THE
SEVEN GABLES

I

THE OLD PYNCHEON FAMILY

HALF-WAY down a by-street of one of our New England towns, stands a rusty wooden house, with seven acutely peaked gables facing towards various points of the compass, and a huge, clustered chimney in the midst. The street is Pyncheon-street; the house is the old Pyncheon-house; and an elm-tree of wide circumference, rooted before the door, is familiar to every town-born child by the title of the Pyncheon-elm. On my occasional visits to the town aforesaid, I seldom fail to turn down Pyncheon-street, for the sake of passing through the shadow of these two antiquities; the great elm-tree, and the weather-beaten edifice.

The aspect of the venerable mansion has always affected me like a human countenance, bearing the traces not merely of outward storm and sunshine, but expressive also of the long lapse of mortal life, and accompanying vicissitudes, that have passed within. Were these to be worthily recounted, they would form a narrative of no small interest and instruction, and possessing, moreover, a certain remarkable unity, which might almost seem the result of artistic arrangement. But the story would include a chain of events, extending over the better part of two centuries, and, written out with reasonable amplitude, would fill a bigger folio volume, or a longer series of duodecimos, than could prudently be appropriated to the annals of all New England, during a similar period. It consequently becomes imperative to make short work with most of the traditionary lore of which the old Pyncheon-house, otherwise known as the House of the Seven Gables, has been the theme. With a brief sketch, therefore, of the circumstances amid which the foundation of the house was laid, and a rapid glimpse at its quaint exterior, as it grew black in the prevalent east-wind—pointing, too, here and there, at some spot of more verdant mossiness on its roof and walls—we shall commence the real action of our tale at an epoch not very remote from the present day. Still, there will be a connection with the long past—a reference to forgotten events and personages, and to manners, feelings, and opinions, almost or wholly obsolete—which, if adequately translated to the reader, would serve to illustrate how much of old material goes to make up the freshest novelty of human life. Hence, too, might be drawn a weighty lesson from the little regarded truth, that the act of the passing generation is the germ which may and must produce good or evil fruit, in a far distant time; that, together with the seed of the merely temporary crop, which mortals term expediency, they inevitably sow the acorns of a more enduring growth, which may darkly overshadow their posterity.

The House of the Seven Gables, antique as it now looks, was not the first habitation erected by civilized man, on precisely the same spot of ground. Pyncheon-street formerly bore the humbler appellation of Maule's Lane, from the name of the original occupant of the soil, before whose cottage-door it was a cow-path. A natural spring of soft and pleasant water—a rare treasure on the sea-girt peninsula, where the Puritan settlement was made—had early induced Matthew Maule to build a hut, shaggy with thatch, at this point, although somewhat too remote from what was then the centre of the village. In the growth of the town, however, after some thirty or forty years, the site covered by this rude hovel had become exceedingly desirable in the eyes of a prominent and powerful personage, who asserted plausible claims to the proprietorship of this, and a large adjacent tract of land, on the strength of a grant from the legislature. Colonel Pyncheon, the claimant, as we gather from whatever traits of him are preserved, was characterized by an iron energy of purpose. Matthew Maule, on the other hand, though an obscure man, was stubborn in the defence of what he considered his right; and, for several years, he succeeded in protecting the acre or two of earth which, with his own toil, he had hewn out of the primeval forest, to be his garden-ground and homestead. No written record of this dispute is known to be in existence. Our acquaintance with the whole subject is derived chiefly from tradition. It would be bold, therefore, and possibly unjust, to venture a decisive opinion as to its merits; although it appears to have been at least a matter of doubt, whether Colonel Pyncheon's claim were not unduly stretched, in order to make it cover the small metes and bounds of Matthew Maule. What greatly strengthens such a suspicion is the fact, that this controversy between two ill-matched antagonists—at a period, moreover, laud it as we may, when personal influence had far more weight than now —remained for years undecided, and came to a close only with the death of the party occupying the disputed soil. The mode of his death, too, affects the mind differently, in our day, from what it did a century and a half ago. It was a death that blasted with strange horror the humble name of the dweller in the cottage, and made it seem almost a religious act to drive the plough over the little area of his habitation, and obliterate his place and memory from among men.

Old Matthew Maule, in a word, was executed for the crime of witchcraft. He was one of the martyrs to that terrible delusion which should teach us, among its other morals, that the influential classes, and those who take upon themselves to be leaders of the people, are fully liable to all the passionate error that has ever characterized the maddest mob. Clergymen, judges, statesmen—the wisest, calmest, holiest persons of their day—stood in the inner circle roundabout the gallows, loudest to applaud the work of blood, latest to confess themselves miserably deceived. If any one part of their proceedings can be said to deserve less blame than another, it was the singular indiscrimination with which they persecuted, not merely the poor and aged, as in former judicial massacres, but people of all ranks; their own equals, brethren, and wives. Amid the disorder of such various ruin, it is not strange that a man of inconsiderable note, like Maule, should have trodden the martyr's path to the hill of execution, almost unremarked in the throng of his fellow-sufferers. But, in after days, when the frenzy of that hideous epoch had subsided, it was remembered how loudly Colonel Pyncheon had joined in the general cry, to purge the land from witchcraft; nor did it fail to be whispered, that there was an invidious acrimony in the zeal with which he had sought the condemnation of Matthew Maule. It was well known, that the victim had recognized the bitterness of personal enmity in his persecutor's conduct towards him, and that he declared himself hunted to death for his spoil. At the moment of execution—with the halter about his neck, and while Colonel Pyncheon sat on horseback, grimly gazing at the scene—Maule had addressed him from the scaffold, and uttered a prophecy, of which history, as well as fireside tradition, has preserved the very words.—"God," said the dying man, pointing his finger with a ghastly look at the undismayed countenance of his enemy, "God will give him blood to drink!"

After the reputed wizard's death, his humble homestead had fallen an easy spoil into Colonel Pyncheon's grasp. When it was understood, however, that the Colonel intended to erect a family-mansion—spacious, ponderously framed of oaken timber, and calculated to endure for many generations of his posterity—over the spot first covered by the log-built hut of Matthew Maule, there was much shaking of the head among the village-gossips. Without absolutely expressing a doubt whether the stalwart Puritan had acted as a man of conscience and integrity, throughout the proceedings which have been sketched, they nevertheless hinted that he was about to build his house over an unquiet grave. His home would include the home of the dead and buried wizard, and would thus afford the ghost of the latter a kind of privilege to haunt its new apartments, and the chambers into which future bridegrooms were to lead their brides, and where children of the Pyncheon blood were to be born. The terror and ugliness of Maule's crime, and the wretchedness of his punishment, would darken the freshly plastered walls, and infect them early with the scent of an old and melancholy house. Why, then—while so much of the soil around him was bestrewn with the virgin forest-leaves—why should Colonel Pyncheon prefer a site that had already been accurst?

But the Puritan soldier and magistrate was not a man to be turned aside from his well-considered scheme, either by dread of the wizard's ghost, or by flimsy sentimentalities of any kind, however specious. Had he been told of a bad air, it might have moved him somewhat; but he was ready to encounter an evil spirit, on his own ground. Endowed with common-sense, as massive and hard as blocks of granite, fastened together by stern rigidity of purpose, as with iron clamps, he followed out his original design, probably without so much as imagining an objection to it. On the score of delicacy, or any scrupulousness which a finer sensibility might have taught him, the Colonel, like most of his breed and generation, was impenetrable. He therefore dug his cellar, and laid the deep foundations of his mansion, on the square of earth whence Matthew Maule, forty years before, had first swept away the fallen leaves. It was a curious, and, as some people thought, an ominous fact, that, very soon after the workmen began their operations, the spring of water, above-mentioned, entirely lost the deliciousness of its pristine quality. Whether its sources were disturbed by the depth of the new cellar, or whatever subtler cause might lurk at the bottom, it is certain that the water of Maule's Well, as it continued to be called, grew hard and brackish. Even such we find it now; and any old woman of the neighborhood will certify, that it is productive of intestinal mischief to those who quench their thirst there.

The reader may deem it singular, that the head-carpenter of the new edifice was no other than the son of the very man, from whose dead gripe the property of the soil had been wrested. Not improbably, he was the best workman of his time; or, perhaps, the Colonel thought it expedient, or was impelled by some better feeling, thus openly to cast aside all animosity against the race of his fallen antagonist. Nor was it out of keeping with the general coarseness and matter-of-fact character of the age, that the son should be willing to earn an honest penny—or rather, a weighty amount of sterling pounds—from the purse of his father's deadly enemy. At all events, Thomas Maule became the architect of the House of the Seven Gables, and performed his duty so faithfully, that the timber frame-work, fastened by his hands, still holds together.

Thus the great house was built. Familiar as it stands in the writer's recollection—for it has been an object of curiosity with him from boyhood, both as a specimen of the best and stateliest architecture of a long-past epoch, and as the scene of events more full of human interest, perhaps, than those of a gray, feudal castle—familiar as it stands, in its rusty old-age, it is therefore only the more difficult to imagine the bright novelty with which it first caught the sunshine. The impression of its actual state, at this distance of a hundred and sixty years, darkens inevitably through the picture which we would fain give of its appearance, on the morning when the Puritan magnate bade all the town to be his guests. A ceremony of consecration, festive, as well as religious, was now to be performed. A prayer and discourse from the Reverend Mr. Higginson, and the outpouring of a psalm from the general throat of the community, was to be made acceptable to the grosser sense by ale, cider, wine, and brandy, in copious effusion, and, as some authorities aver, by an ox roasted whole, or, at least, by the weight and substance of an ox, in more manageable joints and sirloins. The carcass of a deer, shot within twenty miles, had supplied material for the vast circumference of a pasty. A cod-fish of sixty pounds, caught in the bay, had been dissolved into the rich liquid of a chowder. The chimney of the new house, in short, belching forth its kitchen-smoke, impregnated the whole air with the scent of meats, fowls, and fishes, spicily concocted with odoriferous herbs, and onions in abundance. The mere smell of such festivity, making its way to everybody's nostrils, was at once an invitation and an appetite.

Maule's Lane—or Pyncheon-street, as it were now more decorous to call it—was thronged, at the appointed hour, as with a congregation on its way to church. All, as they approached, looked upward at the imposing edifice, which was henceforth to assume its rank among the habitations of mankind. There it rose, a little withdrawn from the line of the street, but in pride, not modesty. Its whole visible exterior was ornamented with quaint figures, conceived in the grotesqueness of a Gothic fancy, and drawn or stamped in the glittering plaster, composed of lime, pebbles, and bits of glass, with which the wood-work of the walls was overspread. On every side, the seven gables pointed sharply towards the sky, and presented the aspect of a whole sisterhood of edifices, breathing through the spiracles of one great chimney. The many lattices, with their small, diamond-shaped panes, admitted the sunlight into hall and chamber; while, nevertheless, the second story, projecting far over the base, and itself retiring beneath the third, threw a shadow and thoughtful gloom into the lower rooms. Carved globes of wood were affixed under the jutting stories. Little, spiral rods of iron beautified each of the seven peaks. On the triangular portion of the gable that fronted next the street, was a dial, put up that very morning, and on which the sun was still marking the passage of the first bright hour in a history, that was not destined to be all so bright. All around were scattered shavings, chips, shingles, and broken halves of bricks; these—together with the lately turned earth, on which the grass had not begun to grow—contributed to the impression of strangeness and novelty, proper to a house that had yet its place to make among men's daily interests.

The principal entrance, which had almost the breadth of a church-door, was in the angle between the two front gables, and was covered by an open porch, with benches beneath its shelter. Under this arched door-way, scraping their feet on the unworn threshold, now trod the clergymen, the elders, the magistrates, the deacons, and whatever of aristocracy there was in town or county. Thither, too, thronged the plebeian classes, as freely as their betters, and in larger number. Just within the entrance, however, stood two serving-men, pointing some of the guests to the neighborhood of the kitchen, and ushering others into the statelier rooms; hospitable alike to all, but still with a scrutinizing regard to the high or low degree of each. Velvet garments, sombre, but rich, stiffly plaited ruffs and bands, embroidered gloves, venerable beards, the mien and countenance of authority, made it easy to distinguish the gentleman of worship, at that period, from the tradesman, with his plodding air, or the laborer in his leathern jerkin, stealing awe-stricken into the house which he had perhaps helped to build.

One inauspicious circumstance there was, which awakened

a hardly concealed displeasure in the breasts of a few of the more punctilious visitors. The founder of this stately mansion —a gentleman noted for the square and ponderous courtesy of his demeanor—ought surely to have stood in his own hall, and to have offered the first welcome to so many eminent personages as here presented themselves, in honor of his solemn festival. He was as yet invisible; the most favored of the guests had not beheld him. This sluggishness on Colonel Pyncheon's part became still more unaccountable, when the second dignitary of the province made his appearance, and found no more ceremonious a reception. The Lieutenant Governor, although his visit was one of the anticipated glories of the day, had alighted from his horse, and assisted his lady from her side-saddle, and crossed the Colonel's threshold, without other greeting than that of the principal domestic.

This person—a gray-headed man of quiet and most respectful deportment—found it necessary to explain that his master still remained in his study, or private apartment; on entering which, an hour before, he had expressed a wish on no account to be disturbed.

"Do not you see, fellow," said the high-sheriff of the county, taking the servant aside, "that this is no less a man than the Lieutenant Governor? Summon Colonel Pyncheon at once! I know that he received letters from England, this morning; and, in the perusal and consideration of them, an hour may have passed away, without his noticing it. But he will be ill-pleased, I judge, if you suffer him to neglect the courtesy due to one of our chief rulers, and who may be said to represent King William, in the absence of the Governor himself. Call your master instantly!"

"Nay, please your worship," answered the man, in much perplexity, but with a backwardness that strikingly indicated the hard and severe character of Colonel Pyncheon's domestic rule, "my master's orders were exceedingly strict; and, as your worship knows, he permits of no discretion in the obedience of those who owe him service. Let who list open yonder door! I dare not, though the Governor's own voice should bid me do it!"

"Pooh, pooh, Master High Sheriff!" cried the Lieutenant Governor, who had overheard the foregoing discussion, and felt himself high enough in station to play a little with his dignity.—"I will take the matter into my own hands. It is time that the good Colonel came forth to greet his friends; else we shall be apt to suspect that he has taken a sip too much of his Canary wine, in his extreme deliberation which cask it were best to broach, in honor of the day! But since he is so much behindhand, I will give him a remembrancer myself!"

Accordingly—with such a tramp of his ponderous riding-boots as might of itself have been audible in the remotest of the seven gables—he advanced to the door, which the servant pointed out, and made its new panels re-echo with a loud, free knock. Then, looking round with a smile to the spectators, he awaited a response. As none came, however, he knocked again, but with the same unsatisfactory result as at first. And, now, being a trifle choleric in his temperament, the Lieutenant Governor uplifted the heavy-hilt of his sword, wherewith he so beat and banged upon the door, that, as some of the bystanders whispered, the racket might have disturbed the dead. Be that as it might, it seemed to produce no awakening effect on Colonel Pyncheon. When the sound subsided, the silence through the house was deep, dreary, and oppressive; notwithstanding that the tongues of many of the guests had already been loosened by a surreptitious cup or two of wine or spirits.

"Strange, forsooth!—very strange!" cried the Lieutenant Governor, whose smile was changed to a frown. "But, seeing that our host sets us the good example of forgetting ceremony, I shall likewise throw it aside, and make free to intrude on his privacy!"

He tried the door, which yielded to his hand, and was flung wide open by a sudden gust of wind that passed, as with a loud sigh, from the outermost portal through all the passages and apartments of the new house. It rustled the silken garments of the ladies, and waved the long curls of the gentlemen's wigs, and shook the window-hangings and the curtains of the bed-chambers; causing everywhere a singular stir, which yet was more like a hush. A shadow of awe and half-fearful anticipation—nobody knew wherefore, nor of what—had all at once fallen over the company.

They thronged, however, to the now open door, pressing the Lieutenant Governor, in the eagerness of their curiosity, into the room in advance of them. At the first glimpse, they beheld nothing extraordinary; a handsomely furnished room of moderate size, somewhat darkened by curtains; books arranged on shelves; a large map on the wall, and likewise a portrait of Colonel Pyncheon, beneath which sat the original Colonel himself, in an oaken elbow-chair, with a pen in his hand. Letters, parchments, and blank sheets of paper were on the table before him. He appeared to gaze at the curious crowd, in front of which stood the Lieutenant Governor; and there was a frown on his dark and massive countenance, as if sternly resentful of the boldness that had impelled them into his private retirement.

A little boy—the Colonel's grandchild, and the only human being that ever dared to be familiar with him—now made his way among the guests and ran towards the seated figure; then pausing half-way, he began to shriek with terror. The company—tremulous as the leaves of a tree, when all are shaking together—drew nearer, and perceived that there was an unnatural distortion in the fixedness of Colonel Pyncheon's stare; that there was blood on his ruff, and that his hoary beard was saturated with it. It was too late to give assistance. The iron-hearted Puritan—the relentless persecutor—the grasping and strong-willed man—was dead! Dead, in his new house! There is a tradition—only worth alluding to, as lending a tinge of superstitious awe to a scene, perhaps gloomy enough without it—that a voice spoke loudly among the guests, the tones of which were like those of old Matthew Maule, the executed wizard:—"God hath given him blood to drink!"

Thus early had that one guest—the only guest who is certain, at one time or another, to find his way into every human dwelling—thus early had Death stept across the threshold of the House of the Seven Gables!

Colonel Pyncheon's sudden and mysterious end made a vast deal of noise in its day. There were many rumors, some of which have vaguely drifted down to the present time, how that appearances indicated violence; that there were the marks of fingers on his throat, and the print of a bloody hand on his plaited ruff; and that his peaked beard was dishevelled, as if it had been fiercely clutched and pulled. It was averred, likewise, that the lattice-window, near the Colonel's chair, was open, and that, only a few minutes before the fatal occurrence, the figure of a man had been seen clambering over the garden-fence, in the rear of the house. But it were folly to lay any stress on stories of this kind, which are sure to spring up around such an event as that now related, and which, as in the present case, sometimes prolong themselves for ages afterwards, like the toadstools that indicate where the fallen and buried trunk of a tree has long since mouldered into the earth. For our own part, we allow them just as little credence as to that other fable of the skeleton hand, which the Lieutenant Governor was said to have seen at the Colonel's throat, but which vanished away, as he advanced farther into the room. Certain it is, however, that there was a great consultation and dispute of doctors over the dead body. One —John Swinnerton by name—who appears to have been a man of eminence, upheld it, if we have rightly understood his terms of art, to be a case of apoplexy. His professional brethren, each for himself, adopted various hypotheses, more or less plausible, but all dressed out in a perplexing mystery of phrase, which, if it do not show a bewilderment of mind in these erudite physicians, certainly causes it in the unlearned peruser of their opinions. The coroner's jury sat upon the corpse, and, like sensible men, returned an unassailable verdict of "Sudden Death!"

It is indeed difficult to imagine that there could have been a serious suspicion of murder, or the slightest grounds for implicating any particular individual as the perpetrator. The rank, wealth, and eminent character of the deceased, must have ensured the strictest scrutiny into every ambiguous circumstance. As none such is on record, it is safe to assume that none existed. Tradition—which sometimes brings down truth that history has let slip, but is oftener the wild babble of the time, such as was formerly spoken at the fireside, and now congeals in newspapers—tradition is responsible for all contrary averments. In Colonel Pyncheon's funeral sermon, which was printed and is still extant, the Reverend Mr. Higginson enumerates, among the many felicities of his distinguished parishioner's earthly career, the happy seasonableness of his death. His duties all performed,—the highest prosperity attained,—his race and future generations fixed on a stable basis, and with a stately roof to shelter them, for centuries to come,—what other upward step remained for this good man to take, save the final step from earth to the golden gate of Heaven! The pious clergyman surely would not have uttered words like these, had he in the least suspected that the Colonel had been thrust into the other world with the clutch of violence upon his throat.

The family of Colonel Pyncheon, at the epoch of his death, seemed destined to as fortunate a permanence as can anywise consist with the inherent instability of human affairs. It might fairly be anticipated that the progress of time would rather increase and ripen their prosperity, than wear away and destroy it. For, not only had his son and heir come into immediate enjoyment of a rich estate, but there was a claim, through an Indian deed, confirmed by a subsequent grant of the General Court, to a vast, and as yet unexplored and unmeasured tract of eastern lands. These possessions—for as such they might almost certainly be reckoned—comprised the greater part of what is now known as Waldo County, in the State of Maine, and were more extensive than many a dukedom, or even a reigning prince's territory, on European soil. When the pathless forest, that still covered this wild principality, should give place—as it inevitably must, though perhaps not till ages hence—to the golden fertility of human culture, it would be the source of incalculable wealth to the Pyncheon blood. Had the Colonel survived only a few weeks longer, it is probable that his great political influence, and powerful connections, at home and abroad, would have consummated all that was necessary to render the claim available. But, in spite of good Mr. Higginson's congratulatory eloquence, this appeared to be the one thing which Colonel Pyncheon, provident and sagacious as he was, had allowed to go at loose ends. So far as the prospective territory was concerned, he unquestionably died too soon. His son lacked not merely the father's eminent position, but the talent and force of character to achieve it; he could therefore effect nothing by dint of political interest; and the bare justice or legality of the claim was not so apparent, after the Colonel's decease, as it had been pronounced in his lifetime. Some connecting link had slipt out of the evidence, and could not anywhere be found.

Efforts, it is true, were made by the Pyncheons, not only then, but, at various periods, for nearly a hundred years afterwards, to obtain what they stubbornly persisted in deeming their right. But, in course of time, the territory was partly re-granted to more favored individuals, and partly cleared and occupied by actual settlers. These last, if they ever heard of the Pyncheon title, would have laughed at the idea of any man's asserting a right—on the strength of mouldy parchments, signed with the faded autographs of governors and legislators, long dead and forgotten—to the lands which they or their fathers had wrested from the wild hand of Nature, by their own sturdy toil. This impalpable claim, therefore, resulted in nothing more solid than to cherish, from generation to generation, an absurd delusion of family importance, which all along characterized the Pyncheons. It caused the poorest member of the race to feel as if he inherited a kind of nobility, and might yet come into the possession of princely wealth to support it. In the better specimens of the breed, this peculiarity threw an ideal grace over the hard material of human life, without stealing away any truly valuable quality. In the baser sort, its effect was to increase the liability to sluggishness and dependence, and induce the victim of a shadowy hope to remit all self-effort, while awaiting the realization of his dreams. Years and years after their claim had passed out of the public memory, the Pyncheons were accustomed to consult the Colonel's ancient map, which had been projected while Waldo County was still an unbroken wilderness. Where the old land-surveyor had put down woods, lakes, and rivers, they marked out the cleared spaces, and dotted the villages and towns, and calculated the progressively increasing value of the territory, as if there were yet a prospect of its ultimately forming a princedom for themselves.

In almost every generation, nevertheless, there happened to be some one descendant of the family, gifted with a portion of the hard, keen sense, and practical energy, that had so remarkably distinguished the original founder. His character, indeed, might be traced all the way down, as distinctly as if the Colonel himself, a little diluted, had been gifted with a sort of intermittent immortality on earth. At two or three epochs, when the fortunes of the family were low, this representative of hereditary qualities had made his appearance, and caused the traditionary gossips of the town to whisper among themselves:—"Here is the old Pyncheon come again! Now the Seven Gables will be new-shingled!" From father to son, they clung to the ancestral house, with singular tenacity of home-attachment. For various reasons, however, and from impressions often too vaguely founded to be put on paper, the writer cherishes the belief that many, if not most, of the successive proprietors of this estate, were troubled with doubts as to their moral right to hold it. Of their legal tenure, there could be no question; but old Matthew Maule, it is to be feared, trode downward from his own age to a far later one, planting a heavy footstep, all the way, on the conscience of a Pyncheon. If so, we are left to dispose of the awful query, whether each inheritor of the property—conscious of wrong, and failing to rectify it—did not commit anew the great guilt of his ancestor, and incur all its original responsibilities. And supposing such to be the case, would it not be a far truer mode of expression to say, of the Pyncheon family, that they inherited a great misfortune, than the reverse?

We have already hinted, that it is not our purpose to trace down the history of the Pyncheon family, in its unbroken connection with the House of the Seven Gables; nor to show, as in a magic picture, how the rustiness and infirmity of age gathered over the venerable house itself. As regards its interior life, a large, dim looking-glass used to hang in one of the rooms, and was fabled to contain within its depths all the shapes that had ever been reflected there; the old Colonel himself, and his many descendants, some in the garb of antique babyhood, and others in the bloom of feminine beauty, or manly prime, or saddened with the wrinkles of frosty age. Had we the secret of that mirror, we would gladly sit down before it, and transfer its revelations to our page. But there was a story, for which it is difficult to conceive any foundation, that the posterity of Matthew Maule had some connection with the mystery of the looking-glass, and that—by what appears to have been a sort of mesmeric process—they could make its inner region all alive with the departed Pyncheons; not as they had shown themselves to the world, nor in their better and happier hours, but as doing over again some deed of sin, or in the crisis of life's bitterest sorrow. The popular imagination, indeed, long kept itself busy with the affair of the old Puritan Pyncheon and the wizard Maule; the curse, which the latter flung from his scaffold, was remembered, with the very important addition, that it had become a part of the Pyncheon inheritance. If one of the family did but gurgle in his throat, a bystander would be likely enough to whisper, between jest and earnest—"He has Maule's blood to drink!"—The sudden death of a Pyncheon, about a hundred years ago, with circumstances very similar to what have been related of the Colonel's exit, was held as giving additional probability to the received opinion on this topic. It was considered, moreover, an ugly and ominous circumstance, that Colonel Pyncheon's picture—in obedience, it was said, to a provision of his will—remained affixed to the wall of the room in which he died. Those stern, immitigable features seemed to symbolize an evil influence, and so darkly to mingle the shadow of their presence with the sunshine of the passing hour, that no good thoughts or purposes could ever spring up and blossom there. To the thoughtful mind, there will be no tinge of superstition in what we figuratively express, by affirming that the ghost of a dead progenitor—perhaps as a portion of his own punishment—is often doomed to become the Evil Genius of his family.

The Pyncheons, in brief, lived along, for the better part of two centuries, with perhaps less of outward vicissitude than has attended most other New England families, during the same period of time. Possessing very distinctive traits of their own, they nevertheless took the general characteristics of the little community in which they dwelt; a town noted for its frugal, discreet, well-ordered, and home-loving inhabitants, as well as for the somewhat confined scope of its sympathies; but in which, be it said, there are odder individuals, and, now and then, stranger occurrences, than one meets with almost anywhere else. During the revolution, the Pyncheon of that epoch, adopting the royal side, became a refugee, but repented, and made his re-appearance, just at the point of time to preserve the House of the Seven Gables from confiscation. For the last seventy years, the most noted event in the Pyncheon annals had been likewise the heaviest calamity that ever befell the race; no less than the violent death—for so it was adjudged—of one member of the family, by the criminal act of another. Certain circumstances, attending this fatal occurrence, had brought the deed irresistibly home to a nephew of the deceased Pyncheon. The young man was tried and convicted of the crime; but either the circumstantial nature of the evidence, and possibly some lurking doubt in the breast of the Executive, or, lastly—an argument of greater weight in a republic, than it could have been under a monarchy—the high respectability and political influence of the criminal's connections, had availed to mitigate his doom from death to perpetual imprisonment. This sad affair had chanced about thirty years before the action of our story commences. Latterly, there were rumors (which few believed, and only one or two felt greatly interested in) that this long-buried man was likely, for some reason or other, to be summoned forth from his living tomb.

It is essential to say a few words respecting the victim of this now almost forgotten murder. He was an old bachelor, and possessed of great wealth, in addition to the house and real estate which constituted what remained of the ancient Pyncheon property. Being of an eccentric and melancholy turn of mind, and greatly given to rummaging old records and hearkening to old traditions, he had brought himself, it is averred, to the conclusion, that Matthew Maule, the wizard, had been foully wronged out of his homestead, if not out of his life. Such being the case, and he, the old bachelor, in possession of the ill-gotten spoil—with the black stain of blood sunken deep into it, and still to be scented by conscientious nostrils—the question occurred, whether it were not imperative upon him, even at this late hour, to make restitution to Maule's posterity. To a man living so much in the past, and so little in the present, as the secluded and antiquarian old bachelor, a century and a half seemed not so vast a period as to obviate the propriety of substituting right for wrong. It was the belief of those who knew him best, that he would positively have taken the very singular step of giving up the House of the Seven Gables to the representative of Matthew Maule, but for the unspeakable tumult which a suspicion of the old gentleman's project awakened among his Pyncheon relatives. Their exertions had the effect of suspending his purpose; but it was feared that he would perform, after death, by the operation of his last will, what he had so hardly been prevented from doing, in his proper lifetime. But there is no one thing which men so rarely do, whatever the provocation or inducement, as to bequeath patrimonial property away from their own blood. They may love other individuals far better than their relatives; they may even cherish dislike, or positive hatred, to the latter; but yet, in view of death, the strong prejudice of propinquity revives, and impels the testator to send down his estate in the line marked out by custom, so immemorial, that it looks like nature. In all the Pyncheons, this feeling had the energy of disease. It was too powerful for the conscientious scruples of the old bachelor; at whose death, accordingly, the mansion-house, together with most of his other riches, passed into the possession of his next legal representative.

This was a nephew; the cousin of the miserable young man who had been convicted of the uncle's murder. The new heir, up to the period of his accession, was reckoned rather a dissipated youth, but had at once reformed, and made himself an exceedingly respectable member of society. In fact, he showed more of the Pyncheon quality, and had won higher eminence in the world, than any of his race since the time of the original Puritan. Applying himself, in earlier manhood, to the study of the law, and having a natural tendency towards office, he had attained, many years ago, to a judicial situation in some inferior court, which gave him, for life, the very desirable and imposing title of Judge. Later, he had engaged in politics, and served a part of two terms in Congress, besides making a considerable figure in both branches of the state legislature. Judge Pyncheon was unquestionably an honor to his race. He had built himself a country-seat, within a few miles of his native town, and there spent such portions of his time as could be spared from public service, in the display of every grace and virtue—as a newspaper phrased it, on the eve of an election—befitting the christian, the good citizen, the horticulturist, and the gentleman!

There were few of the Pyncheons left, to sun themselves in the glow of the Judge's prosperity. In respect to natural increase, the breed had not thriven; it appeared rather to be dying out. The only members of the family, known to be extant, were, first, the Judge himself, and a single surviving son, who was now travelling in Europe; next, the thirty-years' prisoner, already alluded to, and a sister of the latter, who occupied, in an extremely retired manner, the House of the Seven Gables, in which she had a life-estate by the will of the old bachelor. She was understood to be wretchedly poor, and seemed to make it her choice to remain so; inasmuch as her affluent cousin, the Judge, had repeatedly offered her all the comforts of life, either in the old mansion or his own modern residence. The last and youngest Pyncheon was a little country-girl of seventeen, the daughter of another of the Judge's cousins, who had married a young woman of no family or property, and died early, and in poor circumstances. His widow had recently taken another husband.

As for Matthew Maule's posterity, it was supposed now to be extinct. For a very long period after the witchcraft delusion, however, the Maules had continued to inhabit the town, where their progenitor had suffered so unjust a death. To all appearance, they were a quiet, honest, well-meaning race of people, cherishing no malice against individuals or the public, for the wrong which had been done them; or if, at their own fireside, they transmitted, from father to child, any hostile recollection of the wizard's fate, and their lost patrimony, it was never acted upon, nor openly expressed. Nor would it have been singular, had they ceased to remember that the House of the Seven Gables was resting its heavy frame-work on a foundation that was rightfully their own. There is something so massive, stable, and almost irresistibly imposing, in the exterior presentment of established rank and great possessions, that their very existence seems to give them a right to exist; at least, so excellent a counterfeit of right, that few poor and humble men have moral force enough to question it, even in their secret minds. Such is the case now, after so many ancient prejudices have been overthrown; and it was far more so in ante-revolutionary days, when the aristocracy could venture to be proud, and the low were content to be abased. Thus the Maules, at all events, kept their resentments within their own breasts. They were generally poverty-stricken; always plebeian and obscure; working with unsuccessful diligence at handicrafts; laboring on the wharves, or following the sea, as sailors before the mast; living here and there about the town, in hired tenements, and coming finally to the alms house, as the natural home of their old age. At last, after creeping, as it were, for such a length of time, along the utmost verge of the opaque puddle of obscurity, they had taken that downright plunge, which, sooner or later, is the destiny of all families, whether princely or plebeian. For thirty years past, neither town-record, nor grave-stone, nor the directory, nor the knowledge or memory of man, bore any trace of Matthew Maule's descendants. His blood might possibly exist elsewhere; here, where its lowly current could be traced so far back, it had ceased to keep an onward course.

So long as any of the race were to be found, they had been marked out from other men—not strikingly, nor as with a sharp line, but with an effect that was felt, rather than spoken of—by an hereditary character of reserve. Their companions, or those who endeavored to become such, grew conscious of a circle roundabout the Maules, within the sanctity or the spell of which—in spite of an exterior of sufficient frankness and good-fellowship—it was impossible for any man to step. It was this indefinable peculiarity, perhaps, that, by insulating them from human aid, kept them always so unfortunate in life. It certainly operated to prolong, in their case, and to confirm to them, as their only inheritance, those feelings of repugnance and superstitious terror with which the people of the town, even after awakening from their frenzy, continued to regard the memory of the reputed witches. The mantle, or rather, the ragged cloak of old Matthew Maule, had fallen upon his children. They were half-believed to inherit mysterious attributes; the family eye was said to possess strange power. Among other good-for-nothing properties and privileges, one was especially assigned them, of exercising an influence over people's dreams. The Pyncheons, if all stories were true, haughtily as they bore themselves in the noonday streets of their native town, were no better than bond-servants to these plebeian Maules, on entering the topsyturvy commonwealth of sleep. Modern psychology, it may be, will endeavor to reduce these alleged necromancies within a system, instead of rejecting them as altogether fabulous.

A descriptive paragraph or two, treating of the seven-gabled mansion in its more recent aspect, will bring this preliminary chapter to a close. The street, in which it upreared its venerable peaks, has long ceased to be a fashionable quarter of the town; so that, though the old edifice was surrounded by habi-

tations of modern date, they were mostly small, built entirely
of wood, and typical of the most plodding uniformity of common life. Doubtless, however, the whole story of human existence may be latent in each of them, but with no pictur-
esqueness, externally, that can attract the imagination or sympathy to seek it there. But as for the old structure of our story,
its white-oak frame, and its boards, shingles, and crumbling
plaster, and even the huge, clustered chimney in the midst,
seemed to constitute only the least and meanest part of its reality. So much of mankind's varied experience had passed
there—so much had been suffered, and something, too, enjoyed—that the very timbers were oozy, as with the moisture
of a heart. It was itself like a great human heart, with a life
of its own, and full of rich and sombre reminiscences.

The deep projection of the second story gave the house
such a meditative look, that you could not pass it without the
idea that it had secrets to keep, and an eventful history to
moralize upon. In front, just on the edge of the unpaved
sidewalk, grew the Pyncheon-elm, which, in reference to such
trees as one usually meets with, might well be termed gigantic.
It had been planted by a great-grandson of the first Pyncheon,
and, though now fourscore years of age, or perhaps nearer
a hundred, was still in its strong and broad maturity, throwing
its shadow from side to side of the street, overtopping the
seven gables, and sweeping the whole black roof with its
pendent foliage. It gave beauty to the old edifice, and seemed
to make it a part of nature. The street having been widened,
about forty years ago, the front gable was now precisely on
a line with it. On either side extended a ruinous wooden
fence, of open lattice-work, through which could be seen a
grassy yard, and, especially in the angles of the building, an
enormous fertility of burdocks, with leaves, it is hardly an
exaggeration to say, two or three feet long. Behind the house,
there appeared to be a garden, which undoubtedly had once
been extensive, but was now infringed upon by other en-

closures, or shut in by habitations and outbuildings that stood on another street. It would be an omission, trifling, indeed, but unpardonable, were we to forget the green moss that had long since gathered over the projections of the windows, and on the slopes of the roof; nor must we fail to direct the reader's eye to a crop, not of weeds, but flower-shrubs, which were growing aloft in the air not a great way from the chimney, in the nook between two of the gables. They were called Alice's Posies. The tradition was, that a certain Alice Pyncheon had flung up the seeds, in sport, and that the dust of the street and the decay of the roof gradually formed a kind of soil for them, out of which they grew, when Alice had long been in her grave. However the flowers might have come there, it was both sad and sweet to observe how Nature adopted to herself this desolate, decaying, gusty, rusty, old house of the Pyncheon family; and how the ever-returning Summer did her best to gladden it with tender beauty, and grew melancholy in the effort.

There is one other feature, very essential to be noticed, but which, we greatly fear, may damage any picturesque and romantic impression, which we have been willing to throw over our sketch of this respectable edifice. In the front gable, under the impending brow of the second story, and contiguous to the street, was a shop-door, divided horizontally in the midst, and with a window for its upper segment, such as is often seen in dwellings of a somewhat ancient date. This same shop-door had been a subject of no slight mortification to the present occupant of the august Pyncheon-house, as well as to some of her predecessors. The matter is disagreeably delicate to handle; but, since the reader must needs be let into the secret, he will please to understand, that, about a century ago, the head of the Pyncheons found himself involved in serious financial difficulties. The fellow (gentleman as he styled himself) can hardly have been other than a spurious interloper; for, instead of seeking office from the King or the royal Governor, or urging his hereditary claim to eastern lands, he bethought himself of no better avenue to wealth, than by cutting a shop-door through the side of his ancestral residence. It was the custom of the time, indeed, for merchants to store their goods, and transact business, in their own dwellings. But there was something pitifully small in this old Pyncheon's mode of setting about his commercial operations; it was whispered, that, with his own hands, all beruffled as they were, he used to give change for a shilling, and would turn a half-penny twice over, to make sure that it was a good one. Beyond all question, he had the blood of a petty huckster in his veins, through whatever channel it may have found its way there.

Immediately on his death, the shop-door had been locked, bolted, and barred, and, down to the period of our story, had probably never once been opened. The old counter, shelves, and other fixtures of the little shop, remained just as he had left them. It used to be affirmed, that the dead shopkeeper, in a white wig, a faded velvet coat, an apron at his waist, and his ruffles carefully turned back from his wrists, might be seen through the chinks of the shutters, any night of the year, ransacking his till, or poring over the dingy pages of his day-book. From the look of unutterable woe upon his face, it appeared to be his doom to spend eternity in a vain effort to make his accounts balance.

And now—in a very humble way, as will be seen—we proceed to open our narrative.

II

THE LITTLE SHOP-WINDOW

I T STILL lacked half-an-hour of sunrise, when Miss Hepzibah Pyncheon—we will not say awoke; it being doubtful whether the poor lady had so much as closed her eyes, during the brief night of mid-summer—but, at all events, arose from her solitary pillow, and began what it would be mockery to term the adornment of her person. Far from us be the indecorum of assisting, even in imagination, at a maiden lady's toilet! Our story must therefore await Miss Hepzibah at the threshold of her chamber; only presuming, meanwhile, to note some of the heavy sighs that labored from her bosom, with little restraint as to their lugubrious depth and volume of sound, inasmuch as they could be audible to nobody, save a disembodied listener like ourself. The old maid was alone in the old house. Alone, except for a certain respectable and orderly young man, an artist in the daguerreotype line, who, for about three months back, had been a lodger in a remote gable—quite a house by itself, indeed—with locks, bolts, and oaken bars, on all the intervening doors. Inaudible, consequently, were poor Miss Hepzibah's gusty sighs. Inaudible, the creaking joints of her stiffened knees, as she knelt down by the bedside. And inaudible, too, by mortal ear, but heard with all-comprehending love and pity, in the farthest Heaven, that almost agony of prayer—now whispered, now a groan, now a struggling silence—wherewith she besought the Divine assistance through the day! Evidently, this is to be a day of more than ordinary trial to Miss Hepzibah, who, for above a quarter of a century gone-by, has dwelt in strict seclusion; taking no part in the business of life, and just as little in its intercourse and pleasures. Not with such fervor prays the torpid recluse, looking forward to the cold, sunless, stagnant calm of a day that is to be like innumerable yesterdays!

The maiden lady's devotions are concluded. Will she now issue forth over the threshold of our story? Not yet, by many moments. First, every drawer in the tall, old-fashioned bureau is to be opened, with difficulty, and with a succession of spasmodic jerks; then, all must close again, with the same fidgety reluctance. There is a rustling of stiff silks; a tread of backward and forward footsteps, to-and-fro, across the chamber. We suspect Miss Hepzibah, moreover, of taking a step upward into a chair, in order to give heedful regard to her appearance, on all sides, and at full length, in the oval, dingy-framed toilet-glass, that hangs above her table. Truly! Well, indeed! Who would have thought it! Is all this precious time to be lavished on the matutinal repair and beautifying of an elderly person, who never goes abroad—whom nobody ever visits—and from whom, when she shall have done her utmost, it were the best charity to turn one's eyes another way!

Now, she is almost ready. Let us pardon her one other pause; for it is given to the sole sentiment, or we might better say—heightened and rendered intense, as it has been, by sorrow and seclusion—to the strong passion of her life. We heard the turning of a key in a small lock; she has opened a secret drawer of an escritoir, and is probably looking at a certain miniature, done in Malbone's most perfect style, and representing a face worthy of no less delicate a pencil. It was once our good fortune to see this picture. It is the likeness of a young man, in a silken dressing-gown of an old fashion, the soft richness of which is well adapted to the countenance of reverie, with its full, tender lips, and beautiful eyes, that seem to indicate not so much capacity of thought, as gentle and voluptuous emotion. Of the possessor of such features we should have a right to ask nothing, except that he would take the rude world easily, and make himself happy in it. Can it have been an early lover of Miss Hepzibah? No; she never had a lover—poor thing, how could she?—nor ever knew, by her own experience, what love technically means. And yet, her undying faith and trust, her fresh remembrance, and continual devotedness towards the original of that miniature, have been the only substance for her heart to feed upon.

She seems to have put aside the miniature, and is standing again before the toilet-glass. There are tears to be wiped off. A few more footsteps to-and-fro; and here, at last—with another pitiful sigh, like a gust of chill, damp wind out of a long-closed vault, the door of which has accidentally been set ajar—here comes Miss Hepzibah Pyncheon! Forth she steps into the dusky, time-darkened passage; a tall figure, clad in black silk, with a long and shrunken waist, feeling her way towards the stairs like a near-sighted person, as in truth she is.

The sun, meanwhile, if not already above the horizon, was ascending nearer and nearer to its verge. A few clouds, floating high upward, caught some of the earliest light, and threw down its golden gleam on the windows of all the houses in the street; not forgetting the House of the Seven Gables, which—many such sunrises as it had witnessed—looked cheerfully at the present one. The reflected radiance served to show, pretty distinctly, the aspect and arrangement of the room which Hepzibah entered, after descending the stairs. It was a low-studded-room, with a beam across the ceiling, panelled with dark wood, and having a large chimney-piece, set round with pictured tiles, but now closed by an iron fireboard, through which ran the funnel of a modern stove. There was a carpet on the floor, originally of rich texture, but so worn and faded, in these latter years, that its once brilliant figure had quite vanished into one indistinguishable hue. In the way of furniture, there were two tables; one, constructed with perplexing intricacy, and exhibiting as many feet as a centipede; the other, most delicately wrought, with four long and slender legs, so apparently frail, that it was almost incredible what a length of time the ancient tea-table had stood upon them. Half-a-dozen chairs stood about the room, straight and stiff, and so ingeniously contrived for the discomfort of the human person, that they were irksome even to sight, and conveyed the ugliest possible idea of the state of society to which they could have been adapted. One exception there was, however, in a very antique elbow-chair, with a high back, carved elaborately in oak, and a roomy depth within its arms, that made up, by its spacious comprehensiveness, for the lack of any of those artistic curves which abound in a modern chair.

As for ornamental articles of furniture, we recollect but two, if such they may be called. One was a map of the Pyncheon territory at the eastward, not engraved, but the handiwork of some skilful old draftsman, and grotesquely illuminated with pictures of Indians and wild beasts, among which was seen a lion; the natural history of the region being as little known as its geography, which was put down most fantastically awry. The other adornment was the portrait of old Colonel Pyncheon, at two thirds length, representing the stern features of a Puritanic-looking personage, in a scull-cap, with a laced band and a grizzly beard; holding a Bible with one hand, and in the other uplifting an iron sword-hilt. The latter object, being more successfully depicted by the artist, stood out in far greater prominence than the sacred volume. Face to face with this picture, on entering the apartment, Miss Hepzibah Pyncheon came to a pause; regarding it with a singular scowl—a strange contortion of the brow—which, by people who did not know her, would probably have been interpreted as an expression of bitter anger and ill-will. But it was no such thing. She, in fact, felt a reverence for the pictured visage, of which only a far-descended and time-stricken virgin could be susceptible; and this forbidding scowl was the innocent result of her near-sightedness, and an effort so to concentrate her powers of vision, as to substitute a firm outline of the object, instead of a vague one.

We must linger, a moment, on this unfortunate expression of poor Hepzibah's brow. Her scowl—as the world, or such part of it as sometimes caught a transitory glimpse of her at the window, wickedly persisted in calling it—her scowl had done Miss Hepzibah a very ill-office, in establishing her character as an ill-tempered old maid; nor does it appear improbable, that, by often gazing at herself in a dim looking-glass, and perpetually encountering her own frown within its ghostly sphere, she had been led to interpret the expression almost as unjustly as the world did.— "How miserably cross I look!"—she must often have whispered to herself;—and ultimately have fancied herself so, by a sense of inevitable doom. But her heart never frowned. It was naturally tender, sensitive, and full of little tremors and palpitations; all of which weaknesses it retained, while her visage was growing so perversely stern, and even fierce. Nor had Hepzibah ever any hardihood, except what came from the very warmest nook in her affections.

All this time, however, we are loitering faint-heartedly on the threshold of our story. In very truth, we have an invincible reluctance to disclose what Miss Hepzibah Pyncheon was about to do.

It has already been observed, that, in the basement story of the gable fronting on the street, an unworthy ancestor, nearly a century ago, had fitted up a shop. Ever since the old gentleman retired from trade, and fell asleep under his coffin-lid, not only the shop-door, but the inner arrangements, had been suffered to remain unchanged; while the dust of ages gathered inch-deep over the shelves and counter, and

partly filled an old pair of scales, as if it were of value enough
to be weighed.—It treasured itself up, too, in the half-open
till, where there still lingered a base sixpence, worth neither
more nor less than the hereditary pride which had here been
put to shame. Such had been the state and condition of the
little shop, in old Hepzibah's childhood, when she and her
brother used to play at hide-and-seek in its forsaken precincts.
So it had remained, until within a few days past.

But now, though the shop-window was still closely cur-
tained from the public gaze, a remarkable change had taken
place in its interior. The rich and heavy festoons of cobweb,
which it had cost a long ancestral succession of spiders their
life's labor to spin and weave, had been carefully brushed
away from the ceiling. The counter, shelves, and floor had
all been scoured, and the latter was overstrewn with fresh
blue sand. The brown scales, too, had evidently undergone
rigid discipline, in an unavailing effort to rub off the rust,
which, alas! had eaten through and through their substance.
Neither was the little old shop any longer empty of mer-
chantable goods. A curious eye, privileged to take an account
of stock and investigate behind the counter, would have discovered a barrel—yea, two or three barrels and half-ditto—
one containing flour, another apples, and a third, perhaps,
Indian meal. There was likewise a square box of pine-wood,
full of soap in bars; also, another of the same size, in which
were tallow-candles, ten to the pound. A small stock of brown
sugar, some white beans and split peas, and a few other commodities of low price, and such as are constantly in demand,
made up the bulkier portion of the merchandize. It might
have been taken for a ghostly or phantasmagoric reflection of
the old shopkeeper Pyncheon's shabbily provided shelves;
save that some of the articles were of a description and outward form, which could hardly have been known in his day.
For instance, there was a glass pickle-jar, filled with fragments of Gibraltar-rock; not, indeed, splinters of the veritable

stone foundation of the famous fortress, but bits of delectable candy, neatly done up in white paper. Jim Crow, moreover, was seen executing his world-renowned dance, in ginger-bread. A party of leaden dragoons were galloping along one of the shelves, in equipments and uniform of modern cut; and there were some sugar figures, with no strong resemblance to the humanity of any epoch, but less unsatisfactorily representing our own fashions, than those of a hundred years ago. Another phenomenon, still more strikingly modern, was a package of lucifer-matches, which, in old times, would have been thought actually to borrow their instantaneous flame from the nether fires of Tophet.

In short, to bring the matter at once to a point, it was incontrovertibly evident that somebody had taken the shop and fixtures of the long retired and forgotten Mr. Pyncheon, and was about to renew the enterprise of that departed worthy, with a different set of customers. Who could this bold adventurer be? And, of all places in the world, why had he chosen the House of the Seven Gables as the scene of his commercial speculations?

We return to the elderly maiden. She at length withdrew her eyes from the dark countenance of the Colonel's portrait, heaved a sigh—indeed, her breast was a very cave of Æolus, that morning—and stept across the room on tiptoe, as is the customary gait of elderly women. Passing through an intervening passage, she opened a door that communicated with the shop, just now so elaborately described. Owing to the projection of the upper story—and, still more, to the thick shadow of the Pyncheon-elm, which stood almost directly in front of the gable—the twilight, here, was still as much akin to night as morning. Another heavy sigh from Miss Hepzibah! After a moment's pause on the threshold, peering towards the window with her near-sighted scowl, as if frowning down some bitter enemy, she suddenly projected herself into the shop. The haste, and, as it were, the galvanic impulse of the movement, were really quite startling.

Nervously—in a sort of frenzy, we might almost say—she began to busy herself in arranging some children's playthings and other little wares, on the shelves and at the shop-window. In the aspect of this dark-arrayed, pale-faced, ladylike, old figure, there was a deeply tragic character that contrasted irreconcilably with the ludicrous pettiness of her employment. It seemed a queer anomaly, that so gaunt and dismal a personage should take a toy in hand;—a miracle, that the toy did not vanish in her grasp;—a miserably absurd idea, that she should go on perplexing her stiff and sombre intellect with the question how to tempt little boys into her premises! Yet such is undoubtedly her object! Now, she places a ginger-bread elephant against the window, but with so tremulous a touch that it tumbles upon the floor, with the dismemberment of three legs and its trunk; it has ceased to be an elephant, and has become a few bits of musty gingerbread. There, again, she has upset a tumbler of marbles, all of which roll different ways, and each individual marble, devil-directed, into the most difficult obscurity that it can find. Heaven help our poor old Hepzibah, and forgive us for taking a ludicrous view of her position! As her rigid and rusty frame goes down upon its hands and knees, in quest of the absconding marbles, we positively feel so much the more inclined to shed tears of sympathy, from the very fact that we must needs turn aside and laugh at her! For here—and if we fail to impress it suitably upon the reader, it is our own fault, not that of the theme—here is one of the truest points of melancholy interest that occur in ordinary life. It was the final term of what called itself old gentility. A lady—who had fed herself from childhood with the shadowy food of aristocratic reminiscences, and whose religion it was, that a lady's hand soils itself irremediably by doing aught for bread—this born lady, after sixty years of narrowing means, is fain to step down from her pedestal of imaginary rank. Poverty, treading closely at her heels for a lifetime, has come up with her at last. She must earn her own food, or starve! And we have stolen upon Miss Hepzibah Pyncheon, too irreverently, at the instant of time when the patrician lady is to be transformed into the plebeian woman.

In this republican country, amid the fluctuating waves of our social life, somebody is always at the drowning-point. The tragedy is enacted with as continual a repetition as that of a popular drama on a holiday, and, nevertheless, is felt as deeply, perhaps, as when an hereditary noble sinks below his order. More deeply; since, with us, rank is the grosser substance of wealth and a splendid establishment, and has no spiritual existence after the death of these, but dies hopelessly along with them. And, therefore, since we have been unfortunate enough to introduce our heroine at so inauspicious a juncture, we would entreat for a mood of due solemnity in the spectators of her fate. Let us behold, in poor Hepzibah, the immemorial lady—two hundred years old, on this side of the water, and thrice as many, on the other—with her antique portraits, pedigrees, coats of arms, records, and traditions, and her claim, as joint heiress, to that princely territory at the eastward, no longer a wilderness, but a populous fertility—born, too, in Pyncheon-street, under the Pyncheon-elm, and in the Pyncheon-house, where she has spent all her days—reduced now, in that very house, to be the hucksteress of a cent-shop!

This business of setting up a petty shop is almost the only resource of women, in circumstances at all similar to those of our unfortunate recluse. With her near-sightedness, and those tremulous fingers of hers, at once inflexible and delicate, she could not be a seamstress; although her sampler, of fifty years gone-by, exhibited some of the most recondite specimens of ornamental needlework. A school for little children had been often in her thoughts; and, at one time, she had begun a review of her early studies in the New England primer, with a view to prepare herself for the office of instructress. But the love of children had never been quickened in Hepzibah's heart, and was now torpid, if not extinct; she watched the little people of the neighborhood, from her chamber-window, and doubted whether she could tolerate a more intimate acquaintance with them. Besides, in our day, the very A. B. C. has become a science, greatly too abstruse to be any longer taught by pointing a pin from letter to letter. A modern child could teach old Hepzibah more than old Hepzibah could teach the child. So—with many a cold, deep heartquake at the idea of at last coming into sordid contact with the world, from which she had so long kept aloof, while every added day of seclusion had rolled another stone against the cavern-door of her hermitage—the poor thing bethought herself of the ancient shop-window, the rusty scales, and dusty till. She might have held back a little longer; but another circumstance, not yet hinted at, had somewhat hastened her decision. Her humble preparations, therefore, were duly made, and the enterprise was now to be commenced. Nor was she entitled to complain of any remarkable singularity in her fate; for, in the town of her nativity, we might point to several little shops of a similar description; some of them in houses as ancient as that of the seven gables; and one or two, it may be, where a decayed gentlewoman stands behind the counter, as grim an image of family-pride as Miss Hepzibah Pyncheon herself.

It was overpoweringly ridiculous—we must honestly confess it—the deportment of the maiden lady, while setting her shop in order for the public eye. She stole on tiptoe to the window, as cautiously as if she conceived some bloody-minded villain to be watching behind the elm-tree, with intent to take her life. Stretching out her long, lank arm, she put a paper of pearl-buttons, a jewsharp, or whatever the small article might be, in its destined place, and straightway vanished back into the dusk, as if the world need never hope for another glimpse of her. It might have been fancied, indeed, that she expected to minister to the wants of the community, unseen, like a disembodied divinity, or enchantress, holding forth her bargains to the reverential and awe-stricken purchaser, in an invisible hand. But Hepzibah had no such flattering dream. She was well aware that she must ultimately come forward, and stand revealed in her proper individuality; but, like other sensitive persons, she could not bear to be observed in the gradual process, and chose rather to flash forth on the world's astonished gaze, at once.

The inevitable moment was not much longer to be delayed. The sunshine might now be seen stealing down the front of the opposite house, from the windows of which came a reflected gleam, struggling through the boughs of the elm-tree, and enlightening the interior of the shop, more distinctly than heretofore. The town appeared to be waking-up. A baker's cart had already rattled through the street, chasing away the latest vestige of night's sanctity with the jingle-jangle of its dissonant bells. A milkman was distributing the contents of his cans from door to door; and the harsh peal of a fisherman's conch-shell was heard far off, around the corner. None of these tokens escaped Hepzibah's notice. The moment had arrived. To delay longer, would be only to lengthen out her misery. Nothing remained, except to take down the bar from the shop-door, leaving the entrance free—more than free—welcome, as if all were household friends—to every passer-by, whose eyes might be attracted by the commodities at the window. This last act Hepzibah now performed, letting the bar fall, with what smote upon her excited nerves as a most astounding clatter. Then—as if the only barrier betwixt herself and the world had been thrown down, and a flood of evil consequences would come tumbling through the gap—she fled into the inner parlor, threw herself into the ancestral elbow-chair, and wept.

Our miserable old Hepzibah! It is a heavy annoyance to

a writer, who endeavors to represent nature, its various attitudes and circumstances, in a reasonably correct outline and true coloring, that so much of the mean and ludicrous should be hopelessly mixed up with the purest pathos which life anywhere supplies to him. What tragic dignity, for example, can be wrought into a scene like this! How can we elevate our history of retribution for the sin of long ago, when, as one of our most prominent figures, we are compelled to introduce —not a young and lovely woman, nor even the stately remains of beauty, storm-shattered by affliction—but a gaunt, sallow, rusty-jointed maiden, in a long-waisted silk-gown, and with the strange horror of a turban on her head! Her visage is not even ugly. It is redeemed from insignificance only by the contraction of her eyebrows into a near-sighted scowl. And, finally, her great life-trial seems to be, that, after sixty years of idleness, she finds it convenient to earn comfortable bread by setting up a shop, in a small way. Nevertheless, if we look through all the heroic fortunes of mankind, we shall find this same entanglement of something mean and trivial with whatever is noblest in joy or sorrow. Life is made up of marble and mud. And, without all the deeper trust in a comprehensive sympathy above us, we might hence be led to suspect the insult of a sneer, as well as an immitigable frown, on the iron countenance of fate. What is called poetic insight is the gift of discerning, in this sphere of strangely mingled elements, the beauty and the majesty which are compelled to assume a garb so sordid.

III

THE FIRST CUSTOMER

MISS Hepzibah Pyncheon sat in the oaken elbow-chair, with her hands over her face, giving way to that heavy downsinking of the heart which most persons have experienced, when the image of Hope itself seems ponderously moulded of lead, on the eve of an enterprise, at once doubtful and momentous. She was suddenly startled by the tinkling alarum—high, sharp, and irregular—of a little bell. The maiden lady arose upon her feet, as pale as a ghost at cock-crow; for she was an enslaved spirit, and this the talisman to which she owed obedience. This little bell—to speak in plainer terms—being fastened over the shop-door, was so contrived as to vibrate by means of a steel-spring, and thus convey notice to the inner regions of the house, when any customer should cross the threshold. Its ugly and spiteful little din, (heard now for the first time, perhaps, since Hepzibah's periwigged predecessor had retired from trade,) at once set every nerve of her body in responsive and tumultuous vibration. The crisis was upon her! Her first customer was at the door!

Without giving herself time for a second thought, she rushed into the shop, pale, wild, desperate in gesture and expression, scowling portentously, and looking far better qualified to do fierce battle with a housebreaker than to stand smiling behind the counter, bartering small wares for a copper recompense. Any ordinary customer, indeed, would have turned his back, and fled. And yet there was nothing fierce in Hepzibah's poor old heart; nor had she, at the moment, a single bitter thought against the world at large, or one individual man or woman. She wished them all well, but wished, too, that she herself were done with them, and in her quiet grave.

The applicant, by this time, stood within the door-way. Coming freshly, as he did, out of the morning light, he appeared to have brought some of its cheery influences into the shop along with him. It was a slender young man, not more than one or two and twenty years old, with rather a grave and thoughtful expression, for his years, but likewise a springy alacrity and vigor. These qualities were not only perceptible, physically, in his make and motions, but made themselves felt, almost immediately, in his character. A brown beard, not too silken in its texture, fringed his chin, but as yet without completely hiding it; he wore a short moustache, too; and his dark, high-featured countenance looked all the better for these natural ornaments. As for his dress, it was of the simplest kind; a summer sack of cheap and ordinary material, thin checkered pantaloons, and a straw hat, by no means of the finest braid. Oak-hall might have supplied his entire equipment. He was chiefly marked as a gentleman—if such, indeed, he made any claim to be—by the rather remarkable whiteness and nicety of his clean linen.

He met the scowl of old Hepzibah without apparent alarm, as having heretofore encountered it, and found it harmless.

"So, my dear Miss Pyncheon," said the Daguerreotypist—for it was that sole other occupant of the seven-gabled mansion—"I am glad to see that you have not shrunk from your good purpose. I merely look in, to offer my best wishes, and to ask if I can assist you any further in your preparations?"

People in difficulty and distress, or in any manner at odds

with the world, can endure a vast amount of harsh treatment, and perhaps be only the stronger for it; whereas, they give way at once before the simplest expression of what they perceive to be genuine sympathy. So it proved with poor Hepzibah; for when she saw the young man's smile—looking so much the brighter on a thoughtful face—and heard his kindly tone, she broke first into an hysteric giggle, and then began to sob.

"Ah, Mr. Holgrave," cried she, as soon as she could speak, "I never can go through with it! Never, never, never! I wish I were dead, and in the old family-tomb, with all my forefathers! With my father, and my mother, and my sister! Yes; —and with my brother, who had far better find me there than here! The world is too chill and hard—and I am too old, and too feeble, and too hopeless!"

"Oh, believe me, Miss Hepzibah," said the young man quietly, "these feelings will not trouble you any longer, after you are once fairly in the midst of your enterprise. They are unavoidable at this moment, standing, as you do, on the outer verge of your long seclusion, and peopling the world with ugly shapes, which you will soon find to be as unreal as the giants and ogres of a child's story-book. I find nothing so singular in life, as that everything appears to lose its substance, the instant one actually grapples with it. So it will be with what you think so terrible."

"But I am a woman!" said Hepzibah piteously. "I was going to say, a lady,—but I consider that as past."

"Well; no matter if it be past!" answered the artist, a strange gleam of half-hidden sarcasm flashing through the kindliness of his manner. "Let it go! You are the better without it. I speak frankly, my dear Miss Pyncheon:—for are we not friends? I look upon this as one of the fortunate days of your life. It ends an epoch, and begins one. Hitherto, the life-blood has been gradually chilling in your veins, as you sat aloof, within your circle of gentility, while the rest of the world was fighting out its battle with one kind of necessity or another. Henceforth, you will at least have the sense of healthy and natural effort for a purpose, and of lending your strength—be it great or small—to the united struggle of mankind. This is success—all the success that anybody meets with!"

"It is natural enough, Mr. Holgrave, that you should have ideas like these," rejoined Hepzibah, drawing up her gaunt figure with slightly offended dignity.—"You are a man—a young man—and brought up, I suppose, as almost everybody is, now-a-days, with a view to seeking your fortune. But I was born a lady, and have always lived one—no matter in what narrowness of means, always a lady!"

"But I was not born a gentleman; neither have I lived like one," said Holgrave, slightly smiling; "so, my dear Madam, you will hardly expect me to sympathize with sensibilities of this kind; though—unless I deceive myself—I have some imperfect comprehension of them. These names of gentleman and lady had a meaning, in the past history of the world, and conferred privileges, desirable, or otherwise, on those entitled to bear them. In the present—and still more in the future condition of society—they imply, not privilege, but restriction."

"These are new notions," said the old gentlewoman, shaking her head. "I shall never understand them; neither do I wish it."

"We will cease to speak of them, then," replied the artist, with a friendlier smile than his last one; "and I will leave you to feel whether it is not better to be a true woman, than a lady. Do you really think, Miss Hepzibah, that any lady of your family has ever done a more heroic thing, since this house was built, than you are performing in it to-day? Never; —and if the Pyncheons had always acted so nobly, I doubt whether the old wizard Maule's anathema, of which you told me once, would have had much weight with Providence against them."

"Ah!—no, no!" said Hepzibah, not displeased at this allusion to the sombre dignity of an inherited curse. "If old Maule's ghost, or a descendant of his, could see me behind the counter to-day, he would call it the fulfilment of his worst wishes. But I thank you for your kindness, Mr. Holgrave, and will do my utmost to be a good shopkeeper!"

"Pray do," said Holgrave, "and let me have the pleasure of being your first customer. I am about taking a walk to the sea-shore, before going to my rooms, where I misuse Heaven's blessed sunshine by tracing out human features, through its agency. A few of those biscuits, dipt in sea-water, will be just what I need for breakfast. What is the price of half-a-dozen?"

"Let me be a lady a moment longer," replied Hepzibah, with a manner of antique stateliness, to which a melancholy smile lent a kind of grace. She put the biscuits into his hand, but rejected the compensation.—"A Pyncheon must not, at all events, under her forefathers' roof, receive money for a morsel of bread, from her only friend!"

Holgrave took his departure, leaving her, for the moment, with spirits not quite so much depressed. Soon, however, they had subsided nearly to their former dead-level. With a beating heart, she listened to the footsteps of early passengers, which now began to be frequent along the street. Once or twice, they seemed to linger; these strangers, or neighbors, as the case might be, were looking at the display of toys and petty commodities in Hepzibah's shop-window. She was doubly tortured;—in part, with a sense of overwhelming shame, that strange and unloving eyes should have the privilege of gazing;—and, partly, because the idea occurred to her, with ridiculous importunity, that the window was not arranged so skilfully, nor nearly to so much advantage, as it might have been. It seemed as if the whole fortune or failure of her shop might depend on the display of a different set of articles, or substituting a fairer apple for one which appeared to be specked. So she made the change, and straightway fancied that everything was spoiled by it; not recognizing that it was the nervousness of the juncture, and her own native squeamishness, as an old maid, that wrought all the seeming mischief.

Anon, there was an encounter, just at the door-step, betwixt two laboring men, as their rough voices denoted them to be. After some slight talk about their own affairs, one of them chanced to notice the shop-window, and directed the other's attention to it.

"See here!" cried he. "What do you think of this? Trade seems to be looking up, in Pyncheon-street!"

"Well, well, this is a sight, to be sure!" exclaimed the other. "In the old Pyncheon-house, and underneath the Pyncheon-elm! Who would have thought it! Old Maid Pyncheon is setting up a cent-shop!"

"Will she make it go, think you, Dixey?" said his friend. "I don't call it a very good stand. There's another shop, just round the corner."

"Make it go!" cried Dixey, with a most contemptuous expression, as if the very idea were impossible to be conceived. "Not a bit of it! Why, her face—I've seen it; for I dug her garden for her, one year—her face is enough to frighten the Old Nick himself, if he had ever so great a mind to trade with her. People can't stand it, I tell you! She scowls dreadfully, reason or none, out of pure ugliness of temper!"

"Well; that's not so much matter," remarked the other man. "These sour-tempered folks are mostly handy at business, and know pretty well what they are about. But, as you say, I don't think she'll do much. This business of keeping cent-shops is overdone, like all other kinds of trade, handicraft, and bodily labor. I know it, to my cost! My wife kept a cent-shop, three months, and lost five dollars on her outlay!"

"Poor business!" responded Dixey, in a tone as if he were shaking his head.—"Poor business!"

For some reason or other, not very easy to analyze, there had hardly been so bitter a pang in all her previous misery about the matter, as what thrilled Hepzibah's heart, on over-hearing the above conversation. The testimony in regard to her scowl was frightfully important; it seemed to hold up her image, wholly relieved from the false light of her self-partialities, and so hideous that she dared not look at it. She was absurdly hurt, moreover, by the slight and idle effect that her setting-up shop—an event of such breathless interest to herself—appeared to have upon the public, of which these two men were the nearest representatives. A glance; a passing word or two; a coarse laugh;—and she was doubtless forgotten, before they turned the corner! They cared nothing for her dignity, and just as little for her degradation. Then, also, the augury of ill-success, uttered from the sure wisdom of ex-perience, fell upon her half-dead hope, like a clod into a grave. The man's wife had already tried the same experiment, and failed! How could the born lady—the recluse of half-a-lifetime, utterly unpractised in the world, at sixty years of age—how could she ever dream of succeeding, when the hard, vulgar, keen, busy, hackneyed New England woman had lost five dollars on her little outlay? Success presented itself as an impossibility, and the hope of it as a wild hallu-cination.

Some malevolent spirit, doing his utmost to drive Hepzibah mad, unrolled before her imagination a kind of panorama, representing the great thoroughfare of a city, all astir with customers. So many and so magnificent shops as there were! Groceries, toy-shops, dry-goods stores, with their immense panes of plate-glass, their gorgeous fixtures, their vast and complete assortments of merchandize, in which fortunes had been invested; and those noble mirrors at the farther end of each establishment, doubling all this wealth by a brightly burnished vista of unrealities! On one side of the street, this splendid bazaar, with a multitude of perfumed and glossy salesmen, smirking, smiling, bowing, and measuring out the goods! On the other, the dusky old House of the Seven Gables, with the antiquated shop-window under its projecting story, and Hepzibah herself in a gown of rusty black silk, behind the counter, scowling at the world as it went by! This mighty contrast thrust itself forward as a fair expression of the odds against which she was to begin her struggle for a subsistence. Success? Preposterous! She would never think of it again! The house might just as well be buried in an eternal fog, while all other houses had the sunshine on them; for not a foot would ever cross the threshold, nor a hand so much as try the door!

But, at this instant, the shop-bell, right over her head, tinkled as if it were bewitched. The old gentlewoman's heart seemed to be attached to the same steel-spring; for it went through a series of sharp jerks, in unison with the sound. The door was thrust open, although no human form was perceptible on the other side of the half-window. Hepzibah, nevertheless, stood at a gaze, with her hands clasped, looking very much as if she had summoned up an evil spirit, and were afraid, yet resolved, to hazard the encounter.

"Heaven help me!" she groaned mentally. "Now is my hour of need!"

The door, which moved with difficulty on its creaking and rusty hinges, being forced quite open, a square and sturdy little urchin became apparent, with cheeks as red as an apple. He was clad rather shabbily, (but, as it seemed, more owing to his mother's carelessness than his father's poverty,) in a blue apron, very wide and short trowsers, shoes somewhat out at the toes, and a chip-hat, with the frizzles of his curly hair sticking through its crevices. A book and a small slate, under his arm, indicated that he was on his way to school. He stared at Hepzibah, a moment, as an elder customer than himself would have been likely enough to do; not knowing what to make of the tragic attitude and queer scowl, wherewith she regarded him.

"Well, child!" said she, taking heart at sight of a personage so little formidable.—"Well, my child, what did you wish for?"

"That Jim Crow there, in the window!" answered the urchin, holding out a cent, and pointing to the gingerbread figure that had attracted his notice, as he loitered along to school.—"The one that has not a broken foot!"

So Hepzibah put forth her lank arm, and taking the effigy from the shop-window, delivered it to her first customer.

"No matter for the money!" said she, giving him a little push towards the door—for her old gentility was contumaciously squeamish at sight of the copper-coin; and, besides, it seemed such pitiful meanness to take the child's pocket-money, in exchange for a bit of stale gingerbread.—"No matter for the cent! You are welcome to Jim Crow!"

The child—staring with round eyes at this instance of liberality, wholly unprecedented in his large experience of cent-shops—took the man of gingerbread, and quitted the premises. No sooner had he reached the sidewalk (little cannibal that he was!) than Jim Crow's head was in his mouth. As he had not been careful to shut the door, Hepzibah was at the pains of closing it after him, with a pettish ejaculation or two about the troublesomeness of young people, and particularly of small boys. She had just placed another representative of the renowned Jim Crow at the window, when again the shop-bell tinkled clamorously; and again the door being thrust open, with its characteristic jerk and jar, disclosed the same sturdy little urchin who, precisely two minutes ago, had made his exit. The crumbs and discoloration of the cannibal-feast, as yet hardly consummated, were exceedingly visible about his mouth!

"What is it now, child?" asked the maiden lady, rather impatiently.—"Did you come back to shut the door?"

"No!" answered the urchin, pointing to the figure that had just been put up.—"I want that other Jim Crow!"

"Well, here it is for you," said Hepzibah, reaching it down; but, recognizing that this pertinacious customer would not quit her on any other terms, so long as she had a gingerbread figure in her shop, she partly drew back her extended hand—"Where is the cent?"

The little boy had the cent ready, but, like a true-born Yankee, would have preferred the better bargain to the worse. Looking somewhat chagrined, he put the coin into Hepzibah's hand, and departed, sending the second Jim Crow in quest of the former one. The new shopkeeper dropt the first solid result of her commercial enterprise into the till. It was done! The sordid stain of that copper-coin could never be washed away from her palm. The little schoolboy, aided by the impish figure of the negro dancer, had wrought an irreparable ruin. The structure of ancient aristocracy had been demolished by him, even as if his childish gripe had torn down the seven-gabled mansion! Now let Hepzibah turn the old Pyncheon portraits with their faces to the wall, and take the map of her eastern-territory to kindle the kitchen-fire, and blow up the flame with the empty breath of her ancestral traditions! What had she to do with ancestry? Nothing;—no more than with posterity! No lady, now, but simply Hepzibah Pyncheon, a forlorn old maid, and keeper of a cent-shop!

Nevertheless—even while she paraded these ideas somewhat ostentatiously through her mind—it is altogether surprising what a calmness had come over her. The anxiety and misgivings which had tormented her, whether asleep or in melancholy day-dreams, ever since her project began to take an aspect of solidity, had now vanished quite away. She felt the novelty of her position, indeed, but no longer with disturbance or affright. Now and then, there came a thrill of almost youthful enjoyment. It was the invigorating breath of a fresh outward atmosphere, after the long torpor and monotonous seclusion of her life. So wholesome is effort!

So miraculous the strength that we do not know of! The healthiest glow, that Hepzibah had known for years, had come now, in the dreaded crisis, when, for the first time, she had put forth her hand to help herself. That little circlet of the schoolboy's copper-coin—dim and lustreless though it was, with the small services which it had been doing, here and there about the world—had proved a talisman, fragrant with good, and deserving to be set in gold and worn next her heart. It was as potent, and perhaps endowed with the same kind of efficacy, as a galvanic ring! Hepzibah, at all events, was indebted to its subtile operation, both in body and spirit; so much the more, as it inspired her with energy to get some breakfast, at which—still the better to keep up her courage—she allowed herself an extra spoonful in her infusion of black tea.

Her introductory day of shopkeeping did not run on, however, without many and serious interruptions of this mood of cheerful vigor. As a general rule, Providence seldom vouchsafes to mortals any more than just that degree of encouragement, which suffices to keep them at a reasonably full exertion of their powers. In the case of our old gentlewoman, after the excitement of new effort had subsided, the despondency of her whole life threatened, ever and anon, to return. It was like the heavy mass of clouds, which we may often see obscuring the sky, and making a gray twilight everywhere, until, towards nightfall, it yields temporarily to a glimpse of sunshine. But, always, the envious cloud strives to gather again across the streak of celestial azure.

Customers came in, as the forenoon advanced, but rather slowly; in some cases, too, it must be owned, with little satisfaction either to themselves or Miss Hepzibah; nor on the whole, with an aggregate of very rich emolument to the till. A little girl, sent by her mother to match a skein of cotton-thread, of a peculiar hue, took one that the near-sighted old lady pronounced extremely like, but soon came running back, with a blunt and cross message, that it would not do, and, besides, was very rotten! Then there was a pale, care-wrinkled woman, not old, but haggard, and already with streaks of gray among her hair, like silver ribbons; one of those women, naturally delicate, whom you at once recognize as worn to death by a brute—probably, a drunken brute—of a husband, and at least nine children. She wanted a few pounds of flour, and offered the money, which the decayed gentlewoman silently rejected, and gave the poor soul better measure than if she had taken it. Shortly afterwards, a man in a blue cotton-frock, much soiled, came in and bought a pipe; filling the whole shop, meanwhile, with the hot odor of strong drink, not only exhaled in the torrid atmosphere of his breath, but oozing out of his entire system, like an inflammable gas. It was impressed on Hepzibah's mind, that this was the husband of the care-wrinkled woman. He asked for a paper of tobacco; and, as she had neglected to provide herself with the article, her brutal customer dashed down his newly-bought pipe, and left the shop, muttering some unintelligible words, which had the tone and bitterness of a curse. Hereupon, Hepzibah threw up her eyes, unintentionally scowling in the face of Providence!

No less than five persons, during the forenoon, inquired for ginger-beer, or root-beer, or any drink of a similar brewage, and, obtaining nothing of the kind, went off in an exceedingly bad humor. Three of them left the door open; and the other two pulled it so spitefully, in going out, that the little bell played the very deuce with Hepzibah's nerves. A round, bustling, fire-ruddy housewife, of the neighborhood, burst breathless into the shop, fiercely demanding yeast; and when the poor gentlewoman, with her cold shyness of manner, gave her hot customer to understand that she did not keep the article, this very capable housewife took upon herself to administer a regular rebuke.

"A cent-shop, and no yeast!" quoth she. "That will never

do! Who ever heard of such a thing? Your loaf will never rise, no more than mine will to-day. You had better shut up shop at once!"

"Well," said Hepzibah, heaving a deep sigh, "perhaps I had!"

Several times, moreover, besides the above instance, her ladylike sensibilities were seriously infringed upon by the familiar, if not rude tone with which people addressed her. They evidently considered themselves not merely her equals, but her patrons and superiors. Now, Hepzibah had unconsciously flattered herself with the idea, that there would be a gleam or halo of some kind or other, about her person, which would ensure an obeisance to her sterling gentility, or, at least, a tacit recognition of it. On the other hand, nothing tortured her more intolerably than when this recognition was too prominently expressed. To one or two rather officious offers of sympathy, her responses were little short of acrimonious; and, we regret to say, Hepzibah was thrown into a positively unchristian state of mind by the suspicion that one of her customers was drawn to the shop, not by any real need of the article which she pretended to seek, but by a wicked wish to stare at her. The vulgar creature was determined to see for herself what sort of a figure a mildewed piece of aristocracy—after wasting all the bloom and much of the decline of her life, apart from the world—would cut behind a counter. In this particular case—however mechanical and innocuous it might be, at other times—Hepzibah's contortion of brow served her in good stead.

"I never was so frightened in my life!" said the curious customer in describing the incident to one of her acquaintances. "She's a real old vixen, take my word of it. She says little, to be sure;—but if you could only see the mischief in her eye!"

On the whole, therefore, her new experience led our decayed gentlewoman to very disagreeable conclusions as to the temper and manners of what she termed the lower classes, whom, heretofore, she had looked down upon with a gentle and pitying complacence, as herself occupying a sphere of unquestionable superiority. But, unfortunately, she had likewise to struggle against a bitter emotion, of a directly opposite kind; a sentiment of virulence, we mean, towards the idle aristocracy to which it had so recently been her pride to belong. When a lady, in a delicate and costly summer garb, with a floating veil and gracefully swaying gown, and, altogether, an ethereal lightness that made you look at her beautifully slippered feet, to see whether she trod on the dust or floated in the air—when such a vision happened to pass through this retired street, leaving it tenderly and delusively fragrant with her passage, as if a boquet of tea-roses had been borne along—then, again, it is to be feared, old Hepzibah's scowl could no longer vindicate itself entirely on the plea of near-sightedness.

"For what end," thought she, giving vent to that feeling of hostility, which is the only real abasement of the poor, in presence of the rich, "for what good end, in the wisdom of Providence, does that woman live! Must the whole world toil, that the palms of her hands may be kept white and delicate?"

Then, ashamed and penitent, she hid her face.

"May God forgive me!" said she.

Doubtless, God did forgive her. But, taking the inward and outward history of the first half-day into consideration, Hepzibah began to fear that the shop would prove her ruin, in a moral and religious point of view, without contributing very essentially towards even her temporal welfare.

IV

A DAY BEHIND THE COUNTER

TOWARDS noon, Hepzibah saw an elderly gentleman, large and portly, and of remarkably dignified demeanor, passing slowly along, on the opposite side of the white and dusty street. On coming within the shadow of the Pyncheon-elm, he stopt, and (taking off his hat, meanwhile, to wipe the perspiration from his brow) seemed to scrutinize, with especial interest, the dilapidated and rusty-visaged House of the Seven Gables. He himself, in a very different style, was as well worth looking at as the house. No better model need be sought, nor could have been found, of a very high order of respectability, which by some indescribable magic, not merely expressed itself in his looks and gestures, but even governed the fashion of his garments, and rendered them all proper and essential to the man. Without appearing to differ, in any tangible way, from other people's clothes, there was yet a wide and rich gravity about them, that must have been a characteristic of the wearer, since it could not be defined as pertaining either to the cut or material. His gold-headed cane, too—a serviceable staff, of dark, polished wood—had similar traits, and, had it chosen to take a walk by itself, would have been recognized anywhere as a tolerably adequate representative of its master. This character—which showed itself so strikingly in everything about him, and the effect of which we seek to convey to the reader—went no deeper than his station, habits of life, and external circumstances. One perceived him to be a personage of mark, influence, and authority; and, especially, you could feel just as certain that he was opulent, as if he had exhibited his bank account—or as if you had seen him touching the twigs of the Pyncheon-elm, and, Midas-like, transmuting them to gold.

In his youth, he had probably been considered a handsome man; at his present age, his brow was too heavy, his temples too bare, his remaining hair too gray, his eye too cold, his lips too closely compressed, to bear any relation to mere personal beauty. He would have made a good and massive portrait; better now, perhaps, than at any previous period of his life, although his look might grow positively harsh, in the process of being fixed upon the canvass. The artist would have found it desirable to study his face, and prove its capacity for varied expression; to darken it with a frown—to kindle it up with a smile.

While the elderly gentleman stood looking at the Pyncheon-house, both the frown and the smile passed successively over his countenance. His eye rested on the shop-window, and putting up a pair of gold-bowed spectacles, which he held in his hand, he minutely surveyed Hepzibah's little arrangement of toys and commodities. At first, it seemed not to please him—nay, to cause him exceeding displeasure—and yet, the very next moment, he smiled. While the latter expression was yet on his lips, he caught a glimpse of Hepzibah, who had involuntarily bent forward to the window; and then the smile changed from acrid and disagreeable, to the sunniest complaisancy and benevolence. He bowed, with a happy mixture of dignity and courteous kindliness, and pursued his way.

"There he is!" said Hepzibah to herself, gulping down a very bitter emotion, and, since she could not rid herself of it, trying to drive it back into her heart.—"What does he think of it, I wonder? Does it please him? Ah!—he is looking back!"

The gentleman had paused in the street, and turned himself half about, still with his eyes fixed on the shop-window. In fact, he wheeled wholly round, and commenced a step or two, as if designing to enter the shop; but, as it chanced, his purpose was anticipated by Hepzibah's first customer, the little cannibal of Jim Crow, who, staring up at the window, was irresistibly attracted by an elephant of gingerbread. What a grand appetite had this small urchin!—two Jim Crows, immediately after breakfast!—and now an elephant, as a preliminary whet before dinner! By the time this latter purchase was completed, the elderly gentleman had resumed his way, and turned the street-corner.

"Take it as you like, Cousin Jaffrey!" muttered the maiden lady, as she drew back after cautiously thrusting out her head, and looking up and down the street. "Take it as you like! You have seen my little shop-window! Well!—what have you to say?—is not the Pyncheon-house my own, while I'm alive?"

After this incident, Hepzibah retreated to the back parlor, where she at first caught up a half-finished stocking, and began knitting at it with nervous and irregular jerks; but quickly finding herself at odds with the stitches, she threw it aside, and walked hurriedly about the room. At length, she paused before the portrait of the stern old Puritan, her ancestor, and the founder of the house. In one sense, this picture had almost faded into the canvass, and hidden itself behind the duskiness of age; in another, she could not but fancy that it had been growing more prominent, and strikingly expressive, ever since her earliest familiarity with it, as a child. For, while the physical outline and substance were darkening away from the beholder's eye, the bold, hard, and, at the same time, indirect character of the man seemed to be brought out in a kind of spiritual relief. Such an effect may occasionally be observed in pictures of antique date.

They acquire a look which an artist (if he have anything like the complaisancy of artists, now-a-days) would never dream of presenting to a patron as his own characteristic expression, but which, nevertheless, we at once recognize as reflecting the unlovely truth of a human soul. In such cases, the painter's deep conception of his subject's inward traits has wrought itself into the essence of the picture, and is seen, after the superficial coloring has been rubbed off by time.

While gazing at the portrait, Hepzibah trembled under its eye. Her hereditary reverence made her afraid to judge the character of the original so harshly, as a perception of the truth compelled her to do. But still she gazed, because the face of the picture enabled her—at least, she fancied so—to read more accurately, and to a greater depth, the face which she had just seen in the street.

"This is the very man!" murmured she to herself. "Let Jaffrey Pyncheon smile as he will, there is that look beneath! Put on him a scull-cap, and a band, and a black cloak, and a Bible in one hand and a sword in the other—then let Jaffrey smile as he might—nobody would doubt that it was the old Pyncheon come again! He has proved himself the very man to build up a new house! Perhaps, too, to draw down a new curse!"

Thus did Hepzibah bewilder herself with these fantasies of the old time. She had dwelt too much alone—too long in the Pyncheon-house—until her very brain was impregnated with the dry-rot of its timbers. She needed a walk along the noonday street, to keep her sane.

By the spell of contrast, another portrait rose up before her, painted with more daring flattery than any artist would have ventured upon, but yet so delicately touched that the likeness remained perfect. Malbone's miniature, though from the same original, was far inferior to Hepzibah's air-drawn picture, at which affection and sorrowful remembrance wrought together. Soft, mildly and cheerfully contemplative, with full, red lips, just on the verge of a smile, which the eyes seemed to herald by a gentle kindling-up of their orbs! Feminine traits, moulded inseparably with those of the other sex! The miniature, likewise, had this last peculiarity; so that you inevitably thought of the original as resembling his mother; and she, a lovely and loveable woman, with perhaps some beautiful infirmity of character, that made it all the pleasanter to know, and easier to love her.

"Yes," thought Hepzibah, with grief of which it was only the more tolerable portion that welled up from her heart to her eyelids, "they persecuted his mother in him! He never was a Pyncheon!"

But here the shop-bell rang; it was like a sound from a remote distance—so far had Hepzibah descended into the sepulchral depths of her reminiscences. On entering the shop, she found an old man there, a humble resident of Pyncheon-street, and whom, for a great many years past, she had suffered to be a kind of familiar of the house. He was an immemorial personage, who seemed always to have had a white head and wrinkles, and never to have possessed but a single tooth, and that a half-decayed one, in the front of the upper jaw. Well advanced as Hepzibah was, she could not remember when Uncle Venner, as the neighborhood called him, had not gone up and down the street, stooping a little and drawing his feet heavily over the gravel or pavement. But still there was something tough and vigorous about him, that not only kept him in daily breath, but enabled him to fill a place which would else have been vacant, in the apparently crowded world. To go of errands, with his slow and shuffling gait, which made you doubt how he ever was to arrive anywhere; to saw a small household's foot or two of firewood, or knock to pieces an old barrel, or split up a pine board, for kindling-stuff; in summer, to dig the few yards of garden-ground, appertaining to a low-rented tenement, and share the produce of his labor at the halves; in winter, to shovel away the snow from the sidewalk, or open paths to the wood-shed, or along the clothes-line;—such were some of the essential offices which Uncle Venner performed among at least a score of families. Within that circle, he claimed the same sort of privilege, and probably felt as much warmth of interest, as a clergyman does in the range of his parishioners. Not that he laid claim to the tithe pig; but, as an analogous mode of reverence, he went his rounds, every morning, to gather up the crumbs of the table and overflowings of the dinner-pot, as food for a pig of his own.

In his younger days—for, after all, there was a dim tradition that he had been, not young, but younger—Uncle Venner was commonly regarded as rather deficient, than otherwise, in his wits. In truth, he had virtually pleaded guilty to the charge, by scarcely aiming at such success as other men seek, and by taking only that humble and modest part in the intercourse of life, which belongs to the alleged deficiency. But, now, in his extreme old age—whether it were, that his long and hard experience had actually brightened him, or that his decaying judgement rendered him less capable of fairly measuring himself—the venerable man made pretensions to no little wisdom, and really enjoyed the credit of it. There was likewise, at times, a vein of something like poetry in him; it was the moss or wall-flower of his mind in its small dilapidation, and gave a charm to what might have been vulgar and common-place, in his earlier and middle life. Hepzibah had a regard for him, because his name was ancient in the town, and had formerly been respectable. It was a still better reason for awarding him a species of familiar reverence, that Uncle Venner was himself the most ancient existence, whether of man or thing, in Pyncheon-street; except the House of the Seven Gables, and perhaps the elm that overshadowed it.

This patriarch now presented himself before Hepzibah, clad in an old blue coat, which had a fashionable air, and must have accrued to him from the cast-off wardrobe of some dashing clerk. As for his trowsers, they were of tow-cloth, very short in the legs, and bagging down strangely in the rear, but yet having a suitableness to his figure, which his other garment entirely lacked. His hat had relation to no other part of his dress, and but very little to the head that wore it. Thus Uncle Venner was a miscellaneous old gentleman, partly himself, but, in good measure, somebody else; patched together, too, of different epochs; an epitome of times and fashions.

"So, you have really begun trade," said he—"really begun trade! Well, I'm glad to see it. Young people should never live idle in the world, nor old ones neither, unless when the rheumatize gets hold of them. It has given me warning already; and in two or three years longer, I shall think of putting aside business, and retiring to my farm. That's yonder—the great brick house, you know—the work-house, most folks call it; but I mean to do my work first, and go there to be idle and enjoy myself. And I'm glad to see you beginning to do your work, Miss Hepzibah!"

"Thank you, Uncle Venner," said Hepzibah smiling; for she always felt kindly towards the simple and talkative old man. Had he been an old woman, she might probably have repelled the freedom which she now took in good part.—"It is time for me to begin work, indeed! Or, to speak the truth, I have but just begun, when I ought to be giving it up."

"Oh, never say that, Miss Hepzibah," answered the old man. "You are a young woman yet. Why, I hardly thought myself younger than I am now—it seems so little while ago—since I used to see you playing about the door of the old house, quite a small child! Oftener, though, you used to be sitting at the threshold and looking gravely into the street; for you had always a grave kind of way with you—a grown-up air, when you were only the height of my knee. It seems as if I saw you now; and your grandfather, with his red cloak, and his white wig, and his cocked hat, and his cane, coming out of the house, and stepping so grandly up the street! Those old gentlemen, that grew up before the revolution, used to put on grand airs. In my young days, the great man of the town was commonly called King, and his wife—not Queen, to be sure—but Lady. Now-a-days, a man would not dare to be called King; and if he feels himself a little above common folks, he only stoops so much the lower to them. I met your cousin, the Judge, ten minutes ago; and, in my old tow-cloth trowsers, as you see, the Judge raised his hat to me, I do believe! At any rate, the Judge bowed and smiled!"

"Yes," said Hepzibah, with something bitter stealing unawares into her tone; "my Cousin Jaffrey is thought to have a very pleasant smile!"

"And so he has!" replied Uncle Venner. "And that's rather remarkable, in a Pyncheon; for—begging your pardon, Miss Hepzibah—they never had the name of being an easy and agreeable set of folks. There was no getting close to them. But, now, Miss Hepzibah, if an old man may be bold to ask, why don't Judge Pyncheon, with his great means, step forward, and tell his cousin to shut up her little shop at once? It's for your credit to be doing something; but it's not for the Judge's credit to let you!"

"We won't talk of this, if you please, Uncle Venner," said Hepzibah coldly. "I ought to say, however, that, if I choose to earn bread for myself, it is not Judge Pyncheon's fault. Neither will he deserve the blame," added she more kindly, remembering Uncle Venner's privileges of age and humble familiarity, "if I should, by-and-by, find it convenient to retire with you to your farm."

"And it's no bad place neither, that farm of mine!" cried the old man cheerily, as if there were something positively delightful in the prospect.—"No bad place is the great brick farm-house, especially for them that will find a good many old cronies there, as will be my case. I quite long to be among them, sometimes, of the winter evenings; for it is but dull business for a lonesome elderly man, like me, to be nodding, by the hour together, with no company but his air-tight stove. Summer or winter, there's a great deal to be said in favor of my farm! And, take it in the autumn, what can be pleasanter than to spend a whole day, on the sunny side of a barn or a wood-pile, chatting with somebody as old as one's self; or perhaps idling away the time with a natural-born simpleton, who knows how to be idle, because even our busy Yankees have never found out how to put him to any use? Upon my word, Miss Hepzibah, I doubt whether I've ever been so comfortable as I mean to be at my farm, which most folks call the work-house. But you—you're a young woman yet—you never need go there! Something still better will turn up for you. I'm sure of it!"

Hepzibah fancied that there was something peculiar in her venerable friend's look and tone; insomuch that she gazed into his face with considerable earnestness, endeavoring to discover what secret meaning, if any, might be lurking there. Individuals, whose affairs have reached an utterly desperate crisis, almost invariably keep themselves alive with hopes, so much the more airily magnificent, as they have the less of solid matter within their grasp, whereof to mould any judicious and moderate expectation of good. Thus, all the while Hepzibah was projecting the scheme of her little shop, she had cherished an unacknowledged idea that some harlequin-trick of fortune would intervene, in her favor. For example, an uncle—who had sailed for India, fifty years before, and never been heard of since—might yet return, and adopt her to be the comfort of his very extreme and decrepit age, and adorn her with pearls, diamonds, and oriental shawls and turbans, and make her the ultimate heiress of his unreckonable riches. Or the member of parliament, now at the head of the English branch of the family—with which the elder

stock, on this side of the Atlantic, had held little or no intercourse for the last two centuries—this eminent gentleman
might invite Hepzibah to quit the ruinous House of the Seven
Gables, and come over to dwell with her kindred, at Pyncheon
Hall. But, for reasons the most imperative, she could not yield
to his request. It was more probable, therefore, that the descendants of a Pyncheon who had emigrated to Virginia, in
some past generation, and become a great planter there—
hearing of Hepzibah's destitution, and impelled by the splendid generosity of character, with which their Virginian mixture must have enriched the New England blood—would send
her a remittance of a thousand dollars, with a hint of repeating the favor, annually. Or—and, surely, anything so undeniably just could not be beyond the limits of reasonable
anticipation—the great claim to the heritage of Waldo County
might finally be decided in favor of the Pyncheons; so that,
instead of keeping a cent-shop, Hepzibah would build a
palace, and look down from its highest tower on hill, dale,
forest, field, and town, as her own share of the ancestral
territory!

These were some of the fantasies which she had long
dreamed about; and, aided by these, Uncle Venner's casual
attempt at encouragement kindled a strange festal glory in
the poor, bare, melancholy chambers of her brain, as if that
inner world were suddenly lighted up with gas. But either
he knew nothing of her castles in the air—as how should he?
—or else her earnest scowl disturbed his recollection, as it
might a more courageous man's. Instead of pursuing any
weightier topic, Uncle Venner was pleased to favor Hepzibah
with some sage counsel in her shop-keeping capacity.

"Give no credit!"—these were some of his golden maxims—
"Never take paper-money! Look well to your change! Ring
the silver on the four-pound weight! Shove back all English
half-pence and base copper-tokens, such as are very plenty

about town! At your leisure hours, knit children's woollen socks and mittens! Brew your own yeast, and make your own ginger-beer!"

And while Hepzibah was doing her utmost to digest the hard little pellets of his already uttered wisdom, he gave vent to his final, and what he declared to be his all-important advice, as follows:—

"Put on a bright face for your customers, and smile pleasantly as you hand them what they ask for! A stale article, if you dip it in a good, warm, sunny smile, will go off better than a fresh one that you've scowled upon!"

To this last apothegm, poor Hepzibah responded with a sigh, so deep and heavy that it almost rustled Uncle Venner quite away, like a withered leaf, as he was, before an autumnal gale. Recovering himself, however, he bent forward, and, with a good deal of feeling in his ancient visage, beckoned her nearer to him.

"When do you expect him home?" whispered he.

"Whom do you mean?" asked Hepzibah, turning pale.

"Ah!—You don't love to talk about it," said Uncle Venner. "Well, well, we'll say no more, though there's word of it, all over town. I remember him, Miss Hepzibah, before he could run alone!"

During the remainder of the day, poor Hepzibah acquitted herself even less creditably, as a shopkeeper, than in her earlier efforts. She appeared to be walking in a dream; or, more truly, the vivid life and reality, assumed by her emotions, made all outward occurrences unsubstantial, like the teasing phantasms of a half-conscious slumber. She still responded, mechanically, to the frequent summons of the shop-bell, and, at the demand of her customers, went prying with vague eyes about the shop; proffering them one article after another, and thrusting aside—perversely, as most of them supposed—the identical thing they asked for. There is sad confusion, indeed, when the spirit thus flits away into the past, or into the more awful future, or, in any manner, steps across the spaceless boundary betwixt its own region and the actual world; where the body remains to guide itself, as best it may, with little more than the mechanism of animal life. It is like death, without death's quiet privilege; its freedom from mortal care. Worst of all, when the actual duties are comprised in such petty details as now vexed the brooding soul of the old gentlewoman. As the animosity of fate would have it, there was a great influx of custom, in the course of the afternoon. Hepzibah blundered to-and-fro about her small place of business, committing the most unheard of errors; now stringing up twelve, and now seven tallow-candles, instead of ten to the pound; selling ginger for Scotch snuff, pins for needles, and needles for pins; misreckoning her change, sometimes to the public detriment, and much oftener to her own; and thus she went on, doing her utmost to bring chaos back again, until, at the close of the day's labor, to her inexplicable astonishment, she found the money-drawer almost destitute of coin. After all her painful traffic, the whole proceeds were perhaps half-a-dozen coppers, and a questionable ninepence, which ultimately proved to be copper likewise.

At this price, or at whatever price, she rejoiced that the day had reached its end. Never before had she had such a sense of the intolerable length of time that creeps between dawn and sunset, and of the miserable irksomeness of having aught to do, and of the better wisdom that it would be, to lie down at once, in sullen resignation, and let life, and its toils and vexations, trample over one's prostrate body, as they may! Hepzibah's final operation was with the little devourer of Jim Crow and the elephant, who now proposed to eat a camel. In her bewilderment, she offered him first a wooden dragoon, and next a handfull of marbles; neither of which being adapted to his else omnivorous appetite, she hastily held out her whole remaining stock of natural history, in gingerbread, and huddled the small customer out of the shop. She then muffled the bell in an unfinished stocking, and put up the oaken bar across the door.

During the latter process, an omnibus came to a standstill under the branches of the elm-tree. Hepzibah's heart was in her mouth. Remote and dusky, and with no sunshine on all the intervening space, was that region of the Past, whence her only guest might be expected to arrive! Was she to meet him now?

Somebody, at all events, was passing from the farthest interior of the omnibus, towards its entrance. A gentleman alighted; but it was only to offer his hand to a young girl, whose slender figure, nowise needing such assistance, now lightly descended the steps, and made an airy little jump from the final one to the sidewalk. She rewarded her cavalier with a smile, the cheery glow of which was seen reflected on his own face, as he re-entered the vehicle. The girl then turned towards the House of the Seven Gables; to the door of which, meanwhile—not the shop-door, but the antique-portal—the omnibus-man had carried a light trunk and a bandbox. First giving a sharp rap of the old iron knocker, he left his passenger and her luggage at the door-step, and departed.

"Who can it be?" thought Hepzibah, who had been screwing her visual organs into the acutest focus of which they were capable. "The girl must have mistaken the house!"

She stole softly into the hall, and, herself invisible, gazed through the dusty side-lights of the portal at the young, blooming, and very cheerful face, which presented itself for admittance into the gloomy old mansion. It was a face to which almost any door would have opened of its own accord.

The young girl, so fresh, so unconventional, and yet so orderly and obedient to common rules, as you at once recognized her to be, was widely in contrast, at that moment, with everything about her. The sordid and ugly luxuriance of gigantic weeds, that grew in the angle of the house, and the heavy projection that overshadowed her, and the time-worn frame-work of the door;—none of these things belonged to her sphere. But—even as a ray of sunshine, fall into what dismal place it may, instantaneously creates for itself a propriety in being there—so did it seem altogether fit that the girl should be standing at the threshold. It was no less evidently proper, that the door should swing open to admit her. The maiden lady herself, sternly inhospitable in her first purposes, soon began to feel that the bolt ought to be shoved back, and the rusty key be turned in the reluctant lock.

"Can it be Phoebe?" questioned she within herself. "It must be little Phoebe; for it can be nobody else—and there is a look of her father about her, too! But what does she want here? And how like a country-cousin, to come down upon a poor body in this way, without so much as a day's notice, or asking whether she would be welcome! Well; she must have a night's lodging, I suppose; and tomorrow the child shall go back to her mother."

Phoebe, it must be understood, was that one little offshoot of the Pyncheon race to whom we have already referred, as a native of a rural part of New England, where the old fashions and feelings of relationship are still partially kept up. In her own circle, it was regarded as by no means improper for kinsfolk to visit one another, without invitation, or preliminary and ceremonious warning. Yet, in consideration of Miss Hepzibah's recluse way of life, a letter had actually been written and despatched, conveying information of Phoebe's projected visit. This epistle, for three or four days past, had been in the pocket of the penny-postman, who, happening to have no other business in Pyncheon-street, had not yet made it convenient to call at the House of the Seven Gables.

"No!—she can stay only one night," said Hepzibah, unbolting the door. "If Clifford were to find her here, it might disturb him!"

V

MAY AND NOVEMBER

PHOEBE PYNCHEON slept, on the night of her arrival, in a chamber that looked down on the garden of the old house. It fronted towards the east, so that, at a very seasonable hour, a glow of crimson light came flooding through the window, and bathed the dingy ceiling and paper-hangings in its own hue. There were curtains to Phoebe's bed; a dark, antique canopy and ponderous festoons, of a stuff which had been rich, and even magnificent, in its time; but which now brooded over the girl like a cloud, making a night in that one corner, while elsewhere it was beginning to be day. The morning-light, however, soon stole into the aperture at the foot of the bed, betwixt those faded curtains. Finding the new guest there—with a bloom on her cheeks, like the morning's own, and a gentle stir of departing slumber in her limbs, as when an early breeze moves the foliage—the Dawn kissed her brow. It was the caress which a dewy maiden—such as the Dawn is, immortally—gives to her sleeping sister, partly from the impulse of irresistible fondness, and partly as a pretty hint, that it is time now to unclose her eyes.

At the touch of those lips of light, Phoebe quietly awoke, and, for a moment, did not recognize where she was, nor how those heavy curtains chanced to be festooned around

her. Nothing, indeed, was absolutely plain to her, except
that it was now early morning, and that, whatever might
happen next, it was proper, first of all, to get up and say her
prayers. She was the more inclined to devotion, from the
grim aspect of the chamber and its furniture, especially the
tall, stiff chairs; one of which stood close by her bedside,
and looked as if some old-fashioned personage had been sitting there, all night, and had vanished only just in season to
escape discovery.

When Phoebe was quite dressed, she peeped out of the
window, and saw a rose-bush in the garden. Being a very
tall one, and of luxurious growth, it had been propt up
against the side of the house, and was literally covered with
a rare and very beautiful species of white rose. A large portion
of them, as the girl afterwards discovered, had blight or mildew at their hearts; but, viewed at a fair distance, the whole
rose-bush looked as if it had been brought from Eden, that
very summer, together with the mould in which it grew. The
truth was, nevertheless, that it had been planted by Alice
Pyncheon—she was Phoebe's great-great-grand-aunt—in soil
which, reckoning only its cultivation as a garden-plat, was
now unctuous with nearly two hundred years of vegetable
decay. Growing as they did, however, out of the old earth,
the flowers still sent a fresh and sweet incense up to their
Creator; nor could it have been the less pure and acceptable,
because Phoebe's young breath mingled with it, as the fragrance floated past the window. Hastening down the creaking and carpetless staircase, she found her way into the
garden, gathered some of the most perfect of the roses, and
brought them to her chamber.

Little Phoebe was one of those persons who possess, as
their exclusive patrimony, the gift of practical arrangement.
It is a kind of natural magic, that enables these favored ones
to bring out the hidden capabilities of things around them;
and particularly to give a look of comfort and habitableness

to any place which, for however brief a period, may happen to be their home. A wild hut of underbrush, tossed together by wayfarers through the primitive forest, would acquire the home-aspect by one night's lodging of such a woman, and would retain it, long after her quiet figure had disappeared into the surrounding shade. No less a portion of such homely witchcraft was requisite, to reclaim, as it were, Phoebe's waste, cheerless, and dusky chamber, which had been untenanted so long—except by spiders, and mice, and rats, and ghosts—that it was all overgrown with the desolation, which watches to obliterate every trace of man's happier hours. What was precisely Phoebe's process, we find it impossible to say. She appeared to have no preliminary design, but gave a touch here, and another there; brought some articles of furniture to light, and dragged others into the shadow; looped up or let down a window-curtain; and, in the course of half-an-hour, had fully succeeded in throwing a kindly and hospitable smile over the apartment. No longer ago than the night before, it had resembled nothing so much as the old maid's heart; for there was neither sunshine nor household-fire in one nor the other, and, save for ghosts, and ghostly reminiscences, not a guest, for many years gone-by, had entered the heart or the chamber.

There was still another peculiarity of this inscrutable charm. The bed-chamber, no doubt, was a chamber of very great and varied experience, as a scene of human life; the joy of bridal nights had throbbed itself away here; new immortals had first drawn earthly breath here; and here old people had died. But—whether it were the white roses, or whatever the subtile influence might be—a person of delicate instinct would have known, at once, that it was now a maiden's bed-chamber, and had been purified of all former evil and sorrow by her sweet breath and happy thoughts. Her dreams of the past night, being such cheerful ones, had exorcised the gloom, and now haunted the chamber in its stead.

After arranging matters to her satisfaction, Phoebe emerged from her chamber, with a purpose to descend again into the garden. Besides the rose-bush, she had observed several other species of flowers, growing there in a wilderness of neglect, and obstructing one another's developement (as is often the parallel case in human society) by their uneducated entanglement and confusion. At the head of the stairs, however, she met Hepzibah, who, it being still early, invited her into a room which she would probably have called her boudoir, had her education embraced any such French phrase. It was strewn about with a few old books, and a work-basket, and a dusty writing-desk, and had, on one side, a large, black article of furniture, of very strange appearance, which the old gentlewoman told Phoebe was a harpsichord. It looked more like a coffin than anything else; and, indeed—not having been played upon, or opened, for years—there must have been a vast deal of dead music in it, stifled for want of air. Human finger was hardly known to have touched its chords, since the days of Alice Pyncheon, who had learned the sweet accomplishment of melody, in Europe.

Hepzibah bade her young guest sit down, and, herself taking a chair near by, looked as earnestly at Phoebe's trim little figure as if she expected to see right into its springs and motive secrets.

"Cousin Phoebe," said she, at last, "I really can't see my way clear to keep you with me."

These words, however, had not the inhospitable bluntness with which they may strike the reader; for the two relatives, in a talk before bedtime, had arrived at a certain degree of mutual understanding. Hepzibah knew enough to enable her to appreciate the circumstances (resulting from the second marriage of the girl's mother) which made it desirable for Phoebe to establish herself in another home. Nor did she misinterpret Phoebe's character, and the genial activity pervading it—one of the most valuable traits of the true New

England woman—which had impelled her forth, as might be said, to seek her fortune, but with a self-respecting purpose to confer as much benefit as she could anywise receive. As one of her nearest kindred, she had naturally betaken herself to Hepzibah, with no idea of forcing herself on her cousin's protection, but only for a visit of a week or two, which might be indefinitely extended, should it prove for the happiness of both.

To Hepzibah's blunt observation, therefore, Phoebe replied as frankly, and more cheerfully.

"Dear Cousin, I cannot tell how it will be," said she. "But I really think we may suit one another, much better than you suppose."

"You are a nice girl—I see it plainly," continued Hepzibah; "and it is not any question, as to that point, which makes me hesitate. But, Phoebe, this house of mine is but a melancholy place for a young person to be in. It lets in the wind and rain —and the snow, too, in the garret and upper chambers, in winter-time—but it never lets in the sunshine! And as for myself, you see what I am;—a dismal and lonesome old woman (for I begin to call myself old, Phoebe) whose temper, I am afraid, is none of the best, and whose spirits are as bad as can be! I cannot make your life pleasant, Cousin Phoebe; neither can I so much as give you bread to eat."

"You will find me a cheerful little body," answered Phoebe smiling, and yet with a kind of gentle dignity; "and I mean to earn my bread. You know, I have not been brought up a Pyncheon. A girl learns many things in a New England village."

"Ah, Phoebe," said Hepzibah sighing, "your knowledge would do but little for you here! And then it is a wretched thought, that you should fling away your young days in a place like this. Those cheeks would not be so rosy, after a month or two. Look at my face!"—and, indeed, the contrast was very striking—"you see how pale I am! It is my idea that the dust and continual decay of these old houses are unwholesome for the lungs."

"There is the garden—the flowers to be taken care of," observed Phoebe. "I should keep myself healthy with exercise in the open air."

"And, after all, child," exclaimed Hepzibah, suddenly rising, as if to dismiss the subject, "it is not for me to say who shall be a guest, or inhabitant of the old Pyncheon-house! Its master is coming!"

"Do you mean Judge Pyncheon?" asked Phoebe in surprise.

"Judge Pyncheon!" answered her cousin angrily. "He will hardly cross the threshold, while I live. No, no! But, Phoebe, you shall see the face of him I speak of!"

She went in quest of the miniature already described, and returned with it in her hand. Giving it to Phoebe, she watched her features narrowly, and with a certain jealousy as to the mode in which the girl would show herself affected by the picture.

"How do you like the face?" asked Hepzibah.

"It is handsome!—it is very beautiful!" said Phoebe admiringly. "It is as sweet a face as a man's can be, or ought to be. It has something of a child's expression—and yet not childish —only, one feels so very kindly towards him! He ought never to suffer anything. One would bear much, for the sake of sparing him toil or sorrow. Who is it, Cousin Hepzibah?"

"Did you never hear," whispered her cousin, bending towards her, "of Clifford Pyncheon?"

"Never! I thought there were no Pyncheons left, except yourself and our Cousin Jaffrey," answered Phoebe. "And, yet, I seem to have heard the name of Clifford Pyncheon. Yes!—from my father, or my mother—but has he not been a long while dead?"

"Well, well, child, perhaps he has!" said Hepzibah, with a sad, hollow laugh. "But, in old houses like this, you know, dead people are very apt to come back again! We shall see! And, Cousin Phoebe—since, after all that I have said, your courage does not fail you—we will not part so soon. You are welcome, my child, for the present, to such a home as your kinswoman can offer you."

With this measured, but not exactly cold assurance of a hospitable purpose, Hepzibah kissed her cheek.

They now went below stairs, where Phoebe—not so much assuming the office as attracting it to herself, by the magnetism of innate fitness—took the most active part in preparing breakfast. The mistress of the house, meanwhile, as is usual with persons of her stiff and unmalleable cast, stood mostly aside; willing to lend her aid, yet conscious that her natural inaptitude would be likely to impede the business in hand. Phoebe, and the fire that boiled the teakettle, were equally bright, cheerful, and efficient, in their respective offices. Hepzibah gazed forth from her habitual sluggishness, the necessary result of long solitude, as from another sphere. She could not help being interested, however, and even amused, at the readiness with which her new inmate adapted herself to the circumstances, and brought the house, moreover, and all its rusty old appliances, into a suitableness for her purposes. Whatever she did, too, was done without conscious effort, and with frequent outbreaks of song which were exceedingly pleasant to the ear. This natural tunefulness made Phoebe seem like a bird in a shadowy tree; or conveyed the idea that the stream of life warbled through her heart, as a brook sometimes warbles through a pleasant little dell. It betokened the cheeriness of an active temperament, finding joy in its activity, and therefore rendering it beautiful; it was a New England trait—the stern old stuff of Puritanism, with a gold thread in the web.

Hepzibah brought out some old silver spoons, with the family crest upon them, and a China tea-set, painted over with grotesque figures of man, bird, and beast, in as grotesque a landscape. These pictured people were odd humorists, in a world of their own; a world of vivid brilliancy, so far as color went, and still unfaded, although the tea-pot and small cups were as ancient as the custom itself of tea-drinking.

"Your great, great, great, great grandmother had these cups, when she was married," said Hepzibah to Phoebe. "She was a Davenport, of a good family. They were almost the first tea-cups ever seen in the colony; and if one of them were to be broken, my heart would break with it. But it is nonsense to speak so, about a brittle tea-cup, when I remember what my heart has gone through without breaking!"

The cups—not having been used, perhaps, since Hepzibah's youth—had contracted no small burthen of dust, which Phoebe washed away with so much care and delicacy, as to satisfy even the proprietor of this invaluable China.

"What a nice little housewife you are!" exclaimed the latter smiling, and, at the same time, frowning so prodigiously that the smile was sunshine under a thunder-cloud.—"Do you do other things as well? Are you as good at your book as you are at washing tea-cups?"

"Not quite, I am afraid," said Phoebe, laughing at the form of Hepzibah's question.—"But I was schoolmistress for the little children, in our district, last summer, and might have been so still."

"Ah; 'tis all very well!" observed the maiden lady, drawing herself up.—"But these things must have come to you with your mother's blood. I never knew a Pyncheon that had any turn for them!"

It is very queer, but not the less true, that people are generally quite as vain, or even more so, of their deficiencies, than of their available gifts; as was Hepzibah of this native inapplicability, so to speak, of the Pyncheons to any useful purpose. She regarded it as an hereditary trait; and so, perhaps, it was, but, unfortunately, a morbid one, such as is often generated in families that remain long above the surface of society.

Before they left the breakfast-table, the shop-bell rang sharply; and Hepzibah set down the remnant of her final cup of tea, with a look of sallow despair that was truly piteous to behold. In cases of distasteful occupation, the second day is generally worse than the first; we return to the rack, with all the soreness of the preceding torture in our limbs. At all events, Hepzibah had fully satisfied herself of the impossibility of ever becoming wonted to this peevishly obstreperous little bell. Ring as often as it might, the sound always smote upon her nervous system rudely and suddenly. And especially now, while, with her crested tea-spoons and antique China, she was flattering herself with ideas of gentility, she felt an unspeakable disinclination to confront a customer.

"Do not trouble yourself, dear Cousin!" cried Phoebe, starting lightly up. "I am shopkeeper to-day."

"You, child!" exclaimed Hepzibah. "What can a little country-girl know of such matters?"

"Oh, I have done all the shopping for the family, at our village-store," said Phoebe. "And I have had a table at a fancy-fair, and made better sales than anybody. These things are not to be learnt; they depend upon a knack that comes, I suppose," added she smiling, "with one's mother's blood. You shall see that I am as nice a little saleswoman, as I am a housewife!"

The old gentlewoman stole behind Phoebe, and peeped from the passage-way into the shop, to note how she would manage her undertaking. It was a case of some intricacy. A very ancient woman, in a white, short gown, and a green petticoat, with a string of gold beads about her neck, and what looked like a night-cap on her head, had brought a quantity of yarn to barter for the commodities of the shop. She was probably the very last person in town, who still kept the time-honored spinning-wheel in constant revolution. It was worth while to hear the croaking and hollow tones of the old lady and the pleasant voice of Phoebe, mingling in one twisted thread of talk; and still better, to contrast their figures —so light and bloomy—so decrepit and dusky—with only the counter betwixt them, in one sense, but more than threescore years, in another. As for the bargain, it was wrinkled slyness and craft, pitted against native truth and sagacity.

"Was not that well done?" asked Phoebe laughing, when the customer was gone.

"Nicely done, indeed, child!" answered Hepzibah. "I could not have gone through with it nearly so well. As you say, it must be a knack that belongs to you on the mother's side."

It is a very genuine admiration, that with which persons, too shy, or too aukward, to take a due part in the bustling world, regard the real actors in life's stirring scenes;—so genuine, in fact, that the former are usually fain to make it palatable to their self-love, by assuming that these active and forcible qualities are incompatible with others, which they choose to deem higher and more important. Thus, Hepzibah was well content to acknowledge Phoebe's vastly superior gifts as a shopkeeper; she listened, with compliant ear, to her suggestion of various methods whereby the influx of trade might be increased, and rendered profitable, without a hazardous outlay of capital. She consented that the village-maiden should manufacture yeast, both liquid and in cakes; and should brew a certain kind of beer, nectareous to the palate, and of rare stomachic virtues; and, moreover, should bake and exhibit for sale some little spice-cakes, which whosoever tasted, would longingly desire to taste again. All such proofs of a ready mind, and skilful handiwork, were highly acceptable to the aristocratic hucksteress, so long as she could murmur to herself, with a grim smile, and a half-natural sigh, and a sentiment of mixed wonder, pity, and growing affection:—

"What a nice little body she is! If she could only be a lady, too!—but that's impossible! Phoebe is no Pyncheon. She takes everything from her mother!"

As to Phoebe's not being a lady, or whether she were a lady or no, it was a point perhaps difficult to decide, but which could hardly have come up for judgement at all, in any fair and healthy mind. Out of New England, it would be impossible to meet with a person, combining so many ladylike attributes with so many others, that form no necessary, if compatible, part of the character. She shocked no canon of taste; she was admirably in keeping with herself, and never jarred against surrounding circumstances. Her figure, to be sure—so small as to be almost childlike, and so elastic that motion seemed as easy, or easier to it than rest—would hardly have suited one's idea of a countess. Neither did her face—with the brown ringlets on either side, and the slightly piquant nose, and the wholesome bloom, and the clear shade of tan, and the half-a-dozen freckles, friendly remembrancers of the April sun and breeze—precisely give us a right to call her beautiful. But there was both lustre and depth, in her eyes. She was very pretty; as graceful as a bird, and graceful much in the same way; as pleasant, about the house, as a gleam of sunshine falling on the floor through a shadow of twinkling leaves, or as a ray of firelight that dances on the wall, while evening is drawing nigh. Instead of discussing her claim to rank among ladies, it would be preferable to regard Phoebe as the example of feminine grace and availability combined, in a state of society, if there were any such, where ladies did not exist. There, it should be woman's office to move in the midst of practical affairs, and to gild them all—the very homeliest, were it even the scouring of pots and kettles—with an atmosphere of loveliness and joy.

Such was the sphere of Phoebe. To find the born and educated lady, on the other hand, we need look no farther than Hepzibah, our forlorn old maid, in her rustling and rusty silks, with her deeply cherished and ridiculous consciousness of long descent, her shadowy claims to princely territory; and, in the way of accomplishment, her recollections, it may be, of having formerly thrummed on a harpsichord, and walked a minuet, and worked an antique tapestry-stitch on her sampler. It was a fair parallel between new Plebeianism and old Gentility!

It really seemed as if the battered visage of the House of the Seven Gables, black and heavy-browed as it still certainly looked, must have shown a kind of cheerfulness glimmering through its dusky windows, as Phoebe passed to-and-fro in the interior. Otherwise, it is impossible to explain how the people of the neighborhood so soon became aware of the girl's presence. There was a great run of custom, setting steadily in from about ten o'clock until towards noon—relaxing, somewhat, at dinner-time—but re-commencing in the afternoon, and finally dying-away, a half-an-hour or so before the long day's sunset. One of the staunchest patrons was little Ned Higgins, the devourer of Jim Crow and the elephant, who, to-day, had signalized his omnivorous prowess by swallowing two dromedaries and a locomotive. Phoebe laughed, as she summed up her aggregate of sales, upon the slate; while Hepzibah, first drawing on a pair of silk gloves, reckoned over the sordid accumulation of copper-coin, not without silver intermixed, that had jingled into the till.

"We must renew our stock, Cousin Hepzibah!" cried the little saleswoman. "The gingerbread figures are all gone, and so are those Dutch wooden milk-maids, and most of our other playthings. There has been constant inquiry for cheap raisins, and a great cry for whistles, and trumpets, and jewsharps, and at least a dozen little boys have asked for molasses-candy. And we must contrive to get a peck of russet-apples, late in the season as it is. But, dear Cousin, what an enormous heap of copper! Positively a copper-mountain!"

"Well done! Well done! Well done!" quoth Uncle Venner, who had taken occasion to shuffle in and out of the shop, several times in the course of the day. "Here's a girl that will never end her days at my farm! Bless my eyes, what a brisk little soul!"

"Yes!—Phoebe is a nice girl," said Hepzibah, with a scowl of austere approbation. "But, Uncle Venner, you have known the family a great many years. Can you tell me whether there ever was a Pyncheon whom she takes after?"

"I don't believe there ever was," answered the venerable man. "At any rate, it never was my luck to see her like among them, nor—for that matter—anywhere else. I've seen a great deal of the world, not only in people's kitchens and back-yards, but at the street-corners, and on the wharves, and in other places where my business calls me; and I'm free to say, Miss Hepzibah, that I never knew a human creature do her work so much like one of God's angels, as this child Phoebe does!"

Uncle Venner's eulogium, if it appear rather too high-strained for the person and occasion, had nevertheless a sense in which it was both subtle and true. There was a spiritual quality in Phoebe's activity. The life of the long and busy day —spent in occupations that might so easily have taken a squalid and ugly aspect—had been made pleasant, and even lovely, by the spontaneous grace with which these homely duties seemed to bloom out of her character; so that labor, while she dealt with it, had the easy and flexible charm of play. Angels do not toil, but let their good works grow out of them; and so did Phoebe.

The two relatives—the young maid and the old one—found time, before nightfall, in the intervals of trade, to make rapid advances towards affection and confidence. A recluse, like Hepzibah, usually displays remarkable frankness, and at least temporary affability, on being absolutely cornered, and brought to the point of personal intercourse;—like the angel whom Jacob wrestled with, she is ready to bless you, when once overcome.

The old gentlewoman took a dreary and proud satisfaction,

in leading Phoebe from room to room of the house, and re-
counting the traditions with which, as we may say, the walls
were lugubriously frescoed. She showed the indentations,
made by the Lieutenant Governor's sword-hilt, in the door-
panels of the apartment where old Colonel Pyncheon, a dead
host, had received his affrighted visitors with an awful frown.
The dusky terror of that frown, Hepzibah observed, was
thought to be lingering ever since in the passage-way. She
bade Phoebe step into one of the tall chairs, and inspect the
ancient map of the Pyncheon territory, at the eastward. In a
tract of land, on which she laid her finger, there existed a
silver-mine, the locality of which was precisely pointed out in
some memoranda of Colonel Pyncheon himself, but only to
be made known when the family-claim should be recognized
by government. Thus, it was for the interest of all New England that the Pyncheons should have justice done them. She
told, too, how that there was undoubtedly an immense treasure of English guineas, hidden somewhere about the house,
or in the cellar, or possibly in the garden.

"If you should happen to find it, Phoebe," said Hepzibah,
glancing aside at her, with a grim, yet kindly smile, "we will
tie up the shop-bell for good and all!"

"Yes, dear Cousin," answered Phoebe; "but, in the mean-
time, I hear somebody ringing it!"

When the customer was gone, Hepzibah talked rather
vaguely, and at great length, about a certain Alice Pyncheon,
who had been exceedingly beautiful and accomplished, in her
lifetime, a hundred years ago. The fragrance of her rich and
delightful character still lingered about the place where she
had lived, as a dried rosebud scents the drawer where it has
withered and perished. This lovely Alice had met with some
great and mysterious calamity, and had grown thin and white,
and gradually faded out of the world. But, even now, she was
supposed to haunt the House of the Seven Gables, and, a great
many times, especially when one of the Pyncheons was to
die, she had been heard playing sadly and beautifully on the

harpsichord. One of these tunes, just as it sounded from her spiritual touch, had been written down by an amateur of music; it was so exquisitely mournful that nobody, to this day, could bear to hear it played, unless when a great sorrow had made them know the still profounder sweetness of it.

"Was it the same harpsichord that you showed me?" inquired Phoebe.

"The very same," said Hepzibah. "It was Alice Pyncheon's harpsichord. When I was learning music, my father would never let me open it. So, as I could only play on my teacher's instrument, I have forgotten all my music, long ago."

Leaving these antique themes, the old lady began to talk about the Daguerreotypist, whom, as he seemed to be a well-meaning and orderly young man, and in narrow circumstances, she had permitted to take up his residence in one of the seven gables. But, on seeing more of Mr. Holgrave, she hardly knew what to make of him. He had the strangest companions imaginable;—men with long beards, and dressed in linen blouses, and other such new-fangled and ill-fitting garments;—reformers, temperance-lecturers, and all manner of cross-looking philanthropists;—community-men and come-outers, as Hepzibah believed, who acknowledged no law and ate no solid food, but lived on the scent of other people's cookery, and turned up their noses at the fare. As for the Daguerreotypist, she had read a paragraph in a penny-paper, the other day, accusing him of making a speech, full of wild and disorganizing matter, at a meeting of his banditti-like associates. For her own part, she had reason to believe that he practised animal-magnetism, and, if such things were in fashion now-a-days, should be apt to suspect him of studying the Black Art, up there in his lonesome chamber.

"But, dear Cousin," said Phoebe, "if the young man is so dangerous, why do you let him stay? If he does nothing worse, he may set the house on fire!"

"Why, sometimes," answered Hepzibah, "I have seriously

made it a question, whether I ought not to send him away. But, with all his oddities, he is a quiet kind of a person, and has such a way of taking hold of one's mind, that, without exactly liking him, (for I don't know enough of the young man,) I should be sorry to lose sight of him entirely. A woman clings to slight acquaintances, when she lives so much alone as I do."

"But if Mr. Holgrave is a lawless person!" remonstrated Phoebe, a part of whose essence it was, to keep within the limits of law.

"Oh," said Hepzibah carelessly—for, formal as she was, still, in her life's experience, she had gnashed her teeth against human law—"I suppose he has a law of his own!"

VI

MAULE'S WELL

AFTER an early tea, the little country-girl strayed into the garden. The enclosure had formerly been very extensive, but was now contracted within small compass, and hemmed about, partly by high wooden fences, and partly by the outbuildings of houses that stood on another street. In its centre was a grass-plat, surrounding a ruinous little structure, which showed just enough of its original design to indicate that it had once been a summer-house. A hop-vine, springing from last year's root, was beginning to clamber over it, but would be long in covering the roof with its green mantle. Three of the seven gables either fronted, or looked sideways, with a dark solemnity of aspect, down into the garden.

The black, rich soil had fed itself with the decay of a long period of time; such as fallen leaves, the petals of flowers, and the stalks and seed-vessels of vagrant and lawless plants, more useful after their death, than ever while flaunting in the sun. The evil of these departed years would naturally have sprung up again, in such rank weeds (symbolic of the transmitted vices of society) as are always prone to root themselves about human dwellings. Phoebe saw, however, that their growth must have been checked by a degree of careful labor, bestowed daily and systematically on the garden. The white double-rosebush had evidently been propt up anew against the house, since the commencement of the season; and a pear-tree and three damson-trees, which, except a row of currant-bushes, constituted the only varieties of fruit, bore marks of the recent amputation of several superfluous or defective limbs. There were also a few species of antique and hereditary flowers, in no very flourishing condition, but scrupulously weeded; as if some person, either out of love or curiosity, had been anxious to bring them to such perfection as they were capable of attaining. The remainder of the garden presented a well-selected assortment of esculent vegetables, in a praiseworthy state of advancement. Summer-squashes, almost in their golden-blossom; cucumbers, now evincing a tendency to spread away from the main-stock, and ramble far and wide; two or three rows of string-beans, and as many more, that were about to festoon themselves on poles; tomatoes, occupying a site so sheltered and sunny, that the plants were already gigantic, and promised an early and abundant harvest.

Phoebe wondered whose care and toil it could have been, that had planted these vegetables, and kept the soil so clean and orderly. Not, surely, her Cousin Hepzibah's, who had no taste nor spirits for the ladylike employment of cultivating flowers, and—with her recluse habits, and tendency to shelter herself within the dismal shadow of the house—would hardly have come forth, under the speck of open sky, to weed and hoe, among the fraternity of beans and squashes.

It being her first day of complete estrangement from rural objects, Phoebe found an unexpected charm in this little nook of grass, and foliage, and aristocratic flowers, and plebeian vegetables. The eye of Heaven seemed to look down into it, pleasantly, and with a peculiar smile; as if glad to perceive that Nature, elsewhere overwhelmed, and driven out of the dusty town, had here been able to retain a breathing-place. The spot acquired a somewhat wilder grace, and yet a very gentle one, from the fact that a pair of robins had built their nest in the pear-tree, and were making themselves exceedingly busy and happy, in the dark intricacy of its boughs. Bees, too—strange to say—had thought it worth their while to come hither, possibly from the range of hives beside some farm-house, miles away. How many aerial voyages might they have made, in quest of honey, or honey-laden, betwixt dawn and sunset! Yet, late as it now was, there still arose a pleasant hum out of one or two of the squash-blossoms, in the depths of which these bees were plying their golden labor. There was one other object in the garden, which Nature might fairly claim as her inalienable property, in spite of whatever man could do to render it his own. This was a fountain, set round with a rim of old, mossy stones, and paved, in its bed, with what appeared to be a sort of mosaic-work of variously colored pebbles. The play and slight agitation of the water, in its upward gush, wrought magically with these variegated pebbles, and made a continually shifting apparition of quaint figures, vanishing too suddenly to be definable. Thence, welling over the rim of moss-grown stones, the water stole away under the fence, through what we regret to call a gutter, rather than a channel.

Nor must we forget to mention a hen-coop, of very reverend antiquity, that stood in the farther corner of the garden, not a great way from the fountain. It now contained only Chanticleer, his two wives, and a solitary chicken. All of them were pure specimens of a breed which had been transmitted down as an heirloom in the Pyncheon family, and were said, while in their prime, to have attained almost the size of turkeys, and, on the score of delicate flesh, to be fit for a prince's table. In proof of the authenticity of this legendary renown, Hepzibah could have exhibited the shell of a great egg, which an ostrich need hardly have been ashamed of. Be that as it might, the hens were now scarcely larger than pigeons, and had a queer, rusty, withered aspect, and a gouty kind of movement, and a sleepy and melancholy tone throughout all the variations of their clucking and cackling. It was evident that the race had degenerated, like many a noble race besides, in consequence of too strict a watchfulness to keep it pure. These feathered people had existed too long, in their distinct variety; a fact of which the present representatives, judging by their lugubrious deportment, seemed to be aware. They kept themselves alive, unquestionably, and laid now and then an egg, and hatched a chicken, not for any pleasure of their own, but that the world might not absolutely lose what had once been so admirable a breed of fowls. The distinguishing mark of the hens was a crest, of lamentably scanty growth, in these latter days, but so oddly and wickedly analogous to Hepzibah's turban, that Phoebe—to the poignant distress of her conscience, but inevitably—was led to fancy a general resemblance betwixt these forlorn bipeds and her respectable relative.

The girl ran into the house to get some crumbs of bread, cold potatoes, and other such scraps as were suitable to the accommodating appetite of fowls. Returning, she gave a peculiar call, which they seemed to recognize. The chicken crept through the pales of the coop, and ran with some show of liveliness to her feet; while Chanticleer and the ladies of his household regarded her with queer, sidelong glances, and then croaked one to another, as if communicating their sage opinions of her character. So wise as well as antique was their aspect, as to give color to the idea, not merely that they were the descendants of a time-honored race, but that they had existed, in their individual capacity, ever since the House of the Seven Gables was founded, and were somehow mixed up with its destiny. They were a species of tutelary sprite, or Banshee; although winged and feathered differently from most other guardian-angels.

"Here, you odd little chicken!" cried Phoebe. "Here are some nice crumbs for you!"

The chicken, hereupon, though almost as venerable in appearance as its mother—possessing, indeed, the whole antiquity of its progenitors, in miniature—mustered vivacity enough to flutter upward and alight on Phoebe's shoulder.

"That little fowl pays you a high compliment!" said a voice behind Phoebe.

Turning quickly, she was surprised at sight of a young man, who had found access into the garden by a door, opening out of another gable than that whence she had emerged. He held a hoe in his hand, and, while Phoebe was gone in quest of the crumbs, had begun to busy himself with drawing up fresh earth about the roots of the tomatoes.

"The chicken really treats you like an old acquaintance," continued he, in a quiet way, while a smile made his face pleasanter than Phoebe at first fancied it.—"Those venerable personages in the coop, too, seem very affably disposed. You are lucky to be in their good graces so soon! They have known me much longer, but never honor me with any familiarity, though hardly a day passes without my bringing them food. Miss Hepzibah, I suppose, will interweave the fact with her other traditions, and set it down that the fowls know you to be a Pyncheon!"

"The secret is," said Phoebe smiling, "that I have learned how to talk with hens and chickens."

"Ah; but these hens," answered the young man, "these hens of aristocratic lineage would scorn to understand the vulgar language of a barn-door fowl. I prefer to think—and so would Miss Hepzibah—that they recognize the family tone. For you are a Pyncheon?"

"My name is Phoebe Pyncheon," said the girl, with a manner of some reserve; for she was aware that her new acquaintance could be no other than the Daguerreotypist, of whose lawless propensities the old maid had given her a disagreeable idea. "I did not know that my Cousin Hepzibah's garden was under another person's care."

"Yes," said Holgrave, "I dig, and hoe, and weed, in this black old earth, for the sake of refreshing myself with what little nature and simplicity may be left in it, after men have so long sown and reaped here. I turn up the earth by way of pastime. My sober occupation, so far as I have any, is with a lighter material. In short, I make pictures out of sunshine; and, not to be too much dazzled with my own trade, I have prevailed with Miss Hepzibah to let me lodge in one of these dusky gables. It is like a bandage over one's eyes, to come into it. But would you like to see a specimen of my productions?"

"A daguerreotype likeness, do you mean?" asked Phoebe, with less reserve; for, in spite of prejudice, her own youthfulness sprang forward to meet his. "I don't much like pictures of that sort—they are so hard and stern; besides dodging away from the eye, and trying to escape altogether. They are conscious of looking very unamiable, I suppose, and therefore hate to be seen."

"If you would permit me," said the artist, looking at Phoebe, "I should like to try whether the daguerreotype can bring out disagreeable traits on a perfectly amiable face. But there certainly is truth in what you have said. Most of my likenesses do look unamiable; but the very sufficient reason, I fancy, is, because the originals are so. There is a wonderful insight in heaven's broad and simple sunshine. While we give it credit only for depicting the merest surface, it actually brings out the secret character with a truth that no painter would ever venture upon, even could he detect it. There is at least no flattery in my humble line of art. Now, here is a likeness which I have taken, over and over again, and still with no better result. Yet the original wears, to common eyes, a very different expression. It would gratify me to have your judgement on this character."

He exhibited a daguerreotype miniature, in a morocco case. Phoebe merely glanced at it, and gave it back.

"I know the face," she replied; "for its stern eye has been following me about, all day. It is my Puritan ancestor, who hangs yonder in the parlor. To be sure, you have found some way of copying the portrait without its black velvet cap and gray beard, and have given him a modern coat and satin cravat, instead of his cloak and band. I don't think him improved by your alterations."

"You would have seen other differences, had you looked a little longer," said Holgrave, laughing, yet apparently much struck.—"I can assure you that this is a modern face, and one which you will very probably meet. Now, the remarkable point is, that the original wears, to the world's eye—and, for aught I know, to his most intimate friends—an exceedingly pleasant countenance, indicative of benevolence, openness of heart, sunny good humor, and other praiseworthy qualities of that cast. The sun, as you see, tells quite another story, and will not be coaxed out of it, after half-a-dozen patient attempts on my part. Here we have the man, sly, subtle, hard, imperious, and, withal, cold as ice. Look at that eye! Would you like to be at its mercy? At that mouth! Could it ever smile? And yet, if you could only see the benign smile of the original! It is so much the more unfortunate, as he is a public character of some eminence, and the likeness was intended to be engraved."

"Well; I don't wish to see it any more," observed Phoebe, turning away her eyes. "It is certainly very like the old portrait. But my Cousin Hepzibah has another picture; a miniature. If the original is still in the world, I think he might defy the sun to make him look stern and hard."

"You have seen that picture, then?" exclaimed the artist, with an expression of much interest.—"I never did, but have a great curiosity to do so. And you judge favorably of the face?"

"There never was a sweeter one," said Phoebe. "It is almost too soft and gentle for a man's."

"Is there nothing wild in the eye?" continued Holgrave,

so earnestly that it embarrassed Phoebe, as did also the quiet
freedom with which he presumed on their so recent acquaintance. "Is there nothing dark or sinister, anywhere? Could
you not conceive the original to have been guilty of a great
crime?"

"It is nonsense," said Phoebe, a little impatiently, "for us
to talk about a picture which you have never seen. You mistake it for some other. A crime, indeed! Since you are a
friend of my Cousin Hepzibah's, you should ask her to show
you the picture."

"It will suit my purpose still better, to see the original,"
replied the Daguerreotypist coolly. "As to his character, we
need not discuss its points—they have already been settled
by a competent tribunal, or one which called itself competent.—But, stay! Do not go yet, if you please! I have a proposition to make you."

Phoebe was on the point of retreating, but turned back,
with some hesitation; for she did not exactly comprehend his
manner, although, on better observation, its feature seemed
rather to be lack of ceremony, than any approach to offensive
rudeness. There was an odd kind of authority, too, in what
he now proceeded to say; rather as if the garden were his
own, than a place to which he was admitted merely by
Hepzibah's courtesy.

"If agreeable to you," he observed, "it would give me
pleasure to turn over these flowers, and those ancient and
respectable fowls, to your care. Coming fresh from country-
air and occupations, you will soon feel the need of some
such out-of-door employment. My own sphere does not so
much lie among flowers. You can trim and tend them, therefore, as you please; and I will ask only the least trifle of a
blossom, now and then, in exchange for all the good, honest
kitchen-vegetables with which I propose to enrich Miss Hepzibah's table. So, we will be fellow-laborers, somewhat on the
community-system."

Silently, and rather surprised at her own compliance,

Phoebe accordingly betook herself to weeding a flower-bed, but busied herself still more with cogitations respecting this young man, with whom she so unexpectedly found herself on terms approaching to familiarity. She did not altogether like him. His character perplexed the little country-girl, as it might a more practised observer; for, while the tone of his conversation had generally been playful, the impression left on her mind was that of gravity, and, except as his youth modified it, almost sternness. She rebelled, as it were, against a certain magnetic element in the artist's nature, which he exercised towards her, possibly without being conscious of it.

After a little while, the twilight, deepened by the shadows of the fruit-trees and the surrounding buildings, threw an obscurity over the garden.

"There," said Holgrave; "it is time to give over work! That last stroke of the hoe has cut off a bean-stalk. Good night, Miss Phoebe Pyncheon! Any bright day, if you will put one of those rosebuds in your hair, and come to my rooms in Central-street, I will seize the purest ray of sunshine, and make a picture of the flower and its wearer."

He retired towards his own solitary gable, but turned his head, on reaching the door, and called to Phoebe, with a tone which certainly had laughter in it, yet which seemed to be more than half in earnest.

"Be careful not to drink at Maule's Well!" said he. "Neither drink nor bathe your face in it!"

"Maule's Well!" answered Phoebe. "Is that it, with the rim of mossy stones? I have no thought of drinking there—but why not?"

"Oh," rejoined the Daguerreotypist, "because, like an old lady's cup of tea, it is water bewitched!"

He vanished; and Phoebe, lingering a moment, saw a glimmering light, and then the steady beam of a lamp, in a chamber of the gable. On returning into Hepzibah's department of the house, she found the low-studded parlor so dim and dusky, that her eyes could not penetrate the interior. She was indistinctly aware, however, that the gaunt figure of the old gentlewoman was sitting in one of the straight-backed chairs, a little withdrawn from the window, the faint gleam of which showed the blanched paleness of her cheek, turned sideway towards a corner.

"Shall I light a lamp, Cousin Hepzibah?" she asked.

"Do, if you please, my dear child," answered Hepzibah. "But put it on the table in the corner of the passage. My eyes are weak; and I can seldom bear the lamplight on them."

What an instrument is the human voice! How wonderfully responsive to every emotion of the human soul! In Hepzibah's tone, at that moment, there was a certain rich depth and moisture, as if the words, common-place as they were, had been steeped in the warmth of her heart. Again, while lighting the lamp in the kitchen, Phoebe fancied that her cousin spoke to her.

"In a moment, Cousin!" answered the girl. "These matches just glimmer, and go out."

But, instead of a response from Hepzibah, she seemed to hear the murmur of an unknown voice. It was strangely indistinct, however, and less like articulate words than an unshaped sound, such as would be the utterance of feeling and sympathy, rather than of the intellect. So vague was it, that its impression or echo, in Phoebe's mind, was that of unreality. She concluded that she must have mistaken some other sound for that of the human voice; or else that it was altogether in her fancy.

She set the lighted lamp in the passage, and again entered the parlor. Hepzibah's form, though its sable outline mingled with the dusk, was now less imperfectly visible. In the remoter parts of the room, however, its walls being so ill adapted to reflect light, there was nearly the same obscurity as before.

"Cousin," said Phoebe, "did you speak to me just now?"

"No, child!" replied Hepzibah.

Fewer words than before, but with the same mysterious music in them! Mellow, melancholy, yet not mournful, the tone seemed to gush up out of the deep well of Hepzibah's heart, all steeped in its profoundest emotion. There was a tremor in it, too, that—as all strong feeling is electric—partly communicated itself to Phoebe. The girl sat silently for a moment. But soon, her senses being very acute, she became conscious of an irregular respiration in an obscure corner of the room. Her physical organization, moreover, being at once delicate and healthy, gave her a perception, operating with almost the effect of a spiritual medium, that somebody was near at hand.

"My dear Cousin," asked she, overcoming an indefinable reluctance, "is there not some one in the room with us?"

"Phoebe, my dear little girl," said Hepzibah, after a moment's pause, "you were up betimes, and have been busy all day. Pray go to bed; for I am sure you must need rest. I will sit in the parlor, awhile, and collect my thoughts. It has been my custom for more years, child, than you have lived!"

While thus dismissing her, the maiden lady stept forward, kissed Phoebe, and pressed her to her heart, which beat against the girl's bosom with a strong, high, and tumultuous swell. How came there to be so much love in this desolate old heart, that it could afford to well over thus abundantly!

"Good night, Cousin," said Phoebe, strangely affected by Hepzibah's manner. "If you begin to love me, I am glad!"

She retired to her chamber, but did not soon fall asleep, nor then very profoundly. At some uncertain period in the depths of night, and, as it were, through the thin veil of a dream, she was conscious of a footstep mounting the stairs, heavily, but not with force and decision. The voice of Hepzibah, with a hush through it, was going up along with the footsteps; and, again, responsive to her cousin's voice, Phoebe heard that strange, vague murmur, which might be likened to an indistinct shadow of human utterance.

VII

THE GUEST

WHEN Phoebe awoke—which she did with the early twittering of the conjugal couple of robins, in the pear-tree—she heard movements below stairs, and hastening down, found Hepzibah already in the kitchen. She stood by a window, holding a book in close contiguity to her nose; as if with the hope of gaining an olfactory acquaintance with its contents, since her imperfect vision made it not very easy to read them. If any volume could have manifested its essential wisdom, in the mode suggested, it would certainly have been the one now in Hepzibah's hand; and the kitchen, in such an event, would forthwith have steamed with the fragrance of venison, turkeys, capons, larded partridges, puddings, cakes, and Christmas pies, in all manner of elaborate mixture and concoction. It was a Cookery Book, full of innumerable old fashions of English dishes, and illustrated with engravings, which represented the arrangements of the table, at such banquets as it might have befitted a nobleman to give, in the great hall of his castle. And, amid these rich and potent devices of the culinary art, (not one of which, probably, had been tested, within the memory of any man's grandfather,) poor Hepzibah was seeking for some nimble little tidbit, which, with what skill she had, and such materials as were at hand, she might toss up for breakfast!

Soon, with a deep sigh, she put aside the savory volume, and inquired of Phoebe whether old Speckle, as she called one of the hens, had laid an egg, the preceding day. Phoebe ran to see, but returned without the expected treasure in her hand. At that instant, however, the blast of a fishdealer's conch was heard, announcing his approach along the street. With energetic raps at the shop-window, Hepzibah summoned the man in, and made purchase of what he warranted as the finest mackerel in his cart, and as fat a one as ever he felt with his finger, so early in the season. Requesting Phoebe to roast some coffee—which she casually observed was the real Mocha, and so long kept that each of the small berries ought to be worth its weight in gold—the maiden lady heaped fuel into the vast receptacle of the ancient fireplace, in such quantity as soon to drive the lingering dusk out of the kitchen. The country-girl, willing to give her utmost assistance, proposed to make an Indian cake, after her mother's peculiar method, of easy manufacture, and which she could vouch for as possessing a richness, and, if rightly prepared, a delicacy, unequalled by any other mode of breakfast-cake. Hepzibah gladly assenting, the kitchen was soon the scene of savory preparation. Perchance, amid their proper element of smoke, which eddied forth from the ill-constructed chimney, the ghosts of departed cook-maids looked wonderingly on, or peeped down the great breadth of the flue, despising the simplicity of the projected meal, yet ineffectually pining to thrust their shadowy hands into each inchoate dish. The half-starved rats, at any rate, stole visibly out of their hiding-places, and sat on their hind-legs, snuffing the fumy atmosphere, and wistfully awaiting an opportunity to nibble.

Hepzibah had no natural turn for cookery, and, to say the truth, had fairly incurred her present meagerness by often choosing to go without her dinner, rather than be attendant on the rotation of the spit or ebullition of the pot. Her zeal over the fire, therefore, was quite an heroic test of sentiment.

It was touching, and positively worthy of tears, (if Phoebe, the only spectator, except the rats and ghosts aforesaid, had not been better employed than in shedding them,) to see her rake out a bed of fresh and glowing coals, and proceed to broil the mackerel. Her usually pale cheeks were all a-blaze with heat and hurry. She watched the fish with as much tender care, and minuteness of attention, as if—we know not how to express it otherwise—as if her own heart were on the gridiron, and her immortal happiness were involved in its being done precisely to a turn!

Life, within doors, has few pleasanter prospects than a neatly arranged and well-provisioned breakfast-table. We come to it freshly, in the dewy youth of the day, and when our spiritual and sensual elements are in better accord than at a later period; so that the material delights of the morning meal are capable of being fully enjoyed, without any very grievous reproaches, whether gastric or conscientious, for yielding even a trifle overmuch to the animal department of our nature. The thoughts, too, that run around the ring of familiar guests, have a piquancy and mirthfulness, and oftentimes a vivid truth, which more rarely find their way into the elaborate intercourse of dinner. Hepzibah's small and ancient table, supported on its slender and graceful legs, and covered with a cloth of the richest damask, looked worthy to be the scene and centre of one of the cheerfullest of parties. The vapor of the broiled fish arose like incense from the shrine of a barbarian idol; while the fragrance of the Mocha might have gratified the nostrils of a tutelary Lar, or whatever power has scope over a modern breakfast-table. Phoebe's Indian cakes were the sweetest offering of all—in their hue, befitting the rustic altars of the innocent and golden age— or, so brightly yellow were they, resembling some of the bread which was changed to glistening gold, when Midas tried to eat it. The butter must not be forgotten—butter which Phoebe herself had churned, in her own rural home, and brought it to her cousin as a propitiatory gift—smelling of clover-blossoms, and diffusing the charm of pastoral scenery through the dark-panelled parlor. All this, with the quaint gorgeousness of the old China cups and saucers, and the crested spoons, and a silver cream-jug (Hepzibah's only other article of plate, and shaped like the rudest porringer) set out a board, at which the stateliest of old Colonel Pyncheon's guests need not have scorned to take his place. But the Puritan's face scowled down out of the picture, as if nothing on the table pleased his appetite.

By way of contributing what grace she could, Phoebe gathered some roses and a few other flowers, possessing either scent or beauty, and arranged them in a glass-pitcher, which, having long ago lost its handle, was so much the fitter for a flower-vase. The early sunshine—as fresh as that which peeped into Eve's bower, while she and Adam sat at breakfast there—came twinkling through the branches of the pear-tree, and fell quite across the table. All was now ready. There were chairs and plates for three. A chair and plate for Hepzibah—the same for Phoebe:—but what other guest did her cousin look for?

Throughout this preparation, there had been a constant tremor in Hepzibah's frame; an agitation so powerful, that Phoebe could see the quivering of her gaunt shadow, as thrown by the firelight on the kitchen-wall, or by the sunshine on the parlor-floor. Its manifestations were so various, and agreed so little with one another, that the girl knew not what to make of it. Sometimes, it seemed an ecstacy of delight and happiness. At such moments, Hepzibah would fling out her arms, and enfold Phoebe in them, and kiss her cheek, as tenderly as ever her mother had; she appeared to do so by an inevitable impulse, and as if her bosom were oppressed with tenderness, of which she must needs pour out a little, in order to gain breathing-room. The next moment, without any visible cause for the change, her unwonted joy shrank back,

appalled, as it were, and clothed itself in mourning; or it ran
and hid itself, so to speak, in the dungeon of her heart, where
it had long lain chained; while a cold, spectral sorrow took
the place of the imprisoned joy, that was afraid to be enfranchised—a sorrow as black as that was bright. She often
broke into a little, nervous, hysteric laugh, more touching
than any tears could be; and forthwith, as if to try which
was the most touching, a gust of tears would follow; or perhaps the laughter and tears came both at once, and surrounded our poor Hepzibah, in a moral sense, with a kind of
pale, dim rainbow. Towards Phoebe, as we have said, she
was affectionate—far tenderer than ever before, in their brief
acquaintance, except for that one kiss, on the preceding night
—yet with a continually recurring pettishness and irritability.
She would speak sharply to her; then, throwing aside all the
starched reserve of her ordinary manner, ask pardon, and, the
next instant, renew the just forgiven injury.

At last, when their mutual labor was all finished, she took
Phoebe's hand in her own trembling one.

"Bear with me, my dear child," she cried, "for truly my
heart is full to the brim! Bear with me; for I love you, Phoebe,
though I speak so roughly! Think nothing of it, dearest child!
By-and-by, I shall be kind, and only kind!"

"My dearest Cousin, cannot you tell me what has happened?" asked Phoebe, with a sunny and tearful sympathy.
"What is it that moves you so?"

"Hush! hush! He is coming!" whispered Hepzibah, hastily
wiping her eyes. "Let him see you first, Phoebe; for you are
young and rosy, and cannot help letting a smile break out,
whether or no. He always liked bright faces! And mine is
old, now, and the tears are hardly dry on it. He never could
abide tears. There; draw the curtain a little, so that the
shadow may fall across his side of the table! But let there be
a good deal of sunshine, too; for he never was fond of gloom,
as some people are. He has had but little sunshine in his life

—poor Clifford—and, Oh, what a black shadow! Poor, poor, Clifford!"

Thus murmuring, in an undertone, as if speaking rather to her own heart than to Phoebe, the old gentlewoman stept on tiptoe about the room, making such arrangements as suggested themselves at the crisis.

Meanwhile, there was a step in the passage-way, above-stairs. Phoebe recognized it as the same which had passed upward, as through her dream, in the night-time. The approaching guest, whoever it might be, appeared to pause at the head of the staircase; he paused, twice or thrice, in the descent; he paused again at the foot. Each time, the delay seemed to be without purpose, but rather from a forgetfulness of the purpose which had set him in motion, or as if the person's feet came involuntarily to a standstill, because the motive power was too feeble to sustain his progress. Finally, he made a long pause at the threshold of the parlor. He took hold of the knob of the door; then loosened his grasp, without opening it. Hepzibah, her hands convulsively clasped, stood gazing at the entrance.

"Dear Cousin Hepzibah, pray don't look so!" said Phoebe trembling; for her cousin's emotion, and this mysteriously reluctant step, made her feel as if a ghost were coming into the room.—"You really frighten me! Is something awful going to happen?"

"Hush!" whispered Hepzibah. "Be cheerful! Whatever may happen, be nothing but cheerful!"

The final pause at the threshold proved so long, that Hepzibah, unable to endure the suspense, rushed forward, threw open the door, and led in the stranger by the hand. At the first glance, Phoebe saw an elderly personage, in an old-fashioned dressing-gown of faded damask, and wearing his gray, or almost white hair, of an unusual length. It quite overshadowed his forehead, except when he thrust it back, and stared vaguely about the room. After a very brief inspection of his face, it was easy to conceive that his footstep must necessarily be such an one as that which—slowly, and with as indefinite an aim as a child's first journey across a floor—had just brought him hitherward. Yet there were no tokens that his physical strength might not have sufficed for a free and determined gait. It was the spirit of the man, that could not walk. The expression of his countenance—while, notwithstanding, it had the light of reason in it—seemed to waver, and glimmer, and nearly to die away, and feebly to recover itself again. It was like a flame which we see twinkling among half-extinguished embers; we gaze at it, more intently than if it were a positive blaze, gushing vividly upward— more intently, but with a certain impatience, as if it ought either to kindle itself into satisfactory splendor, or be at once extinguished.

For an instant after entering the room, the guest stood still, retaining Hepzibah's hand, instinctively, as a child does that of the grown person who guides it. He saw Phoebe, however, and caught an illumination from her youthful and pleasant aspect, which, indeed, threw a cheerfulness about the parlor, like the circle of reflected brilliancy around the glass vase of flowers that was standing in the sunshine. He made a salutation, or, to speak nearer the truth, an ill-defined, abortive attempt at courtesy. Imperfect as it was, however, it conveyed an idea, or, at least, gave a hint, of indescribable grace, such as no practised art of external manners could have attained. It was too slight to seize upon, at the instant, yet, as recollected afterwards, seemed to transfigure the whole man.

"Dear Clifford," said Hepzibah, in the tone with which one soothes a wayward infant, "this is our Cousin Phoebe— little Phoebe Pyncheon—Arthur's only child, you know! She has come from the country to stay with us awhile; for our old house has grown to be very lonely now."

"Phoebe? — Phoebe Pyncheon! — Phoebe?" repeated the

guest, with a strange, sluggish, ill-defined utterance.—"Arthur's child! Ah, I forget! No matter! She is very welcome!"

"Come, dear Clifford, take this chair," said Hepzibah, leading him to his place.—"Pray, Phoebe, lower the curtain a very little more. Now let us begin breakfast!"

The guest seated himself in the place assigned him, and looked strangely around. He was evidently trying to grapple with the present scene, and bring it home to his mind with a more satisfactory distinctness. He desired to be certain, at least, that he was here, in the low-studded, cross-beamed, oaken-panelled parlor, and not in some other spot, which had stereotyped itself into his senses. But the effort was too great to be sustained with more than a fragmentary success. Continually, as we may express it, he faded away out of his place; or, in other words, his mind and consciousness took their departure, leaving his wasted, gray, and melancholy figure—a substantial emptiness, a material ghost—to occupy his seat at table. Again, after a blank moment, there would be a flickering taper-gleam in his eyeballs. It betokened that his spiritual part had returned, and was doing its best to kindle the heart's household-fire, and light up intellectual lamps in the dark and ruinous mansion, where it was doomed to be a forlorn inhabitant.

At one of these moments of less torpid, yet still imperfect animation, Phoebe became convinced of what she had at first rejected as too extravagant and startling an idea. She saw that the person before her must have been the original of the beautiful miniature in her Cousin Hepzibah's possession. Indeed, with a feminine eye for costume, she had at once identified the damask dressing-gown, which enveloped him, as the same in figure, material, and fashion, with that so elaborately represented in the picture. This old, faded garment, with all its pristine brilliancy extinct, seemed, in some indescribable way, to translate the wearer's untold misfortune, and make it perceptible to the beholder's eye. It was the better to be discerned, by this exterior type, how worn and old were the soul's more immediate garments; that form and countenance, the beauty and grace of which had almost transcended the skill of the most exquisite of artists. It could the more adequately be known, that the soul of the man must have suffered some miserable wrong from its earthly experience. There he seemed to sit, with a dim veil of decay and ruin betwixt him and the world, but through which, at flitting intervals, might be caught the same expression, so refined, so softly imaginative, which Malbone—venturing a happy touch, with suspended breath—had imparted to the miniature! There had been something so innately characteristic in this look, that all the dusky years, and the burthen of unfit calamity which had fallen upon him, did not suffice utterly to destroy it.

Hepzibah had now poured out a cup of deliciously fragrant coffee, and presented it to her guest. As his eyes met hers, he seemed bewildered and disquieted.

"Is this you, Hepzibah?" he murmured sadly; then, more apart, and perhaps unconscious that he was overheard.—"How changed! How changed! And is she angry with me? Why does she bend her brow so!"

Poor Hepzibah! It was that wretched scowl, which time, and her near-sightedness, and the fret of inward discomfort, had rendered so habitual, that any vehemence of mood invariably evoked it. But, at the indistinct murmur of his words, her whole face grew tender, and even lovely, with sorrowful affection; the harshness of her features disappeared, as it were, behind the warm and misty glow.

"Angry!" she repeated. "Angry with you, Clifford!"

Her tone, as she uttered this exclamation, had a plaintive and really exquisite melody thrilling through it, yet without subduing a certain something which an obtuse auditor might still have mistaken for asperity. It was as if some transcendent musician should draw a soul-thrilling sweetness out of a cracked instrument, which makes its physical imperfection heard in the midst of ethereal harmony. So deep was the sensibility that found an organ in Hepzibah's voice!

"There is nothing but love here, Clifford," she added—"nothing but love! You are at home!"

The guest responded to her tone by a smile, which did not half light up his face. Feeble as it was, however, and gone in a moment, it had a charm of wonderful beauty. It was followed by a coarser expression; or one that had the effect of coarseness on the fine mould and outline of his countenance, because there was nothing intellectual to temper it. It was a look of appetite. He ate food with what might almost be termed voracity, and seemed to forget himself, Hepzibah, the young girl, and everything else around him, in the sensual enjoyment which the bountifully spread table afforded. In his natural system, though high-wrought and delicately refined, a sensibility to the delights of the palate was probably inherent. It would have been kept in check, however, and even converted into an accomplishment, and one of the thousand modes of intellectual culture, had his more ethereal characteristics retained their vigor. But, as it existed now, the effect was painful, and made Phoebe droop her eyes.

In a little while, the guest became sensible of the fragrance of the yet untasted coffee. He quaffed it eagerly. The subtle essence acted on him like a charmed draught, and caused the opaque substance of his animal being to grow transparent, or, at least, translucent; so that a spiritual gleam was transmitted through it, with a clearer lustre than hitherto.

"More, more!" he cried, with nervous haste in his utterance, as if anxious to retain his grasp of what sought to escape him. —"This is what I need! Give me more!"

Under this delicate and powerful influence, he sat more erect, and looked out from his eyes with a glance that took note of what it rested on. It was not so much, that his expression grew more intellectual; this, though it had its share, was not the most peculiar effect. Neither was what we call the moral nature so forcibly awakened, as to present itself in remarkable prominence. But a certain fine temper of being was now—not brought out in full relief, but changeably and imperfectly betrayed—of which it was the function to deal with all beautiful and enjoyable things. In a character where it should exist as the chief attribute, it would bestow on its possessor an exquisite taste, and an enviable susceptibility of happiness. Beauty would be his life; his aspirations would all tend towards it; and, allowing his frame and physical organs to be in consonance, his own developements would likewise be beautiful. Such a man should have nothing to do with sorrow; nothing with strife; nothing with the martyrdom which, in an infinite variety of shapes, awaits those who have the heart, and will, and conscience, to fight a battle with the world. To these heroic tempers, such martyrdom is the richest meed in the world's gift. To the individual before us, it could only be a grief, intense in due proportion with the severity of the infliction. He had no right to be a martyr; and, beholding him so fit to be happy, and so feeble for all other purposes, a generous, strong, and noble spirit would, methinks, have been ready to sacrifice what little enjoyment it might have planned for itself—it would have flung down the hopes, so paltry in its regard—if thereby the wintry blasts of our rude sphere might come tempered to such a man.

Not to speak it harshly or scornfully, it seemed Clifford's nature to be a Sybarite. It was perceptible, even there, in the dark, old parlor, in the inevitable polarity with which his eyes were attracted towards the quivering play of sunbeams through the shadowy foliage. It was seen in his appreciating notice of the vase of flowers, the scent of which he inhaled with a zest, almost peculiar to a physical organization so refined that spiritual ingredients are moulded in with it. It was betrayed in the unconscious smile with which he regarded Phoebe, whose fresh and maidenly figure was both sunshine and flowers, their essence, in a prettier and more agreeable mode of manifestation. Not less evident was this love and necessity for the Beautiful, in the instinctive caution with which, even so soon, his eyes turned away from his hostess, and wandered to any quarter, rather than come back. It was Hepzibah's misfortune; not Clifford's fault. How could he—so yellow as she was, so wrinkled, so sad of mien, with that odd uncouthness of a turban on her head, and that most perverse of scowls contorting her brow—how could he love to gaze at her! But, did he owe her no affection for so much as she had silently given? He owed her nothing. A nature like Clifford's can contract no debts of that kind. It is—we say it without censure, nor in diminution of the claim which it indefeasibly possesses on beings of another mould—it is always selfish in its essence; and we must give it leave to be so, and heap up our heroic and disinterested love upon it, so much the more, without a recompense. Poor Hepzibah knew this truth, or, at least, acted on the instinct of it. So long estranged from what was lovely, as Clifford had been, she rejoiced—rejoiced, though with a present sigh, and a secret purpose to shed tears in her own chamber—that he had brighter objects now before his eyes, than her aged and uncomely features. They never possessed a charm; and if they had, the canker of her grief for him would long since have destroyed it.

The guest leaned back in his chair. Mingled in his countenance with a dreamy delight, there was a troubled look of effort and unrest. He was seeking to make himself more fully sensible of the scene around him; or perhaps, dreading it to be a dream, or a play of imagination, was vexing the fair moment with a struggle for some added brilliancy and more durable illusion.

"How pleasant!—How delightful!" he murmured, but not as if addressing any one. "Will it last? How balmy the atmosphere, through that open window! An open window! How beautiful that play of sunshine! Those flowers, how very fragrant! That young girl's face, how cheerful, how bloom-ing; a flower with the dew on it, and sunbeams in the dew-drops! Ah; this must be all a dream! A dream! A dream! But it has quite hidden the four stone-walls!"

Then his face darkened, as if the shadow of a cavern or a dungeon had come over it; there was no more light in its expression than might have come through the iron grates of a prison-window—still lessening, too, as if he were sinking farther into the depths. Phoebe (being of that quickness and activity of temperament that she seldom long refrained from taking a part, and generally a good one, in what was going forward) now felt herself moved to address the stranger.

"Here is a new kind of rose, which I found, this morning, in the garden," said she, choosing a small crimson one from among the flowers in the vase. "There will be but five or six on the bush, this season. This is the most perfect of them all; not a speck of blight or mildew in it. And how sweet it is!—sweet like no other rose! One can never forget that scent!"

"Ah!—let me see!—let me hold it!" cried the guest, eagerly seizing the flower, which, by the spell peculiar to remembered odors, brought innumerable associations along with the fra-grance that it exhaled.—"Thank you! This has done me good. I remember how I used to prize this flower—long ago, I sup-pose, very long ago!—or was it only yesterday? It makes me feel young again! Am I young? Either this remembrance is singularly distinct, or this consciousness strangely dim! But how kind of the fair young girl! Thank you! Thank you!"

The favorable excitement, derived from this little crimson rose, afforded Clifford the brightest moment which he enjoyed at the breakfast-table. It might have lasted longer, but that his eyes happened, soon afterwards, to rest on the face of the old Puritan, who, out of his dingy frame and lustreless canvass, was looking down on the scene like a ghost, and a most ill-tempered and ungenial one. The guest made an impatient gesture of the hand, and addressed Hepzibah with what might easily be recognized as the licensed irritability of a petted member of the family.

"Hepzibah!—Hepzibah!" cried he, with no little force and distinctness. "Why do you keep that odious picture on the wall? Yes, yes!—that is precisely your taste! I have told you, a thousand times, that it was the evil genius of the house!— my evil genius particularly! Take it down at once!"

"Dear Clifford," said Hepzibah sadly, "you know it cannot be!"

"Then, at all events," continued he, still speaking with some energy, "pray cover it with a crimson curtain, broad enough to hang in folds, and with a golden border and tassels! I cannot bear it! It must not stare me in the face!"

"Yes, dear Clifford, the picture shall be covered," said Hepzibah soothingly. "There is a crimson curtain in a trunk above-stairs—a little faded and moth-eaten, I'm afraid—but Phoebe and I will do wonders with it."

"This very day, remember!" said he; and then added, in a low, self-communing voice,—"Why should we live in this dismal house at all? Why not go to the south of France?—to Italy?—Paris, Naples, Venice, Rome? Hepzibah will say, we have not the means. A droll idea, that!"

He smiled to himself, and threw a glance of fine, sarcastic meaning towards Hepzibah.

But the several moods of feeling, faintly as they were marked, through which he had passed, occurring in so brief an interval of time, had evidently wearied the stranger. He was probably accustomed to a sad monotony of life, not so much flowing in a stream, however sluggish, as stagnating in a pool around his feet. A slumberous veil diffused itself over his countenance, and had an effect, morally speaking, on its naturally delicate and elegant outline, like that which a brooding mist, with no sunshine in it, throws over the features of a landscape. He appeared to become grosser; almost cloddish. If aught of interest or beauty—even ruined beauty—had heretofore been visible in this man, the beholder might now begin to doubt it, and to accuse his own imagination of deluding him with whatever grace had flickered over that visage, and whatever exquisite lustre had gleamed in those filmy eyes.

Before he had quite sunken away, however, the sharp and peevish tinkle of the shop-bell made itself audible. Striking most disagreeably on Clifford's auditory organs and the characteristic sensibility of his nerves, it caused him to start upright out of his chair.

"Good Heavens, Hepzibah, what horrible disturbance have we now in the house?" cried he, wreaking his resentful impatience—as a matter of course, and a custom of old—on the one person in the world that loved him. "I have never heard such a hateful clamor! Why do you permit it? In the name of all dissonance, what can it be?"

It was very remarkable into what prominent relief—even as if a dim picture should leap suddenly from its canvass—Clifford's character was thrown by this apparently trifling annoyance. The secret was, that an individual of his temper can always be pricked more acutely through his sense of the beautiful and harmonious, than through his heart. It is even possible—for similar cases have often happened—that if Clifford, in his foregoing life, had enjoyed the means of cultivating his taste to its utmost perfectibility, that subtle attribute might, before this period, have completely eaten out or filed away his affections. Shall we venture to pronounce, therefore, that his long and black calamity may not have had a redeeming drop of mercy, at the bottom?

"Dear Clifford, I wish I could keep the sound from your ears," said Hepzibah patiently, but reddening with a painful suffusion of shame. "It is very disagreeable even to me. But, do you know, Clifford, I have something to tell you? This ugly noise—pray run, Phoebe, and see who is there!—this naughty little tinkle is nothing but our shop-bell!"

"Shop-bell!" repeated Clifford, with a bewildered stare.

"Yes; our shop-bell!" said Hepzibah; a certain natural dignity, mingled with deep emotion, now asserting itself in her manner. "For you must know, dearest Clifford, that we are very poor. And there was no resource, but either to accept assistance from a hand that I would push aside, (and so would you!) were it to offer bread when we were dying for it—no help, save from him, or else to earn our subsistence with my own hands! Alone, I might have been content to starve. But you were to be given back to me! Do you think, then, dear Clifford," added she, with a wretched smile, "that I have brought an irretrievable disgrace on the old house, by opening a little shop in the front gable? Our great, great-grandfather did the same, when there was far less need! Are you ashamed of me?"

"Shame! Disgrace! Do you speak these words to me, Hepzibah?" said Clifford, not angrily, however; for when a man's spirit has been thoroughly crushed, he may be peevish at small offences, but never resentful of great ones. So he spoke with only a grieved emotion.—"It was not kind to say so, Hepzibah! What shame can befall me now?"

And then the unnerved man—he that had been born for enjoyment, but had met a doom so very wretched—burst into a woman's passion of tears. It was but of brief continuance, however; soon leaving him in a quiescent, and, to judge by his countenance, not an uncomfortable state. From this mood, too, he partially rallied, for an instant, and looked at Hepzibah with a smile, the keen, half-derisory purport of which was a puzzle to her.

"Are we so very poor, Hepzibah?" said he.

Finally, his chair being deep and softly cushioned, Clifford fell asleep. Hearing the more regular rise and fall of his breath—(which, however, even then, instead of being strong and full, had a feeble kind of tremor, corresponding with the lack of vigor in his character)—hearing these tokens of settled slumber, Hepzibah seized the opportunity to peruse his face, more attentively than she had yet dared to do. Her heart melted away in tears; her profoundest spirit sent forth a moaning voice, low, gentle, but inexpressibly sad. In this depth of grief and pity, she felt that there was no irreverence in gazing at his altered, aged, faded, ruined face. But, no sooner was she a little relieved, than her conscience smote her for gazing curiously at him, now that he was so changed; and, turning hastily away, Hepzibah let down the curtain over the sunny window, and left Clifford to slumber there.

VIII

THE PYNCHEON OF TO-DAY

PHOEBE, on entering the shop, beheld there the already familiar face of the little devourer—if we can reckon his mighty deeds aright—of Jim Crow, the elephant, the camel, the dromedaries, and the locomotive. Having expended his private fortune, on the two preceding days, in the purchase of the above unheard-of luxuries, the young gentleman's present errand was on the part of his mother, in quest of three eggs and half-a-pound of raisins. These articles Phoebe accordingly supplied, and—as a mark of gratitude for his previous patronage, and a slight, superadded morsel, after breakfast—put likewise into his hand a whale! The great fish —reversing his experience with the prophet of Nineveh—immediately began his progress down the same red pathway of fate, whither so varied a caravan had preceded him. This remarkable urchin, in truth, was the very emblem of old Father Time, both in respect of his all-devouring appetite for men and things, and because he, as well as Time, after engulfing thus much of creation, looked almost as youthful as if he had been just that moment made.

After partly closing the door, the child turned back, and mumbled something to Phoebe which, as the whale was but half-disposed of, she could not perfectly understand.

"What did you say, my little fellow?" asked she.

"Mother wants to know," repeated Ned Higgins, more distinctly, "how Old Maid Pyncheon's brother does? Folks say he has got home!"

"My Cousin Hepzibah's brother!" exclaimed Phoebe, surprised at this sudden explanation of the relationship between Hepzibah and her guest.—"Her brother! And where can he have been!"

The little boy only put his thumb to his broad snub-nose, with that look of shrewdness which a child, spending much of his time in the street, so soon learns to throw over his features, however unintelligent in themselves. Then, as Phoebe continued to gaze at him without answering his mother's message, he took his departure.

As the child went down the steps, a gentleman ascended them, and made his entrance into the shop. It was the portly, and, had it possessed the advantage of a little more height, would have been the stately figure of a man considerably in the decline of life, dressed in a black suit of some thin stuff, resembling broadcloth as closely as possible. A gold-headed cane of rare, oriental wood, added materially to the high respectability of his aspect; as did also a white neckcloth of the utmost snowy purity, and the conscientious polish of his boots. His dark, square countenance, with its almost shaggy depth of eyebrows, was naturally impressive, and would perhaps have been rather stern, had not the gentleman considerately taken upon himself to mitigate the harsh effect by a look of exceeding good-humor and benevolence. Owing, however, to a somewhat massive accumulation of animal substance about the lower region of his face, the look was perhaps unctuous, rather than spiritual, and had, so to speak, a kind of fleshly effulgence, not altogether so satisfactory as he doubtless intended it to be. A susceptible observer, at any rate, might have regarded it as affording very little evidence of the genuine benignity of soul, whereof it purported to be the outward reflection. And if the observer chanced to be ill-natured, as well as acute and susceptible, he would probably suspect, that the smile on the gentleman's face was a good deal akin to the shine on his boots, and that each must have cost him and his boot-black, respectively, a good deal of hard labor to bring out and preserve them.

As the stranger entered the little shop—where the projection of the second story and the thick foliage of the elm-tree, as well as the commodities at the window, created a sort of gray medium—his smile grew as intense as if he had set his heart on counteracting the whole gloom of the atmosphere (besides any moral gloom pertaining to Hepzibah and her inmates) by the unassisted light of his countenance. On perceiving a young rosebud of a girl, instead of the gaunt presence of the old maid, a look of surprise was manifest. He at first knit his brows; then smiled with more unctuous benignity than ever.

"Ah, I see how it is!" said he, in a deep voice—a voice which, had it come from the throat of an uncultivated man, would have been gruff, but, by dint of careful training, was now sufficiently agreeable—"I was not aware that Miss Hepzibah Pyncheon had commenced business under such favorable auspices. You are her assistant, I suppose?"

"I certainly am," answered Phoebe, and added, with a little air of ladylike assumption—(for, civil as the gentleman was, he evidently took her to be a young person serving for wages)—"I am a cousin of Miss Hepzibah, on a visit to her."

"Her cousin?—and from the country? Pray pardon me, then," said the gentleman, bowing and smiling as Phoebe never had been bowed to nor smiled on before.—"In that case, we must be better acquainted; for, unless I am sadly mistaken, you are my own little kinswoman likewise! Let me see—Mary? —Dolly?—Phoebe?—yes, Phoebe is the name! Is it possible that you are Phoebe Pyncheon, only child of my dear cousin and classmate, Arthur? Ah, I see your father now, about your mouth! Yes; yes; we must be better acquainted! I am your kinsman, my dear. Surely you must have heard of Judge Pyncheon?"

As Phoebe courtesied in reply, the Judge bent forward, with the pardonable and even praiseworthy purpose—considering the nearness of blood and the difference of age—of bestowing on his young relative a kiss of acknowledged kindred and natural affection. Unfortunately, (without design, or only with such instinctive design as gives no account of itself to the intellect,) Phoebe, just at the critical moment, drew back; so that her highly respectable kinsman, with his body bent over the counter, and his lips protruded, was betrayed into the rather absurd predicament of kissing the empty air. It was a modern parallel to the case of Ixion embracing a cloud, and was so much the more ridiculous, as the Judge prided himself on eschewing all airy matter, and never mistaking a shadow for a substance. The truth was—and it is Phoebe's only excuse—that, although Judge Pyncheon's glowing benignity might not be absolutely unpleasant to the feminine beholder, with the width of a street or even an ordinary sized room interposed between, yet it became quite too intense, when this dark, full-fed physiognomy (so roughly bearded, too, that no razor could ever make it smooth) sought to bring itself into actual contact with the object of its regards. The man, the sex, somehow or other, was entirely too prominent in the Judge's demonstrations of that sort. Phoebe's eyes sank, and, without knowing why, she felt herself blushing deeply under his look. Yet she had been kissed before, and without any particular squeamishness, by perhaps half-a-dozen different cousins, younger, as well as older, than this dark-browed, grisly bearded, white-neckclothed, and unctuously benevolent Judge! Then why not by him?

On raising her eyes, Phoebe was startled by the change in Judge Pyncheon's face. It was quite as striking, allowing for the difference of scale, as that betwixt a landscape under a broad sunshine, and just before a thunder-storm; not that it had the passionate intensity of the latter aspect, but was cold, hard, immitigable, like a day-long brooding cloud.

"Dear me, what is to be done now?" thought the country-girl to herself.—"He looks as if there were nothing softer in him than a rock, nor milder than the east-wind! I meant no harm! Since he is really my cousin, I would have let him kiss me, if I could!"

Then, all at once, it struck Phoebe, that this very Judge Pyncheon was the original of the miniature, which the Daguerreotypist had shown her in the garden, and that the hard, stern, relentless look, now on his face, was the same that the sun had so inflexibly persisted in bringing out. Was it, therefore, no momentary mood, but, however skilfully concealed, the settled temper of his life? And not merely so, but was it hereditary in him, and transmitted down as a precious heirloom from that bearded ancestor, in whose picture both the expression, and, to a singular degree, the features of the modern Judge, were shown as by a kind of prophecy? A deeper philosopher than Phoebe might have found something very terrible in this idea. It implied that the weaknesses and defects, the bad passions, the mean tendencies, and the moral diseases which lead to crime, are handed down from one generation to another, by a far surer process of transmission than human law has been able to establish, in respect to the riches and honors which it seeks to entail upon posterity.

But, as it happened, scarcely had Phoebe's eyes rested again on the Judge's countenance, than all its ugly sternness vanished; and she found herself quite overpowered by the sultry, dog-day heat, as it were, of benevolence, which this excellent man diffused out of his great heart into the surrounding atmosphere;—very much like a serpent, which, as a preliminary to fascination, is said to fill the air with his peculiar odor.

"I like that, Cousin Phoebe!" cried he, with an emphatic nod of approbation.—"I like it much, my little cousin! You are a good child, and know how to take care of yourself. A young girl—especially if she be a very pretty one—can never be too chary of her lips."

"Indeed, Sir," said Phoebe, trying to laugh the matter off, "I did not mean to be unkind."

Nevertheless, whether or no it were entirely owing to the inauspicious commencement of their acquaintance, she still acted under a certain reserve, which was by no means customary to her frank and genial nature. The fantasy would not quit her, that the original Puritan, of whom she had heard so many sombre traditions—the progenitor of the whole race of New England Pyncheons, the founder of the House of the Seven Gables, and who had died so strangely in it—had now stept into the shop. In these days of off-hand equipment, the matter was easily enough arranged. On his arrival from the other world, he had merely found it necessary to spend a quarter-of-an-hour at a barber's, who had trimmed down the Puritan's full beard into a pair of grizzled whiskers; then, patronizing a ready-made clothing establishment, he had exchanged his velvet doublet and sable cloak, with the richly worked band under his chin, for a white collar and cravat, coat, vest, and pantaloons; and, lastly, putting aside his steel-hilted broadsword to take up a gold-headed cane, the Colonel Pyncheon, of two centuries ago, steps forward as the Judge, of the passing moment!

Of course, Phoebe was far too sensible a girl to entertain this idea in any other way than as matter for a smile. Possibly, also, could the two personages have stood together before her eye, many points of difference would have been perceptible, and perhaps only a general resemblance. The long lapse of intervening years, in a climate so unlike that which had fostered the ancestral Englishman, must inevitably have wrought important changes in the physical system of his descendant. The Judge's volume of muscle could hardly be the same as the Colonel's; there was undoubtedly less beef in him. Though looked upon as a weighty man among his contemporaries, in respect of animal substance; and as favored with a remarkable degree of fundamental developement, well adapting him for the judicial bench, we conceive that the modern Judge Pyncheon, if weighed in the same balance with his ancestor, would have required at least an old-fashioned fifty-six, to keep the scale in equilibrio. Then the Judge's face had lost the ruddy English hue, that showed its warmth through all the duskiness of the Colonel's weatherbeaten cheek, and had taken a sallow shade, the established complexion of his countrymen. If we mistake not, moreover, a certain quality of nervousness had become more or less manifest, even in so solid a specimen of Puritan descent, as the gentleman now under discussion. As one of its effects, it bestowed on his countenance a quicker mobility than the old Englishman's had possessed, and keener vivacity, but at the expense of a sturdier something, on which these acute endowments seemed to act like dissolving acids. This process, for aught we know, may belong to the great system of human progress, which, with every ascending footstep, as it diminishes the necessity for animal force, may be destined gradually to spiritualize us by refining away our grosser attributes of body. If so, Judge Pyncheon could endure a century or two more of such refinement, as well as most other men.

The similarity, intellectual and moral, between the Judge and his ancestor, appears to have been at least as strong as the resemblance of mien and feature would afford reason to anticipate. In old Colonel Pyncheon's funeral discourse, the clergyman absolutely canonized his deceased parishioner, and opening, as it were, a vista through the roof of the church, and thence through the firmament above, showed him seated, harp in hand, among the crowned choristers of the spiritual world. On his tombstone, too, the record is highly eulogistic; nor does history, so far as he holds a place upon its page, assail the consistency and uprightness of his character. So also, as regards the Judge Pyncheon of to-day, neither clergyman, nor legal critic, nor inscriber of tombstones, nor historian of general or local politics, would venture a word against this eminent person's sincerity as a christian, or respectability as a man, or integrity as a judge, or courage and faithfulness as the often-tried representative of his political party. But, besides these cold, formal, and empty words of the chisel that inscribes, the voice that speaks, and the pen that writes for the public eye and for distant time—and which inevitably lose much of their truth and freedom by the fatal consciousness of so doing—there were traditions about the ancestor, and private diurnal gossip about the Judge, remarkably accordant in their testimony. It is often instructive to take the woman's, the private and domestic view, of a public man; nor can anything be more curious than the vast discrepancy between portraits intended for engraving, and the pencil-sketches that pass from hand to hand, behind the original's back.

For example, tradition affirmed that the Puritan had been greedy of wealth; the Judge, too, with all the show of liberal expenditure, was said to be as close-fisted as if his gripe were of iron. The ancestor had clothed himself in a grim assumption of kindliness, a rough heartiness of word and manner, which most people took to be the genuine warmth of nature, making its way through the thick and inflexible hide of a manly character. His descendant, in compliance with the requirements of a nicer age, had etherealized this rude benevolence into that broad benignity of smile, wherewith he shone like a noonday sun along the streets, or glowed like a household fire, in the drawing-rooms of his private acquaintance. The Puritan—if not belied by some singular stories, murmured, even at this day, under the narrator's breath—had fallen into certain transgressions to which men of his great animal developement, whatever their faith or principles, must continue liable, until they put off impurity, along with the gross earthly substance that involves it. We must not stain our page with any contemporary scandal, to a similar purport, that may have been whispered against the Judge. The Puritan, again, an autocrat in his own household, had worn out three wives, and, merely by the remorseless weight and hardness of his character in the conjugal relation, had sent them, one after another, broken hearted, to their graves. Here, the parallel, in some sort, fails. The Judge had wedded but a single wife, and lost her in the third or fourth year of their marriage. There was a fable, however—for such we choose to consider it, though, not impossibly, typical of Judge Pyncheon's marital deportment—that the lady got her death-blow in the honey-moon, and never smiled again, because her husband compelled her to serve him with coffee, every morning, at his bedside, in token of fealty to her liege-lord and master.

But it is too fruitful a subject, this of hereditary resemblances,—the frequent recurrence of which, in a direct line, is truly unaccountable, when we consider how large an accumulation of ancestry lies behind every man, at the distance of one or two centuries. We shall only add, therefore, that the Puritan—so, at least, says chimney-corner tradition, which often preserves traits of character with marvellous fidelity—was bold, imperious, relentless, crafty; laying his purposes deep, and following them out with an inveteracy of pursuit that knew neither rest nor conscience; trampling on the weak, and, when essential to his ends, doing his utmost to beat down the strong. Whether the Judge in any degree resembled him, the farther progress of our narrative may show.

Scarcely any of the items in the above-drawn parallel occurred to Phoebe, whose country-birth and residence, in truth, had left her pitifully ignorant of most of the family traditions, which lingered, like cobwebs and incrustations of smoke, about the rooms and chimney-corners of the House of the Seven Gables. Yet there was a circumstance, very trifling in itself, which impressed her with an odd degree of horror. She had heard of the anathema flung by Maule, the executed wizard, against Colonel Pyncheon and his posterity—that God would give them blood to drink—and likewise of the popular notion, that this miraculous blood might now and then be heard gurgling in their throats. The latter scandal (as became a person of sense, and, more especially, a member of the Pyncheon family) Phoebe had set down for the absurdity which it unquestionably was. But ancient superstitions, after being steeped in human hearts, and embodied in human breath, and passing from lip to ear in manifold repetition, through a series of generations, become imbued with an effect of homely truth. The smoke of the domestic hearth has scented them, through and through. By long transmission among household facts, they grow to look like them, and have such a familiar way of making themselves at home, that their influence is usually greater than we suspect. Thus it happened, that when Phoebe heard a certain noise in Judge Pyncheon's throat—rather habitual with him, not altogether voluntary, yet indicative of nothing, unless it were a slight bronchial complaint, or, as some people hinted, an apoplectic symptom— when the girl heard this queer and aukward ingurgitation, (which the writer never did hear, and therefore cannot describe,) she, very foolishly, started, and clasped her hands.

Of course, it was exceedingly ridiculous in Phoebe to be discomposed by such a trifle, and still more unpardonable to show her discomposure to the individual most concerned in it. But the incident chimed in so oddly with her previous fancies about the Colonel and the Judge, that, for the moment, it seemed quite to mingle their identity.

"What is the matter with you, young woman?" said Judge Pyncheon, giving her one of his harsh looks. "Are you afraid of anything?"

"Oh, nothing, Sir, nothing in the world!" answered Phoebe, with a little laugh of vexation at herself.—"But perhaps you wish to speak with my Cousin Hepzibah. Shall I call her?"

"Stay a moment, if you please!" said the Judge, again beaming sunshine out of his face.—"You seem to be a little nervous, this morning. The town air, Cousin Phoebe, does not agree with your good, wholesome country-habits. Or, has anything happened to disturb you?—anything remarkable in Cousin Hepzibah's family? An arrival, eh? I thought so! No wonder you are out of sorts, my little cousin. To be an inmate with such a guest may well startle an innocent young girl!"

"You quite puzzle me, Sir," replied Phoebe, gazing inquiringly at the Judge. "There is no frightful guest in the house, but only a poor, gentle, childlike man, whom I believe to be Cousin Hepzibah's brother. I am afraid (but you, Sir, will know better than I) that he is not quite in his sound senses; but so mild and quiet, he seems to be, that a mother might trust her baby with him; and I think he would play with the baby as if he were only a few years older than itself. He startle me! Oh, no indeed!"

"I rejoice to hear so favorable and so ingenuous an account of my Cousin Clifford," said the benevolent Judge. "Many years ago, when we were boys and young men together, I had a great affection for him, and still feel a tender interest in all his concerns. You say, Cousin Phoebe, he appears to be weak-minded. Heaven grant him at least enough of intellect to repent of his past sins!"

"Nobody, I fancy," observed Phoebe, "can have fewer to repent of."

"And is it possible, my dear," rejoined the Judge, with a commiserating look, "that you have never heard of Clifford Pyncheon?—that you know nothing of his history? Well; it is all right; and your mother has shown a very proper regard for the good name of the family with which she connected herself. Believe the best you can of this unfortunate person, and hope the best! It is a rule which christians should always follow, in their judgements of one another; and especially is it right and wise among near relatives, whose characters have necessarily a degree of mutual dependence. But is Clifford in the parlor? I will just step in and see!"

"Perhaps, Sir, I had better call my Cousin Hepzibah," said Phoebe; hardly knowing, however, whether she ought to obstruct the entrance of so affectionate a kinsman, into the private regions of the house.—"Her brother seemed to be just falling asleep, after breakfast; and I am sure she would not like him to be disturbed. Pray, Sir, let me give her notice!"

But the Judge showed a singular determination to enter unannounced; and as Phoebe, with the vivacity of a person whose movements unconsciously answer to her thoughts, had stept towards the door, he used little or no ceremony in putting her aside.

"No, no, Miss Phoebe!" said Judge Pyncheon, in a voice as deep as a thunder-growl, and with a frown as black as the cloud whence it issues. "Stay you here! I know the house, and know my Cousin Hepzibah, and know her brother Clifford likewise!—nor need my little country-cousin put herself to the trouble of announcing me!"—in these latter words, by-the-by, there were symptoms of a change from his sudden harshness into his previous benignity of manner—"I am at home here, Phoebe, you must recollect, and you are the stranger. I will just step in, therefore, and see for myself how Clifford is, and assure him and Hepzibah of my kindly feelings and best wishes. It is right, at this juncture, that they should both hear from my own lips how much I desire to serve them. Ha! Here is Hepzibah herself!"

Such was the case. The vibrations of the Judge's voice had reached the old gentlewoman in the parlor, where she sat, with face averted, waiting on her brother's slumber. She now issued forth, as would appear, to defend the entrance, looking, we must needs say, amazingly like the dragon which, in fairy tales, is wont to be the guardian over an enchanted beauty. The habitual scowl of her brow was, undeniably, too fierce, at this moment, to pass itself off on the innocent score of near-sightedness; and it was bent on Judge Pyncheon in a way that seemed to confound, if not alarm him—so inadequately had he estimated the moral force of a deeply grounded antipathy. She made a repelling gesture with her hand, and stood, a perfect picture of Prohibition, at full length, in the dark frame of the door-way. But we must betray Hepzibah's secret, and confess, that the native timorousness of her character even now developed itself, in a quick tremor, which, to her own perception, set each of her joints at variance with its fellow.

Possibly, the Judge was aware how little true hardihood lay behind Hepzibah's formidable front. At any rate, being a gentleman of sturdy nerves, he soon recovered himself, and failed not to approach his cousin with outstretched hand; adopting the sensible precaution, however, to cover his advance with a smile, so broad and sultry, that, had it been only half as warm as it looked, a trellis of grapes might at once have turned purple under its summer-like exposure. It may have been his purpose, indeed, to melt poor Hepzibah, on the spot, as if she were a figure of yellow wax.

"Hepzibah, my beloved Cousin, I am rejoiced!" exclaimed the Judge, most emphatically. "Now, at length, you have something to live for. Yes; and all of us, let me say, your friends and kindred, have more to live for than we had yesterday. I have lost no time in hastening to offer any assistance in my power towards making Clifford comfortable. He belongs to us all. I know how much he requires—how much he used to require—with his delicate taste, and his love of the beautiful. Anything in my house—pictures, books, wine, luxuries of the table—he may command them all! It would afford me a most heartfelt gratification to see him! Shall I step in, this moment?"

"No," replied Hepzibah, her voice quivering too painfully to allow of many words. "He cannot see visitors!"

"A visitor, my dear Cousin?—do you call me so?" cried

the Judge, whose sensibility, it seems, was hurt by the coldness of the phrase. "Nay, then, let me be Clifford's host, and your own likewise. Come at once to my house! The country-air, and all the conveniences—I may say, luxuries—that I have gathered about me, will do wonders for him. And you and I, dear Hepzibah, will consult together, and watch together, and labor together, to make our dear Clifford happy. Come! Why should we make more words about what is both a duty and a pleasure, on my part? Come to me at once!"

On hearing these so hospitable offers, and such generous recognition of the claims of kindred, Phoebe felt very much in the mood of running up to Judge Pyncheon, and giving him, of her own accord, the kiss from which she had so recently shrunk away. It was quite otherwise with Hepzibah; the Judge's smile seemed to operate on her acerbity of heart like sunshine upon vinegar, making it ten times sourer than ever.

"Clifford," said she—still too agitated to utter more than an abrupt sentence—"Clifford has a home here!"

"May Heaven forgive you, Hepzibah," said Judge Pyncheon—reverently lifting his eyes towards that high court of equity to which he appealed—"if you suffer any ancient prejudice or animosity to weigh with you, in this matter! I stand here, with an open heart, willing and anxious to receive yourself and Clifford into it. Do not refuse my good offices—my earnest propositions for your welfare! They are such, in all respects, as it behoves your nearest kinsman to make. It will be a heavy responsibility, Cousin, if you confine your brother to this dismal house and stifled air, when the delightful freedom of my country-seat is at his command."

"It would never suit Clifford," said Hepzibah, as briefly as before.

"Woman," broke forth the Judge, giving way to his resentment, "what is the meaning of all this? Have you other resources? Nay; I suspected as much! Take care, Hepzibah, take care! Clifford is on the brink of as black a ruin as ever befell him yet! But why do I talk with you, woman as you are! Make way! I must see Clifford!"

Hepzibah spread out her gaunt figure across the door, and seemed really to increase in bulk; looking the more terrible, also, because there was so much terror and agitation in her heart. But Judge Pyncheon's evident purpose of forcing a passage was interrupted by a voice from the inner room; a weak, tremulous, wailing voice, indicating helpless alarm, with no more energy for self-defence than belongs to a frightened infant.

"Hepzibah, Hepzibah," cried the voice, "go down on your knees to him! Kiss his feet! Entreat him not to come in! Oh, let him have mercy on me! Mercy!—mercy!"

For the instant, it appeared doubtful whether it were not the Judge's resolute purpose to set Hepzibah aside, and step across the threshold into the parlor, whence issued that broken and miserable murmur of entreaty. It was not pity that restrained him; for, at the first sound of the enfeebled voice, a red fire kindled in his eyes; and he made a quick pace forward, with something inexpressibly fierce and grim, darkening forth, as it were, out of the whole man. To know Judge Pyncheon, was to see him at that moment. After such a revelation, let him smile with what sultriness he would, he could much sooner turn grapes purple, or pumpkins yellow, than melt the iron-branded impression out of the beholder's memory. And it rendered his aspect not the less, but more frightful, that it seemed not to express wrath or hatred, but a certain hot fellness of purpose, which annihilated everything but itself.

Yet, after all, are we not slandering an excellent and amiable man? Look at the Judge now! He is apparently conscious of having erred, in too energetically pressing his deeds of loving-kindness on persons unable to appreciate them. He will await their better mood, and hold himself as ready to assist them, then, as at this moment. As he draws back from the door, an all-comprehensive benignity blazes from his visage, indicating that he gathers Hepzibah, little Phoebe, and the invisible Clifford, all three, together with the whole world besides, into his immense heart, and gives them a warm bath in its flood of affection.

"You do me great wrong, dear Cousin Hepzibah," said he, first kindly offering her his hand, and then drawing on his glove preparatory to departure. "Very great wrong! But I forgive it, and will study to make you think better of me. Of course, our poor Clifford being in so unhappy a state of mind, I cannot think of urging an interview at present. But I shall watch over his welfare, as if he were my own beloved brother; nor do I at all despair, my dear Cousin, of constraining both him and you to acknowledge your injustice. When that shall happen, I desire no other revenge than your acceptance of the best offices in my power to do you."

With a bow to Hepzibah, and a degree of paternal benevolence in his parting nod to Phoebe, the Judge left the shop, and went smiling along the street. As is customary with the rich, when they aim at the honors of a republic, he apologized, as it were, to the people, for his wealth, prosperity, and elevated station, by a free and hearty manner towards those who knew him; putting off the more of his dignity, in due proportion with the humbleness of the man whom he saluted; and thereby proving a haughty consciousness of his advantages, as irrefragably as if he had marched forth, preceded by a troop of lackeys to clear the way. On this particular forenoon, so excessive was the warmth of Judge Pyncheon's kindly aspect, that (such, at least, was the rumor about town) an extra passage of the water-carts was found essential, in order to lay the dust occasioned by so much extra sunshine!

No sooner had he disappeared, than Hepzibah grew deadly white, and staggering towards Phoebe, let her head fall on the young girl's shoulder.

"Oh, Phoebe," murmured she, "that man has been the horror of my life! Shall I never, never have the courage—will my voice never cease from trembling long enough—to let me tell him what he is!"

"Is he so very wicked?" asked Phoebe. "Yet his offers were surely kind!"

"Do not speak of them—he has a heart of iron!" rejoined Hepzibah.—"Go now, and talk to Clifford! Amuse, and keep him quiet! It would disturb him wretchedly, to see me so agitated as I am. There, go, dear child, and I will try to look after the shop!"

Phoebe went, accordingly, but perplexed herself, meanwhile, with queries as to the purport of the scene which she had just witnessed, and also whether judges, clergymen, and other characters of that eminent stamp and respectability, could really, in any single instance, be otherwise than just and upright men. A doubt of this nature has a most disturbing influence, and, if shown to be a fact, comes with fearful and startling effect, on minds of the trim, orderly, and limit-loving class, in which we find our little country-girl. Dispositions more boldly speculative may derive a stern enjoyment from the discovery, since there must be evil in the world, that a high man is as likely to grasp his share of it, as a low one. A wider scope of view, and a deeper insight, may see rank, dignity, and station, all proved illusory, so far as regards their claim to human reverence, and yet not feel as if the universe were thereby tumbled headlong into chaos. But Phoebe, in order to keep the universe in its old place, was fain to smother, in some degree, her own intuitions as to Judge Pyncheon's character. And as for her cousin's testimony in disparagement of it, she concluded that Hepzibah's judgement was embittered by one of those family feuds, which render hatred the more deadly, by the dead and corrupted love that they intermingle with its native poison.

IX

CLIFFORD AND PHOEBE

TRULY was there something high, generous, and noble, in the native composition of our poor old Hepzibah! Or else—and it was quite as probably the case—she had been enriched by poverty, developed by sorrow, elevated by the strong and solitary affection of her life, and thus endowed with heroism, which never could have characterized her in what are called happier circumstances. Through dreary years, Hepzibah had looked forward—for the most part, despairingly, never with any confidence of hope, but always with the feeling that it was her brightest possibility—to the very position in which she now found herself. In her own behalf, she had asked nothing of Providence, but the opportunity of devoting herself to this brother whom she had so loved—so admired for what he was, or might have been—and to whom she had kept her faith, alone of all the world, wholly, unfaulteringly, at every instant, and throughout life. And here, in his late decline, the lost one had come back out of his long and strange misfortune, and was thrown on her sympathy, as it seemed, not merely for the bread of his physical existence, but for everything that should keep him morally alive. She had responded to the call! She had come forward—our poor, gaunt Hepzibah, in her rusty silks, with her rigid joints, and the sad perversity of her scowl—ready to do her utmost, and with affection enough, if that were all, to do a hundred times as much!—There could be few more tearful sights—and Heaven forgive us, if a smile insist on mingling with our conception of it!—few sights with truer pathos in them, than Hepzibah presented, on that first afternoon.

How patiently did she endeavor to wrap Clifford up in her great, warm love, and make it all the world to him, so that he should retain no torturing sense of the coldness and dreariness, without! Her little efforts to amuse him! How pitiful, yet magnanimous, they were!

Remembering his early love of poetry and fiction, she unlocked a bookcase, and took down several books that had been excellent reading, in their day. There was a volume of Pope, with the Rape of the Lock in it, and another of the Tatler, and an odd one of Dryden's Miscellanies, all with tarnished gilding on their covers, and thoughts of tarnished brilliancy, inside. They had no success with Clifford. These, and all such writers of society, whose new works glow like the rich texture of a just-woven carpet, must be content to relinquish their charm, for every reader, after an age or two, and could hardly be supposed to retain any portion of it for a mind, that had utterly lost its estimate of modes and manners. Hepzibah then took up Rasselas, and began to read of the Happy Valley, with a vague idea that some secret of a contented life had there been elaborated, which might at least serve Clifford and herself for this one day. But the Happy Valley had a cloud over it. Hepzibah troubled her auditor, moreover, by innumerable sins of emphasis, which he seemed to detect without any reference to the meaning; nor, in fact, did he appear to take much note of the sense of what she read, but evidently felt the tedium of the lecture without harvesting its profit. His sister's voice, too, naturally harsh, had, in the course of her sorrowful lifetime, contracted a kind of croak, which, when it once gets into the human throat, is as ineradicable as sin. In both sexes, occasionally, this life-long croak, accompanying each word of joy or sorrow, is one of the symptoms of a settled melancholy; and wherever it occurs, the whole history of misfortune is conveyed in its slightest accent. The effect is as if the voice had been dyed black; or—if we must use a more moderate simile—this miserable croak, running through all the variations of the voice, is like a black silken thread, on which the crystal beads of speech are strung, and whence they take their hue. Such voices have put on mourning for dead hopes; and they ought to die and be buried along with them!

Discerning that Clifford was not gladdened by her efforts, Hepzibah searched about the house for the means of more exhilarating pastime. At one time, her eyes chanced to rest on Alice Pyncheon's harpsichord. It was a moment of great peril; for—despite the traditionary awe that had gathered over this instrument of music, and the dirges which spiritual fingers were said to play on it—the devoted sister had solemn thoughts of thrumming on its chords for Clifford's benefit, and accompanying the performance with her voice. Poor Clifford! Poor Hepzibah! Poor harpsichord! All three would have been miserable together. By some good agency—possibly, by the unrecognized interposition of the long-buried Alice, herself—the threatening calamity was averted.

But the worst of all—the hardest stroke of fate for Hepzibah to endure, and perhaps for Clifford too—was his invincible distaste for her appearance. Her features, never the most agreeable, and now harsh with age and grief, and resentment against the world for his sake; her dress, and especially her turban; the queer and quaint manners, which had unconsciously grown upon her in solitude;—such being the poor gentlewoman's outward characteristics, it is no great marvel, although the mournfullest of pities, that the instinctive lover of the Beautiful was fain to turn away his eyes! There was no help for it. It would be the latest impulse to die within him. In his last extremity, the expiring breath stealing faintly through Clifford's lips, he would doubtless press Hepzibah's hand, in fervent recognition of all her lavished love, and close his eyes—but not so much to die, as to be constrained to look no longer on her face! Poor Hepzibah! She took counsel with herself what might be done, and thought of putting ribbons on her turban, but, by the instant rush of several guardian angels, was withheld from an experiment, that could hardly have proved less than fatal to the beloved object of her anxiety.

To be brief, besides Hepzibah's disadvantages of person, there was an uncouthness pervading all her deeds; a clumsy something, that could but ill adapt itself for use, and not at all for ornament. She was a grief to Clifford, and she knew it. In this extremity, the antiquated virgin turned to Phoebe. No grovelling jealousy was in her heart. Had it pleased Heaven to crown the heroic fidelity of her life by making her personally the medium of Clifford's happiness, it would have rewarded her for all the past, by a joy with no bright tints, indeed, but deep and true, and worth a thousand gayer ecstacies. This could not be. She therefore turned to Phoebe, and resigned the task into the young girl's hands. The latter took it up, cheerfully, as she did everything, but with no sense of a mission to perform, and succeeding all the better for that same simplicity.

By the involuntary effect of a genial temperament, Phoebe soon grew to be absolutely essential to the daily comfort, if not the daily life, of her two forlorn companions. The grime and sordidness of the House of the Seven Gables seemed to have vanished, since her appearance there; the gnawing tooth of the dry-rot was stayed, among the old timbers of its skeleton-frame; the dust had ceased to settle down so densely from the antique ceilings, upon the floors and furniture of the rooms below;—or, at any rate, there was a little housewife, as light-footed as the breeze that sweeps a garden-walk, gliding hither and thither, to brush it all away. The shadows

of gloomy events, that haunted the else lonely and desolate apartments; the heavy, breathless scent which Death had
left in more than one of the bed-chambers, ever since his
visits of long ago;—these were less powerful than the purify-
ing influence, scattered throughout the atmosphere of the
household by the presence of one, youthful, fresh, and thoroughly wholesome heart. There was no morbidness in
Phoebe; if there had been, the old Pyncheon-house was the
very locality to ripen it into incurable disease. But, now, her
spirit resembled, in its potency, a minute quantity of attar of
rose in one of Hepzibah's huge, iron-bound trunks, diffusing
its fragrance through the various articles of linen and wrought-
lace, kerchiefs, caps, stockings, folded dresses, gloves, and
whatever else was treasured there. As every article in the
great trunk was the sweeter for the rose-scent, so did all the
thoughts and emotions of Hepzibah and Clifford, sombre as
they might seem, acquire a subtle attribute of happiness from
Phoebe's intermixture with them. Her activity of body, intellect, and heart, impelled her continually to perform the ordinary little toils that offered themselves around her, and to
think the thought, proper for the moment, and to sympathize
—now with the twittering gaiety of the robins in the pear-
tree—and now, to such depth as she could, with Hepzibah's
dark anxiety, or the vague moan of her brother. This facile
adaptation was at once the symptom of perfect health, and
its best preservative.

A nature like Phoebe's has invariably its due influence,
but is seldom regarded with due honor. Its spiritual force,
however, may be partially estimated by the fact of her having
found a place for herself, amid circumstances so stern, as
those which surrounded the mistress of the house; and also
by the effect which she produced on a character of so much
more mass than her own. For the gaunt, bony frame and
limbs of Hepzibah, as compared with the tiny lightsomeness
of Phoebe's figure, were perhaps in some fit proportion with

the moral weight and substance, respectively, of the woman and the girl.

To the guest—to Hepzibah's brother—or Cousin Clifford, as Phoebe now began to call him—she was especially necessary. Not that he could ever be said to converse with her, or often manifest, in any other very definite mode, his sense of a charm in her society. But, if she were a long while absent, he became pettish and nervously restless, pacing the room to-and-fro, with the uncertainty that characterized all his movements; or else would sit broodingly in his great chair, resting his head on his hands, and evincing life only by an electric sparkle of ill-humor, whenever Hepzibah endeavored to arouse him. Phoebe's presence, and the contiguity of her fresh life to his blighted one, was usually all that he required. Indeed, such was the native gush and play of her spirit, that she was seldom perfectly quiet and undemonstrative, any more than a fountain ever ceases to dimple and warble with its flow. She possessed the gift of song, and that too so naturally, that you would as little think of inquiring whence she had caught it, or what master had taught her, as of asking the same questions about a bird, in whose small strain of music we recognize the voice of the Creator, as distinctly as in the loudest accents of His thunder. So long as Phoebe sang, she might stray at her own will about the house. Clifford was content, whether the sweet, airy homeliness of her tones came down from the upper chambers, or along the passage-way from the shop, or was sprinkled through the foliage of the pear-tree, inward from the garden, with the twinkling sunbeams. He would sit quietly, with a gentle pleasure gleaming over his face, brighter now, and now a little dimmer, as the song happened to float near him, or was more remotely heard. It pleased him best, however, when she sat on a low footstool at his knee.

It is perhaps remarkable, considering her temperament, that Phoebe oftener chose a strain of pathos than of gaiety.

But the young and happy are not ill-pleased to temper their life with a transparent shadow. The deepest pathos of Phoebe's voice and song, moreover, came sifted through the golden texture of a cheery spirit, and was somehow so interfused with the quality thence acquired, that one's heart felt all the lighter for having wept at it. Broad mirth, in the sacred presence of dark misfortune, would have jarred harshly and irreverently with the solemn symphony, that rolled its undertone through Hepzibah's and her brother's life. Therefore it was well that Phoebe so often chose sad themes, and not amiss that they ceased to be so sad, while she was singing them.

Becoming habituated to her companionship, Clifford readily showed how capable of imbibing pleasant tints, and gleams of cheerful light from all quarters, his nature must originally have been. He grew youthful, while she sat by him. A beauty—not precisely real, even in its utmost manifestation, and which a painter would have watched long to seize, and fix upon his canvass, and, after all, in vain—beauty, nevertheless, that was not a mere dream, would sometimes play upon and illuminate his face. It did more than to illuminate; it transfigured him with an expression that could only be interpreted as the glow of an exquisite and happy spirit. That gray hair, and those furrows—with their record of infinite sorrow, so deeply written across his brow, and so compressed, as with a futile effort to crowd in all the tale, that the whole inscription was made illegible— these, for the moment, vanished. An eye, at once tender and acute, might have beheld in the man some shadow of what he was meant to be. Anon, as age came stealing, like a sad twilight, back over his figure, you would have felt tempted to hold an argument with Destiny, and affirm, that either this being should not have been made mortal, or mortal existence should have been tempered to his qualities. There seemed no necessity for his having drawn breath, at all;—the world never wanted him;—but, as he had breathed, it ought always to have been the balmiest of summer air. The same perplexity will invariably haunt us with regard to natures, that tend to feed exclusively upon the Beautiful, let their earthly fate be as lenient as it may.

Phoebe, it is probable, had but a very imperfect comprehension of the character, over which she had thrown so beneficent a spell. Nor was it necessary. The fire upon the hearth can gladden a whole semi-circle of faces roundabout it, but need not know the individuality of one among them all. Indeed, there was something too fine and delicate in Clifford's traits, to be perfectly appreciated by one whose sphere lay so much in the Actual as Phoebe's did. For Clifford, however, the reality, and simplicity, and thorough homeliness of the girl's nature, were as powerful a charm as any that she possessed. Beauty, it is true, and beauty almost perfect in its own style, was indispensable. Had Phoebe been coarse in feature, shaped clumsily, of a harsh voice, and uncouthly mannered, she might have been rich with all good gifts, beneath this unfortunate exterior; and still, so long as she wore the guise of woman, she would have shocked Clifford and depressed him by her lack of beauty. But nothing more beautiful—nothing prettier, at least—was ever made, than Phoebe. And, therefore, to this man—whose whole poor and impalpable enjoyment of existence, heretofore, and until both his heart and fancy died within him, had been a dream —whose images of women had more and more lost their warmth and substance, and been frozen, like the pictures of secluded artists, into the chillest ideality—to him, this little figure of the cheeriest household-life was just what he required, to bring him back into the breathing world. Persons who have wandered, or been expelled, out of the common track of things, even were it for a better system, desire nothing so much as to be led back. They shiver in their loneliness, be it on a mountain-top or in a dungeon. Now, Phoebe's presence made a home about her—that very sphere which the outcast, the prisoner, the potentate, the wretch beneath mankind, the wretch aside from it, or the wretch above it, instinctively pines after—a home! She was real! Holding her hand, you felt something; a tender something; a substance, and a warm one; and so long as you should feel its grasp, soft as it was, you might be certain that your place was good in the whole sympathetic chain of human nature. The world was no longer a delusion.

By looking a little farther in this direction, we might suggest an explanation of an often suggested mystery. Why are poets so apt to choose their mates, not for any similarity of poetic endowment, but for qualities which might make the happiness of the rudest handicraftsman, as well as that of the ideal craftsman of the spirit? Because, probably, at his highest elevation, the poet needs no human intercourse; but he finds it dreary to descend, and be a stranger.

There was something very beautiful in the relation that grew up between this pair; so closely and constantly linked together, yet with such a waste of gloomy and mysterious years from his birth-day to hers. On Clifford's part, it was the feeling of a man naturally endowed with the liveliest sensibility to feminine influence, but who had never quaffed the cup of passionate love, and knew that it was now too late. He knew it, with the instinctive delicacy that had survived his intellectual decay. Thus, his sentiment for Phoebe, without being paternal, was not less chaste than if she had been his daughter. He was a man, it is true, and recognized her as a woman. She was his only representative of womankind. He took unfailing note of every charm that appertained to her sex, and saw the ripeness of her lips, and the virginal developement of her bosom. All her little, womanly ways, budding out of her like blossoms on a young fruit-tree, had their effect on him, and sometimes caused his very heart to tingle with the keenest thrills of pleasure. At such moments—

for the effect was seldom more than momentary—the half-torpid man would be full of harmonious life, just as a long-silent harp is full of sound, when the musician's fingers sweep across it. But, after all, it seemed rather a perception, or a sympathy, than a sentiment belonging to himself as an individual. He read Phoebe, as he would a sweet and simple story; he listened to her, as if she were a verse of household poetry, which God, in requital of his bleak and dismal lot, had permitted some angel, that most pitied him, to warble through the house. She was not an actual fact for him, but the interpretation of all that he had lacked on earth, brought warmly home to his conception; so that this mere symbol or lifelike picture had almost the comfort of reality.

But we strive in vain to put the idea into words. No adequate expression of the beauty and profound pathos, with which it impresses us, is attainable. This being, made only for happiness, and heretofore so miserably failing to be happy —his tendencies so hideously thwarted, that, some unknown time ago, the delicate springs of his character, never morally or intellectually strong, had given way, and he was now imbecile—this poor, forlorn voyager from the Islands of the Blest, in a frail bark, on a tempestuous sea, had been flung, by the last mountain-wave of his shipwreck, into a quiet harbor. There, as he lay more than half-lifeless on the strand, the fragrance of an earthly rosebud had come to his nostrils, and, as odors will, had summoned up reminiscences or visions of all the living and breathing beauty, amid which he should have had his home. With his native susceptibility of happy influences, he inhales the slight, ethereal rapture into his soul, and expires!

And how did Phoebe regard Clifford? The girl's was not one of those natures which are most attracted by what is strange and exceptional in human character. The path, which would best have suited her, was the well-worn track of ordinary life; the companions, in whom she would most have delighted, were such as one encounters at every turn. The mystery which enveloped Clifford, so far as it affected her at all, was an annoyance, rather than the piquant charm which many women might have found in it. Still, her native kindliness was brought strongly into play, not by what was darkly picturesque in his situation, nor so much even by the finer grace of his character, as by the simple appeal of a heart so forlorn as his, to one so full of genuine sympathy as hers. She gave him an affectionate regard, because he needed so much love, and seemed to have received so little. With a ready tact, the result of ever-active and wholesome sensibility, she discerned what was good for him, and did it. Whatever was morbid in his mind and experience, she ignored, and thereby kept their intercourse healthy by the incautious, but, as it were, heaven-directed freedom of her whole conduct. The sick in mind, and perhaps in body, are rendered more darkly and hopelessly so, by the manifold reflection of their disease, mirrored back from all quarters, in the deportment of those about them; they are compelled to inhale the poison of their own breath, in infinite repetition. But Phoebe afforded her poor patient a supply of purer air. She impregnated it, too, not with a wild-flower scent—for wildness was no trait of hers—but with the perfume of garden-roses, pinks, and other blossoms of much sweetness, which nature and man have consented together in making grow, from summer to summer, and from century to century. Such a flower was Phoebe, in her relation with Clifford, and such the delight that he inhaled from her.

Yet, it must be said, her petals sometimes drooped a little, in consequence of the heavy atmosphere about her. She grew more thoughtful than heretofore. Looking aside at Clifford's face, and seeing the dim, unsatisfactory elegance, and the intellect almost quenched, she would try to inquire what had been his life. Was he always thus? Had this veil been over him from his birth?—this veil, under which far more of his spirit was hidden than revealed, and through which he so imperfectly discerned the actual world—or was its gray texture woven of some dark calamity? Phoebe loved no riddles, and would have been glad to escape the perplexity of this one. Nevertheless, there was so far a good result of her meditations on Clifford's character, that, when her involuntary conjectures, together with the tendency of every strange circumstance to tell its own story, had gradually taught her the fact, it had no terrible effect upon her. Let the world have done him what vast wrong it might, she knew Cousin Clifford too well—or fancied so—ever to shudder at the touch of his thin, delicate fingers.

Within a few days after the appearance of this remarkable inmate, the routine of life had established itself with a good deal of uniformity in the old house of our narrative. In the morning, very shortly after breakfast, it was Clifford's custom to fall asleep in his chair; nor, unless accidentally disturbed, would he emerge from a dense cloud of slumber, or the thinner mists that flitted to-and-fro, until well towards noonday. These hours of drowsyhead were the season of the old gentlewoman's attendance on her brother, while Phoebe took charge of the shop; an arrangement which the public speedily understood, and evinced their decided preference of the younger shopwoman by the multiplicity of their calls, during her administration of affairs. Dinner over, Hepzibah took her knitting-work—a long stocking of gray yarn, for her brother's winter-wear—and with a sigh, and a scowl of affectionate farewell to Clifford, and a gesture enjoining watchfulness on Phoebe, went to take her seat behind the counter. It was now the young girl's turn to be the nurse, the guardian, the playmate—or whatever is the fitter phrase—of the gray haired man.

X

THE PYNCHEON-GARDEN

CLIFFORD, except for Phoebe's more active instigation, would ordinarily have yielded to the torpor which had crept through all his modes of being, and which sluggishly counselled him to sit in his morning chair, till eventide. But the girl seldom failed to propose a removal to the garden, where Uncle Venner and the Daguerreotypist had made such repairs on the roof of the ruinous arbor, or summer-house, that it was now a sufficient shelter from sunshine and casual showers. The hop-vine, too, had begun to grow luxuriantly over the sides of the little edifice, and made an interior of verdant seclusion, with innumerable peeps and glimpses into the wider solitude of the garden.

Here, sometimes, in this green play-place of flickering light, Phoebe read to Clifford. Her acquaintance, the artist, who appeared to have a literary turn, had supplied her with works of fiction, in pamphlet-form, and a few volumes of poetry, in altogether a different style and taste from those which Hepzibah selected for his amusement. Small thanks were due to the books, however, if the girl's readings were in any degree more successful than her elderly cousin's. Phoebe's voice had always a pretty music in it, and could either enliven Clifford, by its sparkle and gaiety of tone, or soothe him by a continued flow of pebbly and brook-like cadences. But the fictions—in which the country-girl, unused to works of that nature, often became deeply absorbed—interested her strange auditor very little, or not at all. Pictures of life, scenes of passion or sentiment, wit, humor, and pathos, were all thrown away, or worse than thrown away, on Clifford; either because he lacked an experience by which to test their truth, or because his own griefs were a touch-stone of reality that few feigned emotions could withstand. When Phoebe broke into a peal of merry laughter at what she read, he would now and then laugh for sympathy, but oftener respond with a troubled, questioning look. If a tear—a maiden's sunshiny tear, over imaginary woe—dropt upon some melancholy page, Clifford either took it as a token of actual calamity, or else grew peevish, and angrily motioned her to close the volume. And wisely, too! Is not the world sad enough, in genuine earnest, without making a pastime of mock-sorrows?

With poetry, it was rather better. He delighted in the swell and subsidence of the rhythm, and the happily recurring rhyme. Nor was Clifford incapable of feeling the sentiment of poetry—not perhaps where it was highest or deepest—but where it was most flitting and ethereal. It was impossible to foretell in what exquisite verse the awakening spell might lurk; but, on raising her eyes from the page to Clifford's face, Phoebe would be made aware, by the light breaking through it, that a more delicate intelligence than her own had caught a lambent flame from what she read. One glow of this kind, however, was often the precursor of gloom, for many hours afterward, because, when the glow left him, he seemed conscious of a missing sense and power, and groped about for them, as if a blind man should go seeking his lost eyesight.

It pleased him more, and was better for his inward welfare, that Phoebe should talk, and make passing occurrences vivid to his mind by her accompanying description and remarks. The life of the garden offered topics enough for such discourse as suited Clifford best. He never failed to inquire what flowers had bloomed, since yesterday. His feeling for flowers was very exquisite, and seemed not so much a taste, as an emotion; he was fond of sitting with one in his hand, intently observing it, and looking from its petals into Phoebe's face, as if the garden-flower were the sister of the household-maiden. Not merely was there a delight in the flower's perfume, or pleasure in its beautiful form, and the delicacy or brightness of its hue; but Clifford's enjoyment was accompanied with a perception of life, character, and individuality, that made him love these blossoms of the garden, as if they were endowed with sentiment and intelligence. This affection and sympathy for flowers is almost exclusively a woman's trait. Men, if endowed with it by nature, soon lose, forget, and learn to despise it, in their contact with coarser things than flowers. Clifford, too, had long forgotten it, but found it again, now, as he slowly revived from the chill torpor of his life.

It is wonderful how many pleasant incidents continually came to pass in that secluded garden-spot, when once Phoebe had set herself to look for them. She had seen or heard a bee there, on the first day of her acquaintance with the place. And often—almost continually, indeed—since then, the bees kept coming thither, Heaven knows why, or by what pertinacious desire for far-fetched sweets; when, no doubt, there were broad clover-fields, and all kinds of garden-growth, much nearer home than this. Thither the bees came, however, and plunged into the squash-blossoms, as if there were no other squash-vines within a long day's flight, or as if the soil of Hepzibah's garden gave its productions just the very quality which these laborious little wizards wanted, in order to impart the Hymettus odor to their whole hive of New England honey. When Clifford heard their sunny, buzzing murmur, in the heart of the great, yellow blossoms, he looked about him with a joyful sense of warmth, and blue sky, and green grass, and of God's free air in the whole height from earth to heaven. After all, there need be no question why the bees came to that one green nook, in the dusty town. God sent them thither to gladden our poor Clifford! They brought the rich summer with them, in requital of a little honey.

When the bean-vines began to flower on the poles, there was one particular variety which bore a vivid scarlet blossom. The Daguerreotypist had found these beans in a garret, over one of the seven gables, treasured up in an old chest of drawers by some horticultural Pyncheon of days gone-by, who doubtless meant to sow them, the next summer, but was himself first sown in Death's garden-ground. By way of testing whether there was still a living germ in such ancient seeds, Holgrave had planted some of them; and the result of his experiment was a splendid row of bean-vines, clambering early to the full height of the poles, and arraying them, from top to bottom, in a spiral profusion of red blossoms. And, ever since the unfolding of the first bud, a multitude of humming-birds had been attracted thither. At times, it seemed as if, for every one of the hundred blossoms, there was one of these tiniest fowls of the air, a thumb's bigness of burnished plumage, hovering and vibrating about the bean-poles. It was with indescribable interest, and even more than childish delight, that Clifford watched the humming-birds. He used to thrust his head softly out of the arbor, to see them the better; all the while, too, motioning Phoebe to be quiet, and snatching glimpses of the smile upon her face, so as to heap his enjoyment up the higher with her sympathy. He had not merely grown young; he was a child again.

Hepzibah, whenever she happened to witness one of these fits of miniature enthusiasm, would shake her head, with a strange mingling of the mother and sister, and of pleasure and sadness, in her aspect. She said that it had always been thus with Clifford, when the humming-birds came—always, from his babyhood—and that his delight in them had been one of the earliest tokens by which he showed his love for beautiful things. And it was a wonderful coincidence, the good lady thought, that the artist should have planted these scarlet-flowering beans—which the humming-birds sought, far and wide, and which had not grown in the Pyncheon-garden before, for forty years—on the very summer of Clifford's return.

Then would the tears stand in poor Hepzibah's eyes, or overflow them with a too abundant gush, so that she was fain to betake herself into some corner, lest Clifford should espy her agitation. Indeed, all the enjoyments of this period were provocative of tears. Coming so late as it did, it was a kind of Indian summer, with a mist in its balmiest sunshine, and decay and death in its gaudiest delight. The more Clifford seemed to taste the happiness of a child, the sadder was the difference to be recognized. With a mysterious and terrible Past, which had annihilated his memory, and a blank Future before him, he had only this visionary and impalpable Now, which, if you once look closely at it, is nothing. He himself, as was perceptible by many symptoms, lay darkly behind his pleasure, and knew it to be a baby-play, which he was to toy and trifle with, instead of thoroughly believing. Clifford saw, it may be, in the mirror of his deeper consciousness, that he was an example and representative of that great chaos of people, whom an inexplicable Providence is continually putting at cross-purposes with the world; breaking what seems its own promise in their nature; withholding their proper food, and setting poison before them for a banquet; and thus—when it might so easily, as one would think, have been adjusted otherwise—making their existence a strangeness, a solitude, and torment. All his life long, he had been learning how to be wretched, as one learns a foreign tongue; and now, with the lesson thoroughly at heart, he could with difficulty comprehend his little, airy happiness. Frequently, there was a dim shadow of doubt in his eyes.—"Take my hand, Phoebe," he would say, "and pinch it hard with your little fingers! Give me a rose, that I may press its thorns, and prove myself awake, by the sharp touch of pain!"—Evidently, he desired this prick of a trifling anguish, in order to assure himself, by that quality which he best knew to be real, that the garden, and the seven weather-beaten gables, and Hepzibah's scowl and Phoebe's smile, were real, likewise. Without this signet in his flesh, he could have attributed no more substance to them, than to the empty confusion of imaginary scenes with which he had fed his spirit, until even that poor sustenance was exhausted.

The author needs great faith in his reader's sympathy; else he must hesitate to give details so minute, and incidents apparently so trifling, as are essential to make up the idea of this garden-life. It was the Eden of a thunder-smitten Adam, who had fled for refuge thither out of the same dreary and perilous wilderness, into which the original Adam was expelled.

One of the available means of amusement, of which Phoebe made the most, in Clifford's behalf, was that feathered society, the hens, a breed of whom, as we have already said, was an immemorial heirloom in the Pyncheon family. In compliance with a whim of Clifford, as it troubled him to see them in confinement, they had been set at liberty, and now roamed at will about the garden; doing some little mischief, but hindered from escape by buildings, on three sides, and the difficult peaks of a wooden fence, on the other. They spent much of their abundant leisure on the margin of Maule's Well, which was haunted by a kind of snail, evidently a tidbit to their palates; and the brackish water itself, however nauseous to the rest of the world, was so greatly esteemed by these fowls, that they might be seen tasting, turning up their heads, and smacking their bills, with precisely the air of wine-bibbers round a probationary cask. Their generally quiet, yet often brisk, and constantly diversified talk, one to another, or sometimes in soliloquy—as they scratched worms out of the rich, black soil, or pecked at such plants as suited their taste—had such a domestic tone, that it was almost a wonder why you could not establish a regular interchange of ideas about household matters, human and gallinaceous. All hens are well-worth studying, for the piquancy and rich variety of their manners; but by no possibility can there have been other fowls, of such odd appearance and deportment as these ancestral ones. They probably embodied the traditionary peculiarities of their whole line of progenitors, derived through an unbroken succession of eggs; or else this individual Chanticleer and his two wives had grown to be humorists, and a little crack-brained withal, on account of their solitary way of life, and out of sympathy for Hepzibah, their lady-patroness.

Queerly indeed they looked! Chanticleer himself, though stalking on two stilt-like legs, with the dignity of interminable descent in all his gestures, was hardly bigger than an ordinary partridge; his two wives were about the size of quails; and as for the one chicken, it looked small enough to be still in the egg, and, at the same time, sufficiently old, withered, wizened, and experienced, to have been the founder of the antiquated race. Instead of being the youngest of the family, it rather seemed to have aggregated into itself the ages, not only of these living specimens of the breed, but of all its forefathers and fore-mothers, whose united excellencies and oddities were squeezed into its little body. Its mother evidently regarded it as the one chicken of the world, and as necessary, in fact, to the world's continuance, or, at any rate, to the equilibrium of the present system of affairs, whether in church or state. No lesser sense of the infant fowl's importance could have justified, even in a mother's eyes, the perseverance with which she watched over its safety, ruffling her small person to twice its proper size, and flying in everybody's face that so much as looked towards her hopeful

progeny. No lower estimate could have vindicated the indefatigable zeal with which she scratched, and her unscrupu-
lousness in digging up the choicest flower or vegetable, for
the sake of the fat earth-worm at its root. Her nervous cluck,
when the chicken happened to be hidden in the long grass
or under the squash-leaves; her gentle croak of satisfaction,
while sure of it beneath her wing; her note of ill-concealed
fear and obstreperous defiance, when she saw her arch-enemy,
a neighbor's cat, on the top of the high fence;—one or other
of these sounds was to be heard at almost every moment of
the day. By degrees, the observer came to feel nearly as much
interest in this chicken of illustrious race, as the mother-
hen did.

Phoebe, after getting well acquainted with the old hen,
was sometimes permitted to take the chicken in her hand,
which was quite capable of grasping its cubic inch or two
of body. While she curiously examined its hereditary marks—
the peculiar speckle of its plumage, the funny tuft on its
head, and a knob on each of its legs—the little biped, as she
insisted, kept giving her a sagacious wink. The Daguerreotypist once whispered her, that these marks betokened the
oddities of the Pyncheon family, and that the chicken itself
was a symbol of the life of the old house; embodying its interpretation, likewise, although an unintelligible one, as such
clues generally are. It was a feathered riddle; a mystery
hatched out of an egg, and just as mysterious as if the egg
had been addle!

The second of Chanticleer's two wives, ever since Phoebe's
arrival, had been in a state of heavy despondency, caused,
as it afterwards appeared, by her inability to lay an egg. One
day, however, by her self-important gait, the sideway turn
of her head, and the cock of her eye, as she pried into one
and another nook of the garden—croaking to herself, all the
while, with inexpressible complacency—it was made evident
that this identical hen, much as mankind undervalued her,

carried something about her person, the worth of which was not to be estimated either in gold or precious stones. Shortly after, there was a prodigious cackling and gratulation of Chanticleer and all his family, including the wizened chicken, who appeared to understand the matter, quite as well as did his sire, his mother, or his aunt. That afternoon, Phoebe found a diminutive egg—not in the regular nest—it was far too precious to be trusted there—but cunningly hidden under the currant-bushes, on some dry stalks of last year's grass. Hepzibah, on learning the fact, took possession of the egg and appropriated it to Clifford's breakfast, on account of a certain delicacy of flavor, for which, as she affirmed, these eggs had always been famous. Thus unscrupulously did the old gentlewoman sacrifice the continuance, perhaps, of an ancient feathered race, with no better end than to supply her brother with a dainty that hardly filled the bowl of a teaspoon! It must have been in reference to this outrage, that Chanticleer, the next day, accompanied by the bereaved mother of the egg, took his post in front of Phoebe and Clifford, and delivered himself of a harangue that might have proved as long as his own pedigree, but for a fit of merriment on Phoebe's part. Hereupon, the offended fowl stalked away on his long stilts, and utterly withdrew his notice from Phoebe and the rest of human nature; until she made her peace with an offering of spice-cake, which, next to snails, was the delicacy most in favor with his aristocratic taste.

We linger too long, no doubt, beside this paltry rivulet of life that flowed through the garden of the Pyncheon-house. But we deem it pardonable to record these mean incidents, and poor delights, because they proved so greatly to Clifford's benefit. They had the earth-smell in them, and contributed to give him health and substance. Some of his occupations wrought less desirably upon him. He had a singular propensity, for example, to hang over Maule's Well, and look at the constantly shifting phantasmagoria of figures, produced by the agitation of the water over the mosaic-work of colored pebbles, at the bottom. He said that faces looked upward to him there—beautiful faces, arrayed in bewitching smiles—each momentary face so fair and rosy, and every smile so sunny, that he felt wronged at its departure, until the same flitting witchcraft made a new one. But sometimes he would suddenly cry out—"The dark face gazes at me!"—and be miserable, the whole day afterwards. Phoebe, when she hung over the fountain by Clifford's side, could see nothing of all this—neither the beauty nor the ugliness—but only the colored pebbles, looking as if the gush of the water shook and disarranged them. And the dark face, that so troubled Clifford, was no more than the shadow, thrown from a branch of one of the damson-trees, and breaking the inner light of Maule's Well. The truth was, however, that his fancy—reviving faster than his will and judgement, and always stronger than they—created shapes of loveliness that were symbolic of his native character, and now and then a stern and dreadful shape, that typified his fate.

On Sundays, after Phoebe had been at church—for the girl had a church-going conscience, and would hardly have been at ease, had she missed either prayer, singing, sermon, or benediction—after church-time, therefore, there was ordinarily a sober little festival in the garden. In addition to Clifford, Hepzibah, and Phoebe, two guests made up the company. One was the artist, Holgrave, who, in spite of his consociation with reformers, and his other queer and questionable traits, continued to hold an elevated place in Hepzibah's regard. The other, we are almost ashamed to say, was the venerable Uncle Venner, in a clean shirt, and a broadcloth coat, more respectable than his ordinary wear; inasmuch as it was neatly patched on each elbow, and might be called an entire garment, except for a slight inequality in the length of its skirts. Clifford, on several occasions, had seemed to enjoy the old man's intercourse, for the sake of his mellow, cheerful vein, which was like the sweet flavor of a frost-bitten apple, such as one picks up under the tree, in December. A man, at the very lowest point of the social scale, was easier and more agreeable for the fallen gentleman to encounter, than a person at any of the intermediate degrees; and, moreover, as Clifford's young manhood had been lost, he was fond of feeling himself comparatively youthful, now, in apposition with the patriarchal age of Uncle Venner. In fact, it was sometimes observable, that Clifford half wilfully hid from himself the consciousness of being stricken in years, and cherished visions of an earthly future still before him; visions, however, too indistinctly drawn to be followed by disappointment—though, doubtless, by depression—when any casual incident or recollection made him sensible of the withered leaf.

So this oddly composed little social party used to assemble under the ruinous arbor. Hepzibah—stately as ever, at heart, and yielding not an inch of her old gentility, but resting upon it so much the more, as justifying a princesslike condescension —exhibited a not ungraceful hospitality. She talked kindly to the vagrant artist, and took sage counsel, lady as she was, with the wood-sawyer, the messenger of everybody's petty errands, the patched philosopher. And Uncle Venner, who had studied the world at street-corners, and at other posts equally well adapted for just observation, was as ready to give out his wisdom as a town-pump to give water.

"Miss Hepzibah, Ma'am," said he once, after they had all been cheerful together, "I really enjoy these quiet little meetings, of a Sabbath afternoon. They are very much like what I expect to have, after I retire to my farm!"

"Uncle Venner," observed Clifford, in a drowsy, inward tone, "is always talking about his farm. But I have a better scheme for him, by-and-by. We shall see!"

"Ah, Mr. Clifford Pyncheon," said the man of patches, "you may scheme for me as much as you please; but I'm not going to give up this one scheme of my own, even if I never bring it really to pass. It does seem to me that men make a wonderful mistake in trying to heap up property upon property. If I had done so, I should feel as if Providence was not bound to take care of me; and, at all events, the city wouldn't be! I'm one of those people who think that Infinity is big enough for us all—and Eternity long enough!"

"Why, so they are, Uncle Venner," remarked Phoebe after a pause; for she had been trying to fathom the profundity and appositeness of this concluding apothegm. "But, for this short life of ours, one would like a house and a moderate garden-spot of one's own."

"It appears to me," said the Daguerreotypist smiling, "that Uncle Venner has the principles of Fourier at the bottom of his wisdom; only they have not quite so much distinctness, in his mind, as in that of the systematizing Frenchman."

"Come, Phoebe," said Hepzibah, "it is time to bring the currants."

And then, while the yellow richness of the declining sunshine still fell into the open space of the garden, Phoebe brought out a loaf of bread, and a China bowl of currants, freshly gathered from the bushes, and crushed with sugar. These, with water—but not from the fountain of ill-omen, close at hand—constituted all the entertainment. Meanwhile, Holgrave took some pains to establish an intercourse with Clifford; actuated, it might seem, entirely by an impulse of kindliness, in order that the present hour might be cheerfuller than most which the poor recluse had spent, or was destined yet to spend. Nevertheless, in the artist's deep, thoughtful, all-observant eyes, there was now-and-then an expression, not sinister, but questionable; as if he had some other interest in the scene than a stranger, a youthful and unconnected adventurer, might be supposed to have. With great mobility of outward mood, however, he applied himself to the task of enlivening the party, and with so much success, that even dark-hued Hepzibah threw off one tint of melancholy, and made what shift she could with the remaining portion. Phoebe said to herself—"How pleasant he can be!" As for Uncle Venner, as a mark of friendship and approbation, he readily consented to afford the young man his countenance in the way of his profession—not metaphorically, be it understood—but literally, by allowing a daguerreotype of his face, so familiar to the town, to be exhibited at the entrance of Holgrave's studio.

Clifford, as the company partook of their little banquet, grew to be the gayest of them all. Either it was one of those up-quivering flashes of the spirit, to which minds in an abnormal state are liable; or else the artist had subtly touched some chord that made musical vibration. Indeed, what with the pleasant summer-evening, and the sympathy of this little circle of not unkindly souls, it was perhaps natural that a character so susceptible as Clifford's should become animated, and show itself readily responsive to what was said around him. But he gave out his own thoughts, likewise, with an airy and fanciful glow; so that they glistened, as it were, through the arbor, and made their escape among the interstices of the foliage. He had been as cheerful, no doubt, while alone with Phoebe, but never with such tokens of acute, although partial intelligence.

But, as the sunlight left the peaks of the seven gables, so did the excitement fade out of Clifford's eyes. He gazed vaguely and mournfully about him, as if he missed something precious, and missed it the more drearily for not knowing precisely what it was.

"I want my happiness!" at last he murmured hoarsely and indistinctly, hardly shaping out the words. "Many, many years have I waited for it! It is late! It is late! I want my happiness!"

Alas, poor Clifford! You are old, and worn with troubles that ought never to have befallen you. You are partly crazy, and partly imbecile; a ruin, a failure, as almost everybody is—though some in less degree, or less perceptibly, than their fellows. Fate has no happiness in store for you; unless your quiet home in the old family residence, with the faithful Hepzibah, and your long summer-afternoons with Phoebe, and these Sabbath festivals with Uncle Venner and the Daguerreotypist, deserve to be called happiness! Why not? If not the thing itself, it is marvellously like it, and the more so for that ethereal and intangible quality, which causes it all to vanish, at too close an introspection. Take it, therefore, while you may. Murmur not—question not—but make the most of it!

XI

THE ARCHED WINDOW

FROM the inertness, or what we may term the vegetative character of his ordinary mood, Clifford would perhaps have been content to spend one day after another, interminably—or, at least throughout the summer-time—in just the kind of life described in the preceding pages. Fancying, however, that it might be for his benefit occasionally to diversify the scene, Phoebe sometimes suggested that he should look out upon the life of the street. For this purpose, they used to mount the staircase together, to the second story of the house, where, at the termination of a wide entry, there was an arched window of uncommonly large dimensions, shaded by a pair of curtains. It opened above the porch, where there had formerly been a balcony, the balustrade of which had long since gone to decay, and been removed. At this arched window, throwing it open, but keeping himself in comparative obscurity by means of the curtain, Clifford had an opportunity of witnessing such a portion of the great world's movement, as might be supposed to roll through one of the retired streets of a not very populous city. But he and Phoebe made a sight as well worth seeing as any that the city could exhibit. The pale, gray, childish, aged, melancholy, yet often simply cheerful, and sometimes delicately intelligent, aspect of Clifford, peering from behind the faded crim-

son of the curtain—watching the monotony of every-day occurrences with a kind of inconsequential interest and earnestness—and, at every petty throb of his sensibility, turning for
sympathy to the eyes of the bright young girl!

If once he were fairly seated at the window, even Pyncheon-street would hardly be so dull and lonely but that,
somewhere or other along its extent, Clifford might discover
matter to occupy his eye, and titillate, if not engross, his observation. Things, familiar to the youngest child that had
begun its outlook at existence, seemed strange to him. A
cab; an omnibus, with its populous interior, dropping here-and-
there a passenger, and picking up another, and thus typifying
that vast rolling vehicle, the world, the end of whose journey
is everywhere, and nowhere;—these objects he followed
eagerly with his eyes, but forgot them, before the dust, raised
by the horses and wheels, had settled along their track. As
regarded novelties, (among which, cabs and omnibusses were
to be reckoned,) his mind appeared to have lost its proper
gripe and retentiveness. Twice or thrice, for example, during
the sunny hours of the day, a water-cart went along by the
Pyncheon-house, leaving a broad wake of moistened earth,
instead of the white dust that had risen at a lady's lightest
footfall; it was like a summer-shower, which the city-authori-
ties had caught and tamed, and compelled it into the com-
monest routine of their convenience. With the water-cart
Clifford could never grow familiar; it always affected him
with just the same surprise as at first. His mind took an apparently sharp impression from it, but lost the recollection of
this perambulatory shower, before its next re-appearance, as
completely as did the street itself, along which the heat so
quickly strewed white dust again. It was the same with the
railroad. Clifford could hear the obstreperous howl of the
steam-devil, and, by leaning a little way from the arched
window, could catch a glimpse of the trains of cars, flashing
a brief transit across the extremity of the street. The idea of

terrible energy, thus forced upon him, was new at every recurrence, and seemed to affect him as disagreeably, and with almost as much surprise, the hundredth time as the first.

Nothing gives a sadder sense of decay, than this loss or suspension of the power to deal with unaccustomed things and to keep up with the swiftness of the passing moment. It can merely be a suspended animation; for, were the power actually to perish, there would be little use of immortality. We are less than ghosts, for the time being, whenever this calamity befalls us.

Clifford was indeed the most inveterate of conservatives. All the antique fashions of the street were dear to him; even such as were characterized by a rudeness that would naturally have annoyed his fastidious senses. He loved the old rumbling and jolting carts, the former track of which he still found in his long-buried remembrance, as the observer of to-day finds the wheel-tracks of ancient vehicles, in Herculaneum. The butcher's cart, with its snowy canopy, was an acceptable object; so was the fish-cart, heralded by its horn; so, likewise, was the countryman's cart of vegetables, plodding from door to door, with long pauses of the patient horse, while his owner drove a trade in turnips, carrots, summer-squashes, string-beans, green peas, and new potatoes, with half the housewives of the neighborhood. The baker's cart, with the harsh music of its bells, had a pleasant effect on Clifford, because, as few things else did, it jingled the very dissonance of yore. One afternoon, a scissor-grinder chanced to set his wheel a-going, under the Pyncheon-elm, and just in front of the arched window. Children came running with their mothers' scissors, or the carving-knife, or the paternal razor, or anything else that lacked an edge, (except, indeed, poor Clifford's wits,) that the grinder might apply the article to his magic wheel, and give it back as good as new. Round went the busily revolving machinery, kept in motion by the scissor-grinder's foot, and wore away the hard steel against the hard

stone, whence issued an intense and spiteful prolongation of
a hiss, as fierce as those emitted by Satan and his compeers
in Pandemonium, though squeezed into smaller compass. It
was an ugly, little, venomous serpent of a noise, as ever did
petty violence to human ears. But Clifford listened with
rapturous delight. The sound, however disagreeable, had
very brisk life in it, and, together with the circle of curious
children, watching the revolutions of the wheel, appeared to
give him a more vivid sense of active, bustling, and sunshiny
existence, than he had attained in almost any other way.
Nevertheless, its charm lay chiefly in the past; for the scissor-
grinder's wheel had hissed in his childish ears.

He sometimes made doleful complaint, that there were
no stage-coaches, now-a-days. And he asked, in an injured
tone, what had become of all those old square-top chaises,
with wings sticking out on either side, that used to be drawn
by a plough-horse, and driven by a farmer's wife and daughter, peddling whortle-berries and black-berries about the
town. Their disappearance made him doubt, he said, whether
the berries had not left off growing in the broad pastures, and
along the shady country-lanes.

But anything that appealed to the sense of beauty, in however humble a way, did not require to be recommended by
these old associations. This was observable, when one of those
Italian boys (who are rather a modern feature of our streets)
came along, with his barrel-organ, and stopt under the wide
and cool shadows of the elm. With his quick professional
eye, he took note of the two faces watching him from the
arched window, and, opening his instrument, began to scatter
its melodies abroad. He had a monkey on his shoulder,
dressed in a highland plaid; and, to complete the sum of
splendid attractions wherewith he presented himself to the
public, there was a company of little figures, whose sphere
and habitation was in the mahogany case of his organ, and
whose principle of life was the music, which the Italian

made it his business to grind out. In all their variety of occupation—the cobbler, the blacksmith, the soldier, the lady with
her fan, the toper with his bottle, the milk-maid sitting by
her cow—this fortunate little society might truly be said to
enjoy a harmonious existence, and to make life literally a
dance. The Italian turned a crank; and, behold! every one
of these small individuals started into the most curious vivacity. The cobbler wrought upon a shoe; the blacksmith
hammered his iron; the soldier waved his glittering blade;
the lady raised a tiny breeze with her fan; the jolly toper
swigged lustily at his bottle; a scholar opened his book, with
eager thirst for knowledge, and turned his head to-and-fro
along the page; the milk-maid energetically drained her cow;
and a miser counted gold into his strong-box;—all at the same
turning of a crank. Yes; and moved by the self-same impulse,
a lover saluted his mistress on her lips! Possibly, some cynic,
at once merry and bitter, had desired to signify, in this pantomimic scene, that we mortals, whatever our business or
amusement—however serious, however trifling—all dance to
one identical tune, and, in spite of our ridiculous activity,
bring nothing finally to pass. For the most remarkable aspect
of the affair was, that, at the cessation of the music, everybody was petrified at once, from the most extravagant life
into a dead torpor. Neither was the cobbler's shoe finished,
nor the blacksmith's iron shaped out; nor was there a drop
less of brandy in the toper's bottle, nor a drop more of milk
in the milk-maid's pail, nor one additional coin in the miser's
strong-box; nor was the scholar a page deeper in his book.
All were precisely in the same condition as before they made
themselves so ridiculous by their haste to toil, to enjoy, to
accumulate gold, and to become wise. Saddest of all, moreover, the lover was none the happier for the maiden's granted
kiss! But, rather than swallow this last too acrid ingredient,
we reject the whole moral of the show.

The monkey, meanwhile, with a thick tail curling out into

preposterous prolixity from beneath his tartans, took his station at the Italian's feet. He turned a wrinkled and abominable little visage to every passer-by, and to the circle of children that soon gathered round, and to Hepzibah's shopdoor, and upward to the arched window, whence Phoebe and Clifford were looking down. Every moment, also, he took off his highland bonnet, and performed a bow and scrape. Sometimes, moreover, he made personal application to individuals, holding out his small black palm, and otherwise plainly signifying his excessive desire for whatever filthy lucre might happen to be in anybody's pocket. The mean and low, yet strangely man-like expression of his wilted countenance; the prying and crafty glance, that showed him ready to gripe at every miserable advantage; his enormous tail, (too enormous to be decently concealed under his gabardine,) and the deviltry of nature which it betokened;—take this monkey just as he was, in short, and you could desire no better image of the Mammon of copper-coin, symbolizing the grossest form of the love of money. Neither was there any possibility of satisfying the covetous little devil. Phoebe threw down a whole handfull of cents, which he picked up with joyless eagerness, handed them over to the Italian for safe-keeping, and immediately re-commenced a series of pantomimic petitions for more.

Doubtless, more than one New-Englander—or let him be of what country he might, it is as likely to be the case—passed by, and threw a look at the monkey, and went on, without imagining how nearly his own moral condition was here exemplified. Clifford, however, was a being of another order. He had taken childish delight in the music, and smiled, too, at the figures which it set in motion. But, after looking awhile at the long-tailed imp, he was so shocked by his horrible ugliness, spiritual as well as physical, that he actually began to shed tears; a weakness which men of merely delicate endowments—and destitute of the fiercer, deeper, and more tragic power of laughter—can hardly avoid, when the worst and meanest aspect of life happens to be presented to them.

Pyncheon-street was sometimes enlivened by spectacles of more imposing pretensions than the above, and which brought the multitude along with them. With a shivering repugnance at the idea of personal contact with the world, a powerful impulse still seized on Clifford, whenever the rush and roar of the human tide grew strongly audible to him. This was made evident, one day, when a political procession, with hundreds of flaunting banners, and drums, fifes, clarions, and cymbals, reverberating between the rows of buildings, marched all through town, and trailed its length of trampling footsteps, and most infrequent uproar, past the ordinarily quiet House of the Seven Gables. As a mere object of sight, nothing is more deficient in picturesque features than a procession, seen in its passage through narrow streets. The spectator feels it to be fool's play, when he can distinguish the tedious common-place of each man's visage, with the perspiration and weary self-importance on it, and the very cut of his pantaloons, and the stiffness or laxity of his shirt-collar, and the dust on the back of his black coat. In order to become majestic, it should be viewed from some vantage-point, as it rolls its slow and long array through the centre of a wide plain, or the stateliest public square of a city; for then, by its remoteness, it melts all the petty personalities, of which it is made up, into one broad mass of existence—one great life —one collected body of mankind, with a vast, homogeneous spirit animating it. But, on the other hand, if an impressible person, standing alone over the brink of one of these processions, should behold it, not in its atoms, but in its aggregate— as a mighty river of life, massive in its tide, and black with mystery, and, out of its depths, calling to the kindred depth within him—then the contiguity would add to the effect. It might so fascinate him, that he would hardly be restrained from plunging into the surging stream of human sympathies.

So it proved with Clifford. He shuddered; he grew pale,

he threw an appealing look at Hepzibah and Phoebe, who were with him at the window. They comprehended nothing of his emotions, and supposed him merely disturbed by the unaccustomed tumult. At last, with tremulous limbs, he started up, set his foot on the window-sill, and, in an instant more, would have been in the unguarded balcony. As it was, the whole procession might have seen him, a wild, haggard figure, his gray locks floating in the wind that waved their banners; a lonely being, estranged from his race, but now feeling himself man again, by virtue of the irrepressible instinct that possessed him. Had Clifford attained the balcony, he would probably have leaped into the street; but whether impelled by the species of terror, that sometimes urges its victim over the very precipice which he shrinks from, or by a natural magnetism, tending towards the great centre of humanity—it were not easy to decide. Both impulses might have wrought on him at once.

But his companions, affrighted by his gesture—which was that of a man hurried away, in spite of himself—seized Clifford's garment and held him back. Hepzibah shrieked. Phoebe, to whom all extravagance was a horror, burst into sobs and tears.

"Clifford, Clifford, are you crazy?" cried his sister.

"I hardly know, Hepzibah!" said Clifford, drawing a long breath. "Fear nothing—it is over now—but had I taken that plunge, and survived it, methinks it would have made me another man!"

Possibly, in some sense, Clifford may have been right. He needed a shock; or perhaps he required to take a deep, deep plunge into the ocean of human life, and to sink down and be covered by its profoundness, and then to emerge, sobered, invigorated, restored to the world and to himself. Perhaps, again, he required nothing less than the great final remedy—death!

A similar yearning to renew the broken links of brotherhood with his kind sometimes showed itself in a milder form; and once it was made beautiful by the religion that lay even deeper than itself. In the incident now to be sketched, there was a touching recognition, on Clifford's part, of God's care and love towards him—towards this poor, forsaken man, who, if any mortal could, might have been pardoned for regarding himself as thrown aside, forgotten, and left to be the sport of some fiend, whose playfulness was an ecstacy of mischief.

It was the Sabbath morning; one of those bright, calm Sabbaths, with its own hallowed atmosphere, when Heaven seems to diffuse itself over the earth's face in a solemn smile, no less sweet than solemn. On such a Sabbath morn, were we pure enough to be its medium, we should be conscious of the earth's natural worship ascending through our frames, on whatever spot of ground we stood. The church-bells, with various tones, but all in harmony, were calling out, and responding to one another—"It is the Sabbath!—The Sabbath!—Yea; the Sabbath!"—and over the whole city, the bells scattered the blessed sounds, now slowly, now with livelier joy, now one bell alone, now all the bells together, crying earnestly —"It is the Sabbath!"—and flinging their accents afar off, to melt into the air, and pervade it with the holy word. The air, with God's sweetest and tenderest sunshine in it, was meet for mankind to breathe into their hearts, and send it forth again as the utterance of prayer.

Clifford sat at the window, with Hepzibah, watching the neighbors as they stept into the street. All of them, however unspiritual on other days, were transfigured by the Sabbath influence; so that their very garments—whether it were an old man's decent coat, well-brushed for the thousandth time, or a little boy's first sack and trowsers, finished yesterday by his mother's needle—had somewhat of the quality of ascension-robes. Forth, likewise, from the portal of the old house, stept Phoebe, putting up her small, green sunshade, and throwing upward a glance and smile of parting kindness to the faces at the arched window. In her aspect, there was a familiar gladness, and a holiness that you could play with, and yet reverence it as much as ever. She was like a prayer, offered up in the homeliest beauty of one's mother-tongue. Fresh was Phoebe, moreover, and airy and sweet in her apparel; as if nothing that she wore—neither her gown, nor her small straw bonnet, nor her little kerchief, any more than her snowy stockings—had ever been put on, before; or, if worn, were all the fresher for it, and with a fragrance as if they had lain among the rosebuds.

The girl waved her hand to Hepzibah and Clifford, and went up the street; a Religion in herself, warm, simple, true, with a substance that could walk on earth, and a spirit that was capable of Heaven.

"Hepzibah," asked Clifford, after watching Phoebe to the corner, "do you never go to church?"

"No, Clifford," she replied—"not these many, many years!"

"Were I to be there," he rejoined, "it seems to me that I could pray once more, when so many human souls were praying all around me!"

She looked into Clifford's face, and beheld there a soft, natural effusion; for his heart gushed out, as it were, and ran over at his eyes, in delightful reverence for God, and kindly affection for his human brethren. The emotion communicated itself to Hepzibah. She yearned to take him by the hand, and go and kneel down, they two together—both so long separate from the world, and, as she now recognized, scarcely friends with Him above—to kneel down among the people, and be reconciled to God and man at once.

"Dear brother," said she, earnestly, "let us go! We belong nowhere. We have not a foot of space, in any church, to kneel upon; but let us go to some place of worship, even if we stand in the broad aisle. Poor and forsaken as we are, some pew-door will be opened to us!"

So Hepzibah and her brother made themselves ready—as

ready as they could, in the best of their old-fashioned garments, which had hung on pegs, or been laid away in trunks,
so long that the dampness and mouldy smell of the past was
on them—made themselves ready, in their faded bettermost,
to go to church. They descended the staircase together, gaunt,
sallow Hepzibah, and pale, emaciated, age-stricken Clifford!
They pulled open the front-door, and stept across the threshold, and felt, both of them, as if they were standing in the
presence of the whole world, and with mankind's great and
terrible eye on them alone. The eye of their Father seemed
to be withdrawn, and gave them no encouragement. The
warm, sunny air of the street made them shiver. Their hearts
quaked within them, at the idea of taking one step further.

"It cannot be, Hepzibah!—it is too late," said Clifford with
deep sadness.—"We are ghosts! We have no right among
human beings—no right anywhere, but in this old house,
which has a curse on it, and which therefore we are doomed
to haunt. And, besides," he continued, with a fastidious
sensibility, inalienably characteristic of the man, "it would
not be fit nor beautiful, to go! It is an ugly thought, that I
should be frightful to my fellow-beings, and that children
would cling to their mothers' gowns, at sight of me!"

They shrank back into the dusky passage-way, and closed
the door. But, going up the staircase again, they found the
whole interior of the house tenfold more dismal, and the air
closer and heavier, for the glimpse and breath of freedom
which they had just snatched. They could not flee; their jailor
had but left the door ajar, in mockery, and stood behind it,
to watch them stealing out. At the threshold, they felt his
pitiless gripe upon them. For, what other dungeon is so dark
as one's own heart! What jailor so inexorable as one's self!

But it would be no fair picture of Clifford's state of mind,
were we to represent him as continually or prevailingly
wretched. On the contrary, there was no other man in the
city, we are bold to affirm, of so much as half his years, who

enjoyed so many lightsome and griefless moments, as himself. He had no burthen of care upon him; there were none of those questions and contingencies with the future to be settled, which wear away all other lives, and render them not worth having by the very process of providing for their support. In this respect, he was a child; a child for the whole term of his existence, be it long or short. Indeed, his life seemed to be standing still at a period little in advance of childhood, and to cluster all its reminiscences about that epoch; just as, after the torpor of a heavy blow, the sufferer's reviving consciousness goes back to a moment considerably behind the accident that stupefied him. He sometimes told Phoebe and Hepzibah his dreams, in which he invariably played the part of a child, or a very young man. So vivid were they, in his relation of them, that he once held a dispute with his sister as to the particular figure or print of a chintz morning-dress, which he had seen their mother wear, in the dream of the preceding night. Hepzibah, piquing herself on a woman's accuracy in such matters, held it to be slightly different from what Clifford described; but, producing the very gown from an old trunk, it proved to be identical with his remembrance of it. Had Clifford, every time that he emerged out of dreams so lifelike, undergone the torture of transformation from a boy into an old and broken man, the daily recurrence of the shock would have been too much to bear. It would have caused an acute agony to thrill, from the morning twilight, all the day through, until bedtime, and even then would have mingled a dull, inscrutable pain, and pallid hue of misfortune, with the visionary bloom and adolescence of his slumber. But the nightly moonshine interwove itself with the morning mist, and enveloped him as in a robe, which he hugged about his person, and seldom let realities pierce through; he was not often quite awake, but slept open-eyed, and perhaps fancied himself most dreaming, then.

Thus, lingering always so near his childhood, he had sym-

pathies with children, and kept his heart the fresher thereby,
like a reservoir into which rivulets come pouring, not far from
the fountain-head. Though prevented, by a subtle sense of
propriety, from desiring to associate with them, he loved few
things better than to look out of the arched window, and see
a little girl, driving her hoop along the sidewalk, or schoolboys
at a game of ball. Their voices, also, were very pleasant to
him, heard at a distance, all swarming and intermingling together, as flies do in a sunny room.

Clifford would doubtless have been glad to share their
sports. One afternoon, he was seized with an irresistible
desire to blow soap-bubbles; an amusement, as Hepzibah told
Phoebe apart, that had been a favorite one with her brother,
when they were both children. Behold him, therefore, at the
arched window, with an earthen pipe in his mouth! Behold
him, with his gray hair, and a wan, unreal smile over his
countenance, where still hovered a beautiful grace, which his
worst enemy must have acknowledged to be spiritual and immortal, since it had survived so long! Behold him, scattering
airy spheres abroad, from the window into the street! Little,
impalpable worlds, were those soap-bubbles, with the big
world depicted, in hues bright as imagination, on the nothing
of their surface. It was curious to see how the passers-by regarded these brilliant fantasies, as they came floating down,
and made the dull atmosphere imaginative, about them. Some
stopt to gaze, and perhaps carried a pleasant recollection of
the bubbles, onward, as far as the street-corner; some looked
angrily upward, as if poor Clifford wronged them, by setting
an image of beauty afloat so near their dusty pathway. A
great many put out their fingers, or their walking-sticks, to
touch withal, and were perversely gratified, no doubt, when
the bubble, with all its pictured earth and sky scene, vanished
as if it had never been.

At length, just as an elderly gentleman of very dignified
presence happened to be passing, a large bubble sailed majes-

tically down, and burst right against his nose! He looked up
—at first with a stern, keen glance, which penetrated at once
into the obscurity behind the arched window—then with a
smile, which might be conceived as diffusing a dog-day sultriness for the space of several yards about him.

"Aha, Cousin Clifford!" cried Judge Pyncheon. "What!
Still blowing soap-bubbles!"

The tone seemed as if meant to be kind and soothing, but
yet had a bitterness of sarcasm in it. As for Clifford, an absolute palsy of fear came over him. Apart from any definite
cause of dread, which his past experience might have given
him, he felt that native and original horror of the excellent
Judge, which is proper to a weak, delicate, and apprehensive
character, in the presence of massive strength. Strength is incomprehensible by weakness, and therefore the more terrible.
There is no greater bugbear than a strong-willed relative, in
the circle of his own connections.

XII

THE DAGUERREOTYPIST

IT MUST not be supposed that the life of a personage, naturally so active as Phoebe, could be wholly confined within the precincts of the old Pyncheon-house. Clifford's demands upon her time were usually satisfied, in those long days, considerably earlier than sunset. Quiet as his daily existence seemed, it nevertheless drained all the resources by which he lived. It was not physical exercise that overwearied him; for—except that he sometimes wrought a little with a hoe, or paced the garden-walk, or, in rainy weather, traversed a large, unoccupied room—it was his tendency to remain only too quiescent, as regarded any toil of the limbs and muscles. But either there was a smouldering fire within him, that consumed his vital energy, or the monotony, that would have dragged itself with benumbing effect over a mind differently situated, was no monotony to Clifford. Possibly, he was in a state of second growth and recovery, and was constantly assimilating nutriment for his spirit and intellect from sights, sounds, and events, which passed as a perfect void to persons more practised with the world. As all is activity and vicissitude to the new mind of a child, so might it be, likewise, to a mind that had undergone a kind of new creation, after its long-suspended life.

Be the cause what it might, Clifford commonly retired to

rest, thoroughly exhausted, while the sunbeams were still melting through his window-curtains, or were thrown with late lustre on the chamber-wall. And while he thus slept early, as other children do, and dreamed of childhood, Phoebe was free to follow her own tastes for the remainder of the day and evening.

This was a freedom essential to the health even of a character so little susceptible of morbid influences as that of Phoebe. The old house, as we have already said, had both the dry-rot and the damp-rot in its walls; it was not good to breathe no other atmosphere than that. Hepzibah, though she had her valuable and redeeming traits, had grown to be a kind of lunatic, by imprisoning herself so long in one place, with no other company than a single series of ideas, and but one affection, and one bitter sense of wrong. Clifford, the reader may perhaps imagine, was too inert to operate morally on his fellow-creatures, however intimate and exclusive their relations with him. But the sympathy or magnetism among human beings is more subtle and universal, than we think; it exists, indeed, among different classes of organized life, and vibrates from one to another. A flower, for instance, as Phoebe herself observed, always began to droop sooner in Clifford's hand, or Hepzibah's, than in her own; and by the same law, converting her whole daily life into a flower-fragrance for these two sickly spirits, the blooming girl must inevitably droop and fade, much sooner than if worn on a younger and happier breast. Unless she had now and then indulged her brisk impulses, and breathed rural air in a suburban walk, or ocean-breezes along the shore—had occasionally obeyed the impulse of nature, in New England girls, by attending a metaphysical or philosophical lecture, or viewing a seven-mile panorama, or listening to a concert— had gone shopping about the city, ransacking entire depôts of splendid merchandize, and bringing home a ribbon—had enjoyed, likewise, a little time to read the Bible in her chamber, and had stolen a little more, to think of her mother and her native place—unless for such moral medicines as the above, we should soon have beheld our poor Phoebe grow thin, and put on a bleached, unwholesome aspect, and assume strange, shy ways, prophetic of old-maidenhood and a cheerless future.

Even as it was, a change grew visible; a change partly to be regretted, although whatever charm it infringed upon was repaired by another, perhaps more precious. She was not so constantly gay, but had her moods of thought, which Clifford, on the whole, liked better than her former phase of unmingled cheerfulness; because now she understood him better and more delicately, and sometimes even interpreted him to himself. Her eyes looked larger, and darker, and deeper; so deep, at some silent moments, that they seemed like Artesian wells, down, down, into the infinite. She was less girlish than when we first beheld her, alighting from the omnibus; less girlish, but more a woman!

The only youthful mind, with which Phoebe had an opportunity of frequent intercourse, was that of the Daguerreotypist. Inevitably, by the pressure of the seclusion about them, they had been brought into habits of some familiarity. Had they met under different circumstances, neither of these young persons would have been likely to bestow much thought upon the other; unless, indeed, their extreme dissimilarity should have proved a principle of mutual attraction. Both, it is true, were characters proper to New England life, and possessing a common ground, therefore, in their more external developements; but as unlike, in their respective interiors, as if their native climes had been at world-wide distance. During the early part of their acquaintance, Phoebe had held back rather more than was customary with her frank and simple manners, from Holgrave's not very marked advances. Nor was she yet satisfied that she knew him well, although they almost daily met and talked together in a kind, friendly, and what seemed to be a familiar way.

The artist, in a desultory manner, had imparted to Phoebe something of his history. Young as he was, and had his career terminated at the point already attained, there had been enough of incident to fill, very creditably, an autobiographic volume. A romance on the plan of Gil Blas, adapted to American society and manners, would cease to be a romance. The experience of many individuals among us, who think it hardly worth the telling, would equal the vicissitudes of the Spaniard's earlier life; while their ultimate success, or the point whither they tend, may be incomparably higher than any that a novelist would imagine for his hero. Holgrave, as he told Phoebe, somewhat proudly, could not boast of his origin, unless as being exceedingly humble, nor of his education, except that it had been the scantiest possible, and obtained by a few winter-months' attendance at a district-school. Left early to his own guidance, he had begun to be self-dependent while yet a boy; and it was a condition aptly suited to his natural force of will. Though now but twenty-two years old, (lacking some months, which are years, in such a life,) he had already been, first, a country-schoolmaster; next, a salesman in a country-store; and, either at the same time or afterwards, the political-editor of a country-newspaper. He had subsequently travelled New England and the middle states as a pedler, in the employment of a Connecticut manufactory of Cologne water and other essences. In an episodical way, he had studied and practised dentistry, and with very flattering success, especially in many of the factory-towns along our inland-streams. As a supernumerary official, of some kind or other, aboard a packet-ship, he had visited Europe, and found means, before his return, to see Italy, and part of France and Germany. At a later period, he had spent some months in a community of Fourierists. Still more recently, he had been a public lecturer on Mesmerism, for which science (as he assured Phoebe, and, indeed, satisfactorily proved by putting Chanticleer, who happened to be

scratching, near by, to sleep) he had very remarkable endowments.

His present phase, as a Daguerreotypist, was of no more
importance in his own view, nor likely to be more permanent,
than any of the preceding ones. It had been taken up with
the careless alacrity of an adventurer, who had his bread to
earn; it would be thrown aside as carelessly, whenever he
should choose to earn his bread by some other equally digres-
sive means. But what was most remarkable, and perhaps
showed a more than common poise in the young man, was
the fact, that, amid all these personal vicissitudes, he had
never lost his identity. Homeless as he had been—continually
changing his whereabout, and therefore responsible neither
to public opinion nor to individuals—putting off one exterior,
and snatching up another, to be soon shifted for a third—he
had never violated the innermost man, but had carried his
conscience along with him. It was impossible to know Holgrave, without recognizing this to be the fact. Hepzibah had
seen it. Phoebe soon saw it, likewise, and gave him the sort
of confidence which such a certainty inspires. She was
startled, however, and sometimes repelled—not by any doubt
of his integrity to whatever law he acknowledged—but by a
sense that his law differed from her own. He made her un-
easy, and seemed to unsettle everything around her, by his
lack of reverence for what was fixed; unless, at a moment's
warning, it could establish its right to hold its ground.

Then, moreover, she scarcely thought him affectionate in
his nature. He was too calm and cool an observer. Phoebe
felt his eye, often; his heart, seldom or never. He took a certain kind of interest in Hepzibah and her brother, and Phoebe
herself; he studied them attentively, and allowed no slightest
circumstance of their individualities to escape him; he was
ready to do them whatever good he might;—but, after all, he
never exactly made common cause with them, nor gave any
reliable evidence that he loved them better, in proportion as

he knew them more. In his relations with them, he seemed to be in quest of mental food; not heart-sustenance. Phoebe could not conceive what interested him so much in her friends and herself, intellectually, since he cared nothing for them, or comparatively so little, as objects of human affection.

Always, in his interviews with Phoebe, the artist made especial inquiry as to the welfare of Clifford, whom, except at the Sunday festival, he seldom saw.

"Does he still seem happy?" he asked, one day.

"As happy as a child," answered Phoebe, "but—like a child, too—very easily disturbed."

"How disturbed?" inquired Holgrave.—"By things without? —or by thoughts within?"

"I cannot see his thoughts!—How should I?" replied Phoebe, with simple piquancy.—"Very often, his humor changes without any reason that can be guessed at, just as a cloud comes over the sun. Latterly, since I have begun to know him better, I feel it to be not quite right to look closely into his moods. He has had such a great sorrow, that his heart is made all solemn and sacred by it. When he is cheerful—when the sun shines into his mind—then I venture to peep in, just as far as the light reaches, but no farther. It is holy ground where the shadow falls!"

"How prettily you express this sentiment!" said the artist. "I can understand the feeling, without possessing it. Had I your opportunities, no scruples would prevent me from fathoming Clifford to the full depth of my plummet-line!"

"How strange that you should wish it!" remarked Phoebe involuntarily. "What is Cousin Clifford to you?"

"Oh, nothing, of course, nothing!" answered Holgrave with a smile. "Only this is such an odd and incomprehensible world! The more I look at it, the more it puzzles me; and I begin to suspect that a man's bewilderment is the measure of his wisdom. Men and women, and children, too, are such strange creatures, that one never can be certain that he really knows them; nor ever guess what they have been, from what he sees them to be, now. Judge Pyncheon! Clifford! What a complex riddle—a complexity of complexities—do they present! It requires intuitive sympathy, like a young girl's, to solve it. A mere observer, like myself, (who never have any intuitions, and am, at best, only subtile and acute,) is pretty certain to go astray."

The artist now turned the conversation to themes less dark than that which they had touched upon. Phoebe and he were young together; nor had Holgrave, in his premature experience of life, wasted entirely that beautiful spirit of youth, which, gushing forth from one small heart and fancy, may diffuse itself over the universe, making it all as bright as on the first day of creation. Man's own youth is the world's youth; at least, he feels as if it were, and imagines that the earth's granite substance is something not yet hardened, and which he can mould into whatever shape he likes. So it was with Holgrave. He could talk sagely about the world's old age, but never actually believed in what he said; he was a young man still, and therefore looked upon the world—that gray-bearded and wrinkled profligate, decrepit, without being venerable—as a tender stripling, capable of being improved into all that it ought to be, but scarcely yet had shown the remotest promise of becoming. He had that sense, or inward prophecy—which a young man had better never have been born, than not to have, and a mature man had better die at once, than utterly to relinquish—that we are not doomed to creep on forever in the old, bad way, but that, this very now, there are the harbingers abroad of a golden era, to be accomplished in his own lifetime. It seemed to Holgrave—as doubtless it has seemed to the hopeful of every century, since the epoch of Adam's grandchildren—that in this age, more than ever before, the moss-grown and rotten Past is to be torn down, and lifeless institutions to be thrust out of the way, and their dead corpses buried, and everything to begin anew.

As to the main point—may we never live to doubt it!—as to the better centuries that are coming, the artist was surely right. His error lay, in supposing that this age, more than any past or future one, is destined to see the tattered garments of Antiquity exchanged for a new suit, instead of gradually renewing themselves by patchwork; in applying his own little life-span as the measure of an interminable achievement; and, more than all, in fancying that it mattered anything to the great end in view, whether he himself should contend for it or against it. Yet it was well for him to think so. This enthusiasm, infusing itself through the calmness of his character, and thus taking an aspect of settled thought and wisdom, would serve to keep his youth pure, and make his aspirations high. And when, with the years settling down more weightily upon him, his early faith should be modified by inevitable experience, it would be with no harsh and sudden revolution of his sentiments. He would still have faith in man's brightening destiny, and perhaps love him all the better, as he should recognize his helplessness in his own behalf; and the haughty faith, with which he began life, would be well bartered for a far humbler one, at its close, in discerning that man's best-directed effort accomplishes a kind of dream, while God is the sole worker of realities.

Holgrave had read very little, and that little, in passing through the thoroughfare of life, where the mystic language of his books was necessarily mixed up with the babble of the multitude; so that both one and the other were apt to lose any sense, that might have been properly their own. He considered himself a thinker, and was certainly of a thoughtful turn, but, with his own path to discover, had perhaps hardly yet reached the point where an educated man begins to think. The true value of his character lay in that deep consciousness of inward strength, which made all his past vicissitudes seem merely like a change of garments; in that enthusiasm, so quiet that he scarcely knew of its existence, but which gave a warmth to everything that he laid his hand on; in that personal ambition, hidden—from his own as well as other eyes—among his more generous impulses, but in which lurked a certain efficacy, that might solidify him from a theorist into the champion of some practicable cause. Altogether, in his culture and want of culture; in his crude, wild, and misty philosophy, and the practical experience that counteracted some of its tendencies; in his magnanimous zeal for man's welfare, and his recklessness of whatever the ages had established in man's behalf; in his faith, and in his infidelity; in what he had, and in what he lacked—the artist might fitly enough stand forth as the representative of many compeers in his native land.

His career it would be difficult to prefigure. There appeared to be qualities in Holgrave, such as, in a country where everything is free to the hand that can grasp it, could hardly fail to put some of the world's prizes within his reach. But these matters are delightfully uncertain. At almost every step in life, we meet with young men of just about Holgrave's age, for whom we anticipate wonderful things, but of whom, even after much and careful inquiry, we never happen to hear another word. The effervescence of youth and passion, and the fresh gloss of the intellect and imagination, endow them with a false brilliancy, which makes fools of themselves and other people. Like certain chintzes, calicoes, and ginghams, they show finely in their first newness, but cannot stand the sun and rain, and assume a very sober aspect after washing-day.

But our business is with Holgrave, as we find him on this particular afternoon, and in the arbor of the Pyncheon-garden. In that point of view, it was a pleasant sight to behold this young man, with so much faith in himself, and so fair an appearance of admirable powers—so little harmed, too, by the many tests that had tried his metal—it was pleasant to see him in his kindly intercourse with Phoebe. Her thought had scarcely done him justice, when it pronounced him cold; or if so, he had grown warmer, now. Without such purpose, on her part, and unconsciously on his, she made the House of the Seven Gables like a home to him, and the garden a familiar precinct. With the insight on which he prided himself, he fancied that he could look through Phoebe, and all around her, and could read her off like a page of a child's story-book. But these transparent natures are often deceptive in their depth; those pebbles at the bottom of the fountain are farther from us than we think. Thus the artist, whatever he might judge of Phoebe's capacity, was beguiled, by some silent charm of hers, to talk freely of what he dreamed of doing in the world. He poured himself out as to another self. Very possibly, he forgot Phoebe while he talked to her, and was moved only by the inevitable tendency of thought, when rendered sympathetic by enthusiasm and emotion, to flow into the first safe reservoir which it finds. But, had you peeped at them through the chinks of the garden-fence, the young man's earnestness and heightened color might have led you to suppose that he was making love to the young girl!

At length, something was said by Holgrave, that made it apposite for Phoebe to inquire what had first brought him acquainted with her Cousin Hepzibah, and why he now chose to lodge in the desolate old Pyncheon-house. Without directly answering her, he turned from the Future, which had heretofore been the theme of his discourse, and began to speak of the influences of the Past. One subject, indeed, is but the reverberation of the other.

"Shall we never, never get rid of this Past!" cried he, keeping up the earnest tone of his preceding conversation.—"It lies upon the Present like a giant's dead body! In fact, the case is just as if a young giant were compelled to waste all his strength in carrying about the corpse of the old giant, his grandfather, who died a long while ago, and only needs to be

decently buried. Just think, a moment; and it will startle you
to see what slaves we are to by-gone times—to Death, if we
give the matter the right word!"

"But I do not see it," observed Phoebe.

"For example, then," continued Holgrave, "a Dead Man,
if he happen to have made a will, disposes of wealth no longer
his own; or, if he die intestate, it is distributed in accordance
with the notions of men much longer dead than he. A Dead
Man sits on all our judgement-seats; and living judges do
but search out and repeat his decisions. We read in Dead
Men's books! We laugh at Dead Men's jokes, and cry at
Dead Men's pathos! We are sick of Dead Men's diseases,
physical and moral, and die of the same remedies with which
dead doctors killed their patients! We worship the living
Deity, according to Dead Men's forms and creeds! Whatever
we seek to do, of our own free motion, a Dead Man's icy hand
obstructs us! Turn our eyes to what point we may, a Dead
Man's white, immitigable face encounters them, and freezes
our very heart! And we must be dead ourselves, before we can
begin to have our proper influence on our own world, which
will then be no longer our world, but the world of another
generation, with which we shall have no shadow of a right
to interfere. I ought to have said, too, that we live in Dead
Men's houses; as, for instance, in this of the seven gables!"

"And why not," said Phoebe, "so long as we can be comfortable in them?"

"But we shall live to see the day, I trust," went on the
artist, "when no man shall build his house for posterity. Why
should he? He might just as reasonably order a durable suit
of clothes—leather, or gutta percha, or whatever else lasts
longest—so that his great-grandchildren should have the benefit of them, and cut precisely the same figure in the world
that he himself does. If each generation were allowed and
expected to build its own houses, that single change, comparatively unimportant in itself, would imply almost every

reform which society is now suffering for. I doubt whether even our public edifices—our capitols, state-houses, court-houses, city-halls, and churches—ought to be built of such permanent materials as stone or brick. It were better that they should crumble to ruin, once in twenty years, or there-abouts, as a hint to the people to examine into and reform the institutions which they symbolize."

"How you hate everything old!" said Phoebe in dismay. —"It makes me dizzy to think of such a shifting world!"

"I certainly love nothing mouldy," answered Holgrave. "Now this old Pyncheon-house! Is it a wholesome place to live in, with its black shingles, and the green moss that shows how damp they are?—its dark, low-studded rooms?—its grime and sordidness, which are the crystallization on its walls of the human breath, that has been drawn and exhaled here, in discontent and anguish? The house ought to be purified with fire—purified till only its ashes remain!"

"Then why do you live in it?" asked Phoebe, a little piqued.

"Oh, I am pursuing my studies here; not in books, how-ever!" replied Holgrave. "The house, in my view, is expres-sive of that odious and abominable Past, with all its bad influences, against which I have just been declaiming. I dwell in it for awhile, that I may know the better how to hate it. By-the-by, did you ever hear the story of Maule, the wizard, and what happened between him and your immeas-urably great-grandfather?"

"Yes indeed!" said Phoebe. "I heard it long ago from my father, and two or three times from my Cousin Hepzibah, in the month that I have been here. She seems to think that all the calamities of the Pyncheons began from that quarrel with the wizard, as you call him. And you, Mr. Holgrave, look as if you thought so too! How singular, that you should believe what is so very absurd, when you reject many things that are a great deal worthier of credit!"

"I do believe it," said the artist seriously—"not as a super-stition, however—but as proved by unquestionable facts, and as exemplifying a theory. Now, see! Under those seven gables, at which we now look up—and which old Colonel Pyncheon meant to be the home of his descendants, in pros-perity and happiness, down to an epoch far beyond the present—under that roof, through a portion of three centuries, there has been perpetual remorse of conscience, a constantly defeated hope, strife amongst kindred, various misery, a strange form of death, dark suspicion, unspeakable disgrace,— all, or most of which calamity, I have the means of tracing to the old Puritan's inordinate desire to plant and endow a fam-ily. To plant a family! This idea is at the bottom of most of the wrong and mischief which men do. The truth is, that, once in every half-century, at longest, a family should be merged into the great, obscure mass of humanity, and forget all about its ancestors. Human blood, in order to keep its freshness, should run in hidden streams, as the water of an aqueduct is conveyed in subterranean pipes. In the family-existence of these Pyncheons, for instance — forgive me, Phoebe; but I cannot think of you as one of them—in their brief, New England pedigree, there has been time enough to infect them all with one kind of lunacy or another!"

"You speak very unceremoniously of my kindred," said Phoebe, debating with herself whether she ought to take offence.

"I speak true thoughts to a true mind!" answered Holgrave, with a vehemence which Phoebe had not before witnessed in him. "The truth is as I say! Furthermore, the original per-petrator and father of this mischief appears to have perpet-uated himself, and still walks the street—at least, his very image, in mind and body—with the fairest prospect of trans-mitting to posterity as rich, and as wretched, an inheritance as he has received! Do you remember the daguerreotype, and its resemblance to the old portrait?"

"How strangely in earnest you are," exclaimed Phoebe, looking at him with surprise and perplexity, half-alarmed, and partly inclined to laugh. "You talk of the lunacy of the Pyncheons! Is it contagious?"

"I understand you!" said the artist, coloring and laughing. "I believe I am a little mad! This subject has taken hold of my mind with the strangest tenacity of clutch, since I have lodged in yonder old gable. As one method of throwing it off, I have put an incident of the Pyncheon family-history, with which I happen to be acquainted, into the form of a legend, and mean to publish it in a magazine."

"Do you write for the magazines?" inquired Phoebe.

"Is it possible you did not know it?" cried Holgrave.— "Well; such is literary fame! Yes, Miss Phoebe Pyncheon, among the multitude of my marvellous gifts, I have that of writing stories; and my name has figured, I can assure you, on the covers of Graham and Godey, making as respectable an appearance, for aught I could see, as any of the canonized bead-roll with which it was associated. In the humorous line, I am thought to have a very pretty way with me; and as for pathos, I am as provocative of tears as an onion! But shall I read you my story?"

"Yes; if it is not very long," said Phoebe—and added, laughingly—"nor very dull!"

As this latter point was one which the Daguerreotypist could not decide for himself, he forthwith produced his roll of manuscript, and, while the late sunbeams gilded the seven gables, began to read.

XIII

ALICE PYNCHEON

THERE was a message brought, one day, from the worshipful Gervayse Pyncheon to young Matthew Maule, the carpenter, desiring his immediate presence at the House of the Seven Gables.

"And what does your master want with me?" said the carpenter to Mr. Pyncheon's black servant. "Does the house need any repair? Well it may, by this time; and no blame to my father who built it, neither! I was reading the old Colonel's tombstone, no longer ago than last Sabbath; and reckoning from that date, the house has stood seven-and-thirty years. No wonder if there should be a job to do on the roof!"

"Don't know what Massa wants!" answered Scipio. "The house is a berry good house, and old Colonel Pyncheon think so too, I reckon;—else why the old man haunt it so, and frighten a poor nigger, as he does?"

"Well, well, friend Scipio, let your master know that I'm coming," said the carpenter with a laugh. "For a fair, workmanlike job, he'll find me his man. And so the house is haunted, is it? It will take a tighter workman than I am, to keep the spirits out of the seven gables. Even if the Colonel would be quit," he added, muttering to himself, "my old grandfather, the wizard, will be pretty sure to stick to the Pyncheons, as long as their walls hold together!"

"What's that you mutter to yourself, Matthew Maule?" asked Scipio. "And what for do you look so black at me?"

"No matter, darkey!" said the carpenter. "Do you think nobody is to look black but yourself? Go tell your master I'm coming; and if you happen to see Mistress Alice, his daughter, give Matthew Maule's humble respects to her. She has brought a fair face from Italy—fair, and gentle, and proud—has that same Alice Pyncheon!"

"He talk of Mistress Alice!" cried Scipio, as he returned from his errand. "The low carpenter-man! He no business so much as to look at her a great way off!"

This young Matthew Maule, the carpenter, it must be observed, was a person little understood, and not very generally liked, in the town where he resided; not that anything could be alleged against his integrity, or his skill and diligence in the handicraft which he exercised. The aversion (as it might justly be called) with which many persons regarded him, was partly the result of his own character and deportment, and partly an inheritance.

He was the grandson of a former Matthew Maule; one of the early settlers of the town, and who had been a famous and terrible wizard, in his day. This old reprobate was one of the sufferers, when Cotton Mather, and his brother ministers, and the learned judges, and other wise men, and Sir William Phips, the sagacious Governor, made such laudable efforts to weaken the great Enemy of souls, by sending a multitude of his adherents up the rocky pathway of Gallows-Hill. Since those days, no doubt, it had grown to be suspected, that, in consequence of an unfortunate overdoing of a work praiseworthy in itself, the proceedings against the witches had proved far less acceptable to the Beneficent Father, than to that very Arch-Enemy, whom they were intended to distress and utterly overwhelm. It is not the less certain, however, that awe and terror brooded over the memories of those who died for this horrible crime of witchcraft.

Their graves, in the crevices of the rocks, were supposed to be incapable of retaining the occupants, who had been so hastily thrust into them. Old Matthew Maule, especially, was known to have as little hesitation or difficulty in rising out of his grave, as an ordinary man in getting out of bed, and was as often seen at midnight, as living people at noonday. This pestilent wizard (in whom his just punishment seemed to have wrought no manner of amends) had an inveterate habit of haunting a certain mansion, styled the House of the Seven Gables, against the owner of which he pretended to hold an unsettled claim for ground-rent. The ghost, it appears—with the pertinacity which was one of his distinguishing characteristics, while alive—insisted that he was the rightful proprietor of the site upon which the house stood. His terms were, that either the aforesaid ground-rent, from the day when the cellar began to be dug, should be paid down, or the mansion itself given up; else he, the ghostly creditor, would have his finger in all the affairs of the Pyncheons, and make everything go wrong with them, though it should be a thousand years after his death. It was a wild story, perhaps, but seemed not altogether so incredible, to those who could remember what an inflexibly obstinate old fellow this wizard Maule had been!

Now, the wizard's grandson, the young Matthew Maule of our story, was popularly supposed to have inherited some of his ancestor's questionable traits. It is wonderful how many absurdities were promulgated in reference to the young man. He was fabled, for example, to have a strange power of getting into people's dreams, and regulating matters there according to his own fancy, pretty much like the stage-manager of a theatre. There was a great deal of talk among the neighbors, particularly the petticoated ones, about what they called the witchcraft of Maule's eye. Some said, that he could look into people's minds; others, that, by the marvellous power of this eye, he could draw people into his own mind, or send them, if he pleased, to do errands to his grandfather, in the spiritual world; others again, that it was what is termed an Evil Eye, and possessed the valuable faculty of blighting corn, and drying children into mummies with the heart-burn. But, after all, what worked most to the young carpenter's disadvantage was, first, the reserve and sternness of his natural disposition, and next, the fact of his not being a church-communicant, and the suspicion of his holding heretical tenets in matters of religion and polity.

After receiving Mr. Pyncheon's message, the carpenter merely tarried to finish a small job, which he happened to have in hand, and then took his way towards the House of the Seven Gables. This noted edifice, though its style might be getting a little out of fashion, was still as respectable a family residence as that of any gentleman in town. The present owner, Gervayse Pyncheon, was said to have contracted a dislike to the house, in consequence of a shock to his sensibility, in early childhood, from the sudden death of his grandfather. In the very act of running to climb Colonel Pyncheon's knee, the boy had discovered the old Puritan to be a corpse! On arriving at manhood, Mr. Pyncheon had visited England, where he married a lady of fortune, and had subsequently spent many years, partly in the mother-country, and partly in various cities, on the continent of Europe. During this period, the family-mansion had been consigned to the charge of a kinsman, who was allowed to make it his home, for the time being, in consideration of keeping the premises in thorough repair. So faithfully had this contract been fulfilled, that now, as the carpenter approached the house, his practised eye could detect nothing to criticize in its condition. The peaks of the seven gables rose up sharply; the shingled roof looked thoroughly water-tight; and the glittering plaster-work entirely covered the exterior walls, and sparkled in the October sun, as if it had been new only a week ago.

The house had that pleasant aspect of life, which is like the cheery expression of comfortable activity, in the human countenance. You could see at once that there was the stir of a large family within it. A huge load of oak-wood was passing through the gateway, towards the outbuildings in the rear; the fat cook, or probably it might be the housekeeper, stood at the side-door, bargaining for some turkeys and poultry, which a countryman had brought for sale. Now and then, a maid-servant, neatly dressed, and now the shining, sable face of a slave, might be seen bustling across the windows, in the lower part of the house. At an open window of a room in the second story, hanging over some pots of beautiful and delicate flowers—exotics, but which had never known a more genial sunshine than that of the New England autumn—was the figure of a young lady, an exotic, like the flowers, and beautiful and delicate as they. Her presence imparted an indescribable grace and faint witchery to the whole edifice. In other respects, it was a substantial, jolly-looking mansion, and seemed fit to be the residence of a patriarch, who might establish his own head-quarters in the front gable, and assign one of the remainder to each of his six children; while the great chimney, in the centre, should symbolize the old fellow's hospitable heart, which kept them all warm, and made a great whole of the seven smaller ones.

There was a vertical sun-dial on the front gable; and as the carpenter passed beneath it, he looked up and noted the hour.

"Three o'clock!" said he to himself. "My father told me, that dial was put up only an hour before the old Colonel's death. How truly it has kept time, these seven-and-thirty years past! The shadow creeps and creeps, and is always looking over the shoulder of the sunshine!"

It might have befitted a craftsman, like Matthew Maule, on being sent for to a gentleman's house, to go to the back-door, where servants and work-people were usually admitted;

or at least to the side-entrance, where the better class of tradesmen made application. But the carpenter had a great deal of pride and stiffness in his nature; and at this moment, moreover, his heart was bitter with the sense of hereditary wrong, because he considered the great Pyncheon-house to be standing on soil which should have been his own. On this very site, beside a spring of delicious water, his grandfather had felled the pine-trees and built a cottage, in which children had been born to him; and it was only from a dead man's stiffened fingers, that Colonel Pyncheon had wrested away the title-deeds. So young Maule went straight to the principal entrance, beneath a portal of carved oak, and gave such a peal of the iron knocker, that you would have imagined the stern old wizard himself to be standing at the threshold.

Black Scipio answered the summons in a prodigious hurry, but showed the whites of his eyes, in amazement, on beholding only the carpenter.

"Lord-a-mercy, what a great man he be, this carpenter fellow!" mumbled Scipio, down in his throat. "Anybody think he beat on the door with his biggest hammer!"

"Here I am!" said Maule sternly. "Show me the way to your master's parlor!"

As he stept into the house, a note of sweet and melancholy music trilled and vibrated along the passage-way, proceeding from one of the rooms above-stairs. It was the harpsichord which Alice Pyncheon had brought with her from beyond the sea. The fair Alice bestowed most of her maiden leisure between flowers and music, although the former were apt to droop, and the melodies were often sad. She was of foreign education, and could not take kindly to the New England modes of life, in which nothing beautiful had ever been developed.

As Mr. Pyncheon had been impatiently awaiting Maule's arrival, black Scipio, of course, lost no time in ushering the carpenter into his master's presence. The room, in which this gentleman sat, was a parlor of moderate size, looking out upon the garden of the house, and having its windows partly shadowed by the foliage of fruit-trees. It was Mr. Pyncheon's peculiar apartment, and was provided with furniture, in an elegant and costly style, principally from Paris; the floor (which was unusual, at that day) being covered with a carpet, so skilfully and richly wrought, that it seemed to glow as with living flowers. In one corner stood a marble woman, to whom her own beauty was the sole and sufficient garment. Some pictures—that looked old, and had a mellow tinge, diffused through all their artful splendor—hung on the walls. Near the fire-place was a large and very beautiful cabinet of ebony, inlaid with ivory; a piece of antique furniture, which Mr. Pyncheon had bought in Venice, and which he used as the treasure-place for medals, ancient coins, and whatever small and valuable curiosities he had picked up, on his travels. Through all this variety of decoration, however, the room showed its original characteristics; its low stud, its cross-beam, its chimney-piece, with the old-fashioned Dutch tiles; so that it was the emblem of a mind, industriously stored with foreign ideas, and elaborated into artificial refinement, but neither larger, nor, in its proper self, more elegant, than before.

There were two objects that appeared rather out of place in this very handsomely furnished room. One was a large map, or surveyor's plan of a tract of land, which looked as if it had been drawn a good many years ago, and was now dingy with smoke, and soiled, here and there, with the touch of fingers. The other was a portrait of a stern old man, in a Puritan garb, painted roughly, but with a bold effect, and a remarkably strong expression of character.

At a small table, before a fire of English sea-coal, sat Mr. Pyncheon, sipping coffee, which had grown to be a very favorite beverage with him, in France. He was a middle-aged and really handsome man, with a wig flowing down upon his shoulders; his coat was of blue velvet, with lace on the borders and at the button-holes; and the firelight glistened on the spacious breadth of his waistcoat, which was flowered all over with gold. On the entrance of Scipio, ushering in the carpenter, Mr. Pyncheon turned partly round, but resumed his former position, and proceeded deliberately to finish his cup of coffee, without immediate notice of the guest whom he had summoned to his presence. It was not that he intended any rudeness, or improper neglect—which, indeed, he would have blushed to be guilty of—but it never occurred to him that a person in Maule's station had a claim on his courtesy, or would trouble himself about it, one way or the other.

The carpenter, however, stept at once to the hearth, and turned himself about, so as to look Mr. Pyncheon in the face.

"You sent for me!" said he. "Be pleased to explain your business, that I may go back to my own affairs!"

"Ah! excuse me," said Mr. Pyncheon quietly.—"I did not mean to tax your time without a recompense. Your name, I think, is Maule—Thomas or Matthew Maule—a son or grandson of the builder of this house?"

"Matthew Maule," replied the carpenter—"son of him who built the house—grandson of the rightful proprietor of the soil!"

"I know the dispute to which you allude," observed Mr. Pyncheon, with undisturbed equanimity. "I am well aware, that my grandfather was compelled to resort to a suit at law, in order to establish his claim to the foundation-site of this edifice. We will not, if you please, renew the discussion. The matter was settled at the time, and by the competent authorities—equitably, it is to be presumed—and, at all events, irrevocably. Yet, singularly enough, there is an incidental reference to this very subject in what I am now about to say to you. And this same inveterate grudge—excuse me, I mean no offence—this irritability, which you have just shown, is not entirely aside from the matter."

"If you can find anything for your purpose, Mr. Pyncheon," said the carpenter, "in a man's natural resentment for the wrongs done to his blood, you are welcome to it!"

"I take you at your word, Goodman Maule," said the owner of the seven gables, with a smile, "and will proceed to suggest a mode in which your hereditary resentments—justifiable, or otherwise—may have had a bearing on my affairs. You have heard, I suppose, that the Pyncheon family, ever since my grandfather's days, have been prosecuting a still unsettled claim to a very large extent of territory at the eastward?"

"Often," replied Maule—and it is said that a smile came over his face—"very often—from my father!"

"This claim," continued Mr. Pyncheon, after pausing a moment, as if to consider what the carpenter's smile might mean, "appeared to be on the very verge of a settlement and full allowance, at the period of my grandfather's decease. It was well known, to those in his confidence, that he anticipated neither difficulty nor delay. Now, Colonel Pyncheon, I need hardly say, was a practical man, well acquainted with public and private business, and not at all the person to cherish ill-founded hopes, or to attempt the following out of an impracticable scheme. It is obvious to conclude, therefore, that he had grounds—not apparent to his heirs—for his confident anticipation of success in the matter of this eastern claim. In a word, I believe—and my legal advisers coincide in the belief, which, moreover, is authorized, to a certain extent, by the family-traditions—that my grandfather was in possession of some deed, or other document, essential to this claim, but which has since disappeared."

"Very likely," said Matthew Maule—and again, it is said, there was a dark smile on his face—"but what can a poor carpenter have to do with the grand affairs of the Pyncheon family?"

"Perhaps nothing," returned Mr. Pyncheon—"possibly, much!"

Here ensued a great many words between Matthew Maule and the proprietor of the seven gables, on the subject which the latter had thus broached. It seems (although Mr. Pyncheon had some hesitation in referring to stories, so exceedingly absurd in their aspect) that the popular belief pointed to some mysterious connection and dependence, existing between the family of the Maules, and these vast, unrealized possessions of the Pyncheons. It was an ordinary saying, that the old wizard, hanged though he was, had obtained the best end of the bargain, in his contest with Colonel Pyncheon; inasmuch as he had got possession of the great eastern claim, in exchange for an acre or two of garden-ground. A very aged woman, recently dead, had often used the metaphorical expression, in her fireside-talk, that miles and miles of the Pyncheon lands had been shovelled into Maule's grave; which, by-the-by, was but a very shallow nook, between two rocks, near the summit of Gallows-Hill. Again, when the lawyers were making inquiry for the missing document, it was a by-word, that it would never be found, unless in the wizard's skeleton-hand. So much weight had the shrewd lawyers assigned to these fables, that—(but Mr. Pyncheon did not see fit to inform the carpenter of the fact)—they had secretly caused the wizard's grave to be searched. Nothing was discovered, however, except that, unaccountably, the right hand of the skeleton was gone.

Now, what was unquestionably important, a portion of these popular rumors could be traced, though rather doubtfully and indistinctly, to chance words and obscure hints of the executed wizard's son, and the father of this present Matthew Maule. And here Mr. Pyncheon could bring an item of his own personal evidence into play. Though but a child, at the time, he either remembered or fancied, that Matthew's father had had some job to perform, on the day before, or possibly the very morning, of the Colonel's decease, in the private room where he and the carpenter were at this moment talking. Certain papers belonging to Colonel Pyncheon, as his grandson distinctly recollected, had been spread out on the table.

Matthew Maule understood the insinuated suspicion.

"My father," he said—but still there was that dark smile, making a riddle of his countenance—"my father was an honester man than the bloody old Colonel! Not to get his rights back again, would he have carried off one of those papers!"

"I shall not bandy words with you," observed the foreign-bred Mr. Pyncheon, with haughty composure. "Nor will it become me to resent any rudeness towards either my grandfather or myself. A gentleman, before seeking intercourse with a person of your station and habits, will first consider whether the urgency of the end may compensate for the disagreeableness of the means. It does so, in the present instance."

He then renewed the conversation, and made great pecuniary offers to the carpenter, in case the latter should give information leading to the discovery of the lost document, and the consequent success of the eastern claim. For a long time, Matthew Maule is said to have turned a cold ear to these propositions. At last, however, with a strange kind of laugh, he inquired whether Mr. Pyncheon would make over to him the old wizard's homestead-ground, together with the House of the Seven Gables, now standing on it, in requital of the documentary evidence, so urgently required.

The wild, chimney-corner legend (which, without copying all its extravagances, my narrative essentially follows) here gives an account of some very strange behavior on the part of Colonel Pyncheon's portrait. This picture, it must be understood, was supposed to be so intimately connected with the fate of the house, and so magically built into its walls, that, if once it should be removed, that very instant, the whole edifice would come thundering down, in a heap of dusty ruin. All through the foregoing conversation between Mr. Pyncheon and the carpenter, the portrait had been frowning, clenching its fist, and giving many such proofs of excessive discomposure, but without attracting the notice of either of the two colloquists. And finally, at Matthew Maule's audacious suggestion of a transfer of the seven-gabled structure, the ghostly portrait is averred to have lost all patience, and to have shown itself on the point of descending bodily from its frame. But such incredible incidents are merely to be mentioned aside.

"Give up this house!" exclaimed Mr. Pyncheon, in amazement at the proposal. "Were I to do so, my grandfather would not rest quiet in his grave!"

"He never has, if all stories are true," remarked the carpenter, composedly. "But that matter concerns his grandson, more than it does Matthew Maule. I have no other terms to propose."

Impossible as he at first thought it, to comply with Maule's conditions, still, on a second glance, Mr. Pyncheon was of opinion that they might at least be made matter of discussion. He himself had no personal attachment for the house, nor any pleasant associations connected with his childish residence in it. On the contrary, after seven-and-thirty years, the presence of his dead grandfather seemed still to pervade it, as on that morning when the affrighted boy had beheld him, with so ghastly an aspect, stiffening in his chair. His long abode in foreign parts, moreover, and familiarity with many of the castles and ancestral halls of England, and the marble palaces of Italy, had caused him to look contemptuously at the House of the Seven Gables, whether in point of splendor or convenience. It was a mansion exceedingly inadequate to the style of living, which it would be incumbent on Mr. Pyncheon to support, after realizing his territorial rights. His steward might deign to occupy it, but never, certainly, the great landed proprietor himself. In the event of success, indeed, it was his purpose to return to England; nor, to say the truth, would he recently have quitted that more congenial home, had not his own fortune, as well as his deceased wife's, begun to give symptoms of exhaustion. The eastern claim once fairly settled, and put upon the firm basis of actual possession, Mr. Pyncheon's property—to be measured by miles, not acres—would be worth an earldom, and would reasonably entitle him to solicit, or enable him to purchase, that elevated dignity from the British monarch. Lord Pyncheon!—or the Earl of Waldo!—how could such a magnate be expected to contract his grandeur within the pitiful compass of seven shingled gables?

In short, on an enlarged view of the business, the carpenter's terms appeared so ridiculously easy, that Mr. Pyncheon could scarcely forbear laughing in his face. He was quite ashamed, after the foregoing reflections, to propose any diminution of so moderate a recompense for the immense service to be rendered.

"I consent to your proposition, Maule!" cried he. "Put me in possession of the document, essential to establish my rights, and the House of the Seven Gables is your own!"

According to some versions of the story, a regular contract to the above effect was drawn up by a lawyer, and signed and sealed in the presence of witnesses. Others say, that Matthew Maule was contented with a private, written agreement, in which Mr. Pyncheon pledged his honor and integrity to the fulfilment of the terms concluded upon. The gentleman then ordered wine, which he and the carpenter drank together, in confirmation of their bargain. During the whole preceding discussion and subsequent formalities, the old Puritan's portrait seems to have persisted in its shadowy gestures of disapproval, but without effect; except that, as Mr. Pyncheon set down the emptied glass, he thought he beheld his grandfather frown.

"This Sherry is too potent a wine for me;—it has affected

my brain already," he observed, after a somewhat startled look at the picture.—"On returning to Europe, I shall confine myself to the more delicate vintages of Italy and France, the best of which will not bear transportation."

"My Lord Pyncheon may drink what wine he will, and wherever he pleases!" replied the carpenter, as if he had been privy to Mr. Pyncheon's ambitious projects. "But first, Sir, if you desire tidings of this lost document, I must crave the favor of a little talk with your fair daughter Alice!"

"You are mad, Maule!" exclaimed Mr. Pyncheon haughtily; and now, at last, there was anger mixed up with his pride.—"What can my daughter have to do with a business like this?"

Indeed, at this new demand on the carpenter's part, the proprietor of the seven gables was even more thunderstruck, than at the cool proposition to surrender his house. There was, at least, an assignable motive for the first stipulation; there appeared to be none whatever, for the last. Nevertheless, Matthew Maule sturdily insisted on the young lady being summoned, and even gave her father to understand, in a mysterious kind of explanation—which made the matter considerably darker than it looked before—that the only chance of acquiring the requisite knowledge was through the clear, crystal medium of a pure and virgin intelligence, like that of the fair Alice. Not to encumber our story with Mr. Pyncheon's scruples, whether of conscience, pride, or fatherly affection, he at length ordered his daughter to be called. He well knew that she was in her chamber, and engaged in no occupation that could not readily be laid aside; for, as it happened, ever since Alice's name had been spoken, both her father and the carpenter had heard the sad and sweet music of her harpsichord, and the airier melancholy of her accompanying voice.

So Alice Pyncheon was summoned, and appeared. A portrait of this young lady, painted by a Venetian artist and left by her father in England, is said to have fallen into the hands of the present Duke of Devonshire, and to be now preserved at Chatsworth; not on account of any associations with the original, but for its value as a picture, and the high character of beauty, in the countenance. If ever there was a lady born, and set apart from the world's vulgar mass by a certain gentle and cold stateliness, it was this very Alice Pyncheon. Yet there was the womanly mixture in her;— the tenderness, or, at least, the tender capabilities. For the sake of that redeeming quality, a man of generous nature would have forgiven all her pride, and have been content, almost, to lie down in her path, and let Alice set her slender foot upon his heart. All that he would have required, was simply the acknowledgement that he was indeed a man, and a fellow-being, moulded of the same elements as she.

As Alice came into the room, her eyes fell upon the carpenter, who was standing near its centre, clad in a green, woollen jacket, a pair of loose breeches, open at the knees, and with a long pocket for his rule, the end of which protruded; it was as proper a mark of the artizan's calling, as Mr. Pyncheon's full-dress sword, of that gentleman's aristocratic pretensions. A glow of artistic approval brightened over Alice Pyncheon's face; she was struck with admiration— which she made no attempt to conceal—of the remarkable comeliness, strength, and energy of Maule's figure. But that admiring glance (which most other men, perhaps, would have cherished as a sweet recollection, all through life) the carpenter never forgave. It must have been the devil himself that made Maule so subtile in his perception.

"Does the girl look at me as if I were a brute beast!" thought he, setting his teeth. "She shall know whether I have a human spirit; and the worse for her, if it prove stronger than her own!"

"My father, you sent for me," said Alice, in her sweet and harp-like voice. "But, if you have business with this young man, pray let me go again. You know I do not love this room, in spite of that Claude, with which you try to bring back sunny recollections."

"Stay a moment, young lady, if you please!" said Matthew Maule. "My business with your father is over. With yourself, it is now to begin!"

Alice looked towards her father, in surprise and inquiry.

"Yes, Alice," said Mr. Pyncheon, with some disturbance and confusion. "This young man—his name is Matthew Maule—professes, so far as I can understand him, to be able to discover, through your means, a certain paper or parchment, which was missing long before your birth. The importance of the document in question renders it advisable to neglect no possible, even if improbable, method of regaining it. You will therefore oblige me, my dear Alice, by answering this person's inquiries, and complying with his lawful and reasonable requests, so far as they may appear to have the aforesaid object in view. As I shall remain in the room, you need apprehend no rude nor unbecoming deportment, on the young man's part; and, at your slightest wish, of course, the investigation, or whatever we may call it, shall immediately be broken off."

"Mistress Alice Pyncheon," remarked Matthew Maule, with the utmost deference, but yet a half-hidden sarcasm in his look and tone, "will no doubt feel herself quite safe in her father's presence, and under his all-sufficient protection."

"I certainly shall entertain no manner of apprehension, with my father at hand," said Alice, with maidenly dignity. "Neither do I conceive that a lady, while true to herself, can have aught to fear from whomsoever, or in any circumstances!"

Poor Alice! By what unhappy impulse did she thus put herself at once on terms of defiance against a strength which she could not estimate?

"Then, Mistress Alice," said Matthew Maule, handing a

chair—gracefully enough, for a craftsman—"will it please you only to sit down, and do me the favor (though altogether beyond a poor carpenter's deserts) to fix your eyes on mine!"

Alice complied. She was very proud. Setting aside all advantages of rank, this fair girl deemed herself conscious of a power—combined of beauty, high, unsullied purity, and the preservative force of womanhood—that could make her sphere impenetrable, unless betrayed by treachery within. She instinctively knew, it may be, that some sinister or evil potency was now striving to pass her barriers; nor would she decline the contest. So Alice put woman's might against man's might; a match not often equal, on the part of woman.

Her father, meanwhile, had turned away, and seemed absorbed in the contemplation of a landscape by Claude, where a shadowy and sun-streaked vista penetrated so remotely into an ancient wood, that it would have been no wonder if his fancy had lost itself in the picture's bewildering depths. But, in truth, the picture was no more to him, at that moment, than the blank wall against which it hung. His mind was haunted with the many and strange tales which he had heard, attributing mysterious, if not supernatural endowments to these Maules, as well the grandson, here present, as his two immediate ancestors. Mr. Pyncheon's long residence abroad, and intercourse with men of wit and fashion—courtiers, worldlings, and free thinkers—had done much towards obliterating the grim, Puritan superstitions, which no man of New England birth, at that early period, could entirely escape. But, on the other hand, had not a whole community believed Maule's grandfather to be a wizard? Had not the crime been proved? Had not the wizard died for it? Had he not bequeathed a legacy of hatred against the Pyncheons to this only grandson, who, as it appeared, was now about to exercise a subtle influence over the daughter of his enemy's house? Might not this influence be the same that was called witchcraft?

Turning half around, he caught a glimpse of Maule's figure

in the looking-glass. At some paces from Alice, with his arms uplifted in the air, the carpenter made a gesture, as if directing downward a slow, ponderous, and invisible weight upon the maiden.

"Stay, Maule!" exclaimed Mr. Pyncheon, stepping forward. "I forbid your proceeding farther!"

"Pray, my dear father, do not interrupt the young man!" said Alice, without changing her position. "His efforts, I assure you, will prove very harmless."

Again, Mr. Pyncheon turned his eyes towards the Claude. It was then his daughter's will, in opposition to his own, that the experiment should be fully tried. Henceforth, therefore, he did but consent, not urge it. And was it not for her sake, far more than for his own, that he desired its success? That lost parchment once restored, the beautiful Alice Pyncheon, with the rich dowry which he could then bestow, might wed an English duke, or a German reigning-prince, instead of some New England clergyman or lawyer! At the thought, the ambitious father almost consented, in his heart, that, if the devil's power were needed to the accomplishment of this great object, Maule might evoke him! Alice's own purity would be her safe-guard.

With his mind full of imaginary magnificence, Mr. Pyncheon heard a half-uttered exclamation from his daughter. It was very faint and low; so indistinct, that there seemed but half a will to shape out the words, and too undefined a purport, to be intelligible. Yet it was a call for help!—his conscience never doubted it!—and, little more than a whisper to his ear, it was a dismal shriek, and long re-echoed so, in the region round his heart! But, this time, the father did not turn.

After a farther interval, Maule spoke.

"Behold your daughter!" said he.

Mr. Pyncheon came hastily forward. The carpenter was standing erect in front of Alice's chair, and pointing his finger towards the maiden with an expression of triumphant power, the limits of which could not be defined; as, indeed, its scope stretched vaguely towards the unseen and the infinite. Alice sat in an attitude of profound repose, with the long, brown lashes drooping over her eyes.

"There she is!" said the carpenter. "Speak to her!"

"Alice! My daughter!" exclaimed Mr. Pyncheon. "My own Alice!"

She did not stir.

"Louder!" said Maule smiling.

"Alice! Awake!" cried her father. "It troubles me to see you thus! Awake!"

He spoke loudly, with terror in his voice, and close to that delicate ear which had always been so sensitive to every discord. But the sound evidently reached her not. It is indescribable what a sense of remote, dim, unattainable distance, betwixt himself and Alice, was impressed on the father by this impossibility of reaching her with his voice.

"Best touch her!" said Matthew Maule. "Shake the girl, and roughly too! My hands are hardened with too much use of axe, saw, and plane; else I might help you!"

Mr. Pyncheon took her hand, and pressed it with the earnestness of startled emotion. He kissed her, with so great a heart-throb in the kiss, that he thought she must needs feel it. Then, in a gust of anger at her insensibility, he shook her maiden form, with a violence which, the next moment, it affrighted him to remember. He withdrew his encircling arms; and Alice — whose figure, though flexible, had been wholly impassive—relapsed into the same attitude as before these attempts to arouse her. Maule having shifted his position, her face was turned towards him, slightly, but with what seemed to be a reference of her very slumber to his guidance.

Then, it was a strange sight to behold, how the man of conventionalities shook the powder out of his periwig; how the reserved and stately gentleman forgot his dignity; how the gold-embroidered waistcoat flickered and glistened in the firelight, with the convulsion of rage, terror, and sorrow, in the human heart that was beating under it!

"Villain!" cried Mr. Pyncheon, shaking his clenched fist at Maule. "You and the fiend together have robbed me of my daughter! Give her back—spawn of the old wizard!—or you shall climb Gallows-Hill in your grandfather's footsteps!"

"Softly, Mr. Pyncheon!" said the carpenter with scornful composure.—"Softly, an' it please your worship; else you will spoil those rich lace-ruffles, at your wrists! Is it my crime, if you have sold your daughter for the mere hope of getting a sheet of yellow parchment into your clutch? There sits Mistress Alice, quietly asleep! Now let Matthew Maule try whether she be as proud, as the carpenter found her awhile since!"

He spoke; and Alice responded, with a soft, subdued, inward acquiescence, and a bending of her form towards him, like the flame of a torch, when it indicates a gentle draft of air. He beckoned with his hand; and, rising from her chair—blindly, but undoubtingly, as tending to her sure and inevitable centre—the proud Alice approached him. He waved her back; and, retreating, Alice sank again into her seat!

"She is mine!" said Matthew Maule. "Mine, by the right of the strongest spirit!"

In the further progress of the legend, there is a long, grotesque, and occasionally awe-striking account of the carpenter's incantations (if so they are to be called) with a view of discovering the lost document. It appears to have been his object to convert the mind of Alice into a kind of telescopic medium, through which Mr. Pyncheon and himself might obtain a glimpse into the spiritual world. He succeeded, accordingly, in holding an imperfect sort of intercourse, at one remove, with the departed personages, in whose custody the so much valued secret had been carried beyond the precincts of earth. During her trance, Alice described three figures, as being present to her spiritualized perception. One was an aged, dignified, stern-looking gentleman, clad, as for a solemn festival, in grave and costly attire, but with a great blood-stain on his richly wrought band;—the second, an aged man, meanly dressed, with a dark and malign countenance, and a broken halter about his neck;—the third, a person not so advanced in life as the former two, but beyond the middle-age, wearing a coarse woollen tunic and leather-breeches, and with a carpenter's rule sticking out of his side-pocket. These three visionary characters possessed a mutual knowledge of the missing document. One of them, in truth—it was he with the blood-stain on his band—seemed, unless his gestures were misunderstood, to hold the parchment in his immediate keeping, but was prevented, by his two partners in the mystery, from disburthening himself of the trust. Finally, when he showed a purpose of shouting forth the secret, loudly enough to be heard from his own sphere into that of mortals, his companions struggled with him, and pressed their hands over his mouth; and forthwith—whether that he were choked by it, or that the secret itself was of a crimson hue—there was a fresh flow of blood upon his band. Upon this, the two meanly-dressed figures mocked and jeered at the much-abashed old dignitary, and pointed their fingers at the stain!

At this juncture, Maule turned to Mr. Pyncheon.

"It will never be allowed!" said he. "The custody of this secret, that would so enrich his heirs, makes part of your grandfather's retribution. He must choke with it, until it is no longer of any value. And keep you the House of the Seven Gables! It is too dear bought an inheritance, and too heavy, with the curse upon it, to be shifted yet awhile from the Colonel's posterity!"

Mr. Pyncheon tried to speak, but—what with fear and passion—could make only a gurgling murmur in his throat. The carpenter smiled.

"Aha, worshipful Sir! So, you have old Maule's blood to drink!" said he jeeringly.

"Fiend in man's shape, why dost thou keep dominion over my child?" cried Mr. Pyncheon, when his choked utterance could make way.—"Give me back my daughter! Then go thy ways; and may we never meet again!"

"Your daughter!" said Matthew Maule. "Why, she is fairly mine! Nevertheless, not to be too hard with fair Mistress Alice, I will leave her in your keeping; but I do not warrant you, that she shall never have occasion to remember Maule, the carpenter."

He waved his hands with an upward motion; and, after a few repetitions of similar gestures, the beautiful Alice Pyncheon awoke from her strange trance. She awoke, without the slightest recollection of her visionary experience; but as one losing herself in a momentary reverie, and returning to the consciousness of actual life, in almost as brief an interval as the down-sinking flame of the hearth should quiver again up the chimney. On recognizing Matthew Maule, she assumed an air of somewhat cold, but gentle dignity; the rather, as there was a certain peculiar smile on the carpenter's visage, that stirred the native pride of the fair Alice. So ended, for that time, the quest for the lost title-deed of the Pyncheon territory at the eastward; nor, though often subsequently renewed, has it ever yet befallen a Pyncheon to set his eye upon that parchment.

But alas, for the beautiful, the gentle, yet too haughty Alice! A power, that she little dreamed of, had laid its grasp upon her maiden soul. A will, most unlike her own, constrained her to do its grotesque and fantastic bidding. Her father, as it proved, had martyred his poor child to an inordinate desire for measuring his land by miles, instead of acres. And, therefore, while Alice Pyncheon lived, she was Maule's slave, in a bondage more humiliating, a thousand-fold, than that which binds its chain around the body. Seated by his humble fireside, Maule had but to wave his hand; and, wherever the proud lady chanced to be—whether in her chamber, or entertaining her father's stately guests, or worshipping at church—whatever her place or occupation, her spirit passed from beneath her own control, and bowed itself to Maule. "Alice, laugh!"—the carpenter, beside his hearth, would say; or perhaps intensely will it, without a spoken word. And, even were it prayer-time, or at a funeral, Alice must break into wild laughter. "Alice, be sad!"—and, at the instant, down would come her tears, quenching all the mirth of those around her, like sudden rain upon a bonfire. "Alice, dance!" —and dance she would, not in such court-like measures as she had learned abroad, but some high-paced jig, or hop-skip rigadoon, befitting the brisk lasses at a rustic merry-making. It seemed to be Maule's impulse, not to ruin Alice, nor to visit her with any black or gigantic mischief, which would have crowned her sorrow with the grace of tragedy, but to wreak a low, ungenerous scorn upon her. Thus all the dignity of life was lost. She felt herself too much abased, and longed to change natures with some worm!

One evening, at a bridal party—(but not her own; for, so lost from self-control, she would have deemed it sin to marry) —poor Alice was beckoned forth by her unseen despot, and constrained, in her gossamer white dress and satin slippers, to hasten along the street to the mean dwelling of a laboring-man. There was laughter and good cheer, within; for Matthew Maule, that night, was to wed the laborer's daughter, and had summoned proud Alice Pyncheon to wait upon his bride. And so she did; and when the twain were one, Alice awoke out of her enchanted sleep. Yet, no longer proud—humbly, and with a smile, all steeped in sadness—she kissed Maule's wife, and went her way. It was an inclement night; the south-east wind drove the mingled snow and rain into her thinly sheltered bosom; her satin slippers were wet through and through, as she trod the muddy sidewalks. The next day, a cold; soon, a settled cough; anon, a hectic cheek, a wasted form, that sat beside the harpsichord, and filled the house with music! Music, in which a strain of the heavenly choristers was echoed! Oh, joy! For Alice had borne her last humiliation! Oh, greater joy! For Alice was penitent of her one earthly sin, and proud no more!

The Pyncheons made a great funeral for Alice. The kith and kin were there, and the whole respectability of the town besides. But, last in the procession, came Matthew Maule, gnashing his teeth, as if he would have bitten his own heart in twain; the darkest and wofullest man that ever walked behind a corpse. He meant to humble Alice, not to kill her;—but he had taken a woman's delicate soul into his rude gripe, to play with;—and she was dead!

XIV

PHOEBE'S GOOD BYE

HOLGRAVE, plunging into his tale with the energy and absorption natural to a young author, had given a good deal of action to the parts capable of being developed and exemplified in that manner. He now observed that a certain remarkable drowsiness (wholly unlike that with which the reader possibly feels himself affected) had been flung over the senses of his auditress. It was the effect, unquestionably, of the mystic gesticulations, by which he had sought to bring bodily before Phoebe's perception the figure of the mesmerizing carpenter. With the lids drooping over her eyes—now lifted, for an instant, and drawn down again, as with leaden weights—she leaned slightly towards him, and seemed almost to regulate her breath by his. Holgrave gazed at her, as he rolled up his manuscript, and recognized an incipient stage of that curious psychological condition, which, as he had himself told Phoebe, he possessed more than an ordinary faculty of producing. A veil was beginning to be muffled about her, in which she could behold only him, and live only in his thoughts and emotions. His glance, as he fastened it on the young girl, grew involuntarily more concentrated; in his attitude, there was the consciousness of power, investing his hardly mature figure with a dignity that did not belong to its physical manifestation. It was evident, that, with but one wave of his hand and a corresponding effort of his will, he could complete his mastery over Phoebe's yet free and virgin spirit; he could establish an influence over this good, pure, and simple child, as dangerous, and perhaps as disastrous, as that which the carpenter of his legend had acquired and exercised over the ill-fated Alice.

To a disposition like Holgrave's, at once speculative and active, there is no temptation so great as the opportunity of acquiring empire over the human spirit; nor any idea more seductive to a young man, than to become the arbiter of a young girl's destiny. Let us, therefore—whatever his defects of nature and education, and in spite of his scorn for creeds and institutions—concede to the Daguerreotypist the rare and high quality of reverence for another's individuality. Let us allow him integrity, also, forever after to be confided in; since he forbade himself to twine that one link more, which might have rendered his spell over Phoebe indissoluble.

He made a slight gesture upward, with his hand.

"You really mortify me, my dear Miss Phoebe!" he exclaimed, smiling half sarcastically at her. "My poor story, it is but too evident, will never do for Godey or Graham! Only think of your falling asleep, at what I hoped the newspaper critics would pronounce a most brilliant, powerful, imaginative, pathetic, and original winding up! Well; the manuscript must serve to light lamps with;—if, indeed, being so imbued with my gentle dulness, it is any longer capable of flame!"

"Me asleep! How can you say so?" answered Phoebe, as unconscious of the crisis through which she had passed, as an infant of the precipice to the verge of which it has rolled. "No, no! I consider myself as having been very attentive; and though I don't remember the incidents quite distinctly, yet I have an impression of a vast deal of trouble and calamity —so, no doubt, the story will prove exceedingly attractive."

By this time, the sun had gone down, and was tinting the clouds towards the zenith with those bright hues, which are not seen there until some time after sunset, and when the horizon has quite lost its richer brilliancy. The moon, too, which had long been climbing overhead, and unobtrusively melting its disk into the azure—like an ambitious demagogue, who hides his aspiring purpose by assuming the prevalent hue of popular sentiment—now began to shine out, broad and oval, in its middle pathway. These silvery beams were already powerful enough to change the character of the lingering daylight. They softened and embellished the aspect of the old house; although the shadows fell deeper into the angles of its many gables, and lay brooding under the projecting story, and within the half-open door. With the lapse of every moment, the garden grew more picturesque; the fruit-trees, shrubbery, and flower-bushes had a dark obscurity among them. The common-place characteristics—which, at noontide, it seemed to have taken a century of sordid life to accumulate —were now transfigured by a charm of romance. A hundred mysterious years were whispering among the leaves, whenever the slight sea-breeze found its way thither, and stirred them. Through the foliage that roofed the little summer-house, the moonlight flickered to-and-fro, and fell, silvery white, on the dark floor, the table, and the circular bench, with a continual shift and play, according as the chinks and wayward crevices among the twigs admitted or shut out the glimmer.

So sweetly cool was the atmosphere, after all the feverish day, that the summer Eve might be fancied as sprinkling dews and liquid moonlight, with a dash of icy temper in them, out of a silver vase. Here and there, a few drops of this freshness were scattered on a human heart, and gave it youth again, and sympathy with the eternal youth of nature. The artist chanced to be one, on whom the reviving influence fell. It made him feel—what he sometimes almost forgot, thrust so early, as he had been, into the rude struggle of man with man—how youthful he still was.

"It seems to me," he observed, "that I never watched the

coming of so beautiful an eve, and never felt anything so very much like happiness as at this moment. After all, what a good world we live in! How good, and beautiful! How young it is, too, with nothing really rotten or age-worn in it! This old house, for example, which sometimes has positively oppressed my breath with its smell of decaying timber! And this garden, where the black mould always clings to my spade, as if I were a sexton, delving in a grave-yard! Could I keep the feeling that now possesses me, the garden would every day be virgin soil, with the earth's first freshness in the flavor of its beans and squashes; and the house!—it would be like a bower in Eden, blossoming with the earliest roses that God ever made. Moonlight, and the sentiment in man's heart, responsive to it, is the greatest of renovators and reformers. And all other reform and renovation, I suppose, will prove to be no better than moonshine!"

"I have been happier than I am now—at least, much gayer," said Phoebe thoughtfully. "Yet I am sensible of a great charm in this brightening moonlight; and I love to watch how the day, tired as it is, lags away reluctantly, and hates to be called yesterday, so soon. I never cared much about moonlight before. What is there, I wonder, so beautiful in it, to-night?"

"And you have never felt it before?" inquired the artist, looking earnestly at the girl, through the twilight.

"Never," answered Phoebe; "and life does not look the same, now that I have felt it so. It seems as if I had looked at everything, hitherto, in broad daylight, or else in the ruddy light of a cheerful fire, glimmering and dancing through a room. Ah, poor me!" she added, with a half-melancholy laugh. "I shall never be so merry as before I knew Cousin Hepzibah and poor Cousin Clifford. I have grown a great deal older, in this little time. Older, and, I hope, wiser, and —not exactly sadder—but, certainly, with not half so much lightness in my spirits! I have given them my sunshine, and have been glad to give it; but, of course, I cannot both give and keep it. They are welcome, notwithstanding!"

"You have lost nothing, Phoebe, worth keeping, nor which it was possible to keep," said Holgrave, after a pause. "Our first youth is of no value; for we are never conscious of it, until after it is gone. But sometimes—always, I suspect, unless one is exceedingly unfortunate—there comes a sense of second youth, gushing out of the heart's joy at being in love; or, possibly, it may come to crown some other grand festival in life, if any other such there be. This bemoaning of one's self (as you do now) over the first, careless, shallow gaiety of youth departed, and this profound happiness at youth regained—so much deeper and richer than that we lost—are essential to the soul's developement. In some cases, the two states come almost simultaneously, and mingle the sadness and the rapture in one mysterious emotion."

"I hardly think I understand you," said Phoebe.

"No wonder," replied Holgrave, smiling; "for I have told you a secret which I hardly began to know, before I found myself giving it utterance. Remember it, however; and when the truth becomes clear to you, then think of this moonlight scene!"

"It is entirely moonlight now; except only a little flush of faint crimson, upward from the west, between those buildings," remarked Phoebe. "I must go in. Cousin Hepzibah is not quick at figures, and will give herself a headache over the day's accounts, unless I help her."

But Holgrave detained her a little longer.

"Miss Hepzibah tells me," observed he, "that you return to the country, in a few days."

"Yes; but only for a little while," answered Phoebe; "for I look upon this as my present home. I go to make a few arrangements, and to take a more deliberate leave of my mother and friends. It is pleasant to live where one is much desired, and very useful; and I think I may have the satisfaction of feeling myself so, here."

"You surely may, and more than you imagine," said the artist. "Whatever health, comfort, and natural life, exists in the house, is embodied in your person. These blessings came along with you, and will vanish when you leave the threshold. Miss Hepzibah, by secluding herself from society, has lost all true relation with it, and is in fact dead; although she galvanizes herself into a semblance of life, and stands behind her counter, afflicting the world with a greatly-to-be-deprecated scowl. Your poor Cousin Clifford is another dead and long-buried person, on whom the Governor and Council have wrought a necromantic miracle. I should not wonder if he were to crumble away, some morning, after you are gone, and nothing be seen of him more, except a heap of dust. Miss Hepzibah, at any rate, will lose what little flexibility she has. They both exist by you!"

"I should be very sorry to think so," answered Phoebe, gravely. "But it is true that my small abilities were precisely what they needed; and I have a real interest in their welfare— an odd kind of motherly sentiment—which I wish you would not laugh at! And let me tell you frankly, Mr. Holgrave, I am sometimes puzzled to know whether you wish them well or ill."

"Undoubtedly," said the Daguerreotypist, "I do feel an interest in this antiquated, poverty-stricken, old maiden lady; and this degraded and shattered gentleman—this abortive lover of the Beautiful. A kindly interest too, helpless old children that they are! But you have no conception what a different kind of heart mine is from your own. It is not my impulse—as regards these two individuals—either to help or hinder; but to look on, to analyze, to explain matters to myself, and to comprehend the drama which, for almost two hundred years, has been dragging its slow length over the ground, where you and I now tread. If permitted to witness the close, I doubt not to derive a moral satisfaction from it, go matters how they may. There is a conviction within me, that the end draws nigh. But, though Providence sent you hither to help, and sends me only as a privileged and meet spectator, I pledge myself to lend these unfortunate beings whatever aid I can!"

"I wish you would speak more plainly," cried Phoebe, perplexed and displeased;—"and, above all, that you would feel more like a christian and a human being! How is it possible to see people in distress, without desiring, more than anything else, to help and comfort them? You talk as if this old house were a theatre; and you seem to look at Hepzibah's and Clifford's misfortunes, and those of generations before them, as a tragedy, such as I have seen acted in the hall of a country-hotel; only the present one appears to be played exclusively for your amusement! I do not like this. The play costs the performers too much—and the audience is too cold-hearted!"

"You are severe!" said Holgrave, compelled to recognize a degree of truth in this piquant sketch of his own mood.

"And then," continued Phoebe, "what can you mean by your conviction, which you tell me of, that the end is drawing near? Do you know of any new trouble hanging over my poor relatives? If so, tell me at once, and I will not leave them!"

"Forgive me, Phoebe!" said the Daguerreotypist, holding out his hand, to which the girl was constrained to yield her own. "I am somewhat of a mystic, it must be confessed. The tendency is in my blood, together with the faculty of mesmerism, which might have brought me to Gallows-Hill, in the good old times of witchcraft. Believe me, if I were really aware of any secret, the disclosure of which would benefit your friends—who are my own friends, likewise—you should learn it, before we part. But I have no such knowledge."

"You hold something back!" said Phoebe.

"Nothing—no secrets, but my own," answered Holgrave. "I can perceive, indeed, that Judge Pyncheon still keeps his eye on Clifford, in whose ruin he had so large a share. His motives and intentions, however, are a mystery to me. He is a determined and relentless man, with the genuine character of an inquisitor; and had he any object to gain by putting Clifford to the rack, I verily believe that he would wrench his joints from their sockets in order to accomplish it. But, so wealthy and eminent as he is—so powerful in his own strength, and in the support of society on all sides—what can Judge Pyncheon have to hope or fear from the imbecile, branded, half-torpid Clifford?"

"Yet," urged Phoebe, "you did speak as if misfortune were impending!"

"Oh, that was because I am morbid!" replied the artist. "My mind has a twist aside, like almost everybody's mind, except your own. Moreover, it is so strange to find myself an inmate of this old Pyncheon-house, and sitting in this old garden—(hark, how Maule's Well is murmuring!)—that, were it only for this one circumstance, I cannot help fancying that Destiny is arranging its fifth act for a catastrophe."

"There!" cried Phoebe with renewed vexation; for she was by nature as hostile to mystery, as the sunshine to a dark corner. "You puzzle me more than ever!"

"Then let us part friends!" said Holgrave, pressing her hand. "Or, if not friends, let us part before you entirely hate me. You, who love everybody else in the world!"

"Good bye, then," said Phoebe frankly. "I do not mean to be angry a great while, and should be sorry to have you think so. There has Cousin Hepzibah been standing in the shadow of the door-way, this quarter-of-an-hour past! She thinks I stay too long in the damp garden. So, good night, and good bye!"

On the second morning thereafter, Phoebe might have been seen, in her straw bonnet, with a shawl on one arm and a little carpet-bag on the other, bidding adieu to Hepzibah and Cousin Clifford. She was to take a seat in the next train of cars, which would transport her to within half-a-dozen miles of her country village.

The tears were in Phoebe's eyes; a smile, dewy with affectionate regret, was glimmering around her pleasant mouth. She wondered how it came to pass, that her life of a few weeks, here in this heavy-hearted old mansion, had taken such hold of her, and so melted into her associations, as now to seem a more important centre-point of remembrance than all which had gone before. How had Hepzibah—grim, silent, and irresponsive to her overflow of cordial sentiment—contrived to win so much love? And Clifford—in his abortive decay, with the mystery of fearful crime upon him, and the close prison-atmosphere yet lurking in his breath—how had he transformed himself into the simplest child, whom Phoebe felt bound to watch over, and be, as it were, the Providence of his unconsidered hours! Everything, at that instant of farewell, stood out prominently to her view. Look where she would, lay her hand on what she might, the object responded to her consciousness, as if a moist human heart were in it.

She peeped from the window into the garden, and felt herself more regretful at leaving this spot of black earth, vitiated with such an age-long growth of weeds, than joyful at the idea of again scenting her pine-forests and fresh clover-fields. She called Chanticleer, his two wives, and the venerable chicken, and threw them some crumbs of bread from the breakfast-table. These being hastily gobbled up, the chicken spread its wings, and alighted close by Phoebe on the window-sill, where it looked gravely into her face and vented its emotions in a croak. Phoebe bade it be a good old chicken, during her absence, and promised to bring it a little bag of buckwheat.

"Ah, Phoebe," remarked Hepzibah, "you do not smile so naturally as when you came to us! Then, the smile chose to shine out;—now, you choose it should. It is well that you are going back, for a little while, into your native air! There has been too much weight on your spirits. The house is too gloomy and lonesome; the shop is full of vexations; and as for me, I have no faculty of making things look brighter than they are. Dear Clifford has been your only comfort!"

"Come hither, Phoebe!" suddenly cried her Cousin Clifford, who had said very little, all the morning.—"Close!—closer!—and look me in the face!"

Phoebe put one of her small hands on each elbow of his chair, and leaned her face towards him, so that he might peruse it as carefully as he would. It is probable that the latent emotions of this parting hour had revived, in some degree, his bedimmed and enfeebled faculties. At any rate, Phoebe soon felt that, if not the profound insight of a seer, yet a more than feminine delicacy of appreciation was making her heart the subject of its regard. A moment before, she had known nothing which she would have sought to hide. Now, as if some secret were hinted to her own consciousness through the medium of another's perception, she was fain to let her eyelids droop beneath Clifford's gaze. A blush, too— the redder, because she strove hard to keep it down—ascended higher and higher, in a tide of fitful progress, until even her brow was all suffused with it.

"It is enough, Phoebe!" said Clifford, with a melancholy smile. "When I first saw you, you were the prettiest little maiden in the world; and now you have deepened into beauty! Girlhood has passed into womanhood; the bud is a bloom! Go, now! I feel lonelier than I did."

Phoebe took leave of the desolate couple, and passed through the shop, twinkling her eyelids to shake off a dew-drop; for—considering how brief her absence was to be, and therefore the folly of being cast down about it—she would not so far acknowledge her tears as to dry them with her handkerchief. On the door-step, she met the little urchin, whose marvellous feats of gastronomy have been recorded in the earlier pages of our narrative. She took from the window some specimen or other of natural history—her eyes being too dim with moisture to inform her accurately whether it was a rabbit or a hippopotamus—put it into the child's hand, as a parting gift, and went her way. Old Uncle Venner was just coming out of his door, with a wood-horse and saw on his shoulder; and, trudging along the street, he scrupled not to keep company with Phoebe, so far as their paths lay together; nor, in spite of his patched coat and rusty beaver, and the curious fashion of his tow-cloth trowsers, could she find it in her heart to outwalk him.

"We shall miss you, next Sabbath afternoon," observed the street-philosopher. "It is unaccountable how little while it takes some folks to grow just as natural to a man as his own breath; and, begging your pardon, Miss Phoebe, (though there can be no offence in an old man's saying it,) that's just what you've grown, to me! My years have been a great many, and your life is but just beginning; and yet, you are somehow as familiar to me as if I had found you at my mother's door, and you had blossomed, like a running vine, all along my pathway since. Come back soon, or I shall be gone to my farm; for I begin to find these wood-sawing jobs a little too tough for my back-ache."

"Very soon, Uncle Venner," replied Phoebe.

"And let it be all the sooner, Phoebe, for the sake of those poor souls yonder," continued her companion. "They can never do without you, now—never, Phoebe, never!—no more than if one of God's angels had been living with them, and making their dismal house pleasant and comfortable. Don't it seem to you they'd be in a sad case, if, some pleasant summer morning like this, the angel should spread his wings, and fly to the place he came from? Well; just so they feel, now that you're going home by the railroad! They can't bear it, Miss Phoebe; so be sure to come back!"

"I am no angel, Uncle Venner," said Phoebe, smiling, as she offered him her hand at the street-corner. "But, I suppose, people never feel so much like angels as when they are doing what little good they may. So I shall certainly come back!"

Thus parted the old man and the rosy girl; and Phoebe took the wings of the morning, and was soon flitting almost as rapidly away, as if endowed with the aerial locomotion of the angels, to whom Uncle Venner had so graciously compared her.

XV

THE SCOWL AND SMILE

SEVERAL days passed over the seven gables, heavily and drearily enough. In fact (not to attribute the whole gloom of sky and earth to the one inauspicious circumstance of Phoebe's departure) an easterly storm had set in, and indefatigably applied itself to the task of making the black roof and walls of the old house look more cheerless than ever before. Yet was the outside not half so cheerless as the interior. Poor Clifford was cut off, at once, from all his scanty resources of enjoyment. Phoebe was not there; nor did the sunshine fall upon the floor. The garden, with its muddy walks and the chill, dripping foliage of its summer-house, was an image to be shuddered at. Nothing flourished in the cold, moist, pitiless atmosphere, drifting with the brackish scud of sea-breezes, except the moss along the joints of the shingle-roof, and the great bunch of weeds, that had lately been suffering from drought, in the angle between the two front gables.

As for Hepzibah, she seemed not merely possessed with the east-wind, but to be, in her very person, only another phase of this gray and sullen spell of weather; the East-Wind itself, grim and disconsolate, in a rusty black silk-gown, and with a turban of cloud-wreaths on its head! The custom of the shop fell off, because a story got abroad that she soured her small beer and other damageable commodities, by scowling on them. It is perhaps true, that the public had something reasonably to complain of in her deportment; but towards Clifford she was neither ill-tempered nor unkind, nor felt less warmth of heart than always, had it been possible to make it reach him. The inutility of her best efforts, however, palsied the poor old gentlewoman. She could do little else than sit silently in a corner of the room, where the wet pear-tree branches, sweeping across the small windows, created a noonday dusk, which Hepzibah unconsciously darkened with her wo-begone aspect. It was no fault of Hepzibah's. Everything—even the old chairs and tables, that had known what weather was, for three or four such lifetimes as her own—looked as damp and chill as if the present were their worst experience. The picture of the Puritan Colonel shivered on the wall. The house itself shivered, from every attic of its seven gables, down to the great kitchen-fireplace, which served all the better as an emblem of the mansion's heart, because, though built for warmth, it was now so comfortless and empty.

Hepzibah attempted to enliven matters by a fire in the parlor. But the storm-demon kept watch above, and, whenever a flame was kindled, drove the smoke back again, choking the chimney's sooty throat with its own breath. Nevertheless, during four days of this miserable storm, Clifford wrapt himself in an old cloak, and occupied his customary chair. On the morning of the fifth, when summoned to breakfast, he responded only by a broken-hearted murmur, expressive of a determination not to leave his bed. His sister made no attempt to change his purpose. In fact, entirely as she loved him, Hepzibah could hardly have borne any longer the wretched duty—so impracticable by her few and rigid faculties—of seeking pastime for a still sensitive, but ruined mind, critical, and fastidious, without force or volition. It was, at least, something short of positive despair, that, to-day, she might sit shivering alone, and not suffer continually a new grief, and unreasonable pang of remorse, at every fitful sigh of her fellow-sufferer.

But Clifford, it seemed, though he did not make his appearance below stairs, had, after all, bestirred himself in quest of amusement. In the course of the forenoon, Hepzibah heard a note of music, which (there being no other tuneful contrivance in the House of the Seven Gables) she knew must proceed from Alice Pyncheon's harpsichord. She was aware that Clifford, in his youth, had possessed a cultivated taste for music, and a considerable degree of skill in its practice. It was difficult, however, to conceive of his retaining an accomplishment to which daily exercise is so essential, in the measure indicated by the sweet, airy, and delicate, though most melancholy strain, that now stole upon her ear. Nor was it less marvellous, that the long silent instrument should be capable of so much melody. Hepzibah involuntarily thought of the ghostly harmonies, prelusive of death in the family, which were attributed to the legendary Alice. But it was, perhaps, proof of the agency of other than spiritual fingers, that, after a few touches, the chords seemed to snap asunder with their own vibrations, and the music ceased.

But a harsher sound succeeded to the mysterious notes; nor was the easterly day fated to pass without an event, sufficient in itself to poison, for Hepzibah and Clifford, the balmiest air that ever brought the humming-birds along with it. The final echoes of Alice Pyncheon's performance, (or Clifford's, if his we must consider it,) were driven away by no less vulgar a dissonance than the ringing of the shop-bell. A foot was heard scraping itself on the threshold, and thence somewhat ponderously stepping on the floor. Hepzibah delayed, a moment, while muffling herself in a faded shawl, which had been her defensive armor in a forty years' warfare against the east-wind. A characteristic sound, however—neither a cough nor a hem, but a kind of rumbling and reverberating spasm in somebody's capacious depth of chest—impelled her to hurry forward, with that aspect of fierce faint-heartedness, so common to women in cases of perilous emergency. Few of her sex, on such occasions, have ever looked so terrible as our poor scowling Hepzibah. But the visitor quietly closed the shop-door behind him, stood up his umbrella against the counter, and turned a visage of composed benignity, to meet the alarm and anger which his appearance had excited.

Hepzibah's presentiment had not deceived her. It was no other than Judge Pyncheon, who, after in vain trying the front-door, had now effected his entrance into the shop.

"How do you do, Cousin Hepzibah?—and how does this most inclement weather affect our poor Clifford?" began the Judge; and wonderful it seemed, indeed, that the easterly storm was not put to shame, or, at any rate, a little mollified, by the genial benevolence of his smile. "I could not rest without calling to ask, once more, whether I can in any manner promote his comfort, or your own!"

"You can do nothing," said Hepzibah, controlling her agitation as well as she could. "I devote myself to Clifford. He has every comfort which his situation admits of."

"But, allow me to suggest, dear Cousin," rejoined the Judge, "you err—in all affection and kindness, no doubt, and with the very best intentions—but you do err, nevertheless, in keeping your brother so secluded. Why insulate him thus from all sympathy and kindness? Clifford, alas! has had too much of solitude. Now let him try society—the society, that is to say, of kindred and old friends. Let me, for instance, but see Clifford; and I will answer for the good effect of the interview."

"You cannot see him," answered Hepzibah. "Clifford has kept his bed since yesterday."

"What! How! Is he ill?" exclaimed Judge Pyncheon, starting with what seemed to be angry alarm; for the very frown of the old Puritan darkened through the room as he spoke.

"Nay, then, I must and will see him! What if he should die?"

"He is in no danger of death," said Hepzibah—and added, with bitterness that she could repress no longer, "None;— unless he shall be persecuted to death, now, by the same man who long ago attempted it!"

"Cousin Hepzibah," said the Judge, with an impressive earnestness of manner, which grew even to tearful pathos as he proceeded, "is it possible that you do not perceive how unjust, how unkind, how unchristian, is this constant, this long-continued bitterness against me, for a part which I was constrained by duty and conscience, by the force of law, and at my own peril, to act? What did I do, in detriment to Clifford, which it was possible to leave undone? How could you, his sister—if, for your never-ending sorrow, as it has been for mine, you had known what I did—have shown greater tenderness? And do you think, Cousin, that it has cost me no pang? —that it has left no anguish in my bosom, from that day to this, amidst all the prosperity with which Heaven has blessed me?—or that I do not now rejoice, when it is deemed consistent with the dues of public justice and the welfare of society, that this dear kinsman, this early friend, this nature so delicately and beautifully constituted—so unfortunate, let us pronounce him, and forbear to say, so guilty—that our own Clifford, in fine, should be given back to life and its possibilities of enjoyment? Ah, you little know me, Cousin Hepzibah! You little know this heart! It now throbs at the thought of meeting him! There lives not the human being—(except yourself; and you not more than I)—who has shed so many tears for Clifford's calamity! You behold some of them now. There is none who would so delight to promote his happiness! Try me, Hepzibah!—try me, Cousin!—try the man whom you have treated as your enemy and Clifford's!—try Jaffrey Pyncheon, and you shall find him true, to the heart's core!"

"In the name of Heaven," cried Hepzibah, provoked only to intenser indignation by this outgush of the inestimable tenderness of a stern nature—"in God's name, whom you insult—and whose power I could almost question, since He hears you utter so many false words, without palsying your tongue—give over, I beseech you, this loathsome pretence of affection for your victim! You hate him! Say so, like a man! You cherish, at this moment, some black purpose against him, in your heart! Speak it out, at once!—or, if you hope so to promote it better, hide it, till you can triumph in its success. But never speak again of your love for my poor brother! I cannot bear it! It will drive me beyond a woman's decency! It will drive me mad! Forbear! Not another word! It will make me spurn at you!"

For once, Hepzibah's wrath had given her courage. She had spoken. But, after all, was this unconquerable distrust of Judge Pyncheon's integrity—and this utter denial, apparently, of his claim to stand in the ring of human sympathies—were they founded in any just perception of his character, or merely the offspring of a woman's unreasoning prejudice, deduced from nothing?

The Judge, beyond all question, was a man of eminent respectability. The church acknowledged it; the state acknowledged it. It was denied by nobody. In all the very extensive sphere of those who knew him, whether in his public or private capacities, there was not an individual—except Hepzibah, and some lawless mystic like the Daguerreotypist, and possibly a few political opponents—who would have dreamed of seriously disputing his claim to a high and honorable place in the world's regard. Nor, we must do him the further justice to say, did Judge Pyncheon himself, probably, entertain many or very frequent doubts, that his enviable reputation accorded with his deserts. His conscience, therefore—usually considered the surest witness to a man's integrity—his conscience, unless, it might be for the little space of five minutes in the twenty-four hours, or, now and then, some black day in the whole year's circle—his conscience bore an accordant testimony with the world's laudatory voice. And yet, strong as this evidence may seem to be, we should hesitate to peril our own conscience on the assertion, that the Judge and the consenting world were right, and that poor Hepzibah, with her solitary prejudice, was wrong. Hidden from mankind—forgotten by himself, or buried so deeply under a sculptured and ornamented pile of ostentatious deeds, that his daily life could take no note of it—there may have lurked some evil and unsightly thing. Nay; we could almost venture to say farther, that a daily guilt might have been acted by him, continually renewed, and reddening forth afresh, like the miraculous blood-stain of a murder, without his necessarily, and at every moment, being aware of it.

Men of strong minds, great force of character, and a hard texture of the sensibilities, are very capable of falling into mistakes of this kind. They are ordinarily men to whom forms are of paramount importance. Their field of action lies among the external phenomena of life. They possess vast ability in grasping, and arranging, and appropriating to themselves, the big, heavy, solid unrealities, such as gold, landed estate, offices of trust and emolument, and public honors. With these materials, and with deeds of goodly aspect, done in the public eye, an individual of this class builds up, as it were, a tall and stately edifice, which, in the view of other people, and ultimately in his own view, is no other than the man's character, or the man himself. Behold, therefore, a palace! Its splendid halls and suites of spacious apartments are floored with a mosaic-work of costly marbles; its windows, the whole height of each room, admit the sunshine through the most transparent of plate-glass; its high cornices are gilded, and its ceilings gorgeously painted; and a lofty dome—through which, from the central pavement, you may gaze up to the sky, as with no obstructing medium between—surmounts the whole. With what fairer and nobler emblem could any man desire to shadow forth his character? Ah; but in some low and obscure nook—some narrow closet on the ground floor, shut, locked, and bolted, and the key flung away—or beneath the marble pavement, in a stagnant water-puddle, with the richest pattern of mosaic-work above—may lie a corpse, half-decayed, and still decaying, and diffusing its death-scent all through the palace! The inhabitant will not be conscious of it; for it has long been his daily breath! Neither will the visitors; for they smell only the rich odors which the master sedulously scatters through the palace, and the incense which they bring, and delight to burn before him! Now and then, perchance, comes in a seer, before whose sadly gifted eye the whole structure melts into thin air, leaving only the hidden nook, the bolted closet, with the cobwebs festooned over its forgotten door, or the deadly hole under the pavement, and the decaying corpse within. Here, then, we are to seek the true emblem of the man's character, and of the deed that gives whatever reality it possesses, to his life. And, beneath the show of a marble palace, that pool of stagnant water, foul with many impurities, and perhaps tinged with blood—that secret abomination, above which, possibly, he may say his prayers, without remembering it—is this man's miserable soul!

To apply this train of remark somewhat more closely to Judge Pyncheon! We might say (without, in the least, imputing crime to a personage of his eminent respectability) that there was enough of splendid rubbish in his life to cover up and paralyze a more active and subtile conscience than the Judge was ever troubled with. The purity of his judicial character, while on the bench; the faithfulness of his public service in subsequent capacities; his devotedness to his party, and the rigid consistency with which he had adhered to its principles, or, at all events, kept pace with its organized movements; his remarkable zeal as president of a Bible society; his unimpeachable integrity as treasurer of a Widow's and Orphan's fund; his benefits to horticulture, by

producing two much-esteemed varieties of the pear, and to
agriculture, through the agency of the famous Pyncheon-
bull; the cleanliness of his moral deportment, for a great
many years past; the severity with which he had frowned
upon, and finally cast off, an expensive and dissipated son,
delaying forgiveness until within the final quarter of an hour
of the young man's life; his prayers at morning and eventide,
and graces at mealtime; his efforts in furtherance of the
temperance-cause; his confining himself, since the last attack
of the gout, to five diurnal glasses of old Sherry wine; the
snowy whiteness of his linen, the polish of his boots, the
handsomeness of his gold-headed cane, the square and roomy
fashion of his coat, and the fineness of its material, and, in
general, the studied propriety of his dress and equipment;
the scrupulousness with which he paid public notice, in the
street, by a bow, a lifting of the hat, a nod, or a motion of the
hand, to all and sundry his acquaintances, rich or poor; the
smile of broad benevolence wherewith he made it a point to
gladden the whole world;—what room could possibly be found
for darker traits, in a portrait made up of lineaments like
these! This proper face was what he beheld in the looking-
glass. This admirably arranged life was what he was conscious of, in the progress of every day. Then, might not he
claim to be its result and sum, and say to himself and the
community—"Behold Judge Pyncheon, there"?

And, allowing that, many, many years ago, in his early
and reckless youth, he had committed some one wrong act—
or that, even now, the inevitable force of circumstances
should occasionally make him do one questionable deed,
among a thousand praiseworthy, or, at least, blameless ones—
would you characterize the Judge by that one necessary deed,
and that half-forgotten act, and let it overshadow the fair
aspect of a lifetime! What is there so ponderous in evil, that
a thumb's bigness of it should outweigh the mass of things
not evil, which were heaped into the other scale! This scale

and balance system is a favorite one with people of Judge Pyncheon's brotherhood. A hard, cold man, thus unfortunately situated, seldom or never looking inward, and resolutely taking his idea of himself from what purports to be his image, as reflected in the mirror of public opinion, can scarcely arrive at true self-knowledge, except through loss of property and reputation. Sickness will not always help him to it; not always the death-hour!

But our affair, now, is with Judge Pyncheon, as he stood confronting the fierce outbreak of Hepzibah's wrath. Without premeditation, to her own surprise, and indeed terror, she had given vent, for once, to the inveteracy of her resentment, cherished against this kinsman, for thirty years.

Thus far, the Judge's countenance had expressed mild forbearance—grave and almost gentle deprecation of his cousin's unbecoming violence—free and christianlike forgiveness of the wrong inflicted by her words. But, when those words were irrevocably spoken, his look assumed sternness, the sense of power, and immitigable resolve; and this with so natural and imperceptible a change, that it seemed as if the iron man had stood there from the first, and the meek man not at all. The effect was as when the light vapory clouds, with their soft coloring, suddenly vanish from the stony brow of a precipitous mountain, and leave there the frown which you at once feel to be eternal. Hepzibah almost adopted the insane belief, that it was her old Puritan ancestor, and not the modern Judge, on whom she had just been wreaking the bitterness of her heart. Never did a man show stronger proof of the lineage attributed to him, than Judge Pyncheon, at this crisis, by his unmistakeable resemblance to the picture in the inner room.

"Cousin Hepzibah," said he, very calmly, "it is time to have done with this."

"With all my heart!" answered she. "Then why do you

persecute us any longer? Leave poor Clifford and me in peace. Neither of us desires anything better!"

"It is my purpose to see Clifford before I leave this house," continued the Judge. "Do not act like a madwoman, Hepzibah! I am his only friend, and an all-powerful one. Has it never occurred to you—are you so blind as not to have seen—that, without not merely my consent, but my efforts, my representations, the exertion of my whole influence, political, official, personal—Clifford would never have been what you call free? Did you think his release a triumph over me? Not so, my good Cousin; not so, by any means! The farthest possible from that! No; but it was the accomplishment of a purpose long entertained on my part. I set him free!"

"You!" answered Hepzibah. "I never will believe it! He owed his dungeon to you; his freedom, to God's providence!"

"I set him free!" re-affirmed Judge Pyncheon, with the calmest composure. "And I come hither now to decide whether he shall retain his freedom. It will depend upon himself. For this purpose, I must see him."

"Never!—it would drive him mad!" exclaimed Hepzibah, but with an irresoluteness, sufficiently perceptible to the keen eye of the Judge; for, without the slightest faith in his good intentions, she knew not whether there was most to dread in yielding, or resistance. "And why should you wish to see this wretched, broken man, who retains hardly a fraction of his intellect, and will hide even that from an eye which has no love in it?"

"He shall see love enough in mine, if that be all!" said the Judge, with well-grounded confidence in the benignity of his aspect. "But, Cousin Hepzibah, you confess a great deal, and very much to the purpose. Now, listen, and I will frankly explain my reasons for insisting on this interview. At the death, thirty years since, of our Uncle Jaffrey, it was found—I know not whether the circumstance ever attracted much of your attention, among the sadder interests that clustered round that event—but it was found that his visible estate, of every kind, fell far short of any estimate ever made of it. He was supposed to be immensely rich. Nobody doubted that he stood among the weightiest men of his day. It was one of his eccentricities, however—and not altogether a folly, neither—to conceal the amount of his property by making distant and foreign investments, perhaps under other names than his own, and by various means, familiar enough to capitalists, but unnecessary here to be specified. By Uncle Jaffrey's last will and testament, as you are aware, his entire property was bequeathed to me, with the single exception of a life-interest, to yourself, in this old family-mansion, and the strip of patrimonial estate, remaining attached to it."

"And do you seek to deprive us of that?" asked Hepzibah, unable to restrain her bitter contempt. "Is this your price for ceasing to persecute poor Clifford?"

"Certainly not, my dear Cousin!" answered the Judge, smiling benevolently. "On the contrary, as you must do me the justice to own, I have constantly expressed my readiness to double or treble your resources, whenever you should make up your mind to accept any kindness of that nature, at the hands of your kinsman. No, no! But here lies the gist of the matter. Of my Uncle's unquestionably great estate, as I have said, not the half—no, not one third, as I am fully convinced—was apparent after his death. Now, I have the best possible reasons for believing, that your brother Clifford can give me a clue to the recovery of the remainder!"

"Clifford?—Clifford know of any hidden wealth?—Clifford have it in his power to make you rich?" cried the old gentle-woman, affected with a sense of something like ridicule, at the idea. "Impossible! You deceive yourself! It is really a thing to laugh at!"

"It is as certain as that I stand here!" said Judge Pyncheon, striking his gold-headed cane on the floor, and at the same time stamping his foot, as if to express his conviction the more forcibly by the whole emphasis of his substantial person.—"Clifford told me so himself!"

"No, no!" exclaimed Hepzibah incredulously. "You are dreaming, Cousin Jaffrey!"

"I do not belong to the dreaming class of men," said the Judge quietly. "Some months before my Uncle's death, Clifford boasted to me of the possession of the secret of incalculable wealth. His purpose was to taunt me, and excite my curiosity. I know it well. But, from a pretty distinct recollection of the particulars of our conversation, I am thoroughly convinced that there was truth in what he said. Clifford, at this moment, if he chooses—and choose he must—can inform me where to find the schedule, the documents, the evidences, in whatever shape they exist, of the vast amount of Uncle Jaffrey's missing property. He has the secret. His boast was no idle word. It had a directness, an emphasis, a particularity, that showed a backbone of solid meaning within the mystery of his expression."

"But what could have been Clifford's object," asked Hepzibah, "in concealing it so long?"

"It was one of the bad impulses of our fallen nature," replied the Judge, turning up his eyes. "He looked upon me as his enemy. He considered me as the cause of his overwhelming disgrace, his imminent peril of death, his irretrievable ruin. There was no great probability, therefore, of his volunteering information, out of his dungeon, that should elevate me still higher on the ladder of prosperity. But the moment has now come, when he must give up his secret."

"And what if he should refuse?" inquired Hepzibah. "Or—as I steadfastly believe—what if he has no knowledge of this wealth?"

"My dear Cousin," said Judge Pyncheon, with a quietude which he had the power of making more formidable than any violence, "since your brother's return, I have taken the precaution (a highly proper one in the near kinsman and natural guardian of an individual so situated) to have his deportment and habits constantly and carefully overlooked. Your neighbors have been eye-witnesses to whatever has passed in the garden. The butcher, the baker, the fish-monger, some of the customers of your shop, and many a prying old woman, have told me several of the secrets of your interior. A still larger circle—I myself among the rest—can testify to his extravagances, at the arched window. Thousands beheld him, a week or two ago, on the point of flinging himself thence into the street. From all this testimony, I am led to apprehend—reluctantly, and with deep grief—that Clifford's misfortunes have so affected his intellect, never very strong, that he cannot safely remain at large. The alternative, you must be aware—and its adoption will depend entirely on the decision which I am now about to make—the alternative is his confinement, probably for the remainder of his life, in a public asylum for persons in his unfortunate state of mind."

"You cannot mean it!" shrieked Hepzibah.

"Should my Cousin Clifford," continued Judge Pyncheon, wholly undisturbed, "from mere malice, and hatred of one whose interests ought naturally to be dear to him—a mode of passion that, as often as any other, indicates mental dis-ease—should he refuse me the information, so important to myself, and which he assuredly possesses, I shall consider it the one needed jot of evidence, to satisfy my mind of his insanity. And, once sure of the course pointed out by conscience, you know me too well, Cousin Hepzibah, to entertain a doubt that I shall pursue it."

"Oh, Jaffrey—Cousin Jaffrey," cried Hepzibah, mournfully, not passionately—"it is you that are diseased in mind, not Clifford! You have forgotten that a woman was your mother! —that you have had sisters, brothers, children of your own!— or that there ever was affection between man and man, or pity from one man to another, in this miserable world! Else, how could you have dreamed of this? You are not young, Cousin Jaffrey—no, nor middle-aged—but already an old man.

The hair is white upon your head! How many years have you to live? Are you not rich enough for that little time? Shall you be hungry?—shall you lack clothes, or a roof to shelter you, between this point and the grave? No; but, with the half of what you now possess, you could revel in costly food and wines, and build a house twice as splendid as you now inhabit, and make a far greater show to the world—and yet leave riches to your only son, to make him bless the hour of your death! Then why should you do this cruel, cruel thing? —so mad a thing, that I know not whether to call it wicked! Alas, Cousin Jaffrey, this hard and grasping spirit has run in our blood, these two hundred years! You are but doing over again, in another shape, what your ancestor before you did, and sending down to your posterity the curse inherited from him!"

"Talk sense, Hepzibah, for Heaven's sake!" exclaimed the Judge, with the impatience natural to a reasonable man, on hearing anything so utterly absurd as the above, in a discussion about matters of business. "I have told you my determination. I am not apt to change. Clifford must give up his secret, or take the consequences. And let him decide quickly; for I have several affairs to attend to, this morning, and an important dinner-engagement with some political friends."

"Clifford has no secret!" answered Hepzibah. "And God will not let you do the thing you meditate!"

"We shall see!" said the unmoved Judge. "Meanwhile, choose whether you will summon Clifford, and allow this business to be amicably settled by an interview between two kinsmen; or drive me to harsher measures, which I should be most happy to feel myself justified in avoiding. The responsibility is altogether on your part."

"You are stronger than I," said Hepzibah, after a brief consideration; "and you have no pity in your strength. Clifford is not now insane; but the interview, which you insist upon, may go far to make him so. Nevertheless, knowing you as I do, I believe it to be my best course to allow you to judge for yourself as to the improbability of his possessing any valuable secret. I will call Clifford. Be merciful in your dealings with him!—be far more merciful than your heart bids you be!—for God is looking at you, Jaffrey Pyncheon!"

The Judge followed his cousin from the shop, where the foregoing conversation had passed, into the parlor, and flung himself heavily into the great, ancestral chair. Many a former Pyncheon had found repose in its capacious arms;—rosy children, after their sports, young men, dreamy with love, grown men, weary with cares, old men, burthened with winters;—they had mused, and slumbered, and departed, to a yet profounder sleep. It had been a long tradition, though a doubtful one, that this was the very chair, seated in which, the earliest of the Judge's New England forefathers—he whose picture still hung upon the wall—had given a dead man's silent and stern reception to the throng of distinguished guests. From that hour of evil omen, until the present, it may be—though we know not the secret of his heart—but it may be, that no wearier and sadder man had ever sunk into the chair, than this same Judge Pyncheon, whom we have just beheld so immitigably hard and resolute. Surely, it must have been at no slight cost, that he had thus fortified his soul with iron! Such calmness is a mightier effort than the violence of weaker men. And there was yet a heavy task for him to do! Was it a little matter—a trifle, to be prepared for in a single moment, and to be rested from, in another moment—that he must now, after thirty years, encounter a kinsman risen from a living tomb, and wrench a secret from him, or else consign him to a living tomb again?

"Did you speak?" asked Hepzibah, looking in from the threshold of the parlor; for she imagined that the Judge had uttered some sound, which she was anxious to interpret as a relenting impulse. "I thought you called me back!"

"No, no!" gruffly answered Judge Pyncheon, with a harsh

frown, while his brow grew almost a black purple, in the shadow of the room. "Why should I call you back? Time flies! Bid Clifford come to me!"

The Judge had taken his watch from his vest-pocket, and now held it in his hand, measuring the interval which was to ensue before the appearance of Clifford.

XVI

CLIFFORD'S CHAMBER

NEVER had the old house appeared so dismal to poor Hepzibah, as when she departed on that wretched errand. There was a strange aspect in it. As she trode along the foot-worn passages, and opened one crazy door after another, and ascended the creaking staircase, she gazed wistfully and fearfully around. It would have been no marvel, to her excited mind, if, behind or beside her, there had been the rustle of dead people's garments, or pale visages awaiting her on the landing place above. Her nerves were set all ajar by the scene of passion and terror, through which she had just struggled. Her colloquy with Judge Pyncheon, who so perfectly represented the person and attributes of the founder of the family, had called back the dreary past. It weighed upon her heart. Whatever she had heard from legendary aunts and grandmothers, concerning the good or evil fortunes of the Pyncheons—stories, which had heretofore been kept warm in her remembrance by the chimney-corner glow, that was associated with them—now recurred to her, sombre, ghastly, cold, like most passages of family history, when brooded over in melancholy mood. The whole seemed little else but a series of calamity, reproducing itself in successive generations, with one general hue, and varying in little save the outline. But Hepzibah now felt as if the Judge, and Clifford, and herself—they three together—were on the point of adding another incident to the annals of the house, with a bolder relief of wrong and sorrow, which would cause it to stand out from all the rest. Thus it is, that the grief of the passing moment takes upon itself an individuality, and a character of climax, which it is destined to lose, after awhile, and to fade into the dark gray tissue, common to the grave or glad events of many years ago. It is but for a moment, comparatively, that anything looks strange or startling;—a truth, that has the bitter and the sweet in it!

But Hepzibah could not rid herself of the sense of something unprecedented, at that instant passing, and soon to be accomplished. Her nerves were in a shake. Instinctively, she paused before the arched window, and looked out upon the street, in order to seize its permanent objects with her mental grasp, and thus to steady herself from the reel and vibration which affected her more immediate sphere. It brought her up, as we may say, with a kind of shock, when she beheld everything under the same appearance as the day before, and numberless preceding days, except for the difference between sunshine and sullen storm. Her eyes travelled along the street, from door-step to door-step, noting the wet sidewalks, with here and there a puddle in hollows that had been imperceptible, until filled with water. She screwed her dim optics to their acutest point in the hope of making out, with greater distinctness, a certain window, where she half saw, half guessed, that a tailor's seamstress was sitting at her work. Hepzibah flung herself upon that unknown woman's companionship, even thus far off. Then she was attracted by a chaise rapidly passing, and watched its moist and glistening top, and its splashing wheels, until it had turned the corner, and refused to carry any further her idly trifling, because appalled and overburthened mind. When the vehicle had disappeared, she allowed herself still another loitering moment; for the patched figure of good Uncle Venner was now visible, coming slowly from the head of the street downward, with a rheumatic limp, because the east-wind had got into his joints. Hepzibah wished that he would pass yet more slowly, and befriend her shivering solitude, a little longer. Anything that would take her out of the grievous present, and interpose human beings betwixt herself and what was nearest to her—whatever would defer, for an instant, the inevitable errand on which she was bound—all such impediments were welcome. Next to the lightest heart, the heaviest is apt to be most playful.

Hepzibah had little hardihood for her own proper pain, and far less for what she must inflict on Clifford. Of so slight a nature, and so shattered by his previous calamities, it could not well be short of utter ruin, to bring him face to face with the hard, relentless man, who had been his Evil Destiny through life. Even had there been no bitter recollections, nor any hostile interest now at stake between them, the mere natural repugnance of the more sensitive system to the massive, weighty, and unimpressible one, must in itself have been disastrous to the former. It would be like flinging a porcelain vase, with already a crack in it, against a granite column. Never before had Hepzibah so adequately estimated the powerful character of her Cousin Jaffrey;—powerful by intellect, energy of will, the long habit of acting among men, and, as she believed, by his unscrupulous pursuit of selfish ends through evil means. It did but increase the difficulty, that Judge Pyncheon was under a delusion as to the secret which he supposed Clifford to possess. Men of his strength of purpose, and customary sagacity, if they chance to adopt a mistaken opinion in practical matters, so wedge it and fasten it among things known to be true, that to wrench it out of their minds is hardly less difficult than pulling up an oak. Thus, as the Judge required an impossibility of Clifford, the latter, as he could not perform it, must needs perish. For what, in the grasp of a man like this, was to become of Clifford's soft, poetic nature, that never should have had a task more stubborn than to set a life of beautiful enjoyment to the flow and rhythm of musical cadences! Indeed, what had become of it, already? Broken! Blighted! All but annihilated! Soon to be wholly so!

For a moment, the thought crossed Hepzibah's mind, whether Clifford might not really have such knowledge of their deceased uncle's vanished estate, as the Judge imputed to him. She remembered some vague intimations, on her brother's part, which—if the supposition were not essentially preposterous—might have been so interpreted. There had been schemes of travel and residence abroad, day-dreams of brilliant life at home, and splendid castles in the air, which it would have required boundless wealth to build and realize. Had this wealth been in her power, how gladly would Hepzibah have bestowed it all upon her iron-hearted kinsman, to buy for Clifford the freedom and seclusion of the desolate old house! But she believed that her brother's schemes were as destitute of actual substance and purpose, as a child's pictures of its future life, while sitting in a little chair by its mother's knee. Clifford had none but shadowy gold at his command; and it was not the stuff to satisfy Judge Pyncheon!

Was there no help in their extremity? It seemed strange that there should be none, with a city roundabout her. It would be so easy to throw up the window and send forth a shriek, at the strange agony of which, everybody would come hastening to the rescue, well understanding it to be the cry of a human soul, at some dreadful crisis! But how wild, how almost laughable the fatality—and yet how continually it comes to pass, thought Hepzibah, in this dull delirium of a world—that whosoever, and with however kindly a purpose, should come to help, they would be sure to help the strongest side! Might and wrong combined, like iron magnetized, are endowed with irresistible attraction. There would be Judge Pyncheon; a person eminent in the public view, of high sta-

tion and great wealth, a philanthropist, a member of Congress
and of the church, and intimately associated with whatever
else bestows good name; so imposing, in these advantageous
lights, that Hepzibah herself could hardly help shrinking
from her own conclusions as to his hollow integrity! The
Judge, on one side! And who, on the other? The guilty
Clifford! Once, a by-word! Now, an indistinctly remembered
ignominy!

Nevertheless, in spite of this perception that the Judge
would draw all human aid to his own behalf, Hepzibah was
so unaccustomed to act for herself, that the least word of
counsel would have swayed her to any mode of action. Little
Phoebe Pyncheon would at once have lighted up the whole
scene, if not by any available suggestion, yet simply by the
warm vivacity of her character. The idea of the artist occurred to Hepzibah. Young and unknown, mere vagrant
adventurer as he was, she had been conscious of a force in
Holgrave, which might well adapt him to be the champion
of a crisis. With this thought in her mind, she unbolted a
door, cobwebbed and long disused, but which had served as
a former medium of communication between her own part
of the house, and the gable where the wandering Daguerreotypist had now established his temporary home. He was not
there. A book, face downward on the table, a roll of manuscript, a half-written sheet, a newspaper, some tools of his
present occupation, and several rejected daguerreotypes, conveyed an impression as if he were close at hand. But, at this
period of the day, as Hepzibah might have anticipated, the
artist was at his public rooms. With an impulse of idle curiosity, that flickered among her heavy thoughts, she looked at
one of the daguerreotypes, and beheld Judge Pyncheon
frowning at her! Fate stared her in the face. She turned back
from her fruitless quest, with a heart-sinking sense of disappointment. In all her years of seclusion, she had never felt,
as now, what it was to be alone. It seemed as if the house

stood in a desert, or, by some spell, was made invisible to those who dwelt around, or passed beside it; so that any mode of misfortune, miserable accident, or crime, might happen in it, without the possibility of aid. In her grief and wounded pride, Hepzibah had spent her life in divesting herself of friends;—she had wilfully cast off the support which God has ordained His creatures to need from one another;—and it was now her punishment, that Clifford and herself would fall the easier victims to their kindred enemy.

Returning to the arched window, she lifted her eyes—scowling, poor, dim-sighted Hepzibah, in the face of Heaven!—and strove hard to send up a prayer through the dense, gray pavement of clouds. Those mists had gathered, as if to symbolize a great, brooding mass of human trouble, doubt, confusion, and chill indifference, between earth and the better regions. Her faith was too weak; the prayer too heavy to be thus uplifted. It fell back, a lump of lead, upon her heart. It smote her with the wretched conviction, that Providence intermeddled not in these petty wrongs of one individual to his fellow, nor had any balm for these little agonies of a solitary soul, but shed its justice, and its mercy, in a broad, sunlike sweep, over half the universe at once. Its vastness made it nothing. But Hepzibah did not see, that, just as there comes a warm sunbeam into every cottage-window, so comes a love-beam of God's care and pity, for every separate need.

At last, finding no other pretext for deferring the torture that she was to inflict on Clifford, her reluctance to which was the true cause of her loitering at the window, her search for the artist, and even her abortive prayer—dreading also to hear the stern voice of Judge Pyncheon from below stairs, chiding her delay—she crept slowly, a pale, grief-stricken figure, a dismal shape of woman, with almost torpid limbs, slowly to her brother's door, and knocked.

There was no reply!

And how should there have been! Her hand, tremulous

with the shrinking purpose which directed it, had smitten so feebly against the door that the sound could hardly have gone inward. She knocked again. Still, no response! Nor was it to be wondered at. She had struck with the entire force of her heart's vibration, communicating by some subtle magnetism her own terror to the summons. Clifford would turn his face to the pillow, and cover his head beneath the bed-clothes, like a startled child at midnight. She knocked a third time, three regular strokes, gentle, but perfectly distinct, and with meaning in them; for, modulate it with what cautious art we will, the hand cannot help playing some tune of what we feel, upon the senseless wood.

Clifford returned no answer.

"Clifford! Dear brother!" said Hepzibah. "Shall I come in?"

A silence!

Two or three times, and more, Hepzibah repeated his name, without result; till, thinking her brother's sleep unwontedly profound, she undid the door, and entering, found the chamber vacant. How could he have come forth, and when, without her knowledge? Was it possible that, in spite of the stormy day, and worn out with the irksomeness within doors, he had betaken himself to his customary haunt, in the garden, and was now shivering under the cheerless shelter of the summer-house? She hastily threw up a window, thrust forth her turbaned head and the half of her gaunt figure, and searched the whole garden through, as completely as her dim vision would allow. She could see the interior of the summer-house, and its circular seat, kept moist by the droppings of the roof. It had no occupant. Clifford was not thereabouts; unless, indeed, he had crept for concealment—(as, for a moment, Hepzibah fancied might be the case)—into a great, wet mass of tangled and broad-leaved shadow, where the squash-vines were clambering tumultuously upon an old wooden frame-work, set casually aslant against the fence. This could not be, however; he was not there; for, while Hepzibah was looking, a strange Grimalkin stole forth from the very spot, and picked his way across the garden. Twice, he paused to snuff the air, and then anew directed his course towards the parlor-window. Whether it was only on account of the stealthy, prying manner common to the race, or that this cat seemed to have more than ordinary mischief in his thoughts, the old gentlewoman, in spite of her much perplexity, felt an impulse to drive the animal away, and accordingly flung down a window-stick. The cat stared up at her, like a detected thief or murderer, and, the next instant, took to flight. No other living creature was visible in the garden. Chanticleer and his family had either not left their roost, disheartened by the interminable rain, or had done the next wisest thing, by seasonably returning to it. Hepzibah closed the window.

But where was Clifford? Could it be, that, aware of the presence of his Evil Destiny, he had crept silently down the staircase, while the Judge and Hepzibah stood talking in the shop, and had softly undone the fastenings of the outer door, and made his escape into the street? With that thought, she seemed to behold his gray, wrinkled, yet childlike aspect, in the old-fashioned garments which he wore about the house; a figure such as one sometimes imagines himself to be, with the world's eye upon him, in a troubled dream. This figure of her wretched brother would go wandering through the city, attracting all eyes, and everybody's wonder and repugnance, like a ghost, the more to be shuddered at because visible at noontide. To incur the ridicule of the younger crowd, that knew him not; the harsher scorn and indignation of a few old men, who might recall his once familiar features! To be the sport of boys, who, when old enough to run about the streets, have no more reverence for what is beautiful and holy, nor pity for what is sad—no more sense of sacred misery, sanctifying the human shape in which it embodies itself— than if Satan were the father of them all! Goaded by their taunts, their loud, shrill cries, and cruel laughter—insulted by the filth of the public ways, which they would fling upon him—or, as it might well be, distracted by the mere strangeness of his situation, though nobody should afflict him with so much as a thoughtless word—what wonder if Clifford were to break into some wild extravagance, which was certain to be interpreted as lunacy? Thus Judge Pyncheon's fiendish scheme would be ready accomplished to his hands!

Then Hepzibah reflected that the town was almost completely water-girdled. The wharves stretched out towards the centre of the harbor, and, in this inclement weather, were deserted by the ordinary throng of merchants, laborers, and sea-faring men; each wharf a solitude, with the vessels moored stem and stern, along its misty length. Should her brother's aimless footsteps stray thitherward, and he but bend, one moment, over the deep, black tide, would he not bethink himself that here was the sure refuge within his reach, and that, with a single step, or the slightest overbalance of his body, he might be forever beyond his kinsman's gripe? Oh, the temptation! To make of his ponderous sorrow a security! To sink, with its leaden weight upon him, and never rise again!

The horror of this last conception was too much for Hepzibah. Even Jaffrey Pyncheon must help her now! She hastened down the staircase, shrieking as she went.

"Clifford is gone!" she cried. "I cannot find my brother! Help, Jaffrey Pyncheon! Some harm will happen to him!"

She threw open the parlor-door. But, what with the shade of branches across the windows, and the smoke-blackened ceiling, and the dark oak-panelling of the walls, there was hardly so much daylight in the room that Hepzibah's imperfect sight could accurately distinguish the Judge's figure. She was certain, however, that she saw him sitting in the ancestral arm-chair, near the centre of the floor, with his face somewhat averted, and looking towards a window. So firm and quiet is the nervous system of such men as Judge Pyncheon, that he had perhaps stirred not more than once since her departure, but, in the hard composure of his temperament, retained the position into which accident had thrown him.

"I tell you, Jaffrey," cried Hepzibah impatiently, as she turned from the parlor-door to search other rooms, "my brother is not in his chamber! You must help me seek him!"

But Judge Pyncheon was not the man to let himself be startled from an easy-chair, with haste ill-befitting either the dignity of his character or his broad personal basis, by the alarm of an hysteric woman. Yet, considering his own interest in the matter, he might have bestirred himself with a little more alacrity!

"Do you hear me, Jaffrey Pyncheon?" screamed Hepzibah, as she again approached the parlor-door, after an ineffectual search elsewhere. "Clifford is gone!"

At this instant, on the threshold of the parlor, emerging from within, appeared Clifford himself! His face was preternaturally pale; so deadly white, indeed, that, through all the glimmering indistinctness of the passage-way, Hepzibah could discern his features, as if a light fell on them alone. Their vivid and wild expression seemed likewise sufficient to illuminate them; it was an expression of scorn and mockery, coinciding with the emotions indicated by his gesture. As Clifford stood on the threshold, partly turning back, he pointed his finger within the parlor, and shook it slowly, as though he would have summoned not Hepzibah alone, but the whole world, to gaze at some object inconceivably ridiculous. This action, so ill-timed and extravagant—accompanied, too, with a look that showed more like joy than any other kind of excitement—compelled Hepzibah to dread that her stern kinsman's ominous visit had driven her poor brother to absolute insanity. Nor could she otherwise account for the Judge's quiescent mood, than by supposing him craftily on the watch, while Clifford developed these symptoms of a distracted mind.

"Be quiet, Clifford!" whispered his sister, raising her hand to impress caution. "Oh, for Heaven's sake, be quiet!"

"Let him be quiet!—What can he do better?" answered Clifford, with a still wilder gesture, pointing into the room which he had just quitted. "As for us, Hepzibah, we can dance now!—we can sing, laugh, play, do what we will! The weight is gone, Hepzibah; it is gone off this weary old world; and we may be as light-hearted as little Phoebe herself!"

And, in accordance with his words, he began to laugh, still pointing his finger at the object, invisible to Hepzibah, within the parlor. She was seized with a sudden intuition of some horrible thing. She thrust herself past Clifford, and disappeared into the room, but almost immediately returned, with a cry choking in her throat. Gazing at her brother, with an affrighted glance of inquiry, she beheld him all in a tremor and a quake, from head to foot; while, amid these commoted elements of passion or alarm, still flickered his gusty mirth.

"My God, what is to become of us!" gasped Hepzibah.

"Come!" said Clifford, in a tone of brief decision, most unlike what was usual with him. "We stay here too long! Let us leave the old house to our Cousin Jaffrey! He will take good care of it!"

Hepzibah now noticed that Clifford had on a cloak—a garment of long ago—in which he had constantly muffled himself during these days of easterly storm. He beckoned with his hand, and intimated, so far as she could comprehend him, his purpose that they should go together from the house. There are chaotic, blind, or drunken moments, in the lives of persons who lack real force of character—moments of test, in which courage would most assert itself—but where these individuals, if left to themselves, stagger aimlessly along, or follow implicitly whatever guidance may befall them, even if it be a child's. No matter how preposterous or insane, a purpose is a god-send to them. Hepzibah had reached this point. Unaccustomed to action or responsibility—full of horror at what she had seen, and afraid to inquire, or almost to imagine, how it had come to pass—affrighted at the fatality which seemed to pursue her brother—stupefied by the dim, thick, stifling atmosphere of dread, which filled the house as with a death-smell, and obliterated all definiteness of thought —she yielded without a question, and on the instant, to the will which Clifford expressed. For herself, she was like a person in a dream, when the will always sleeps. Clifford, ordinarily so destitute of this faculty, had found it in the tension of the crisis.

"Why do you delay so?" cried he sharply. "Put on your cloak and hood, or whatever it pleases you to wear! No matter what;—you cannot look beautiful nor brilliant, my poor Hepzibah! Take your purse, with money in it, and come along!"

Hepzibah obeyed these instructions, as if nothing else were to be done or thought of. She began to wonder, it is true, why she did not wake up, and at what still more intolerable pitch of dizzy trouble her spirit would struggle out of the maze, and make her conscious that nothing of all this had actually happened. Of course, it was not real; no such black, easterly day as this had yet begun to be; Judge Pyncheon had not talked with her; Clifford had not laughed, pointed, beckoned her away with him; but she had merely been afflicted — as lonely sleepers often are—with a great deal of unreasonable misery in a morning dream!

"Now—now—I shall certainly awake!" thought Hepzibah, as she went to-and-fro, making her little preparations. "I can bear it no longer! I must wake up now!"

But it came not, that awakening moment! It came not, even when, just before they left the house, Clifford stole to the parlor-door, and made a parting obeisance to the sole occupant of the room.

"What an absurd figure the old fellow cuts now!" whispered he to Hepzibah. "Just when he fancied he had me completely under his thumb! Come, come; make haste; or he will start up like Giant Despair in pursuit of Christian and Hopeful, and catch us yet!"

As they passed into the street, Clifford directed Hepzibah's attention to something on one of the posts of the front-door. It was merely the initials of his own name, which, with somewhat of his characteristic grace about the forms of the letters, he had cut there, when a boy. The brother and sister departed, and left Judge Pyncheon sitting in the old home of his forefathers, all by himself; so heavy and lumpish that we can liken him to nothing better than a defunct nightmare, which had perished in the midst of its wickedness, and left its flabby corpse on the breast of the tormented one, to be gotten rid of as it might!

XVII

THE FLIGHT OF TWO OWLS

SUMMER as it was, the east-wind set poor Hepzibah's few remaining teeth chattering in her head, as she and Clifford faced it, on their way up Pyncheon-street, and towards the centre of the town. Not merely was it the shiver which this pitiless blast brought to her frame, (although her feet and hands, especially, had never seemed so death-a-cold as now,) but there was a moral sensation, mingling itself with the physical chill, and causing her to shake more in spirit than in body. The world's broad, bleak atmosphere was all so comfortless! Such, indeed, is the impression which it makes on every new adventurer, even if he plunge into it while the warmest tide of life is bubbling through his veins. What then must it have been to Hepzibah and Clifford—so time-stricken as they were, yet so like children in their inexperience—as they left the door-step, and passed from beneath the wide shelter of the Pyncheon-elm! They were wandering all abroad, on precisely such a pilgrimage as a child often meditates, to the world's end, with perhaps a sixpence and a biscuit in his pocket. In Hepzibah's mind, there was the wretched consciousness of being adrift. She had lost the faculty of self-guidance, but, in view of the difficulties around her, felt it hardly worth an effort to regain it, and was, moreover, incapable of making one.

As they proceeded on their strange expedition, she now and then cast a look sidelong at Clifford, and could not but observe that he was possessed and swayed by a powerful excitement. It was this, indeed, that gave him the control which he had at once, and so irresistibly, established over her movements. It not a little resembled the exhilaration of wine. Or it might more fancifully be compared to a joyous piece of music, played with wild vivacity, but upon a disordered instrument. As the cracked, jarring note might always be heard, and as it jarred loudest amid the loftiest exultation of the melody, so was there a continual quake through Clifford, causing him most to quiver while he wore a triumphant smile, and seemed almost under a necessity to skip in his gait.

They met few people abroad, even on passing from the retired neighborhood of the House of the Seven Gables into what was ordinarily the more thronged and busier portion of the town. Glistening sidewalks, with little pools of rain, here and there, along their unequal surface; umbrellas, displayed ostentatiously in the shop-windows, as if the life of trade had concentred itself in that one article; wet leaves of the horse-chestnut or elm-trees, torn off untimely by the blast, and scattered along the public-way; an unsightly accumulation of mud in the middle of the street, which perversely grew the more unclean for its long and laborious washing;— these were the more definable points of a very sombre picture. In the way of movement, and human life, there was the hasty rattle of a cab or coach, its driver protected by a water-proof cap over his head and shoulders; the forlorn figure of an old man, who seemed to have crept out of some subterranean sewer, and was stooping along the kennel, and poking the wet rubbish with a stick, in quest of rusty nails; a merchant or two, at the door of the post-office, together with an editor, and a miscellaneous politician, awaiting a dilatory mail; a few visages of retired sea-captains at the window of an Insurance Office, looking out vacantly at the vacant street, blaspheming at the weather, and fretting at the dearth as well of public news as local gossip. What a treasure-trove to these venerable quidnuncs, could they have guessed the secret which Hepzibah and Clifford were carrying along with them! But their two figures attracted hardly so much notice as that of a young girl, who passed, at the same instant, and happened to raise her skirt a trifle too high above her ancles. Had it been a sunny and cheerful day, they could hardly have gone through the streets without making themselves obnoxious to remark. Now, probably, they were felt to be in keeping with the dismal and bitter weather, and therefore did not stand out in strong relief, as if the sun were shining on them, but melted into the gray gloom, and were forgotten as soon as gone.

Poor Hepzibah! Could she have understood this fact, it would have brought her some little comfort; for, to all her other troubles—strange to say!—there was added the womanish and old-maidenlike misery, arising from a sense of unseemliness in her attire. Thus, she was fain to shrink deeper into herself, as it were, as if in the hope of making people suppose that here was only a cloak and hood, threadbare and wofully faded, taking an airing in the midst of the storm, without any wearer!

As they went on, the feeling of indistinctness and unreality kept dimly hovering roundabout her, and so diffusing itself into her system that one of her hands was hardly palpable to the touch of the other. Any certainty would have been preferable to this. She whispered to herself, again and again— 'Am I awake?—Am I awake?'—and sometimes exposed her face to the chill spatter of the wind, for the sake of its rude assurance, that she was. Whether it were Clifford's purpose, or only chance had led them thither, they now found themselves passing beneath the arched entrance of a large structure of gray stone. Within, there was a spacious breadth, and an airy height from floor to roof, now partially filled with smoke and steam, which eddied voluminously upward, and formed a mimic cloud-region over their heads. A train of cars was just ready for a start; the locomotive was fretting and fuming, like a steed impatient for a headlong rush; and the bell rang out its hasty peal, so well expressing the brief summons which life vouchsafes to us, in its hurried career. Without question or delay—with the irresistible decision, if not rather to be called recklessness, which had so strangely taken possession of him, and through him of Hepzibah—Clifford impelled her towards the cars, and assisted her to enter. The signal was given; the engine puffed forth its short, quick breaths; the train began its movement; and, along with a hundred other passengers, these two unwonted travellers sped onward like the wind.

At last, therefore, and after so long estrangement from everything that the world acted or enjoyed, they had been drawn into the great current of human life, and were swept away with it, as by the suction of fate itself.

Still haunted with the idea that not one of the past incidents, inclusive of Judge Pyncheon's visit, could be real, the recluse of the seven gables murmured in her brother's ear:—

"Clifford! Clifford! Is not this a dream?"

"A dream, Hepzibah!" repeated he, almost laughing in her face. "On the contrary, I have never been awake before!"

Meanwhile, looking from the window, they could see the world racing past them. At one moment, they were rattling through a solitude;—the next, a village had grown up around them;—a few breaths more, and it had vanished, as if swallowed by an earthquake. The spires of meeting-houses seemed set adrift from their foundations; the broad-based hills glided away. Everything was unfixed from its age-long rest, and moving at whirlwind speed in a direction opposite to their own.

Within the car, there was the usual interior life of the railroad, offering little to the observation of other passengers, but full of novelty for this pair of strangely enfranchised prisoners. It was novelty enough, indeed, that there were fifty human beings in close relation with them, under one long and narrow roof, and drawn onward by the same mighty influence that had taken their two selves into its grasp. It seemed marvellous how all these people could remain so quietly in their seats, while so much noisy strength was at work in their behalf. Some, with tickets in their hats, (long travellers these, before whom lay a hundred miles of railroad,) had plunged into the English scenery and adventures of pamphlet-novels, and were keeping company with dukes and earls. Others, whose briefer span forbade their devoting themselves to studies so abstruse, beguiled the little tedium of the way with penny-papers. A party of girls, and one young man, on opposite sides of the car, found huge amusement in a game of ball. They tossed it to-and-fro, with peals of laughter that might be measured by mile-lengths; for, faster than the nimble ball could fly, the merry players fled unconsciously along, leaving the trail of their mirth afar behind, and ending their game under another sky than had witnessed its commencement. Boys, with apples, cakes, candy, and rolls of variously tinctured lozenges—merchandize that reminded Hepzibah of her deserted shop—appeared at each momentary stopping-place, doing up their business in a hurry, or breaking it short off, lest the market should ravish them away with it. New people continually entered. Old acquaintances—for such they soon grew to be, in this rapid current of affairs—continually departed. Here and there, amid the rumble and the tumult, sat one asleep. Sleep; sport; business; graver or lighter study;—and the common and inevitable movement onward! It was life itself!

Clifford's naturally poignant sympathies were all aroused. He caught the color of what was passing about him, and threw it back more vividly than he received it, but mixed, nevertheless, with a lurid and portentous hue. Hepzibah, on the other hand, felt herself more apart from humankind than even in the seclusion which she had just quitted.

"You are not happy, Hepzibah!" said Clifford apart, in a

tone of reproach. "You are thinking of that dismal old house, and of Cousin Jaffrey"—here came the quake through him—"and of Cousin Jaffrey sitting there, all by himself! Take my advice—follow my example—and let such things slip aside. Here we are, in the world, Hepzibah!—in the midst of life!—in the throng of our fellow-beings! Let you and I be happy! As happy as that youth, and those pretty girls, at their game of ball!"

"Happy!" thought Hepzibah, bitterly conscious, at the word, of her dull and heavy heart, with the frozen pain in it. "Happy! He is mad already; and, if I could once feel myself broad awake, I should go mad too!"

If a fixed idea be madness, she was perhaps not remote from it. Fast and far as they had rattled and clattered along the iron track, they might just as well, as regarded Hepzibah's mental images, have been passing up and down Pyncheon-street. With miles and miles of varied scenery between, there was no scene for her, save the seven old gable-peaks, with their moss, and the tuft of weeds in one of the angles, and the shop-window, and a customer shaking the door, and compelling the little bell to jingle fiercely, but without disturbing Judge Pyncheon! This one old house was everywhere! It transported its great, lumbering bulk, with more than railroad speed, and set itself phlegmatically down on whatever spot she glanced at. The quality of Hepzibah's mind was too unmalleable to take new impressions so readily as Clifford's. He had a winged nature; she was rather of the vegetable kind, and could hardly be kept long alive, if drawn up by the roots. Thus it happened, that the relation heretofore existing between her brother and herself was changed. At home, she was his guardian; here, Clifford had become hers, and seemed to comprehend whatever belonged to their new position, with a singular rapidity of intelligence. He had been startled into manhood and intellectual vigor; or, at least, into a condition that resembled them, though it might be both diseased and transitory.

The conductor now applied for their tickets; and Clifford, who had made himself the purse-bearer, put a bank-note into his hand, as he had observed others do.

"For the lady and yourself?" asked the conductor. "And how far?"

"As far as that will carry us," said Clifford. "It is no great matter. We are riding for pleasure, merely!"

"You choose a strange day for it, Sir!" remarked a gimlet-eyed old gentleman, on the other side of the car, looking at Clifford and his companion as if curious to make them out.—"The best chance of pleasure in an easterly rain, I take it, is in a man's own house, with a nice little fire in the chimney."

"I cannot precisely agree with you," said Clifford, courteously bowing to the old gentleman, and at once taking up the clue of conversation which the latter had proffered.—"It had just occurred to me, on the contrary, that this admirable invention of the railroad—with the vast and inevitable improvements to be looked for, both as to speed and convenience—is destined to do away with those stale ideas of home and fireside, and substitute something better."

"In the name of common sense," asked the old gentleman, rather testily, "what can be better for a man than his own parlor and chimney-corner?"

"These things have not the merit which many good people attribute to them," replied Clifford. "They may be said, in few and pithy words, to have ill-served a poor purpose! My impression is, that our wonderfully increased, and still increasing, facilities of locomotion are destined to bring us round again to the nomadic state. You are aware, my dear Sir—you must have observed it, in your own experience—that all human progress is in a circle; or, to use a more accurate and beautiful figure, in an ascending spiral curve. While we fancy ourselves going straight forward, and attaining, at every step, an entirely new position of affairs, we do actually return to something long ago tried and abandoned, but which we now find etherealized, refined, and perfected to its ideal. The past is but a coarse and sensual prophecy of the present and the future. To apply this truth to the topic now under discussion! In the early epochs of our race, men dwelt in temporary huts, or bowers of branches, as easily constructed as a bird's nest, and which they built—if it should be called building, when such sweet homes of a summer-solstice rather grew, than were made with hands—which Nature, we will say, assisted them to rear, where fruit abounded, where fish and game were plentiful, or, most especially, where the sense of beauty was to be gratified by a lovelier shade than elsewhere, and a more exquisite arrangement of lake, wood, and hill. This life possessed a charm, which, ever since man quitted it, has vanished from existence. And it typified something better than itself. It had its drawbacks; such as hunger and thirst, inclement weather, hot sunshine, and weary and foot-blistering marches over barren and ugly tracts, that lay between the sites desirable for their fertility and beauty. But, in our ascending spiral, we escape all this. These railroads—could but the whistle be made musical, and the rumble and the jar got rid of—are positively the greatest blessing that the ages have wrought out for us. They give us wings; they annihilate the toil and dust of pilgrimage; they spiritualize travel! Transition being so facile, what can be any man's inducement to tarry in one spot? Why, therefore, should he build a more cumbrous habitation than can readily be carried off with him? Why should he make himself a prisoner for life in brick, and stone, and old worm-eaten timber, when he may just as easily dwell, in one sense, nowhere—in a better sense, wherever the fit and beautiful shall offer him a home?"

Clifford's countenance glowed, as he divulged this theory; a youthful character shone out from within, converting the wrinkles and pallid duskiness of age into an almost transparent mask. The merry girls let their ball drop upon the floor, and gazed at him. They said to themselves, perhaps, that, before his hair was gray and the crow's feet tracked his temples, this now decaying man must have stamped the impress of his features on many a woman's heart. But, alas, no woman's eye had seen his face, while it was beautiful!

"I should scarcely call it an improved state of things," observed Clifford's new acquaintance, "to live everywhere, and nowhere!"

"Would you not?" exclaimed Clifford, with singular energy. "It is as clear to me as sunshine—were there any in the sky—that the greatest possible stumbling-blocks in the path of human happiness and improvement, are these heaps of bricks, and stones, consolidated with mortar, or hewn timber, fastened together with spike-nails, which men painfully contrive for their own torment, and call them house and home! The soul needs air; a wide sweep and frequent change of it. Morbid influences, in a thousand-fold variety, gather about hearths, and pollute the life of households. There is no such unwholesome atmosphere as that of an old home, rendered poisonous by one's defunct forefathers and relatives! I speak of what I know! There is a certain house within my familiar recollection—one of those peaked-gable, (there are seven of them,) projecting-storied edifices, such as you occasionally see, in our elder towns—a rusty, crazy, creaky, dry-rotted, damp-rotted, dingy, dark, and miserable old dungeon, with an arched window over the porch, and a little shop-door on one side, and a great, melancholy elm before it. Now, Sir, whenever my thoughts recur to this seven-gabled mansion—(the fact is so very curious that I must needs mention it)—immediately, I have a vision or image of an elderly man, of remarkably stern countenance, sitting in an oaken elbow-chair, dead, stone-dead, with an ugly flow of blood upon his shirt-bosom. Dead, but with open eyes! He taints the whole house, as I remember it. I could never flourish there, nor be happy, nor do nor enjoy what God meant me to do and enjoy!"

His face darkened, and seemed to contract, and shrivel itself up, and wither into age.

"Never, Sir!" he repeated. "I could never draw cheerful breath there!"

"I should think not," said the old gentleman, eyeing Clifford earnestly and rather apprehensively. "I should conceive not, Sir, with that notion in your head!"

"Surely not," continued Clifford; "and it were a relief to me, if that house could be torn down, or burnt up, and so the earth be rid of it, and grass be sown abundantly over its foundation. Not that I should ever visit its site again! For, Sir, the farther I get away from it, the more does the joy, the lightsome freshness, the heart-leap, the intellectual dance, the youth, in short—yes, my youth, my youth!—the more does it come back to me. No longer ago than this morning, I was old. I remember looking in the glass, and wondering at my own gray hair, and the wrinkles, many and deep, right across my brow, and the furrows down my cheeks, and the prodigious trampling of crow's feet about my temples! It was too soon! I could not bear it! Age had no right to come! I had not lived! But now do I look old? If so, my aspect belies me strangely; for—a great weight being off my mind—I feel in the very hey-day of my youth, with the world and my best days before me!"

"I trust you may find it so," said the old gentleman, who seemed rather embarrassed, and desirous of avoiding the observation which Clifford's wild talk drew on them both. "You have my best wishes for it!"

"For Heaven's sake, dear Clifford, be quiet!" whispered his sister. "They think you mad!"

"Be quiet yourself, Hepzibah!" returned her brother. "No matter what they think! I am not mad. For the first time in thirty years, my thoughts gush up and find words ready for them. I must talk, and I will!"

He turned again towards the old gentleman, and renewed the conversation.

"Yes, my dear Sir," said he, "it is my firm belief and hope, that these terms of roof and hearth-stone, which have so long been held to embody something sacred, are soon to pass out of men's daily use, and be forgotten. Just imagine, for a moment, how much of human evil will crumble away, with this one change! What we call real estate—the solid ground to build a house on—is the broad foundation on which nearly all the guilt of this world rests. A man will commit almost any wrong—he will heap up an immense pile of wickedness, as hard as granite, and which will weigh as heavily upon his soul, to eternal ages—only to build a great, gloomy, dark-chambered mansion, for himself to die in, and for his posterity to be miserable in. He lays his own dead corpse beneath the underpinning, as one may say, and hangs his frowning picture on the wall, and, after thus converting himself into an Evil Destiny, expects his remotest great-grandchildren to be happy there! I do not speak wildly. I have just such a house in my mind's eye."

"Then, Sir," said the old gentleman, getting anxious to drop the subject, "you are not to blame for leaving it."

"Within the lifetime of the child already born," Clifford went on, "all this will be done away. The world is growing too ethereal and spiritual to bear these enormities a great while longer. To me—though, for a considerable period of time, I have lived chiefly in retirement, and know less of such things than most men—even to me, the harbingers of a better era are unmistakeable. Mesmerism, now! Will that effect nothing, think you, towards purging away the grossness out of human life?"

"All a humbug!" growled the old gentleman.

"These rapping spirits that little Phoebe told us of, the other day," said Clifford. "What are these but the messengers

of the spiritual world, knocking at the door of substance?
And it shall be flung wide open!"

"A humbug, again!" cried the old gentleman, growing more
and more testy at these glimpses of Clifford's metaphysics.—
"I should like to rap, with a good stick, on the empty pates
of the dolts who circulate such nonsense!"

"Then there is electricity;—the demon, the angel, the
mighty physical power, the all-pervading intelligence!" exclaimed Clifford. "Is that a humbug, too? Is it a fact—or have
I dreamt it—that, by means of electricity, the world of matter
has become a great nerve, vibrating thousands of miles in a
breathless point of time? Rather, the round globe is a vast
head, a brain, instinct with intelligence! Or, shall we say, it
is itself a thought, nothing but thought, and no longer the
substance which we deemed it?"

"If you mean the telegraph," said the old gentleman, glancing his eye towards its wire, alongside the rail-track, "it is an
excellent thing;—that is, of course, if the speculators in cotton
and politics don't get possession of it. A great thing indeed,
Sir; particularly as regards the detection of bank-robbers and
murderers!"

"I don't quite like it, in that point of view," replied Clifford.
"A bank-robber—and what you call a murderer, likewise—
has his rights, which men of enlightened humanity and
conscience should regard in so much the more liberal spirit,
because the bulk of society is prone to controvert their existence. An almost spiritual medium, like the electric telegraph,
should be consecrated to high, deep, joyful, and holy missions.
Lovers, day by day—hour by hour, if so often moved to do it—
might send their heart-throbs from Maine to Florida, with
some such words as these—'I love you forever!'—'My heart
runs over with love!'—'I love you more than I can!'—and,
again, at the next message—'I have lived an hour longer, and
love you twice as much!' Or, when a good man has departed,
his distant friend should be conscious of an electric thrill, as
from the world of happy spirits, telling him—'Your dear friend

is in bliss!' Or, to an absent husband, should come tidings thus—'An immortal being, of whom you are the father, has this moment come from God!'—and immediately its little voice would seem to have reached so far, and to be echoing in his heart. But for these poor rogues, the bank-robbers—who, after all, are about as honest as nine people in ten, except that they disregard certain formalities, and prefer to transact business at midnight, rather than 'Change-hours—and for these murderers, as you phrase it, who are often excusable in the motives of their deed, and deserve to be ranked among public benefactors, if we consider only its result—for unfortunate individuals like these, I really cannot applaud the enlistment of an immaterial and miraculous power in the universal world-hunt at their heels!"

"You can't, hey?" cried the old gentleman, with a hard look.

"Positively, no!" answered Clifford. "It puts them too miserably at disadvantage. For example, Sir, in a dark, low, cross-beamed, panelled room of an old house, let us suppose a dead man, sitting in an arm-chair, with a blood-stain on his shirt-bosom—and let us add to our hypothesis another man, issuing from the house, which he feels to be over-filled with the dead man's presence—and let us lastly imagine him fleeing, Heaven knows whither, at the speed of a hurricane, by railroad! Now, Sir,—if the fugitive alight in some distant town, and find all the people babbling about that self-same dead man, whom he has fled so far to avoid the sight and thought of—will you not allow that his natural rights have been infringed? He has been deprived of his city of refuge, and, in my humble opinion, has suffered infinite wrong!"

"You are a strange man, Sir!" said the old gentleman, bringing his gimlet-eye to a point on Clifford, as if determined to bore right into him.—"I can't see through you!"

"No, I'll be bound you can't!" cried Clifford laughing. "And yet, my dear Sir, I am as transparent as the water of Maule's Well! But, come, Hepzibah! We have flown far enough for once. Let us alight, as the birds do, and perch ourselves on the nearest twig, and consult whither we shall fly next!"

Just then, as it happened, the train reached a solitary way-station. Taking advantage of the brief pause, Clifford left the car, and drew Hepzibah along with him. A moment afterwards, the train—with all the life of its interior, amid which Clifford had made himself so conspicuous an object—was gliding away in the distance, and rapidly lessening to a point, which, in another moment, vanished. The world had fled away from these two wanderers. They gazed drearily about them. At a little distance stood a wooden church, black with age, and in a dismal state of ruin and decay, with broken windows, a great rift through the main-body of the edifice, and a rafter dangling from the top of the square tower. Farther off was a farm-house in the old style, as venerably black as the church, with a roof sloping downward from the three-story peak to within a man's height of the ground. It seemed uninhabited. There were the relics of a wood-pile, indeed, near the door, but with grass sprouting up among the chips and scattered logs. The small rain-drops came down aslant; the wind was not turbulent, but sullen, and full of chilly moisture.

Clifford shivered from head to foot. The wild effervescence of his mood—which had so readily supplied thoughts, fantasies, and a strange aptitude of words, and impelled him to talk from the mere necessity of giving vent to this bubbling up-gush of ideas—had entirely subsided. A powerful excitement had given him energy and vivacity. Its operation over, he forthwith began to sink.

"You must take the lead now, Hepzibah!" murmured he, with a torpid and reluctant utterance. "Do with me as you will!"

She knelt down upon the platform where they were standing, and lifted her clasped hands to the sky. The dull, gray

weight of clouds made it invisible; but it was no hour for dis-
belief;—no juncture this, to question that there was a sky
above, and an Almighty Father looking down from it!

"Oh, God!"—ejaculated poor, gaunt Hepzibah—then
paused a moment, to consider what her prayer should be—
"Oh, God—our Father—are we not thy children? Have mercy
on us!"

XVIII

GOVERNOR PYNCHEON

JUDGE PYNCHEON, while his two relatives have fled away with such ill-considered haste, still sits in the old parlor, keeping house, as the familiar phrase is, in the absence of its ordinary occupants. To him, and to the venerable House of the Seven Gables, does our story now betake itself, like an owl, bewildered in the daylight, and hastening back to his hollow tree.

The Judge has not shifted his position for a long while, now. He has not stirred hand or foot—nor withdrawn his eyes, so much as a hair's breadth, from their fixed gaze towards the corner of the room—since the footsteps of Hepzibah and Clifford creaked along the passage, and the outer door was closed cautiously behind their exit. He holds his watch in his left hand, but clutched in such a manner that you cannot see the dial-plate. How profound a fit of meditation! Or, supposing him asleep, how infantile a quietude of conscience, and what wholesome order in the gastric region, are betokened by slumber so entirely undisturbed with starts, cramp, twitches, muttered dream-talk, trumpet-blasts through the nasal organ, or any, the slightest, irregularity of breath! You must hold your own breath, to satisfy yourself whether he breathes at all. It is quite inaudible. You hear the ticking of his watch; his breath you do not hear. A most refreshing slumber, doubtless! And yet the Judge cannot be asleep. His eyes are open! A veteran politician, such as he, would never fall asleep with wide-open eyes; lest some enemy or mischief-maker, taking him thus at unawares, should peep through these windows into his consciousness, and make strange discoveries among the reminiscences, projects, hopes, apprehensions, weaknesses, and strong points, which he has heretofore shared with nobody. A cautious man is proverbially said to sleep with one eye open. That may be wisdom. But not with both; for this were heedlessness! No, no! Judge Pyncheon cannot be asleep.

It is odd, however, that a gentleman so burthened with engagements—and noted, too, for punctuality—should linger thus in an old, lonely mansion, which he has never seemed very fond of visiting. The oaken chair, to be sure, may tempt him with its roominess. It is, indeed, a spacious, and—allowing for the rude age that fashioned it—a moderately easy seat, with capacity enough, at all events, and offering no restraint to the Judge's breadth of beam. A bigger man might find ample accommodation in it. His ancestor, now pictured upon the wall, with all his English beef about him, used hardly to present a front extending from elbow to elbow of this chair, or a base that would cover its whole cushion. But there are better chairs than this—mahogany, black walnut, rosewood, spring-seated and damask-cushioned, with varied slopes, and innumerable artifices to make them easy, and obviate the irksomeness of too tame an ease;—a score of such might be at Judge Pyncheon's service. Yes; in a score of drawing-rooms, he would be more than welcome. Mamma would advance to meet him, with outstretched hand; the virgin daughter, elderly as he has now got to be—an old widower, as he smilingly describes himself—would shake up the cushion for the Judge, and do her pretty little utmost to make him comfortable. For the Judge is a prosperous man. He cherishes his schemes, moreover, like other people, and reasonably brighter than most others; or did so, at least, as he lay abed, this morning, in an agreeable half-drowse, planning the business of the day, and speculating on the probabilities of the next fifteen years. With his firm health, and the little inroad that age has made upon him, fifteen years, or twenty—yes, or perhaps five-and-twenty!—are no more than he may fairly call his own. Five-and-twenty years for the enjoyment of his real estate in town and country, his railroad, bank, and insurance shares, his United States stock, his wealth, in short, however invested, now in possession, or soon to be acquired; together with the public honors that have fallen upon him, and the weightier ones that are yet to fall! It is good! It is excellent! It is enough!

Still lingering in the old chair! If the Judge has a little time to throw away, why does not he visit the Insurance Office, as is his frequent custom, and sit awhile in one of their leathern-cushioned arm-chairs, listening to the gossip of the day, and dropping some deeply designed chance-word, which will be certain to become the gossip of tomorrow? And have not the Bank Directors a meeting, at which it was the Judge's purpose to be present, and his office to preside? Indeed they have; and the hour is noted on a card, which is, or ought to be, in Judge Pyncheon's right vest-pocket. Let him go thither, and loll at ease upon his money-bags! He has lounged long enough in the old chair.

This was to have been such a busy day! In the first place, the interview with Clifford. Half-an-hour, by the Judge's reckoning, was to suffice for that; it would probably be less, but—taking into consideration that Hepzibah was first to be dealt with, and that these women are apt to make many words where a few would do much better—it might be safest to allow half-an-hour. Half-an-hour? Why, Judge, it is already two hours, by your own undeviatingly accurate chronometer! Glance your eye down at it, and see. Ah; he will not give himself the trouble either to bend his head, or elevate his hand, so as to bring the faithful timekeeper within his range of vision. Time, all at once, appears to have become a matter of no moment with the Judge!

And has he forgotten all the other items of his memoranda? Clifford's affair arranged, he was to meet a State-street broker, who has undertaken to procure a heavy per-centage, and the best of paper, for a few loose thousands which the Judge happens to have by him, uninvested. The wrinkled note-shaver will have taken his railroad trip in vain. Half-an-hour later, in the street next to this, there was to be an auction of real estate, including a portion of the old Pyncheon property, originally belonging to Maule's garden-ground. It has been alienated from the Pyncheons, these fourscore years; but the Judge had kept it in his eye, and had set his heart on re-annexing it to the small demesne still left around the seven gables;— and now, during this odd fit of oblivion, the fatal hammer must have fallen, and transferred our ancient patrimony to some alien possessor! Possibly, indeed, the sale may have been postponed till fairer weather. If so, will the Judge make it convenient to be present, and favor the auctioneer with his bid, on the proximate occasion?

The next affair was to buy a horse for his own driving. The one, heretofore his favorite, stumbled, this very morning, on the road to town, and must be at once discarded. Judge Pyncheon's neck is too precious to be risked on such a contingency as a stumbling steed. Should all the above business be seasonably got through with, he might attend the meeting of a charitable society; the very name of which, however, in the multiplicity of his benevolence, is quite forgotten; so that this engagement may pass unfulfilled, and no great harm done. And if he have time, amid the press of more urgent matters, he must take measures for the renewal of Mrs. Pyncheon's tombstone, which, the sexton tells him, has fallen on its marble face, and is cracked quite in twain. She was a praiseworthy woman enough, thinks the Judge, in spite of her nervousness,

and the tears that she was so oozy with, and her foolish behavior about the coffee; and as she took her departure so seasonably, he will not grudge the second tombstone. It is better,
at least, than if she had never needed any! The next item on
his list was to give orders for some fruit-trees, of a rare variety,
to be deliverable at his country-seat, in the ensuing autumn.
Yes; buy them, by all means; and may the peaches be luscious
in your mouth, Judge Pyncheon! After this, comes something
more important. A committee of his political party has besought him for a hundred or two of dollars, in addition to his
previous disbursements, towards carrying on the fall-cam-
paign. The Judge is a patriot; the fate of the country is staked
on the November election; and besides, as will be shadowed
forth in another paragraph, he has no trifling stake of his own,
in the same great game. He will do what the committee asks;
nay, he will be liberal beyond their expectations; they shall
have a check for five hundred dollars, and more anon, if it be
needed. What next? A decayed widow, whose husband was
Judge Pyncheon's early friend, has laid her case of destitution
before him, in a very moving letter. She and her fair daughter
have scarcely bread to eat. He partly intends to call on her,
to-day—perhaps so—perhaps not—accordingly as he may happen to have leisure, and a small bank-note.

Another business, which, however, he puts no great weight
on—(it is well, you know, to be heedful, but not over anxious,
as respects one's personal health)—another business, then, was
to consult his family-physician. About what, for Heaven's
sake? Why, it is rather difficult to describe the symptoms. A
mere dimness of sight and dizziness of brain, was it?—or a
disagreeable choking, or stifling, or gurgling, or bubbling, in
the region of the thorax, as the anatomists say?—or was it a
pretty severe throbbing and kicking of the heart, rather cred-
itable to him than otherwise, as showing that the organ had
not been left out of the Judge's physical contrivance? No
matter what it was. The Doctor, probably, would smile at the

statement of such trifles to his professional ear; the Judge would smile, in his turn; and meeting one another's eyes, they would enjoy a hearty laugh, together! But, a fig for medical advice! The Judge will never heed it.

Pray, pray, Judge Pyncheon, look at your watch, now! What, not a glance? It is within ten minutes of the dinner-hour! It surely cannot have slipt your memory, that the dinner of to-day is to be the most important, in its consequences, of all the dinners you ever ate. Yes; precisely the most important; although, in the course of your somewhat eminent career, you have been placed high towards the head of the table, at splendid banquets, and have poured out your festive eloquence to ears yet echoing with Webster's mighty organ-tones. No public dinner this, however. It is merely a gathering of some dozen or so of friends from several districts of the State; men of distinguished character and influence, assembling, almost casually, at the house of a common friend, likewise distinguished, who will make them welcome to a little better than his ordinary fare. Nothing in the way of French cookery, but an excellent dinner, nevertheless! Real turtle, we understand, and salmon, tautog, canvass-backs, pig, English mutton, good roast-beef, or dainties of that serious kind, fit for substantial country-gentlemen, as these honorable persons mostly are. The delicacies of the season, in short, and flavored by a brand of old Madeira which has been the pride of many seasons. It is the Juno brand; a glorious wine, fragrant, and full of gentle might; a bottled-up happiness, put by for use; a golden liquid, worth more than liquid gold; so rare and admirable, that veteran wine-bibbers count it among their epochs to have tasted it! It drives away the heart-ache, and substitutes no head-ache! Could the Judge but quaff a glass, it might enable him to shake off the unaccountable lethargy, which—(for the ten intervening minutes, and five to boot, are already past)—has made him such a laggard at this momentous dinner. It would all but revive a dead man! Would you like to sip it now, Judge Pyncheon?

Alas, this dinner! Have you really forgotten its true object? Then let us whisper it, that you may start at once out of the oaken chair, which really seems to be enchanted, like the one in Comus, or that in which Moll Pitcher imprisoned your own grandfather. But ambition is a talisman more powerful than witchcraft. Start up, then, and hurrying through the streets, burst in upon the company, that they may begin before the fish is spoiled! They wait for you; and it is little for your interest that they should wait. These gentlemen—need you be told it?—have assembled, not without purpose, from every quarter of the State. They are practised politicians, every man of them, and skilled to adjust those preliminary measures, which steal from the people, without its knowledge, the power of choosing its own rulers. The popular voice, at the next gubernatorial election, though loud as thunder, will be really but an echo of what these gentlemen shall speak, under their breath, at your friend's festive board. They meet to decide upon their candidate. This little knot of subtle schemers will control the Convention, and, through it, dictate to the party. And what worthier candidate—more wise and learned, more noted for philanthropic liberality, truer to safe principles, tried oftener by public trusts, more spotless in private character, with a larger stake in the common welfare, and deeper grounded, by hereditary descent, in the faith and practice of the Puritans—what man can be presented for the suffrage of the people, so eminently combining all these claims to the chief-rulership, as Judge Pyncheon here before us?

Make haste, then! Do your part! The meed for which you have toiled, and fought, and climbed, and crept, is ready for your grasp! Be present at this dinner!—drink a glass or two of that noble wine!—make your pledges in as low a whisper as you will!—and you rise up from table, virtually governor of the glorious old State! Governor Pyncheon of Massachusetts!

And is there no potent and exhilarating cordial in a certainty like this? It has been the grand purpose of half your lifetime to attain it. Now, when there needs little more than to signify your acceptance, why do you sit so lumpishly in your great-great-grandfather's oaken chair, as if preferring it to the gubernatorial one? We have all heard of King Log; but, in these jostling times, one of that royal kindred will hardly win the race for an elective chief-magistracy!

Well; it is absolutely too late for dinner. Turtle, salmon, tautog, woodcock, boiled turkey, Southdown mutton, pig, roast-beef, have vanished, or exist only in fragments, with lukewarm potatoes, and gravies crusted over with cold fat. The Judge, had he done nothing else, would have achieved wonders with his knife and fork. It was he, you know, of whom it used to be said, in reference to his ogre-like appetite, that his Creator made him a great animal, but that the dinner-hour made him a great beast. Persons of his large sensual endowments must claim indulgence, at their feeding-time. But, for once, the Judge is entirely too late for dinner. Too late, we fear, even to join the party at their wine! The guests are warm and merry; they have given up the Judge; and, concluding that the Free Soilers have him, they will fix upon another candidate. Were our friend now to stalk in among them, with that wide-open stare, at once wild and stolid, his ungenial presence would be apt to change their cheer. Neither would it be seemly in Judge Pyncheon, generally so scrupulous in his attire, to show himself at a dinner-table with that crimson stain upon his shirt-bosom. By-the-by, how came it there? It is an ugly sight, at any rate; and the wisest way for the Judge is to button his coat closely over his breast, and, taking his horse and chaise from the livery-stable, to make all speed to his own house. There, after a glass of brandy and water, and a mutton-chop, a beef-steak, a broiled fowl, or some such hasty little dinner and supper, all in one, he had better spend the evening by the fireside. He must toast his slippers a long while, in order to get rid of the chilliness, which the air of this vile old house has sent curdling through his veins.

Up, therefore, Judge Pyncheon, up! You have lost a day. But tomorrow will be here anon. Will you rise, betimes, and make the most of it? Tomorrow! Tomorrow! Tomorrow! We, that are alive, may rise betimes tomorrow. As for him that has died to-day, his morrow will be the resurrection-morn.

Meanwhile the twilight is glooming upward out of the corners of the room. The shadows of the tall furniture grow deeper, and at first become more definite; then, spreading wider, they lose their distinctness of outline in the dark, gray tide of oblivion, as it were, that creeps slowly over the various objects, and the one human figure sitting in the midst of them. The gloom has not entered from without; it has brooded here all day, and now, taking its own inevitable time, will possess itself of everything. The Judge's face, indeed, rigid, and singularly white, refuses to melt into this universal solvent. Fainter and fainter grows the light. It is as if another double-handfull of darkness had been scattered through the air. Now it is no longer gray, but sable. There is still a faint appearance at the window; neither a glow, nor a gleam, nor a glimmer—any phrase of light would express something far brighter than this doubtful perception, or sense, rather, that there is a window there. Has it yet vanished? No!—yes!—not quite! And there is still the swarthy whiteness —we shall venture to marry these ill-agreeing words—the swarthy whiteness of Judge Pyncheon's face. The features are all gone; there is only the paleness of them left. And how looks it now? There is no window! There is no face! An infinite, inscrutable blackness has annihilated sight! Where is our universe? All crumbled away from us; and we, adrift in chaos, may hearken to the gusts of homeless wind, that go sighing and murmuring about, in quest of what was once a world!

Is there no other sound? One other, and a fearful one. It is the ticking of the Judge's watch, which, ever since Hepzibah left the room in search of Clifford, he has been holding in his hand. Be the cause what it may, this little, quiet, never-ceasing throb of Time's pulse, repeating its small strokes with such busy regularity, in Judge Pyncheon's motionless hand, has an effect of terror, which we do not find in any other accompaniment of the scene.

But, listen! That puff of the breeze was louder; it had a tone unlike the dreary and sullen one, which has bemoaned itself, and afflicted all mankind with miserable sympathy, for five days past. The wind has veered about! It now comes boisterously from the north-west, and, taking hold of the aged frame-work of the seven gables, gives it a shake, like a wrestler that would try strength with his antagonist. Another, and another sturdy tustle with the blast! The old house creaks again, and makes a vociferous, but somewhat unintelligible bellowing in its sooty throat—(the big flue, we mean, of its wide chimney)—partly in complaint at the rude wind, but rather, as befits their century-and-a-half of hostile intimacy, in tough defiance. A rumbling kind of a bluster roars behind the fire-board. A door has slammed above-stairs. A window, perhaps, has been left open, or else is driven in by an unruly gust. It is not to be conceived, beforehand, what wonderful wind-instruments are these old timber-mansions, and how haunted with the strangest noises, which immediately begin to sing, and sigh, and sob, and shriek—and to smite with sledge-hammers, airy, but ponderous, in some distant chamber—and to tread along the entries as with stately footsteps, and rustle up and down the staircase, as with silks miraculously stiff—whenever the gale catches the house with a window open, and gets fairly into it. Would that we were not an attendant spirit, here! It is too awful! This clamor of the wind through the lonely house; the Judge's quietude, as he sits invisible; and that pertinacious ticking of his watch!

As regards Judge Pyncheon's invisibility, however, that matter will soon be remedied. The north-west wind has swept the sky clear. The window is distinctly seen. Through its panes, moreover, we dimly catch the sweep of the dark, clustering foliage, outside, fluttering with a constant irregularity of movement, and letting in a peep of starlight, now here, now there. Oftener than any other object, these glimpses illuminate the Judge's face. But here comes more effectual light. Observe that silvery dance upon the upper branches of the pear-tree, and now a little lower, and now on the whole mass of boughs, while, through their shifting intricacies, the moonbeams fall aslant into the room. They play over the Judge's figure, and show that he has not stirred throughout the hours of darkness. They follow the shadows, in changeful sport, across his unchanging features. They gleam upon his watch. His grasp conceals the dial-plate; but we know that the faithful hands have met; for one of the city-clocks tells midnight.

A man of sturdy understanding, like Judge Pyncheon, cares no more for twelve o'clock at night, than for the corresponding hour of noon. However just the parallel, drawn in some of the preceding pages, between his Puritan ancestor and himself, it fails in this point. The Pyncheon of two centuries ago, in common with most of his contemporaries, professed his full belief in spiritual ministrations, although reckoning them chiefly of a malignant character. The Pyncheon of to-night, who sits in yonder chair, believes in no such nonsense. Such, at least, was his creed, some few hours since. His hair will not bristle, therefore, at the stories which—in times when chimney-corners had benches in them, where old people sat poking into the ashes of the past, and raking out traditions, like live coals—used to be told about this very room of his ancestral house. In fact, these tales are too absurd to bristle even childhood's hair. What sense, meaning, or moral, for example, such as even ghost-stories should be susceptible of, can be traced in the ridiculous legend, that, at midnight, all the dead Pyncheons are bound to assemble in this parlor! And, pray, for what? Why, to see whether the portrait of their ancestor still keeps its place upon the wall, in compliance with his testamentary directions! Is it worth while to come out of their graves for that?

We are tempted to make a little sport with the idea. Ghost-stories are hardly to be treated seriously, any longer. The family-party of the defunct Pyncheons, we presume, goes off in this wise.

First comes the ancestor himself, in his black cloak, steeple-hat, and trunk-breeches, girt about the waist with a leathern belt, in which hangs his steel-hilted sword; he has a long staff in his hand, such as gentlemen in advanced life used to carry, as much for the dignity of the thing, as for the support to be derived from it. He looks up at the portrait; a thing of no substance, gazing at its own painted image! All is safe. The picture is still there. The purpose of his brain has been kept sacred, thus long after the man himself has sprouted up in grave-yard grass. See; he lifts his ineffectual hand, and tries the frame. All safe! But, is that a smile?—is it not, rather, a frown of deadly import, that darkens over the shadow of his features? The stout Colonel is dissatisfied! So decided is his look of discontent as to impart additional distinctness to his features; through which, nevertheless, the moonlight passes, and flickers on the wall beyond. Something has strangely vexed the ancestor! With a grim shake of the head, he turns away. Here come other Pyncheons, the whole tribe, in their half-a-dozen generations, jostling and elbowing one another, to reach the picture. We behold aged men and grandames, a clergyman, with the Puritanic stiffness still in his garb and mien, and a red-coated officer of the Old French War; and there comes the shopkeeping Pyncheon of a century ago, with the ruffles turned back from his wrists; and there the periwigged and brocaded gentleman of the artist's legend, with the beautiful and pensive Alice, who brings no pride, out of her virgin grave. All try the picture-frame. What do these ghostly people seek? A mother lifts her child, that his little hands may touch it! There is evidently a mystery about the picture, that perplexes these poor Pyncheons when they ought to be at rest. In a corner, meanwhile, stands the figure of an elderly man, in a leather jerkin and breeches, with a carpenter's rule sticking out of his side-pocket; he points his finger at the bearded Colonel and his descendants, nodding, jeering, mocking, and finally bursting into obstreperous, though inaudible laughter.

Indulging our fancy in this freak, we have partly lost the power of restraint and guidance. We distinguish an unlooked-for figure in our visionary scene. Among those ancestral people, there is a young man, dressed in the very fashion of to-day; he wears a dark frock-coat, almost destitute of skirts, gray pantaloons, gaiter-boots of patent leather, and has a finely wrought gold chain across his breast, and a little silver-headed whalebone-stick in his hand. Were we to meet this figure at noonday, we should greet him as young Jaffrey Pyncheon, the Judge's only surviving child, who has been spending the last two years in foreign travel. If still in life, how comes his shadow hither? If dead, what a misfortune! The old Pyncheon property, together with the great estate, acquired by this young man's father, would devolve on whom? On poor, foolish Clifford, gaunt Hepzibah, and rustic little Phoebe! But another, and a greater marvel greets us! Can we believe our eyes? A stout, elderly gentleman has made his appearance; he has an aspect of eminent respectability, wears a black coat and pantaloons, of roomy width, and might be pronounced scrupulously neat in his attire, but for a broad crimson-stain, across his snowy neckcloth and down his shirt-bosom. Is it the Judge, or no? How can it be Judge Pyncheon? We discern his figure, as plainly as the flickering moonbeams can show us anything, still seated in the oaken chair! Be the apparition whose it may, it advances to the picture, seems to seize the frame, tries to peep behind it, and turns away, with a frown as black as the ancestral one.

The fantastic scene, just hinted at, must by no means be considered as forming an actual portion of our story. We were betrayed into this brief extravagance by the quiver of the moonbeams; they dance hand-in-hand with shadows, and are reflected in the looking-glass, which, you are aware, is always a kind of window or door-way into the spiritual world. We needed relief, moreover, from our too long and exclusive contemplation of that figure in the chair. This wild wind, too, has tossed our thoughts into strange confusion, but without tearing them away from their one determined centre. Yonder leaden Judge sits immoveably upon our soul. Will he never stir again? We shall go mad, unless he stirs! You may the better estimate his quietude by the fearlessness of a little mouse, which sits on its hind-legs, in a streak of moonlight, close by Judge Pyncheon's foot, and seems to meditate a journey of exploration over this great, black bulk. Ha! What has startled the nimble little mouse? It is the visage of Grimalkin, outside of the window, where he appears to have posted himself for a deliberate watch. This Grimalkin has a very ugly look. Is it a cat watching for a mouse, or the Devil for a human soul? Would we could scare him from the window!

Thank Heaven, the night is well-nigh past! The moonbeams have no longer so silvery a gleam, nor contrast so strongly with the blackness of the shadows among which they fall. They are paler, now; the shadows look gray, not black. The boisterous wind is hushed. What is the hour? Ah! The watch has at last ceased to tick; for the Judge's forgetful fingers neglected to wind it up, as usual, at ten o'clock, being half-an-hour, or so, before his ordinary bed-time;—and it has run down, for the first time in five years. But the great world-clock of Time still keeps its beat. The dreary night—for, Oh, how dreary seems its haunted waste, behind us!—gives place to a fresh, transparent, cloudless morn. Blessed, blessed radiance! The day-beam—even what little of it finds its way into this always dusky parlor—seems part of the universal benediction, annulling evil, and rendering all goodness possible, and happiness attainable. Will Judge Pyncheon now rise up from his chair? Will he go forth, and receive the early sunbeams on his brow? Will he begin this new day—which God has smiled upon, and blessed, and given to mankind—will he begin it with better purposes than the many that have been spent amiss? Or are all the deep-laid schemes of yesterday as stubborn in his heart, and as busy in his brain, as ever?

In this latter case, there is much to do. Will the Judge still insist with Hepzibah on the interview with Clifford? Will he buy a safe, elderly gentleman's horse? Will he persuade the purchaser of the old Pyncheon property to relinquish the bargain, in his favor? Will he see his family-physician, and obtain a medicine that shall preserve him, to be an honor and blessing to his race, until the utmost term of patriarchal longevity? Will Judge Pyncheon, above all, make due apologies to that company of honorable friends, and satisfy them that his absence from the festive board was unavoidable, and so fully retrieve himself in their good opinion, that he shall yet be Governor of Massachusetts? And, all these great purposes accomplished, will he walk the streets again, with that dog-day smile of elaborate benevolence, sultry enough to tempt flies to come and buzz in it? Or will he—after the tomblike seclusion of the past day and night—go forth a humbled and repentant man, sorrowful, gentle, seeking no profit, shrinking from worldly honor, hardly daring to love God, but bold to love his fellow-man, and to do him what good he may? Will he bear about with him—no odious grin of feigned benignity, insolent in its pretence, and loathsome in its falsehood—but the tender sadness of a contrite heart, broken, at last, beneath its own weight of sin? For it is our belief, whatever show of honor he may have piled upon it, that there was heavy sin at the base of this man's being.

Rise up, Judge Pyncheon! The morning sunshine glimmers through the foliage, and, beautiful and holy as it is, shuns not to kindle up your face. Rise up, thou subtile, worldly, selfish, iron-hearted hypocrite, and make thy choice, whether still to be subtile, worldly, selfish, iron-hearted, and hypocritical, or to tear these sins out of thy nature, though they bring the life-blood with them! The Avenger is upon thee! Rise up, before it be too late!

What! Thou art not stirred by this last appeal? No; not a jot! And there we see a fly—one of your common house-flies, such as are always buzzing on the window-pane—which has smelt out Governor Pyncheon, and alights now on his forehead, now on his chin, and now, Heaven help us, is creeping over the bridge of his nose, towards the would-be chief-magistrate's wide-open eyes! Canst thou not brush the fly away? Art thou too sluggish? Thou man, that hadst so many busy projects, yesterday! Art thou too weak, that wast so powerful? Not brush away a fly! Nay, then, we give thee up!

And, hark! the shop-bell rings. After hours like these latter ones, through which we have borne our heavy tale, it is good to be made sensible that there is a living world, and that even this old, lonely mansion retains some manner of connection with it. We breathe more freely, emerging from Judge Pyncheon's presence into the street before the seven gables.

XIX

ALICE'S POSIES

U NCLE VENNER, trundling a wheelbarrow, was the
earliest person stirring in the neighborhood, the day
after the storm.

Pyncheon-street, in front of the House of the Seven Gables,
was a far pleasanter scene than a by-lane, confined by shabby
fences, and bordered with wooden dwellings of the meaner
class, could reasonably be expected to present. Nature made
sweet amends, that morning, for the five unkindly days which
had preceded it. It would have been enough to live for,
merely to look up at the wide benediction of the sky, or as
much of it as was visible between the houses, genial once
more with sunshine. Every object was agreeable, whether to
be gazed at in the breadth, or examined more minutely. Such,
for example, were the well-washed pebbles and gravel of the
sidewalk; even the sky-reflecting pools in the centre of the
street; and the grass, now freshly verdant, that crept along
the base of the fences, on the other side of which, if one
peeped over, was seen the multifarious growth of gardens.
Vegetable productions, of whatever kind, seemed more than
negatively happy, in the juicy warmth and abundance of
their life. The Pyncheon-elm, throughout its great circumference, was all alive, and full of the morning sun and a
sweetly tempered little breeze, which lingered within this

verdant sphere, and set a thousand leafy tongues a-whispering all at once. This aged tree appeared to have suffered nothing from the gale. It had kept its boughs unshattered, and its full complement of leaves, and the whole in perfect verdure, except a single branch, that, by the earlier change with which the elm-tree sometimes prophesies the autumn, had been transmuted to bright gold. It was like the golden branch, that gained Æneas and the Sibyl admittance into Hades.

This one mystic branch hung down before the main-entrance of the seven gables, so nigh the ground, that any passer-by might have stood on tiptoe and plucked it off. Presented at the door, it would have been a symbol of his right to enter, and be made acquainted with all the secrets of the house. So little faith is due to external appearance, that there was really an inviting aspect over the venerable edifice, conveying an idea that its history must be a decorous and happy one, and such as would be delightful for a fireside-tale. Its windows gleamed cheerfully in the slanting sunlight. The lines and tufts of green moss, here and there, seemed pledges of familiarity and sisterhood with Nature; as if this human dwelling-place, being of such old date, had established its prescriptive title among primeval oaks, and whatever other objects, by virtue of their long continuance, have acquired a gracious right to be. A person of imaginative temperament, while passing by the house, would turn, once and again, and peruse it well;—its many peaks, consenting together in the clustered chimney; the deep projection over its basement story; the arched window, imparting a look, if not of grandeur, yet of antique gentility, to the broken portal over which it opened; the luxuriance of gigantic burdocks, near the threshold,—he would note all these characteristics, and be conscious of something deeper than he saw. He would conceive the mansion to have been the residence of the stubborn old Puritan, Integrity, who, dying in some forgotten generation, had left a blessing in all its rooms and chambers, the efficacy of which was to be seen in the religion, honesty, moderate competence, or upright poverty, and solid happiness, of his descendants, to this day.

One object, above all others, would take root in the imaginative observer's memory. It was the great tuft of flowers—weeds, you would have called them, only a week ago—the tuft of crimson-spotted flowers, in the angle between the two front gables. The old people used to give them the name of Alice's Posies, in remembrance of fair Alice Pyncheon, who was believed to have brought their seeds from Italy. They were flaunting in rich beauty and full bloom, to-day, and seemed, as it were, a mystic expression that something within the house was consummated.

It was but little after sunrise, when Uncle Venner made his appearance, as aforesaid, impelling a wheelbarrow along the street. He was going his matutinal rounds to collect cabbage-leaves, turnip-tops, potato-skins, and the miscellaneous refuse of the dinner-pot, which the thrifty housewives of the neighborhood were accustomed to put aside, as fit only to feed a pig. Uncle Venner's pig was fed entirely and kept in prime order on these eleemosynary contributions; insomuch that the patched philosopher used to promise that, before retiring to his farm, he would make a feast of the portly grunter, and invite all his neighbors to partake of the joints and spare-ribs which they had helped to fatten. Miss Hepzibah Pyncheon's house-keeping had so greatly improved, since Clifford became a member of the family, that her share of the banquet would have been no lean one; and Uncle Venner, accordingly, was a good deal disappointed not to find the large earthen pan, full of fragmentary eatables, that ordinarily awaited his coming, at the back-doorstep of the seven gables.

"I never knew Miss Hepzibah so forgetful before," said the patriarch to himself. "She must have had a dinner, yesterday—no question of that! She always has one, now-a-days.

So where's the pot-liquor and potato-skins, I ask? Shall I knock, and see if she's stirring yet? No, no—'twon't do! If little Phoebe was about the house, I should not mind knocking; but Miss Hepzibah, likely as not, would scowl down at me, out of the window, and look cross, even if she felt pleasantly. So I'll come back at noon."

With these reflections, the old man was shutting the gate of the little back-yard. Creaking on its hinges, however, like every other gate and door about the premises, the sound reached the ears of the occupant of the northern gable; one of the windows of which had a side-view towards the gate.

"Good morning, Uncle Venner!" said the Daguerreotypist, leaning out of the window.—"Do you hear nobody stirring?"

"Not a soul!" said the man of patches. "But that's no wonder. 'Tis barely half-an-hour past sunrise, yet. But I'm really glad to see you, Mr. Holgrave! There's a strange, lonesome look about this side of the house; so that my heart misgave me, somehow or other, and I felt as if there was nobody alive in it. The front of the house looks a good deal cheerier; and Alice's Posies are blooming there beautifully; and if I were a young man, Mr. Holgrave, my sweetheart should have one of those flowers in her bosom, though I risked my neck climbing for it! Well!—and did the wind keep you awake, last night?"

"It did indeed!" answered the artist smiling. "If I were a believer in ghosts—and I don't quite know whether I am, or not—I should have concluded that all the old Pyncheons were running riot in the lower rooms; especially in Miss Hepzibah's part of the house. But it is very quiet, now."

"Yes; Miss Hepzibah will be apt to oversleep herself, after being disturbed, all night, with the racket," said Uncle Venner. "But it would be odd, now—wouldn't it?—if the Judge had taken both his cousins into the country along with him. I saw him go into the shop, yesterday."

"At what hour?" inquired Holgrave.

"Oh, along in the forenoon," said the old man. "Well, well; I must go my rounds, and so must my wheelbarrow. But I'll be back here at dinner-time; for my pig likes a dinner as well as a breakfast. No meal-time, and no sort of victuals, ever seems to come amiss to my pig. Good morning to you! And, Mr. Holgrave, if I were a young man, like you, I'd get one of Alice's Posies, and keep it in water till Phoebe comes back."

"I have heard," said the Daguerreotypist, as he drew in his head, "that the water of Maule's Well suits those flowers best."

Here the conversation ceased, and Uncle Venner went on his way. For half-an-hour longer, nothing disturbed the repose of the seven gables, nor was there any visitor, except a carrier-boy, who, as he passed the front-doorstep, threw down one of his newspapers; for Hepzibah, of late, had regularly taken it in. After awhile, there came a fat woman, making prodigious speed, and stumbling as she ran up the steps of the shop-door. Her face glowed with fire-heat; and, it being a pretty warm morning, she bubbled and hissed, as it were, as if all a-fry with chimney-warmth, and summer-warmth, and the warmth of her own corpulent velocity. She tried the shop-door; it was fast. She tried it again, with so angry a jar that the bell tinkled angrily back at her.

"The deuce take Old Maid Pyncheon!" muttered the irascible housewife. "Think of her pretending to set up a cent-shop, and then lying abed till noon! These are what she calls gentlefolk's airs, I suppose! But I'll either start her ladyship, or break the door down!"

She shook it accordingly; and the bell, having a spiteful little temper of its own, rang obstreperously, making its remonstrances heard—not, indeed, by the ears for which they were intended—but by a good lady on the opposite side of the street. She opened her window, and addressed the impatient applicant.

"You'll find nobody there, Mrs. Gubbins."

"But I must and will find somebody here!" cried Mrs. Gubbins, inflicting another outrage on the bell. "I want a half-pound of pork, to fry some first-rate flounders for Mr. Gubbins's breakfast; and, lady or not, Old Maid Pyncheon shall get up and serve me with it!"

"But do hear reason, Mrs. Gubbins!" responded the lady opposite.—"She, and her brother too, have both gone to their cousin, Judge Pyncheon's, at his country-seat. There's not a soul in the house but that young daguerreotype-man, that sleeps in the north-gable. I saw old Hepzibah and Clifford go away, yesterday; and a queer couple of ducks they were, paddling through the mud-puddles! They're gone, I'll assure you."

"And how do you know they're gone to the Judge's?" asked Mrs. Gubbins.—"He's a rich man; and there's been a quarrel between him and Hepzibah, this many a day, because he won't give her a living. That's the main reason of her setting up a cent-shop."

"I know that well enough," said the neighbor. "But they're gone—that's one thing certain. And who but a blood-relation, that couldn't help himself, I ask you, would take in that awful-tempered Old Maid, and that dreadful Clifford? That's it, you may be sure!"

Mrs. Gubbins took her departure, still brimming over with hot wrath against the absent Hepzibah. For another half-hour, or perhaps considerably more, there was almost as much quiet on the outside of the house, as within. The elm, however, made a pleasant, cheerful, sunny sigh, responsive to the breeze that was elsewhere imperceptible; a swarm of insects buzzed merrily under its drooping shadow, and became specks of light, whenever they darted into the sunshine; a locust sang, once or twice, in some inscrutable seclusion of the tree; and a solitary little bird, with plumage of pale gold, came and hovered about Alice's Posies.

At last, our small acquaintance Ned Higgins trudged up the street, on his way to school; and happening, for the first time in a fortnight, to be the possessor of a cent, he could by no means get past the shop-door of the seven gables. But it would not open. Again and again, however, and half-a-dozen other agains, with the inexorable pertinacity of a child, intent upon some object important to itself, did he renew his efforts for admittance. He had doubtless set his heart upon an elephant; or, possibly, with Hamlet, he meant to eat a crocodile. In response to his more violent attacks, the bell gave now-and-then a moderate tinkle, but could not be stirred into clamor by any exertion of the little fellow's childish and tiptoe strength. Holding by the door-handle, he peeped through a crevice of the curtain, and saw that the inner door, communicating with the passage towards the parlor, was closed.

"Miss Pyncheon!" screamed the child, rapping on the window-pane. "I want an elephant!"

There being no answer to several repetitions of the summons, Ned began to grow impatient; and his little pot of passion quickly boiling over, he picked up a stone, with a naughty purpose to fling it through the window; at the same time blubbering and sputtering with wrath. A man, one of two who happened to be passing by, caught the urchin's arm.

"What's the trouble, old gentleman?" he asked.

"I want old Hepzibah, or Phoebe, or any of them!" answered Ned, sobbing. "They won't open the door; and I can't get my elephant!"

"Go to school, you little scamp!" said the man. "There's another cent-shop round the corner. 'Tis very strange, Dixey," added he to his companion, "what's become of all these Pyncheons! Smith, the livery-stable keeper, tells me Judge Pyncheon put his horse up, yesterday, to stand till after dinner, and has not taken him away, yet. And one of the Judge's hired men has been in, this morning, to make inquiry about him. He's a kind of person, they say, that seldom breaks his habits, or stays out o'nights."

"Oh, he'll turn up safe enough!" said Dixey. "And as for

Old Maid Pyncheon, take my word for it, she has run in debt, and gone off from her creditors. I foretold, you remember, the first morning she set up shop, that her devilish scowl would frighten away customers. They couldn't stand it!"

"I never thought she'd make it go," remarked his friend. "This business of cent-shops is overdone among the women-folks. My wife tried it, and lost five dollars on her outlay!"

"Poor business!" said Dixey, shaking his head. "Poor business!"

In the course of the morning, there were various other attempts to open a communication with the supposed inhabitants of this silent and impenetrable mansion. The man of root-beer came, in his neatly painted wagon, with a couple of dozen full bottles, to be exchanged for empty ones; the baker, with a lot of crackers which Hepzibah had ordered for her retail-custom; the butcher, with a nice tidbit which he fancied she would be eager to secure for Clifford. Had any observer of these proceedings been aware of the fearful secret, hidden within the house, it would have affected him with a singular shape and modification of horror, to see the current of human life making this small eddy hereabouts; —whirling sticks, straws, and all such trifles, round and round, right over the black depth where a dead corpse lay unseen.

The butcher was so much in earnest with his sweetbread of lamb, or whatever the dainty might be, that he tried every accessible door of the seven gables, and at length came round again to the shop, where he ordinarily found admittance.

"It's a nice article, and I know the old lady would jump at it," said he to himself.—"She can't be gone away! In fifteen years that I have driven my cart through Pyncheon-street, I've never known her to be away from home; though, often enough, to be sure, a man might knock all day without bringing her to the door. But that was when she'd only herself to provide for."

Peeping through the same crevice of the curtain where,

only a little while before, the urchin of elephantine appetite had peeped, the butcher beheld the inner door, not closed, as the child had seen it, but ajar, and almost wide open. However it might have happened, it was the fact. Through the passage-way there was a dark vista into the lighter, but still obscure, interior of the parlor. It appeared to the butcher that he could pretty clearly discern what seemed to be the stalwart legs, clad in black pantaloons, of a man sitting in a large oaken chair, the back of which concealed all the remainder of his figure. This contemptuous tranquillity on the part of an occupant of the house, in response to the butcher's indefatigable efforts to attract notice, so piqued the man of flesh that he determined to withdraw.

"So," thought he, "there sits Old Maid Pyncheon's bloody brother, while I've been giving myself all this trouble! Why, if a hog hadn't more manners, I'd stick him! I call it demeaning a man's business to trade with such people; and from this time forth, if they want a sausage or an ounce of liver, they shall run after the cart for it!"

He tossed the tidbit angrily into his cart, and drove off in a pet.

Not a great while afterwards, there was a sound of music turning the corner, and approaching down the street, with several intervals of silence, and then a renewed and nearer outbreak of brisk melody. A mob of children was seen moving onward, or stopping, in unison with the sound, which appeared to proceed from the centre of the throng; so that they were loosely bound together by slender strains of harmony, and drawn along captive; with ever and anon an accession of some little fellow in an apron and straw hat, capering forth from door or gateway. Arriving under the shadow of the Pyncheon-elm, it proved to be the Italian boy, who, with his monkey and show of puppets, had once before played his hurdy-gurdy beneath the arched window. The pleasant face of Phœbe—and doubtless, too, the liberal recompense which she had flung him—still dwelt in his remembrance. His expressive features kindled up, as he recognized the spot where this trifling incident of his erratic life had chanced. He entered the neglected yard, (now wilder than ever, with its growth of hogweed and burdock,) stationed himself on the door-step of the main-entrance, and opening his show-box, began to play. Each individual of the automatic community forthwith set to work, according to his or her proper vocation; the monkey, taking off his highland bonnet, bowed and scraped to the bystanders, most obsequiously, with ever an observant eye to pick up a stray cent; and the young foreigner himself, as he turned the crank of his machine, glanced upward to the arched window, expectant of a presence that would make his music the livelier and sweeter. The throng of children stood near; some on the sidewalk; some within the yard; two or three establishing themselves on the very door-step; and one squatting on the threshold. Meanwhile, the locust kept singing, in the great, old Pyncheon-elm.

"I don't hear anybody in the house," said one of the children to another. "The monkey won't pick up anything here."

"There is somebody at home," affirmed the urchin on the threshold. "I heard a step!"

Still the young Italian's eye turned sidelong upward; and it really seemed as if the touch of genuine, though slight and almost playful emotion, communicated a juicier sweetness to the dry, mechanical process of his minstrelsy. These wanderers are readily responsive to any natural kindness—be it no more than a smile, or a word, itself not understood, but only a warmth in it—which befalls them on the roadside of life. They remember these things, because they are the little enchantments which, for the instant—for the space that reflects a landscape in a soap-bubble—build up a home about them. Therefore, the Italian boy would not be discouraged

by the heavy silence, with which the old house seemed resolute to clog the vivacity of his instrument. He persisted in his
melodious appeals; he still looked upward, trusting that his
dark, alien countenance would soon be brightened by
Phoebe's sunny aspect. Neither could he be willing to depart
without again beholding Clifford, whose sensibility, like
Phoebe's smile, had talked a kind of heart's language to the
foreigner. He repeated all his music, over and over again,
until his auditors were getting weary. So were the little
wooden-people in his show-box, and the monkey most of all.
There was no response, save the singing of the locust.

"No children live in this house," said a schoolboy, at last.
"Nobody lives here but an old maid and an old man. You'll
get nothing here! Why don't you go along?"

"You fool, you, why do you tell him?" whispered a shrewd
little Yankee, caring nothing for the music, but a good deal
for the cheap rate at which it was had. "Let him play as long
as he likes. If there's nobody to pay him, that's his own
look-out!"

Once more, however, the Italian ran over his round of
melodies. To the common observer—who could understand
nothing of the case, except the music and the sunshine on
the hither side of the door—it might have been amusing to
watch the pertinacity of the street-performer. Will he succeed
at last? Will that stubborn door be suddenly flung open?
Will a group of joyous children, the young ones of the house,
come dancing, shouting, laughing, into the open air, and
cluster round the show-box, looking with eager merriment at
the puppets, and tossing each a copper for long-tailed Mammon, the monkey, to pick up?

But, to us, who know the inner heart of the seven gables,
as well as its exterior face, there is a ghastly effect in this repetition of light popular tunes at its door-step. It would be an
ugly business, indeed, if Judge Pyncheon (who would not
have cared a fig for Paganini's fiddle, in his most harmonious

mood) should make his appearance at the door, with a bloody shirt-bosom, and a grim frown on his swarthily white visage, and motion the foreign vagabond away! Was ever before such a grinding-out of jigs and waltzes, where nobody was in the cue to dance? Yes; very often. This contrast, or intermingling of tragedy with mirth, happens daily, hourly, momently. The gloomy and desolate old house, deserted of life, and with awful Death sitting sternly in its solitude, was the emblem of many a human heart, which, nevertheless, is compelled to hear the trill and echo of the world's gaiety around it.

Before the conclusion of the Italian's performance, a couple of men happened to be passing, on their way to dinner.

"I say, you young French fellow!" called out one of them, —"come away from that door-step, and go somewhere else with your nonsense! The Pyncheon family live there; and they are in great trouble, just about this time. They don't feel musical to-day. It is reported, all over town, that Judge Pyncheon, who owns the house, has been murdered; and the City Marshal is going to look into the matter. So be off with you at once!"

As the Italian shouldered his hurdy-gurdy, he saw on the door-step a card, which had been covered, all the morning, by the newspaper that the carrier had flung upon it, but was now shuffled into sight. He picked it up, and perceiving something written in pencil, gave it to the man to read. In fact, it was an engraved card of Judge Pyncheon's, with certain pencilled memoranda on the back, referring to various businesses which it had been his purpose to transact during the preceding day. It formed a prospective epitome of the day's history; only that affairs had not turned out altogether in accordance with the programme. The card must have been lost from the Judge's vest-pocket, in his preliminary attempt to gain access by the main-entrance of the house. Though well-soaked with rain, it was still partially legible.

"Look here, Dixey!" cried the man. "This has something

to do with Judge Pyncheon. See;—here's his name printed on it; and here, I suppose, is some of his handwriting."

"Let's go to the City Marshal with it!" said Dixey. "It may give him just the clue he wants. After all," whispered he in his companion's ear, "it would be no wonder if the Judge has gone into that door, and never come out again! A certain cousin of his may have been at his old tricks. And Old Maid Pyncheon having got herself in debt by the cent-shop—and the Judge's pocket-book being well-filled—and bad blood amongst them already! Put all these things together, and see what they make!"

"Hush, hush!" whispered the other. "It seems like a sin to be the first to speak of such a thing. But I think, with you, that we had better go to the City Marshal."

"Yes, yes!" said Dixey. "Well!—I always said there was something devilish in that woman's scowl!"

The men wheeled about, accordingly, and retraced their steps up the street. The Italian, also, made the best of his way off, with a parting glance up at the arched window. As for the children, they took to their heels, with one accord, and scampered, as if some giant or ogre were in pursuit; until, at a good distance from the house, they stopt as suddenly and simultaneously as they had set out. Their susceptible nerves took an indefinite alarm from what they had over-heard. Looking back at the grotesque peaks and shadowy angles of the old mansion, they fancied a gloom diffused about it, which no brightness of the sunshine could dispel. An imaginary Hepzibah scowled and shook her finger at them, from several windows at the same moment. An imaginary Clifford—for (and it would have deeply wounded him to know it) he had always been a horror to these small people —stood behind the unreal Hepzibah, making awful gestures, in a faded dressing-gown. Children are even more apt, if possible, than grown people, to catch the contagion of a panic terror. For the rest of the day, the more timid went whole streets about, for the sake of avoiding the seven gables; while the bolder signalized their hardihood by challenging their comrades to race past the mansion, at full speed.

It could not have been more than half-an-hour after the disappearance of the Italian boy, with his unseasonable melodies, when a cab drove down the street. It stopt beneath the Pyncheon-elm; the cabman took a trunk, a canvass-bag, and a bandbox, from the top of his vehicle, and deposited them on the door-step of the old house; a straw bonnet, and then the pretty figure of a young girl, came into view from the interior of the cab. It was Phoebe! Though not altogether so blooming as when she first tript into our story—for, in the few intervening weeks, her experiences had made her graver, more womanly, and deeper-eyed, in token of a heart that had begun to suspect its depths—still there was the quiet glow of natural sunshine over her. Neither had she forfeited her proper gift of making things look real, rather than fantastic, within her sphere. Yet we feel it to be a questionable venture, even for Phoebe, at this juncture, to cross the threshold of the seven gables. Is her healthful presence potent enough to chase away the crowd of pale, hideous, and sinful phantoms, that have gained admittance there, since her departure? Or will she, likewise, fade, sicken, sadden, and grow into deformity, and be only another pallid phantom, to glide noiselessly up and down the stairs, and affright children, as she pauses at the window?

At least, we would gladly forewarn the unsuspecting girl, that there is nothing in human shape or substance to receive her, unless it be the figure of Judge Pyncheon, who—wretched spectacle that he is, and frightful in our remembrance, since our night-long vigil with him!—still keeps his place in the oaken chair.

Phoebe first tried the shop-door. It did not yield to her

hand; and the white curtain, drawn across the window which formed the upper section of the door, struck her quick perceptive faculty as something unusual. Without making another effort to enter here, she betook herself to the great portal, under the arched window. Finding it fastened, she knocked. A reverberation came from the emptiness within. She knocked again, and a third time, and, listening intently, fancied that the floor creaked, as if Hepzibah were coming, with her ordinary tiptoe movement, to admit her. But so dead a silence ensued upon this imaginary sound, that she began to question whether she might not have mistaken the house, familiar as she thought herself with its exterior.

Her notice was now attracted by a child's voice, at some distance. It appeared to call her name. Looking in the direction whence it proceeded, Phoebe saw little Ned Higgins, a good way down the street, stamping, shaking his head violently, making deprecatory gestures with both hands, and shouting to her at mouth-wide screech.

"No, no, Phoebe!" he screamed. "Don't you go in! There's something wicked there! Don't—don't—don't go in!"

But, as the little personage could not be induced to approach near enough to explain himself, Phoebe concluded that he had been frightened, on some of his visits to the shop, by her Cousin Hepzibah; for the good lady's manifestations, in truth, ran about an equal chance of scaring children out of their wits, or compelling them to unseemly laughter. Still, she felt the more, for this incident, how unaccountably silent and impenetrable the house had become. As her next resort, Phoebe made her way into the garden, where, on so warm and bright a day as the present, she had little doubt of finding Clifford, and perhaps Hepzibah also, idling away the noontide in the shadow of the arbor. Immediately on her entering the garden-gate, the family of hens half ran, half flew, to meet her; while a strange Grimalkin, which was prowling under the parlor-window, took to his heels, clambered hastily over the fence, and vanished. The arbor was vacant, and its floor, table, and circular bench, were still damp, and bestrewn with twigs, and the disarray of the past storm. The growth of the garden seemed to have got quite out of bounds; the weeds had taken advantage of Phoebe's absence, and the long-continued rain, to run rampant over the flowers and kitchen-vegetables. Maule's Well had overflowed its stone-border, and made a pool of formidable breadth, in that corner of the garden.

The impression of the whole scene was that of a spot, where no human foot had left its print, for many preceding days—probably, not since Phoebe's departure—for she saw a side-comb of her own under the table of the arbor, where it must have fallen, on the last afternoon when she and Clifford sat there.

The girl knew that her two relatives were capable of far greater oddities, than that of shutting themselves up in their old house, as they appeared now to have done. Nevertheless, with indistinct misgivings of something amiss, and apprehensions to which she could not give shape, she approached the door that formed the customary communication between the house and garden. It was secured within, like the two which she had already tried. She knocked, however; and, immediately, as if the application had been expected, the door was drawn open, by a considerable exertion of some unseen person's strength, not widely, but far enough to afford her a sidelong entrance. As Hepzibah, in order not to expose herself to inspection from without, invariably opened a door in this manner, Phoebe necessarily concluded that it was her cousin who now admitted her.

Without hesitation, therefore, she stept across the threshold, and had no sooner entered, than the door closed behind her.

XX

THE FLOWER OF EDEN

PHOEBE, coming so suddenly from the sunny daylight, was altogether bedimmed in such density of shadow as lurked in most of the passages of the old house. She was not at first aware by whom she had been admitted. Before her eyes had adapted themselves to the obscurity, a hand grasped her own, with a firm, but gentle and warm pressure, thus imparting a welcome which caused her heart to leap and thrill with an undefinable shiver of enjoyment. She felt herself drawn along, not towards the parlor, but into a large and unoccupied apartment, which had formerly been the grand reception-room of the seven gables. The sunshine came freely into all the uncurtained windows of this room, and fell upon the dusty floor; so that Phoebe now clearly saw—what, indeed, had been no secret, after the encounter of a warm hand with hers—that it was not Hepzibah nor Clifford, but Holgrave, to whom she owed her reception. The subtle, intuitive communication, or, rather, the vague and formless impression of something to be told, had made her yield unresistingly to his impulse. Without taking away her hand, she looked eagerly in his face, not quick to forebode evil, but unavoidably conscious that the state of the family had changed, since her departure, and therefore anxious for an explanation.

The artist looked paler than ordinary; there was a thought-

ful and severe contraction of his forehead, tracing a deep,
vertical line between the eyebrows. His smile, however, was
full of genuine warmth, and had in it a joy, by far the most
vivid expression that Phoebe had ever witnessed, shining out
of the New England reserve with which Holgrave habitually
masked whatever lay near his heart. It was the look wherewith a man, brooding alone over some fearful object, in a
dreary forest or illimitable desert, would recognize the familiar aspect of his dearest friend, bringing up all the peaceful ideas that belong to home, and the gentle current of
every-day affairs. And yet, as he felt the necessity of responding to her look of inquiry, the smile disappeared.

"I ought not to rejoice that you have come, Phoebe!" said
he. "We meet at a strange moment!"

"What has happened?" she exclaimed. "Why is the house
so deserted? Where are Hepzibah and Clifford?"

"Gone! I cannot imagine where they are!" answered Holgrave. "We are alone in the house!"

"Hepzibah and Clifford gone?" cried Phoebe. "It is not
possible! And why have you brought me into this room,
instead of the parlor? Ah, something terrible has happened!
I must run and see!"

"No, no, Phoebe!" said Holgrave, holding her back. "It
is as I have told you. They are gone, and I know not whither.
A terrible event has indeed happened, but not to them,
nor, as I undoubtingly believe, through any agency of theirs.
If I read your character rightly, Phoebe," he continued, fixing
his eyes on hers with stern anxiety, intermixed with tenderness, "gentle as you are, and seeming to have your sphere
among common things, you yet possess remarkable strength.
You have wonderful poise, and a faculty which, when tested,
will prove itself capable of dealing with matters that fall far
out of the ordinary rule."

"Oh, no, I am very weak!" replied Phoebe trembling. "But
tell me what has happened!"

"You are strong!" persisted Holgrave. "You must be both

strong and wise; for I am all astray, and need your counsel. It may be, you can suggest the one right thing to do!"

"Tell me!—tell me!" said Phoebe, all in a tremble. "It oppresses—it terrifies me—this mystery! Anything else, I can bear!"

The artist hesitated. Notwithstanding what he had just said, and most sincerely, in regard to the self-balancing power with which Phoebe impressed him, it still seemed almost wicked to bring the awful secret of yesterday to her knowledge. It was like dragging a hideous shape of death into the cleanly and cheerful space before a household fire, where it would present all the uglier aspect, amid the decorousness of everything about it. Yet it could not be concealed from her; she must needs know it.

"Phoebe," said he, "do you remember this?"

He put into her hand a daguerreotype; the same that he had shown her at their first interview, in the garden, and which so strikingly brought out the hard and relentless traits of the original.

"What has this to do with Hepzibah and Clifford?" asked Phoebe, with impatient surprise that Holgrave should so trifle with her, at such a moment. "It is Judge Pyncheon! You have shown it to me before!"

"But here is the same face, taken within this half-hour," said the artist, presenting her with another miniature. "I had just finished it, when I heard you at the door."

"This is death!" shuddered Phoebe, turning very pale. "Judge Pyncheon dead!"

"Such as there represented," said Holgrave, "he sits in the next room. The Judge is dead, and Clifford and Hepzibah have vanished! I know no more. All beyond is conjecture. On returning to my solitary chamber, last evening, I noticed no light, either in the parlor, or Hepzibah's room, or Clifford's;—no stir nor footstep about the house. This morning, there was the same deathlike quiet. From my window, I overheard the testimony of a neighbor, that your relatives were seen leaving the house, in the midst of yesterday's storm. A rumor reached me, too, of Judge Pyncheon being missed. A feeling which I cannot describe—an indefinite sense of some catastrophe, or consummation—impelled me to make my way into this part of the house, where I discovered what you see. As a point of evidence that may be useful to Clifford—and also as a memorial valuable to myself; for, Phoebe, there are hereditary reasons that connect me strangely with that man's fate—I used the means at my disposal to preserve this pictorial record of Judge Pyncheon's death."

Even in her agitation, Phoebe could not help remarking the calmness of Holgrave's demeanor. He appeared, it is true, to feel the whole awfulness of the Judge's death, yet had received the fact into his mind without any mixture of surprise, but as an event pre-ordained, happening inevitably, and so fitting itself into past occurrences, that it could almost have been prophesied.

"Why have not you thrown open the doors, and called in witnesses?" inquired she, with a painful shudder. "It is terrible to be here alone!"

"But Clifford!" suggested the artist. "Clifford and Hepzibah! We must consider what is best to be done in their behalf. It is a wretched fatality, that they should have disappeared. Their flight will throw the worst coloring over this event, of which it is susceptible. Yet how easy is the explanation, to those who know them! Bewildered and terror-stricken by the similarity of this death to a former one, which was attended with such disastrous consequences to Clifford, they have had no idea but of removing themselves from the scene. How miserably unfortunate! Had Hepzibah but shrieked aloud—had Clifford flung wide the door, and proclaimed Judge Pyncheon's death—it would have been, however awful in itself, an event fruitful of good consequences to them. As I view it, it would have gone far towards obliterating the black stain on Clifford's character."

"And how," asked Phoebe, "could any good come from what is so very dreadful?"

"Because," said the artist, "if the matter can be fairly considered, and candidly interpreted, it must be evident that Judge Pyncheon could not have come unfairly to his end. This mode of death has been an idiosyncrasy with his family, for generations past; not often occurring, indeed, but—when it does occur—usually attacking individuals of about the Judge's time of life, and generally in the tension of some mental crisis, or perhaps in an access of wrath. Old Maule's prophecy was probably founded on a knowledge of this physical predisposition in the Pyncheon race. Now, there is a minute and almost exact similarity in the appearances, connected with the death that occurred yesterday, and those recorded of the death of Clifford's uncle, thirty years ago. It is true, there was a certain arrangement of circumstances, unnecessary to be recounted, which made it possible—nay, as men look at these things, probable, or even certain—that old Jaffrey Pyncheon came to a violent death, and by Clifford's hands."

"Whence came those circumstances?" exclaimed Phoebe— "he being innocent, as we know him to be!"

"They were arranged," said Holgrave—"at least, such has long been my conviction—they were arranged, after the uncle's death, and before it was made public, by the man who sits in yonder parlor. His own death, so like that former one, yet attended with none of those suspicious circumstances, seems the stroke of God upon him, at once a punishment for his wickedness, and making plain the innocence of Clifford. But this flight—it distorts everything! He may be in concealment, near at hand. Could we but bring him back, before the discovery of the Judge's death, the evil might be rectified."

"We must not hide this thing, a moment longer!" said

Phoebe. "It is dreadful to keep it so closely in our hearts. Clifford is innocent. God will make it manifest! Let us throw open the doors, and call all the neighborhood to see the truth!"

"You are right, Phoebe," rejoined Holgrave. "Doubtless, you are right."

Yet the artist did not feel the horror, which was proper to Phoebe's sweet and order-loving character, at thus finding herself at issue with society, and brought in contact with an event that transcended ordinary rules. Neither was he in haste, like her, to betake himself within the precincts of common life. On the contrary, he gathered a wild enjoyment —as it were, a flower of strange beauty, growing in a desolate spot, and blossoming in the wind—such a flower of momentary happiness he gathered from his present position. It separated Phoebe and himself from the world, and bound them to each other, by their exclusive knowledge of Judge Pyncheon's mysterious death, and the counsel which they were forced to hold respecting it. The secret, so long as it should continue such, kept them within the circle of a spell, a solitude in the midst of men, a remoteness as entire as that of an island in mid-ocean;—once divulged, the ocean would flow betwixt them, standing on its widely sundered shores. Meanwhile, all the circumstances of their situation seemed to draw them together; they were like two children who go hand in hand, pressing closely to one another's side, through a shadow-haunted passage. The image of awful Death, which filled the house, held them united by his stiffened grasp.

These influences hastened the developement of emotions, that might not otherwise have flowered so soon. Possibly, indeed, it had been Holgrave's purpose to let them die in their undeveloped germs.

"Why do we delay so?" asked Phoebe. "This secret takes away my breath! Let us throw open the doors!"

"In all our lives, there can never come another moment like this!" said Holgrave. "Phoebe, is it all terror?—nothing but terror? Are you conscious of no joy, as I am, that has made this the only point of life, worth living for?"

"It seems a sin," replied Phoebe trembling, "to think of joy, at such a time!"

"Could you but know, Phoebe, how it was with me, the hour before you came!" exclaimed the artist. "A dark, cold, miserable hour! The presence of yonder dead man threw a great black shadow over everything; he made the universe, so far as my perception could reach, a scene of guilt, and of retribution more dreadful than the guilt. The sense of it took away my youth. I never hoped to feel young again! The world looked strange, wild, evil, hostile;—my past life, so lonesome and dreary; my future, a shapeless gloom, which I must mould into gloomy shapes! But, Phoebe, you crossed the threshold; and hope, warmth, and joy, came in with you! The black moment became at once a blissful one. It must not pass without the spoken word. I love you!"

"How can you love a simple girl, like me?" asked Phoebe, compelled by his earnestness to speak. "You have many, many thoughts, with which I should try in vain to sympathize. And I—I, too—I have tendencies with which you would sympathize as little. That is less matter. But I have not scope enough to make you happy."

"You are my only possibility of happiness!" answered Holgrave. "I have no faith in it, except as you bestow it on me!"

"And then—I am afraid!" continued Phoebe, shrinking towards Holgrave, even while she told him so frankly the doubts with which he affected her. "You will lead me out of my own quiet path. You will make me strive to follow you, where it is pathless. I cannot do so. It is not my nature. I shall sink down, and perish!"

"Ah, Phoebe!" exclaimed Holgrave, with almost a sigh, and a smile that was burthened with thought. "It will be far otherwise than as you forebode. The world owes all its onward impulse to men ill at ease. The happy man inevitably confines himself within ancient limits. I have a presentiment, that, hereafter, it will be my lot to set out trees, to make fences—perhaps, even, in due time, to build a house for another generation—in a word, to conform myself to laws, and the peaceful practice of society. Your poise will be more powerful than any oscillating tendency of mine."

"I would not have it so!" said Phoebe earnestly.

"Do you love me?" asked Holgrave. "If we love one another, the moment has room for nothing more. Let us pause upon it, and be satisfied. Do you love me, Phoebe?"

"You look into my heart," replied she, letting her eyes droop. "You know I love you!"

And it was in this hour, so full of doubt and awe, that the one miracle was wrought, without which every human existence is a blank. The bliss, which makes all things true, beautiful, and holy, shone around this youth and maiden. They were conscious of nothing sad nor old. They transfigured the earth, and made it Eden again, and themselves the two first dwellers in it. The dead man, so close beside them, was forgotten. At such a crisis, there is no Death; for Immortality is revealed anew, and embraces everything in its hallowed atmosphere.

But how soon the heavy earth-dream settled down again!

"Hark!" whispered Phoebe. "Somebody is at the street-door!"

"Now let us meet the world!" said Holgrave. "No doubt, the rumor of Judge Pyncheon's visit to this house, and the flight of Hepzibah and Clifford, is about to lead to the investigation of the premises. We have no way but to meet it. Let us open the door at once!"

But, to their surprise, before they could reach the street-door—even before they quitted the room in which the foregoing interview had passed—they heard footsteps in the farther passage. The door, therefore, which they supposed to be securely locked—which Holgrave, indeed, had seen to be so, and at which Phoebe had vainly tried to enter—must have been opened from without. The sound of footsteps was not harsh, bold, decided, and intrusive, as the gait of strangers would naturally be, making authoritative entrance into a dwelling where they knew themselves unwelcome. It was feeble, as of persons either weak or weary; there was the mingled murmur of two voices, familiar to both the listeners.

"Can it be!" whispered Holgrave.

"It is they!" answered Phoebe. "Thank God!—thank God!"

And then, as if in sympathy with Phoebe's whispered ejaculation, they heard Hepzibah's voice, more distinctly.

"Thank God, my brother, we are at home!"

"Well!—Yes!—thank God!" responded Clifford. "A dreary home, Hepzibah! But you have done well to bring me hither! Stay! That parlor-door is open. I cannot pass by it! Let me go and rest me in the arbor, where I used—Oh, very long ago, it seems to me, after what has befallen us—where I used to be so happy with little Phoebe!"

But the house was not altogether so dreary as Clifford imagined it. They had not made many steps—in truth, they were lingering in the entry, with the listlessness of an accomplished purpose, uncertain what to do next—when Phoebe ran to meet them. On beholding her, Hepzibah burst into tears. With all her might, she had staggered onward beneath the burden of grief and responsibility, until now that it was safe to fling it down. Indeed, she had not energy to fling it down, but only ceased to uphold it, and suffered it to press her to the earth. Clifford appeared the stronger of the two.

"It is our own little Phoebe!—Ah! and Holgrave with her," exclaimed he, with a glance of keen and delicate insight, and a smile, beautiful, kind, but melancholy. "I thought of you both, as we came down the street, and beheld Alice's Posies in full bloom. And so the flower of Eden has bloomed, likewise, in this old, darksome house, to-day!"

XXI

THE DEPARTURE

THE SUDDEN DEATH of so prominent a member of the social world, as the Honorable Judge Jaffrey Pyncheon, created a sensation (at least, in the circles more immediately connected with the deceased) which had hardly quite subsided in a fortnight.

It may be remarked, however, that, of all the events which constitute a person's biography, there is scarcely one—none, certainly, of anything like a similar importance—to which the world so easily reconciles itself, as to his death. In most other cases and contingencies, the individual is present among us, mixed up with the daily revolution of affairs, and affording a definite point for observation. At his decease, there is only a vacancy, and a momentary eddy—very small, as compared with the apparent magnitude of the ingurgitated object—and a bubble or two, ascending out of the black depth, and bursting at the surface. As regarded Judge Pyncheon, it seemed probable, at first blush, that the mode of his final departure might give him a larger and longer posthumous vogue, than ordinarily attends the memory of a distinguished man. But when it came to be understood, on the highest professional authority, that the event was a natural, and—except for some unimportant particulars, denoting a slight idiosyncrasy—by no means an unusual form of death, the public, with its customary alacrity, proceeded to forget that he had ever lived. In short, the honorable Judge was beginning to be a stale subject, before half the county-newspapers had found time to put their columns in mourning, and publish his exceedingly eulogistic obituary.

Nevertheless, creeping darkly through the places which this excellent person had haunted in his lifetime, there was a hidden stream of private talk, such as it would have shocked all decency to speak loudly at the street-corners. It is very singular, how the fact of a man's death often seems to give people a truer idea of his character, whether for good or evil, than they have ever possessed while he was living and acting among them. Death is so genuine a fact that it excludes falsehood, or betrays its emptiness; it is a touch-stone that proves the gold, and dishonors the baser metal. Could the departed, whoever he may be, return in a week after his decease, he would almost invariably find himself at a higher or lower point than he had formerly occupied, on the scale of public appreciation. But the talk, or scandal, to which we now allude, had reference to matters of no less old a date than the supposed murder, thirty or forty years ago, of the late Judge Pyncheon's uncle. The medical opinion, with regard to his own recent and regretted decease, had almost entirely obviated the idea that a murder was committed, in the former case. Yet, as the record showed, there were circumstances irrefragably indicating that some person had gained access to old Jaffrey Pyncheon's private apartments, at or near the moment of his death. His desk and private drawers, in a room contiguous to his bed-chamber, had been ransacked; money and valuable articles were missing; there was a bloody hand-print on the old man's linen; and, by a powerfully welded chain of deductive evidence, the guilt of the robbery and apparent murder had been fixed on Clifford, then residing with his uncle in the House of the Seven Gables.

Whencesoever originating, there now arose a theory that

undertook so to account for these circumstances as to exclude the idea of Clifford's agency. Many persons affirmed, that the history and elucidation of the facts, long so mysterious, had been obtained by the Daguerreotypist from one of those mesmerical seers, who, now-a-days, so strangely perplex the aspect of human affairs, and put everybody's natural vision to the blush, by the marvels which they see with their eyes shut.

According to this version of the story, Judge Pyncheon, exemplary as we have portrayed him in our narrative, was, in his youth, an apparently irreclaimable scapegrace. The brutish, the animal instincts, as is often the case, had been developed earlier than the intellectual qualities, and the force of character, for which he was afterwards remarkable. He had shown himself wild, dissipated, addicted to low pleasures, little short of ruffianly in his propensities, and recklessly expensive, with no other resources than the bounty of his uncle. This course of conduct had alienated the old bachelor's affection, once strongly fixed upon him. Now, it is averred—but whether on authority available in a court of justice, we do not pretend to have investigated—that the young man was tempted by the devil, one night, to search his uncle's private drawers, to which he had unsuspected means of access. While thus criminally occupied, he was startled by the opening of the chamber-door. There stood old Jaffrey Pyncheon, in his night-clothes! The surprise of such a discovery, his agitation, alarm, and horror, brought on the crisis of a disorder to which the old bachelor had an hereditary liability; he seemed to choke with blood, and fell upon the floor, striking his temple a heavy blow against the corner of a table. What was to be done? The old man was surely dead! Assistance would come too late! What a misfortune, indeed, should it come too soon; since his reviving consciousness would bring the recollection of the ignominious offence, which he had beheld his nephew in the very act of committing!

But he never did revive. With the cool hardihood, that always pertained to him, the young man continued his search of the drawers, and found a will of recent date, in favor of Clifford—which he destroyed—and an older one in his own favor, which he suffered to remain. But, before retiring, Jaffrey bethought himself of the evidence, in these ransacked drawers, that some one had visited the chamber with sinister purposes. Suspicion, unless averted, might fix upon the real offender. In the very presence of the dead man, therefore, he laid a scheme that should free himself at the expense of Clifford, his rival, for whose character he had at once a contempt and a repugnance. It is not probable, be it said, that he acted with any set purpose of involving Clifford in a charge of murder; knowing that his uncle did not die by violence, it may not have occurred to him, in the hurry of the crisis, that such an inference might be drawn. But, when the affair took this darker aspect, Jaffrey's previous steps had already pledged him to those which remained. So craftily had he arranged the circumstances, that, at Clifford's trial, his cousin hardly found it necessary to swear to anything false, but only to withhold the one decisive explanation, by refraining to state what he had himself done and witnessed.

Thus, Jaffrey Pyncheon's inward criminality, as regarded Clifford, was indeed black and damnable; while its mere outward show and positive commission was the smallest that could possibly consist with so great a sin. This is just the sort of guilt that a man of eminent respectability finds it easiest to dispose of. It was suffered to fade out of sight, or be reckoned a venial matter, in the Honorable Judge Pyncheon's long subsequent survey of his own life. He shuffled it aside, among the forgotten and forgiven frailties of his youth, and seldom thought of it again.

We leave the Judge to his repose. He could not be styled fortunate, at the hour of death. Unknowingly, he was a childless man, while striving to add more wealth to his only child's inheritance. Hardly a week after his decease, one of the Cunard steamers brought intelligence of the death, by cholera, of Judge Pyncheon's son, just at the point of embarkation for his native land. By this misfortune, Clifford became rich; so did Hepzibah; so did our little village-maiden, and through her, that sworn foe of wealth and all manner of conservatism —the wild reformer—Holgrave!

It was now far too late in Clifford's life for the good opinion of society to be worth the trouble and anguish of a formal vindication. What he needed was the love of a very few; not the admiration, or even the respect, of the unknown many. The latter might probably have been won for him, had those, on whom the guardianship of his welfare had fallen, deemed it advisable to expose Clifford to a miserable resuscitation of past ideas, when the condition of whatever comfort he might expect lay in the calm of forgetfulness. After such wrong as he had suffered, there is no reparation. The pitiable mockery of it, which the world might have been ready enough to offer, coming so long after the agony had done its utmost work, would have been fit only to provoke bitterer laughter than poor Clifford was ever capable of. It is a truth (and it would be a very sad one, but for the higher hopes which it suggests) that no great mistake, whether acted or endured, in our mortal sphere, is ever really set right. Time, the continual vicissitude of circumstances, and the invariable inopportunity of death, render it impossible. If, after long lapse of years, the right seems to be in our power, we find no niche to set it in. The better remedy is for the sufferer to pass on, and leave what he once thought his irreparable ruin far behind him.

The shock of Judge Pyncheon's death had a permanently invigorating and ultimately beneficial effect on Clifford. That strong and ponderous man had been Clifford's nightmare. There was no free breath to be drawn, within the sphere of so malevolent an influence. The first effect of freedom, as we have witnessed in Clifford's aimless flight, was a tremulous exhilaration. Subsiding from it, he did not sink into his former intellectual apathy. He never, it is true, attained to nearly the full measure of what might have been his faculties. But he recovered enough of them partially to light up his character, to display some outline of the marvellous grace that was abortive in it, and to make him the object of no less deep, although less melancholy interest than heretofore. He was evidently happy. Could we pause to give another picture of his daily life, with all the appliances now at command to gratify his instinct for the Beautiful, the garden-scenes, that seemed so sweet to him, would look mean and trivial in comparison.

Very soon after their change of fortune, Clifford, Hepzibah, and little Phoebe, with the approval of the artist, concluded to remove from the dismal old House of the Seven Gables, and take up their abode, for the present, at the elegant country-seat of the late Judge Pyncheon. Chanticleer and his family had already been transported thither; where the two hens had forthwith begun an indefatigable process of egg-laying, with an evident design, as a matter of duty and conscience, to continue their illustrious breed under better auspices than for a century past. On the day set for their departure, the principal personages of our story, including good Uncle Venner, were assembled in the parlor.

"The country-house is certainly a very fine one, so far as the plan goes," observed Holgrave, as the party were discussing their future arrangements.—"But I wonder that the late Judge—being so opulent, and with a reasonable prospect of transmitting his wealth to descendants of his own—should not have felt the propriety of embodying so excellent a piece of domestic architecture in stone, rather than in wood. Then, every generation of the family might have altered the interior, to suit its own taste and convenience; while the exterior, through the lapse of years, might have been adding venerableness to its original beauty, and thus giving that impression of permanence, which I consider essential to the happiness of any one moment."

"Why," cried Phœbe, gazing into the artist's face with infinite amazement, "how wonderfully your ideas are changed! A house of stone, indeed! It is but two or three weeks ago, that you seemed to wish people to live in something as fragile and temporary as a bird's nest!"

"Ah, Phœbe, I told you how it would be!" said the artist, with a half-melancholy laugh. "You find me a conservative already! Little did I think ever to become one. It is especially unpardonable in this dwelling of so much hereditary misfortune, and under the eye of yonder portrait of a model-conservative, who, in that very character, rendered himself so long the Evil Destiny of his race."

"That picture!" said Clifford, seeming to shrink from its stern glance. "Whenever I look at it, there is an old, dreamy recollection haunting me, but keeping just beyond the grasp of my mind. Wealth, it seems to say!—boundless wealth!— unimaginable wealth! I could fancy, that, when I was a child, or a youth, that portrait had spoken, and told me a rich secret, or had held forth its hand, with the written record of hidden opulence. But those old matters are so dim with me, now-a-days! What could this dream have been!"

"Perhaps I can recall it," answered Holgrave.—"See! There are a hundred chances to one, that no person, unacquainted with the secret, would ever touch this spring."

"A secret spring!" cried Clifford. "Ah, I remember now! I did discover it, one summer afternoon, when I was idling and dreaming about the house, long, long ago. But the mystery escapes me."

The artist put his finger on the contrivance to which he had referred. In former days, the effect would probably have been, to cause the picture to start forward. But, in so long a period of concealment, the machinery had been eaten through with rust; so that, at Holgrave's pressure, the portrait, frame and all, tumbled suddenly from its position, and lay face downward on the floor. A recess in the wall was thus brought to light, in which lay an object so covered with a century's dust, that it could not immediately be recognized as a folded sheet of parchment. Holgrave opened it, and displayed an ancient deed, signed with the hieroglyphics of several Indian sagamores, and conveying to Colonel Pyncheon and his heirs, forever, a vast extent of territory at the eastward.

"This is the very parchment, the attempt to recover which cost the beautiful Alice Pyncheon her happiness and life," said the artist, alluding to his legend. "It is what the Pyncheons sought in vain, while it was valuable; and now that they find the treasure, it has long been worthless."

"Poor Cousin Jaffrey! This is what deceived him," exclaimed Hepzibah. "When they were young together, Clifford probably made a kind of fairy-tale of this discovery. He was always dreaming hither and thither about the house, and lighting up its dark corners with beautiful stories. And poor Jaffrey, who took hold of everything as if it were real, thought my brother had found out his uncle's wealth. He died with this delusion in his mind!"

"But," said Phoebe, apart to Holgrave, "how came you to know the secret?"

"My dearest Phoebe," said Holgrave, "how will it please you to assume the name of Maule? As for the secret, it is the only inheritance that has come down to me from my ancestors. You should have known sooner, (only that I was afraid of frightening you away,) that, in this long drama of wrong and retribution, I represent the old wizard, and am probably as much of a wizard as ever he was. The son of the executed Matthew Maule, while building this house, took the opportunity to construct that recess, and hide away the Indian deed, on which depended the immense land-claim of the Pyncheons. Thus, they bartered their eastern-territory for Maule's garden-ground."

"And now," said Uncle Venner, "I suppose their whole claim is not worth one man's share in my farm yonder!"

"Uncle Venner," cried Phoebe, taking the patched philosopher's hand, "you must never talk any more about your farm! You shall never go there, as long as you live! There is a cottage in our new garden—the prettiest little, yellowish-brown cottage you ever saw; and the sweetest-looking place, for it looks just as if it were made of gingerbread—and we are going to fit it up and furnish it, on purpose for you. And you shall do nothing but what you choose, and shall be as happy as the day is long, and shall keep Cousin Clifford in spirits with the wisdom and pleasantness, which is always dropping from your lips!"

"Ah, my dear child," quoth good Uncle Venner, quite overcome, "if you were to speak to a young man as you do to an old one, his chance of keeping his heart, another minute, would not be worth one of the buttons on my waistcoat! And —soul alive!—that great sigh, which you made me heave, has burst off the very last of them! But never mind! It was the happiest sigh I ever did heave; and it seems as if I must have drawn in a gulp of heavenly breath, to make it with. Well, well, Miss Phoebe! They'll miss me in the gardens, hereabouts, and round by the back-doors; and Pyncheon-street, I'm afraid, will hardly look the same without old Uncle Venner, who remembers it with a mowing-field on one side, and the garden of the seven gables on the other. But either I must go to your country-seat, or you must come to my farm—that's one of two things certain; and I leave you to choose which!"

"Oh, come with us, by all means, Uncle Venner!" said Clifford, who had a remarkable enjoyment of the old man's mellow, quiet, and simple spirit. "I want you always to be within five minutes' saunter of my chair. You are the only philosopher I ever knew of, whose wisdom has not a drop of bitter essence at the bottom!"

"Dear me!" cried Uncle Venner, beginning partly to realize

what manner of man he was.—"And yet folks used to set me down among the simple ones, in my younger days! But I suppose I am like a Roxbury russet—a great deal the better, the longer I can be kept. Yes; and my words of wisdom, that you and Phoebe tell me of, are like the golden dandelions, which never grow in the hot months, but may be seen glistening among the withered grass, and under the dry leaves, sometimes as late as December. And you are welcome, friends, to my mess of dandelions, if there were twice as many!"

A plain, but handsome, dark-green barouche had now drawn up in front of the ruinous portal of the old mansion-house. The party came forth, and (with the exception of good Uncle Venner, who was to follow in a few days) proceeded to take their places. They were chatting and laughing very pleasantly together; and—as proves to be often the case, at moments when we ought to palpitate with sensibility— Clifford and Hepzibah bade a final farewell to the abode of their forefathers, with hardly more emotion than if they had made it their arrangement to return thither at tea-time. Several children were drawn to the spot, by so unusual a spectacle as the barouche and pair of gray horses. Recognizing little Ned Higgins among them, Hepzibah put her hand into her pocket, and presented the urchin, her earliest and staunchest customer, with silver enough to people the Domdaniel cavern of his interior with as various a procession of quadrupeds, as passed into the ark.

Two men were passing, just as the barouche drove off.

"Well, Dixey," said one of them, "what do you think of this? My wife kept a cent-shop, three months, and lost five dollars on her outlay. Old Maid Pyncheon has been in trade just about as long, and rides off in her carriage with a couple of hundred thousand—reckoning her share, and Clifford's, and Phoebe's—and some say twice as much! If you choose to call it luck, it is all very well; but if we are to take it as the will of Providence, why, I can't exactly fathom it!"

"Pretty good business!" quoth the sagacious Dixey. "Pretty good business!"

Maule's Well, all this time, though left in solitude, was throwing up a succession of kaleidoscopic pictures, in which a gifted eye might have seen fore-shadowed the coming fortunes of Hepzibah, and Clifford, and the descendant of the legendary wizard, and the village-maiden, over whom he had thrown love's web of sorcery. The Pyncheon-elm moreover, with what foliage the September gale had spared to it, whispered unintelligible prophecies. And wise Uncle Venner, passing slowly from the ruinous porch, seemed to hear a strain of music, and fancied that sweet Alice Pyncheon—after witnessing these deeds, this by-gone woe, and this present happiness, of her kindred mortals—had given one farewell touch of a spirit's joy upon her harpsichord, as she floated heavenward from the HOUSE OF THE SEVEN GABLES!

The End.

APPENDIXES

TEXTUAL NOTES

24.16–17 horticulturist] Both the manuscript and first edition concur in the nonce word "horticulturalist". It is barely possible that Hawthorne was satirizing newspaper grandiloquent style that came out a little wrong. On the other hand, the slip was more likely his own. In view of his use of "agriculturalists" (an acceptable form) in *The Blithedale Romance* 65.27, it is probable that he was unaware that "horticulturalist" was not an analogue.

24.23 thirty-years'] Although the apostrophe to show the plural possessive is wanting in the manuscript and first edition, the emendation may be justified from the concurrence of both authorities in "a forty years' warfare" (225.32) and "a few winter-months' attendance" (176.15).

24.31 The] It is interesting to observe that the extremely wide spacing of the line in the first edition (30.1) indicates that manuscript "In fine, the" was originally set and then altered in proof. The change, then, must be authoritative.

30.13 old maid] Editorial emendation here brings the capitals of manuscript and first-edition "Old Maid" into conformity with the otherwise established usage of the first edition, which in this case must be authoritative. Hawthorne wrote "Old Maid" throughout the inscription of the manuscript but in a late stage of revision substituted a number of paraphrases. However, in the few examples where the phrase is retained, the first edition reduces the manuscript capitals to lower case and retains the capitals only when Hepzibah is being titled in dialogue about her. That the reduction of the capitals in the print at 47.4, 72.19–20, 90.33, and 117.14 is authoritative and almost certainly made in the proof may be evidenced by the proof-alteration at 80.32 from manuscript "Hepzibah" to first-edition "old maid", a form that we may fairly believe is an accurate setting of Hawthorne's proof-marking. Incidentally, at this place the manuscript "Hepzibah" had been interlined above deleted "Old Maid".

31.29 heard] The reading "heard" of the manuscript and first edition can be defended against an impulse to emend to "hear". By the use of the preterite Hawthorne is catching up the chronology of his narrative. The pause for which he was willing to pardon Hepzibah occurred *after* he heard the turning of the key in the lock.

32.4 should] The first-edition change to "shall" from manuscript "should" is odd, since it ought to have been complemented by the alteration of following "would take" to "will take" if the author in proof had decided to introduce the idea that the person of the miniature would appear later in the narrative. But such an anticipation is clumsy indeed, and even out of place at this point. In the manuscript "should" is not written very clearly, and King might have misread it. On the whole, the manuscript reading is better retained and the hypothesis rejected that "shall" is an authorial change in proof.

37.30 term] The first edition reads, vividly, "throe"; but, carefully examined, the letters do not form this word in the manuscript and the reading is definitely "term". Since the "e" is a tall one that could be mistaken for the loop of an "h", compositor King must have made a bold guess at the word, which, in fact, requires careful study to decipher. The general sense of "period of time" is well expressed by "term", and the several legal meanings add flavor. On reflection, one can see that "throe" is more violent than the context encourages. Because of the lack of legibility in the manuscript, there is small chance that "throe" represents a Hawthorne proof-alteration.

43.30 Daguerreotypist] In the earlier pages of the manuscript this word, as here, is never capitalized, and the first edition follows in heading it with a lower-case letter. However, Hawthorne then changed his mind since after Centenary 94.30 the manuscript invariably capitalizes although the first edition continues (wrongly) its use of lower case.

45.12 have always lived one] This seems to be an idiom that parallels the common phrase "I was brought up a lady" or "I was raised a lady." Holgrave, it is true, answers, "But I was not born a gentleman; neither have I lived like one". But his use of "like" should not encourage a suspicion that Hawthorne inadvertently omitted a word in manuscript (overlooked also in proof) and that Hepzibah should also say, "and have always lived like one". Holgrave was not a gentleman, and so, if he had chosen, he could only have lived "like" one. But Hepzibah was born a lady and has "lived one", i.e., "was raised one". The use of "like" in her case would be quite possible but it would destroy a good idiom and would blunt the distinction (which Holgrave recognizes) she is drawing between them.

45.33 the old] The first-edition reading "an old wizard" for manuscript "the old wizard" is tempting to accept as a delicate touch, not untypical of Hawthorne's narrative care, that introduces a subtle vagueness into Holgrave's allusion. The inference would be that he was unacquainted with the story except from Hepzibah's lips, and so could not speak familiarly of "the wizard" as a received and detailed tradition. However, the "the" in the manuscript is so carelessly formed as to invite misreading; hence a slip by compositor Whittle seems, unfortunately, to be the most probable explanation for the difference in the authorities. At 31.33 King set "a" for manuscript "the", but there the "the" is clearly formed and the change seems to have been a memorial lapse.

52.4 That] Since in the manuscript "That" is mended, not too clearly, from original "The", the first-edition "The" seems to represent Loring's misreading, not a change in proof.

55.3 complacence] The dictionary that Hawthorne used, *A New Critical Pronouncing Dictionary* (1813), defines "complaisant" as "civil, affable, soft". Webster's of 1828 defines it as "civil, courteous, obliging, kind", and "complacent" as "cheerful, civil, affable, soft, kind". Although these definitions make the two words interchangeable in most circumstances, the context indicates that Hawthorne is approaching very close to the idea of undue self-satisfaction, being overpleased with oneself, which according to the OED had begun to tinge "complacent" (but not "complaisant") in the eighteenth century. On the evidence of 57.30 and 59.2, where Hawthorne's manuscript spelling (followed by the first edition) is "complacency" when he clearly means "complaisancy", it follows that at 55.3 his manuscript (and first-edition) spelling "complaisance" is precisely wrong. To these occurrences may be added the evidence of *The Blithedale Romance* of the next year, which quite clearly confuses the two words in a manner indicating that Hawthorne was aware of the distinction that had developed between them but reversed the two in error (see *The Blithedale Romance* textual note to 165.27, Centenary pp. 254–55). Editorial emendation in *The House of the Seven Gables* is required in 55.3, 57.30, and 59.2 to restore the right sense. The weight of the evidence in the two texts is too strong, it would seem, to allow 152.34, where "complacency" seems to be correctly used (although the idea of cheerfulness or softness is not to be ruled out completely) to affect this reasoning.

62.26 but] The first-edition omission of this manuscript word must represent a rare lapse by compositor Letts since the word is necessary for the sense.

64.10 have never] There is no reason to suppose that the first edition's alteration of this manuscript reading to "never have" is anything but Loring's memory failure or sophistication.

64.25 projecting] The ambiguous formation of the letters in the manuscript indicates sufficiently that the first-edition "perfecting" is a simple misreading by Loring.

65.8 become] The letter "o" is not clearly formed, but careful examination of the manuscript reveals that "become" is definitely the word and that first-edition "became" is Loring's misreading or sophistication.

69.6 bolt] The first-edition substitution of "door" for manuscript "bolt", which is clearly required, may be explained best as

Jackman's memorial failure by contamination from "door" in 69.4. Hawthorne was careless not to catch this error in the proof.

83.6 visitors] Although Hawthorne's dictionary has no other spelling than "visiter", and "visiter" is the invariable spelling of the first edition, the manuscript always uses the modern spelling "-or" except here and at 127.35 and 127.36.

84.1 sounded] The first-edition addition of "had" in "had sounded" is awkward and seems to have been Loring's memorial error affected by the use of "had" in context at 83.36 and 84.2.

88.20 welling] First-edition "swelling" is Letts's misreading caused by a clumsy mending of the first minim of the "w" in manuscript "welling". See 96.27 for another use of "well over".

89.34 cried] Ordinarily one might accept as Hawthorne's proof-alteration a change like the first-edition "said" for manuscript "cried". But here the word "cried" is so badly written in the manuscript as to make "said" almost demonstrably Jackman's misreading.

90.27 barn-door fowl] According to the OED this is good idiom at least as late as Sir Walter Scott. Hence the first-edition change to "barn-yard fowl" away from the manuscript seems to be a clear case of compositorial sophistication by Jackman.

103.23 step] First-edition "stop" for manuscript "step" appears to be Fox's misreading of a not too plainly written word. The "step" has been described throughout the paragraph; moreover, as the description continues, it must be this "step" that is like a ghost's, not a "stop".

106.26 murmur] The first-edition substitution of "manner" must represent Jackman's misreading or memorial failure: the sense is markedly inferior, and manuscript "murmur" refers back to 106.19.

106.31 this] The manuscript is not at all clearly inscribed for this word, which could easily be misread "the", as set by Jackman in the first edition.

111.16 I'm] Nothing is easier than for a compositor to read manuscript "I am" and set "I'm" by memorial failure, as may have happened in the first edition here. Moreover, it is suspicious indeed that the only other case of variance in contracted forms between the two authorities (though in reverse) was also set by King at 291.31, although there something may be said for the authority of the change from manuscript "I've" to first-edition "I have" (see Textual Note). Thus conservative editorial procedure might well suggest a preference for manuscript authority in these two readings were it not for the significant evidence of the change in a late state of the proof in *The Blithedale Romance* 232.13 of manuscript "I'm" to "I am" (see Centenary Textual Introduction, pp. xliv–xlvii) that demonstrates that Hawthorne was concerned with speech-rhythms affected by contractions or non-contractions. Under the circumstances, although the evidence is most uncertain at best, the assumption may hold that the alteration here was made in proof. Hepzibah had previously used the contractions "can't" (73.25), " 'tis" (77.26), and "don't" (85.4).

111.20 south] Although the manuscript "s" is much larger than usual, and might seem to be intended as a capital, it is not formed like Hawthorne's characteristic majuscule and seems to be a regular minuscule. The first edition reads "south".

113.4 no resource] "No other resource" is such standard idiom that King seems by memorial lapse, or a belief that he was "correcting" the manuscript, to have added "other" to manuscript "no resource", just as at 137.23 he set "such a depth" for manuscript "such depth". Actually, the sophistication makes nonsense of the sentence. Hepzibah had *no resource* except to take Jaffrey's charity or to earn her living. To have *no other resource* except these two is to state that she had adopted a third choice. These two examples in King's pages, and one in Loring's at 84.1, are the only additions of words in the first edition, except for the obvious correction of a manuscript error at 181.2–3.

117.24–26 —(for . . . wages)—] The first dash is clear in the manuscript but the second is smudged as if partly wiped out, and a not very certain mark after it, which also seems to be smudged, looks something like a comma. Although there is a chance that Hawthorne started to alter his original dashes-plus-parentheses construction (for a similar construction see 113.32–34 and its note in the Alterations in the Manuscript list), the incompleteness of the change makes the final intention doubtful; hence the manuscript dashes have been preferred to the first edition's omission of the first dash and substitution of a comma for the second.

123.16–17 resemblances,–] A rare case of Hawthorne's use of a comma before a dash, a practice favored by the house style of the period but seldom found in Hawthorne's manuscripts.

127.11 fellow] The substitution in the first edition of plural "fellows" for manuscript singular seems to be Willis' sophistication dependent upon a misinterpretation of the meaning. That is, Hepzibah's tremor resulted from one joint shaking at variance with the fellow into which it fitted, within a series of joints, and not from one set of fitted joints remaining firm in their two parts but shaking at variance with other sets elsewhere.

137.8 Pyncheon-house] Despite the absence of the hyphen in the manuscript here and in several other noted places where the Centenary text supplies from the first edition, the hyphenated form is found in the manuscript, for example, in 5.6, 6.5–6, 28.28, 38.26, 182.25. This hyphenation agrees with other hyphenated compounds involving "Pyncheon" like "Pyncheon-street", "Pyncheon-elm", and "Pyncheon-garden". Although "Pyncheon-bull" appears only once (231.2–3) and is not hyphenated in the manuscript, the first-edition hyphenated form has also been adopted. "Pyncheon family" is the most prominent of the compounds that are exempt.

144.20 drowsyhead] Although the manuscript does not perfectly join the two parts of this compound, the sense requires the complete word instead of the mistaken "drowsy head" of the first edition.

149.25 chaos] The manuscript definitely reads "chaos". In view of such parallels as "There are chaotic, blind, or drunken moments, in the lives of persons" (250.28–29) and "we, adrift in chaos, may hearken to the gusts of homeless wind" (276.33–34), first-edition "class", with its blander sense, is evidently a misreading or sophistication.

151.26 fore-mothers] Despite the unhyphenated "forefathers" two words before, Hawthorne intended the form "fore-mothers". The manuscript shows that he began, originally, to inscribe "foremothers"; but after writing the "mo" he wiped out the letters, added the hyphen, and only then continued with the inscription of "mothers".

165.12 infrequent] Hawthorne's dictionary defines this word as "rare, uncommon", which must be the meaning here; see "the unaccustomed tumult" at 166.4.

169.31 one's self] The odds would seem to favor the first-edition reading, adopted here instead of manuscript "one's own self", as more likely to represent Hawthorne's removal of a too ostentatiously rhetorical repetition for effect than the compositor King's memory failure or eyeskip. This view would seem to be strengthened by a similar removal of rhetorical repetition in a Henderson page (see 276.8 and its Textual Note). In addition to the present, the Centenary text accepts removal of words in proof at 24.31 (Letts), 234.3 (King), 276.8 (Henderson), and 309.2 (Letts). Of these, King's at 234.3 is the most doubtful, followed by Henderson's at 276.8. On the other hand, the five rejected cases of dropped words in the first edition do not involve King or Henderson: 62.26 (Letts), 127.32 (Willis), 179.19 (Jackman), 228.12 (Jackman), 304.11 (Willis). It is probable that 169.31 and 276.8 should stand or fall together. That they tend to support each other, however, is incontestable, the more especially since two compositors are involved.

170.9 its] Although the first-edition substitution of "his" for manuscript "its" occurs on the same page as accepted 169.31, the case for automatic acceptance on this evidence is not a particularly strong one (see, for example, the mixture in sheet 21). The meaning is relatively indifferent although the sense with "its" is somewhat contorted. However, Hawthorne wrote "its" in the manuscript, and one can see how King could easily have been influenced, whether consciously or inadvertently, to keep the system of reference superficially represented by "his life", "the sufferer's reviving consciousness", and "stupefied him".

171.2 come] First-edition "were" is an obvious case of Loring's misreading. Hawthorne's "co" is often extraordinarily like "wo" or "we", a fact that accounts for certain misprints in *The Marble Faun.*

179.19 believed in what] The manuscript reading, retained here, must be correct. Holgrave was not lying, as he would be in the first-edition version, "believed what he said"; instead, his talk was more hypothetical than proceeding from any firm conviction. Some slight smudging in the manuscript may have misled Jackman to believe that the word "in" was intended to be excised.

185.5 home] Although the word in the manuscript is definitely "home", at first sight it might perhaps be misread as "house", as appears in the first edition. It is unlikely that a change was made in proof. The connotations of "home" are important here, as in Clifford's: "There is no such unwholesome atmosphere as that of an old home, rendered poisonous by one's defunct forefathers and relatives! I speak of what I know! There is a certain house within my familiar recollection . . . " (261.18–22).

228.12 spurn at you] An argument in favor of adopting the first-edition variant "spurn you" as a proof correction would go as follows: in the manuscript "spurn" was interlined above deleted "spit"; when Hawthorne made this change, he neglected to remove the following "at" which had been associated with "spit", but he did so when the phrase caught his attention in proof. On the other hand, parallels to such a failure to delete the whole of a rejected phrase are wanting in the manuscript. "Spit" might have struck Hawthorne as too ungenteel, even given the force of Hepzibah's emotions. But it is perfectly appropriate for her to use the somewhat archaic phrase "spurn at" in the *OED* sense of being tempted to "strike or thrust with the foot", still a violent enough action to substitute for "spit". Jackman may have been unacquainted with the old-fashioned phrase and thought he was "correcting" an error.

234.3 fell far] It is a truly indifferent variant as between the first edition's "fell far short" and the manuscript's "fell very far short". The omission could well represent an eyeskip by compositor King, although his only other omission of a word is the accepted variant at 169.31 (see Textual Note). According to the Judge's calculation that perhaps as little as one-third of the estate had been found, the adjective "very" is certainly justified. On the other hand, "very" is not a strong word, and the phrase "fell far short" might have seemed to Hawthorne to be more impressive and characteristic of the Judge in its monosyllabic understatement. One may notice in this sentence "event", "visible", "every", "very", "ever". Just possibly Hawthorne omitted the "very" in proof to reduce the alliteration and the slightly awkward sequence of "every", "very", "ever". Yet, on the whole, small grounds exist here to support any decision, and the case for accepting the first-edition variant is perhaps the weakest in the text, together with 266.17.

240.21 series of calamity] This common reading of first edition and of manuscript is shown to be right by the continuation "reproducing itself in successive generations, with one general hue, and varying in little save the outline." The referent of "itself" is "calamity", not "series". That is, the evil fortunes of the family were each one a calamity, and together they constituted a series that formed the family history. For a similar idiom, see *The Scarlet Letter*, 19.10, "series of enjoyment".

261.3–4 no woman's eye . . . while it was beautiful!] This is the reading of the manuscript (with no changes during or after inscription), and it is the reading of the first edition except that an exclamation point is substituted in the print for the comma after "alas" and the comma before "while" is omitted. As it stands, the sentence cannot be literally intended. If, however, we assume that the difficulty rests not in a corruption made while copying the manuscript and overlooked in proof, nor in some hypothetical moment of forgetfulness, we must suppose that Hawthorne had some meaning in mind that was not clearly expressed. It is certainly possible that he intended the reader to equate the woman's eye in line 4 that had not seen Clifford's beauty with the woman's heart in line 3 that had not had his features impressed on it (in other words, fallen in love with him) through the eye contemplating his beauty. Thus Hawthorne may be regretting that the eye of no woman *in love* had seen his face (and had its features impressed) while it was still beautiful before the years in prison had done their work. But whether this or some other meaning was intended, the method of expression is far from precise. See 141.23–24: [Clifford] "had never quaffed the cup of passionate love. . . . "

266.17 the three-story] This first-edition change from manuscript "a three-story" is so indifferent that it could result from Letts's memorial lapse as readily as from an author's change in proof. Just slightly in favor of proof-alteration is the fact that "the" interrupts a slightly awkward series of "a's" in the original form of "with *a* roof sloping downward from *a* three-story peak to within *a* man's height of the ground." An interesting parallel comes immediately above in the description, "At a little distance stood a wooden church, black with age, and in a dismal state of ruin and decay, with broken windows, a great rift through the main-body of the edifice, and a rafter dangling from the top of *the* square tower." In each case, the singular or structural feature "the square tower" and "the three-story peak" is identified as "the", as in "the main-body" where it is required. However, these arguments need be no more than rationalization of a printer's error, despite the fact that Letts is a singularly trustworthy compositor.

266.27–28 bubbling up-gush] The position of the hyphen is clear in the manuscript; thus it would seem that the first edition's "bubbling-up gush" is a sophistication. In favor of the manuscript idiom one may compare "upward gush" (88.17), "to gush up out of the deep well" (96.5), "up-quivering flashes of the spirit" (157.12), and especially "this outgush of the inestimable tenderness" (227.35).

276.8 morrow] The first-edition substitution adopted here for manuscript "tomorrow" seems to represent an attempt to vary for effect the extreme repetition of "tomorrow" in lines 5–7. One may notice that the change to "morrow" also sharpens the parallel with following "morn" and produces a more effective and subtle rhetorical touch. For a similar case of assumed proof-alteration to vary rhetorical repetition, see 169.31 and its Textual Note.

278.30 in yonder chair] The manuscript reads "in yonder in chair", altered in the first edition to "in yonder arm-chair". That the chair was indeed an arm-chair is indicated by such references as "elbow-chair" 15.18, and "the ancestral arm-chair" 248.33. Hence the first-edition correction is not wrong in fact. On the other hand, since we must suppose that "arm-" does not represent an authorial proof-correction for compositor King's exact setting of the manuscript error, it is almost inevitable that "arm-chair" was this compositor's rationalization of the mistake. The only way in which "arm-chair" could be authorial is to conjecture that it was present in the manuscript that Hawthorne was copying but that the "in" before preceding "the" blotted it out from his eye. Such a hypothesis is not impossible, but no evidence exists to support it, whereas a parallel in error is found in the copying of the manuscript at 242.16, "Even had there had been no bitter recollections" for correct "Even had there been no bitter recollections". The errors at 221.33 and 244.12 may also be mentioned, although they are not true parallels.

287.31 with] To be "disturbed with" 'the racket is more colloquial and less elegant idiom than to be "disturbed by" and thus the change of manuscript "by" to first-edition "with" is appropriate for Uncle Venner's speech. If this argument seems too fine-spun, one can list various rough parallels in the text where "with" is preferred to "by" or some other possible preposition: "thronged . . . as with a congregation on its way to church" (11.22–23), "Miss Hepzibah, by secluding herself from society, has lost all true relation with it" (216.7–8), "this spot of black earth, vitiated with such an age-long growth of weeds" (219.19–20), or "His own death . . . attended with none of those suspicious circumstances" (304.28–29). The inference is not that Fox (the second most reliable compositor) introduced his own idiom inadvertently but that Hawthorne altered the manuscript form to suit his taste.

291.31 I have] The first-edition substitution of the full form "I have" for manuscript "I've" may represent an authorial attempt to avoid two contractions in the same sentence, although the rhythmic improvement may seem obscure. King may have made the change inadvertently, but see the Textual Note to 111.16 for a discussion.

299.22 within] Manuscript "inside" is interlined above deleted "within". Interestingly, Hawthorne appears to have restored the original reading in proof, and so one may exonerate King.

303.20 not you] The naturalness of the first edition's "Why have you not" instead of manuscript "Why have not you" should promote a suspicion that the compositor Willis was responsible for the "improvement". Phoebe is speaking under great stress and the comparative harshness of the word-order is appropriate. Something of a parallel is Phoebe's "Was not that well done?" (79.8). Although this change takes place in sheet 21, which was certainly proof-corrected by Hawthorne, five other rejected variants appear in this sheet (304.11, 306.35, 307.11, 307.12, 308.27) as well as the two accepted alterations (299.22, 309.2). Willis, who has a bad record for corrupting copy, was responsible for the error at 304.11, also.

304.11 of] The correctness of the manuscript "individuals of about the Judge's time of life" as against the first-edition omission of "of" before "about" may be attested by the phrase "of just about Holgrave's age" (181.19).

307.11 replied] First-edition "said" for manuscript "replied" is not likely to be a misreading, as was the change of a similar word at 89.34 (see Textual Note). Hawthorne occasionally adjusted such words connected with dialogue while copying the manuscript (see Alterations in the Manuscript 287.25 and 306.3) and could be presumed to have continued the process sometimes in proof. Thus one might be tempted to impute this change to a proof-alteration were it not that it occurs in the first edition only one line above the indubitable error of "drop" for manuscript "droop". That Hawthorne's eye could be caught by a triviality like "replied-said" and miss the unidiomatic reading immediately below is not impossible, but it may seem more implausible than a Henderson compositorial error, whether memorial or sophisticating.

307.12 droop] The correctness of the manuscript reading as against first-edition "drop" may be demonstrated by the same phrase "droop her eyes" in both manuscript and first edition at 107.22. One might also compare *The Blithedale Romance* 28.5–6, "she drooped down upon her knees", which was corrupted to "dropped" in the third edition.

EDITORIAL EMENDATIONS IN THE COPY-TEXT

(NOTE: Except for such silent typographical alterations as are remarked in the appendix on general textual procedures as applying to all Centenary texts, supplemented by the statement at the end of the Textual Introduction, every editorial change made from the final inscription of the printer's-copy manuscript of *The House of the Seven Gables* is listed here. Only the immediate source of the emendation, with its antecedents, is noticed; the Historical Collation may be consulted for the complete history, within the editions collated, of any substantive readings that qualify for inclusion in that listing. An alteration assigned to CENTENARY is made for the first time in the present edition if by "the first time" is understood "the first time in respect to the editions chosen for collation." Asterisked readings are discussed in the Textual Notes. The following texts are referred to: MS (the Houghton Library, Harvard University, manuscript), I (1851 first American edition), II (1876 Little Classics Edition), III (1883 Riverside Edition), IV (1899 illustrated edition), and V (1900 Autograph Edition). The wavy dash ~ represents the same word that appears before the bracket and is used in recording punctuation variants. An inferior caret ʌ indicates the absence of a punctuation mark.)

1.5	Novel] I; novel MS
7.23	period,] I; ~ ʌ MS
7.24	far] I; infinitely MS
8.5-7	statesmen— . . . day— . . . gallows, . . . blood,] CENTENARY; ~ , . . . ~ , . . . ~ — . . . ~ — MS; ~ ,— . . . ~ ,— . . . ~ , . . . ~ , I-V

18.8	State] I; state MS
21.31	New England] I; New-England MS
22.10	befell] I; befel MS
*24.16–17	horticulturist] II; horticulturalist MS, I
*24.23	-years'] II; -years $_\wedge$ MS, I
*24.31	The] I; In fine, the MS
24.31–32	country-girl] I; $\sim_\wedge\sim$ MS
25.29	alms house] CENTENARY; alm's house MS; almshouse I–V
28.22	front gable] I; front-gable MS
29.18	shopkeeper] I; shokeeper MS
30.1	half-an-hour] CENTENARY; $\sim_\wedge\sim_\wedge\sim$ MS, I–V
30.7–8	maiden lady's] I; maiden-lady's MS
*30.13	old maid] CENTENARY; Old Maid MS, I–V
31.13	fidgety] I; fidgetty MS
*31.29	heard] stet MS, I
*32.4	should] stet MS
32.14	to-and-fro] CENTENARY; $\sim$-$\sim_\wedge\sim$ MS; $\sim_\wedge\sim_\wedge\sim$ I–V
32.19	black silk] I; MS doubtfully black-silk
32.26	sunrises] I; sun-rises MS
32.30	ceiling] I; cieling MS
33.7	Half-a-dozen] CENTENARY; $\sim_\wedge\sim_\wedge\sim$ MS, I–V
33.26	Puritanic-] II; puritanic- MS, I
33.27	Bible] I; bible MS
35.14	ceiling] I; cieling MS
35.31	shopkeeper] I; shokeeper MS
*37.30	term] stet MS
38.18	entreat] I; intreat MS
41.11	silk-gown] CENTENARY; $\sim_\wedge\sim$ MS, I–V
41.14	near-sighted] I; $\sim_\wedge\sim$ MS
43.1	bartering] I; batering MS
43.9	door-way] I; doorway MS
*43.30	Daguerreotypist] CENTENARY; daguerreotypist MS, I–V
45.10	everybody] I; every body MS
*45.12	have always lived one] stet MS
45.14	have I] I; have I have I MS

45.15	Madam] CENTENARY; madam MS, I–V
*45.33	the old] *stet* MS
47.4	old maid] I; Old Maid MS
47.17	Dixey'] I; ~ , MS
48.18	half-a-lifetime] CENTENARY; half-a life time MS; half a lifetime I–V
48.29	dry-goods] I; dry-good MS
48.34	unrealities] I; unrealaties MS
50.15	copper-coin] CENTENARY; ~ ∧ ~ MS, I–V
50.17	gingerbread.–] CENTENARY; ~ ∧ – MS; ~ . ∧ I–V
*52.4	That] *stet* MS
*55.3	complacence] CENTENARY; complaisance MS, I–V
56.6	seemed ∧ . . . scrutinize,] I; ~ , . . . ~ ∧ MS
57.30	complaisancy] CENTENARY; complacency MS, I–V
58.21	up] I; up up MS
59.2	complaisancy] CENTENARY; complacency MS, I–V
61.1	sidewalk] II; side-walk MS, I
61.20	judgement] CENTENARY; judgment MS, I–V
*62.26	but] *stet* MS
64.5	autumn] I; Autumn MS
*64.10	have never] *stet* MS
*64.25	projecting] *stet* MS
*65.8	become] *stet* MS
65.24	chambers] I; chamber's MS
66.20	Venner.] I; ~ ∧ MS
67.31	handfull] CENTENARY; handful MS, I–V
*69.6	bolt] *stet* MS
70.5	ceiling] I; cieling MS
71.11	rose-bush] I; rose bush MS (*hyphen just possible*)
71.17	rose-bush] I; rosebush MS
72.19–20	old maid's] I; Old Maid's MS
73.12	writing-desk;] I; ~ ∧ ~ , MS
74.11	Cousin] CENTENARY; cousin MS, I–V

80.15	half-a-dozen] CENTENARY; $\sim_\wedge\sim_\wedge\sim$ MS, I–V
80.32	old maid] I; Hepzibah MS
81.1	accomplishment] I; accomplisment MS
81.26	milk-maids] CENTENARY; milkmaids MS, I–V
81.31	Cousin] CENTENARY; cousin MS, I–V
*83.6	visitors] II; visiters MS, I
83.23	Cousin] CENTENARY; cousin MS, I–V
*84.1	sounded] stet MS
84.13, 84.25	Daguerreotypist] CENTENARY; daguerreotypist MS, I–V
84.30	now-a-days] I; now-a $_\wedge$ days MS
87.4	currant-] I; current- MS
88.2	pear-tree] I; $\sim_\wedge\sim$ MS
88.15	-work] I; -word MS
*88.20	welling] stet MS
*89.34	cried] stet MS
*90.27	barn-door] stet MS
90.32	Daguerreotypist] CENTENARY; daguerreotypist MS, I–V
90.33	old maid] I; Old Maid MS
91.19	me,] I; $\sim_\wedge$ MS
92.17	half-a-dozen] CENTENARY; $\sim_\wedge\sim_\wedge\sim$ MS, I–V
92.33	face?"] I; $\sim$? $_\wedge$ MS
93.12	Daguerreotypist] CENTENARY; daguerreotypist MS, I–V
93.33	-vegetables] I; -vegetable MS
94.25, 94.27	Well] CENTENARY; well MS, I–V
94.30	Daguerreotypist] CENTENARY; daguerreotypist MS, I–V
98.12	turkeys] I; turkies MS
101.28	ecstacy] CENTENARY; ecstasy MS, I–V
102.24	dearest] I; dear MS
103.7–8	above-stairs] CENTENARY; $\sim_\wedge\sim$ MS, I–V
*103.23	step] stet MS
105.27	that] I; that that MS
105.28	Cousin] CENTENARY; cousin MS, I–V

*106.26	murmur] *stet* MS
*106.31	this] *stet* MS
110.14	garden,] I; ~ ∧ MS
*111.16	I'm] I; I am MS
111.19	voice,—] I; ~ .— MS
*111.20	south] *stet* MS, I
*113.4	no resource] *stet* MS
117.7	second story] I; second-story MS
117.14	old maid] I; Old Maid MS
*117.24–26	—(for . . . wages)—] *stet* MS
118.28	half-a-dozen] CENTENARY; ~ ∧ ~ ∧ ~ MS, I–V
120.17	quarter-of-an-hour] CENTENARY; ~ ∧ ~ ∧ ~ ∧ ~ MS, I–V
*123.16–17	resemblances,—] *stet* MS
125.1	Cousin] CENTENARY; cousin MS, I–V
125.32	shown] I; shewn MS
125.35	christians] CENTENARY; Christians MS, I–V
126.22	by-the-by] I; ~ ∧ ~ ∧ ~ MS
*127.11	fellow] *stet* MS
127.35	visitors] II; visiters MS, I
127.36	visitor] II; visiter MS, I
136.6	ribbons ∧] I; ~ , MS
136.32	ceilings] I; cielings MS
*137.8	Pyncheon-house] I; ~ ∧ ~ MS
138.23	His] CENTENARY; his MS, I–V
141.4	real! ∧] I; ~ !— MS
141.21	hers] I; her's MS
142.11	earth,] I; ~ ; MS
*144.20	drowsyhead] *stet* MS
145.20	successful] I; successul MS
147.32	New England] I; New-England MS
149.5	Pyncheon-garden] I; ~ ∧ ~ MS
*149.25	chaos] *stet* MS
150.22	Pyncheon family] I; Pyncheon-family MS
*151.26	fore-mothers] *stet* MS
152.24	although] I; athough MS
152.31	sideway] II; side-way MS, I
153.9	currant-bushes] I; ~ ∧ ~ MS

153.13	unscrupulously] I; unscrupously MS
153.28	Pyncheon-house] I; $\sim_\wedge\sim$ MS
154.1–2	mosaic-work] I; $\sim_\wedge\sim$ MS
161.30	mothers'] I; mother's MS
163.27	milk-maid's] CENTENARY; $\sim_\wedge\sim$ MS; milkmaid's I–V
164.7	highland bonnet] II; highland-bonnet MS, I
*165.12	infrequent] stet MS, I–V
168.7	straw bonnet] I; straw-bonnet MS
*169.31	one's self] I; one's own self MS
*170.9	its] stet MS
170.23	torture of] I; torture of of MS
*171.2	come] stet MS
173.3	Pyncheon-house] I; $\sim_\wedge\sim$ MS
178.26	opportunities] I; opportunites MS
*179.19	believed in what] stet MS
181.2–3	well as other] I; well other MS
181.5–6	Altogether] I; Atogether MS
181.8	in his] I; in his his MS
181.32	himself] I; him self MS
182.26	her] I; he MS
183.3	word!"] I; $\sim!_\wedge$ MS
184.11	Pyncheon-house] I; $\sim_\wedge\sim$ MS
184.21	view,] I; $\sim_\wedge$ MS
184.25	By-the-by] I; $\sim_\wedge\sim_\wedge\sim$ MS
*185.5	home] stet MS
186.1	Phoebe] I; Phobe MS
186.24	laughingly] I; laughing MS
189.7	wizard$_\wedge$] I; $\sim$, MS
191.7	turkeys] I; turkies MS (interlined above deleted 'turkeys')
191.14	New England] I; New-England MS
191.20	front gable] I; front-gable MS
192.5	Pyncheon-house] I; $\sim_\wedge\sim$ MS
192.19	Anybody] I; Any body MS
192.25	above-stairs] CENTENARY; $\sim_\wedge\sim$ MS, I–V
194.2	firelight] II; fire-light MS, I
194.20	house?"] I; $\sim?_\wedge$ MS
195.8	Pyncheon family] I; Pyncheon-family MS

195.33	family?"] I; ∼ ?∧ MS
196.35	were] I; where MS
198.17	propose."] I; ∼ .∧ MS
198.23	seven-and-thirty] I; ∼ ∧∼ ∧∼ MS
199.35	Sherry] CENTENARY; sherry MS, I–V
203.24–25	fashion— . . . thinkers—] CENTENARY; ∼ , . . . ∼ , MS; ∼ ,— . . . ∼ ,– I–V
203.26	Puritan] I; puritan MS
206.6	Gallows-Hill] CENTENARY; Gallows-hill MS; Gallows Hill I–V
206.8	an'] I; an MS
206.26	incantations ∧] I; ∼ , MS
209.25	Maule,] I; ∼ ∧ MS
210.9	wofullest] I; woefullest MS
211	GOOD BYE] CENTENARY; GOOD-BYE MS; GOOD-BY I–V
213.4	demagogue] I; demaagogue MS
214.22	to-night] I; ∼ ∧∼ MS
214.27–28	ruddy light of a cheerful fire] I; light of a ruddy, cheerful fire MS
216.26	maiden lady] II; maiden-lady MS, I
218.24, 218.29	good bye] CENTENARY; good-bye MS; good-by I, III–V; good by II
218.34	half-a-dozen] CENTENARY; ∼ ∧∼ ∧∼ MS, I–V
221.1	hippopotamus] I; hippopotamas MS
221.33	him her] I; him at her MS
223.19	east-wind] CENTENARY; ∼ ∧∼ MS, I–V
223.20	East-Wind] CENTENARY; ∼ ∧∼ MS, I; east wind II–V
224.9	noonday] II; noon-day MS, I
224.15	Colonel] II; colonel MS, I
225.25	humming-birds] I; ∼ ∧∼ MS
225.27	it,) ∧] CENTENARY; ∼ ∧), MS; ∼ ∧) ∧ I–V
227.3	longer,] I; ∼ . MS
227.28	I)—] CENTENARY; ∼ —) MS; ∼) ∧ I–V
227.31	Cousin] CENTENARY; cousin MS, I–V
228.2	He] CENTENARY; he MS, I–V
*228.12	spurn at you] *stet* MS

229.31	ceilings] I; cielings MS
230.20	blood ∧ —] CENTENARY; ~ ,— MS, I–V
231.2–3	Pyncheon-bull]] I; ~ ∧ ~ MS
231.25	there"?] I; ~ ?" MS
233.9	personal—] CENTENARY; ~ ,— MS; ~ , ∧ I–V
233.11	Cousin] CENTENARY; cousin MS, I–V
*234.3	fell far] I; fell very far MS
235.6	Uncle's] CENTENARY; uncle's MS, I–V
236.7	arched window] I; arched-window MS
236.18	Cousin] CENTENARY; *doubtful in* MS; cousin I–V
236.28	Cousin] I; MS *doubtfully* cousin
237.7	world—] CENTENARY; ~ .— MS; ~ ,— I–V
*240.21	series of calamity] *stet* MS, I
242.15	Evil Destiny] CENTENARY; evil destiny MS, I–V
242.16	there been] I; there had been MS
242.23	Cousin] II; cousin MS, I
243.3	rhythm] I; rhythhm MS
244.1	Congress] II; congress MS, I
244.12	swayed her] I; swayed to her MS
245.7	His] CENTENARY; his MS, I–V
248.29	ceiling] I; cieling MS
251.34	Hepzibah.] I; ~ ∧ MS
254.30	kennel] I; *just possibly* MS *reads* kennels
*261.3–4	no woman's eye . . . while it was beautiful!] *stet* MS
262.25	so,] I; ~ . MS
264.29	day ∧ —] CENTENARY; ~ ,— MS, I–V
264.31–265.3	'I . . . forever!'—'My . . . love!'—'I . . . can!'. . . 'I . . . much!' . . . 'Your . . . bliss!' . . . 'An . . . God!'] I; *double quotation marks in* MS
*266.17	the three-story] I; a three-story MS
*266.27–28	bubbling up-gush] *stet* MS
270.27, 271.9	Half-an-hour] CENTENARY; ~ ∧ ~ ∧ ~ MS, I–V
273.14	this,] I; ~ ; MS

275.28	By-the-by] I; $\sim_\wedge\sim_\wedge\sim$ MS
*276.8	morrow] I; tomorrow MS
*278.30	in yonder chair] CENTENARY; in yonder in chair MS; in yonder arm-chair I
279.35	shopkeeping] CENTENARY; shop-keeping MS, I–V
280.9	side-pocket] I; $\sim_\wedge\sim$ MS
280.21	noonday] II; noon-day MS, I
281.25	Devil] CENTENARY; devil MS, I–V
281.25	could] I; could could MS
282.1	keeps] I; keep MS
283.2	may have piled] I; may piled MS
285.8	Sibyl] II; Sybil MS, I
285.9	main-entrance] CENTENARY; $\sim_\wedge\sim$ MS, I–V
285.26	again] I; agai MS
285.28	basement story] CENTENARY; basement-story MS, I–V
285.34	Puritan] I; puritan MS
*287.31	with] I; by MS
287.35	Holgrave.] I; $\sim_\wedge$ MS
288.21	chimney-warmth] I; $\sim_\wedge\sim$ MS
290.24	want] I; wan't MS
*291.31	I have] I; I've MS
293.7, 293.17–18, 294.33	door-step] I; doorstep MS
293.20	anybody] I; any body MS
294.34–295.1	Pyncheon $_\wedge$ (. . . mood $_\wedge$)] I; $\sim$,(. . . $\sim$,) MS
295.15	Pyncheon family] I; Pyncheon-family MS
297.5	half-an-hour] CENTENARY; $\sim_\wedge\sim_\wedge\smile$ MS, I–V
297.10	door-step] I; doorstep MS
298.24	Cousin] CENTENARY; cousin MS, I–V
299.19	indistinct] I; indististinct MS
*299.22	within] I; inside MS
299.27	sidelong] IV; side-long MS, I–III
301.12	inquiry] I; enquiry MS
303.18	into] I; in	to MS

*303.20   not you] *stet* MS
*304.11   of] *stet* MS
*307.11   replied] *stet* MS
*307.12   droop] *stet* MS
309.2   social world] I; social and political world
                 MS
310.9   street-corners] I; $\sim_\wedge\sim$ MS
310.24   that a murder] I; that a | a murder MS
310.26   indicating] I; showing MS
310.29   bed-chamber] CENTENARY; bedchamber
                 MS, I–V
316.34   eastern-territory] CENTENARY; $\sim_\wedge\sim$ MS,
                 I–V
318.15   and—as] I; and—and, as MS

REJECTED FIRST-EDITION
SUBSTANTIVE READINGS

(NOTE: Although the readings below are listed in the Historical Collation, they are given separately here since the information is of critical importance. An asterisk indicates that a Textual Note discusses the reading.)

31.33	the] MS; a I
*32.4	should] MS; shall I
*37.30	term] MS; throe I
44.7	an] MS; a I
*45.33	the] MS; an I
*52.4	That] MS; The I
*62.26	but] MS; *omit* I
*64.10	have never] MS; never have I
*64.25	projecting] MS; perfecting I
*65.8	become] MS; became I
*69.6	bolt] MS; door I
79.19	choose] MS; chose I
81.17	Higgins] MS; Wiggins I
*84.1	it sounded] MS; it had sounded I
*88.20	welling] MS; swelling I
*89.34	cried] MS; said I
*90.27	barn-door] MS; barn-yard I
*103.23	step] MS; stop I
*106.26	murmur] MS; manner I
*106.31	this] MS; the I
*113.4	no resource] MS; no other resource I

*127.11	fellow] MS; fellows I
127.14	sturdy] MS; steady I
127.32	a] MS; *omit* I
129.14	your] MS; you I
137.23	such depth] MS; such a depth I
*144.20	drowsyhead] MS; drowsy head I
*149.25	chaos] MS; class I
151.26	excellencies] excellences I
*170.9	its] MS; his I
*171.2	come] MS; were I
171.22	on] MS; or I
174.34–35	enjoyed] MS; employed I
*179.19	believed in what] MS; believed what I
*185.5	home] MS; house I
192.24	trilled] MS; thrilled I
209.15	sorrow] MS; sorrows I
214.14	is] MS; are I
224.8	where] MS; when I
*228.12	spurn at you] MS; spurn you I
228.18	unreasoning] MS; unreasonable I
254.5	her] MS; his I
255.31	were] MS; was I
*266.27–28	bubbling up-gush] MS; bubbling-up gush I
275.3	attain] MS; obtain I
*278.30	in yonder chair] CENTENARY; in yonder arm-chair I
280.26	this] MS; the I
300.8	undefinable] indefinable I
*303.20	not you] MS; you not I
*304.11	of] MS; *omit* I
306.35	impulse] MS; impulses I
*307.11	replied] MS; said I
*307.12	droop] MS; drop I
308.27	only] MS; had I

WORD-DIVISION

1. *End-of-the-Line Hyphenation in the Centenary Edition*

(NOTE: No hyphenation of a possible compound at the end of a line in the Centenary text is present in the manuscript except for the following readings, which are hyphenated within the line in the manuscript. Hyphenated compounds in which both elements are capitalized are not included.)

5.9	Pyncheon-|street	53.18	newly-|bought
7.13	garden-|ground	57.19	Pyncheon-|house
10.3	above-|mentioned	59.33	air-|drawn
10.32	old-|age	64.26	harlequin-|trick
14.14	riding-|boots	67.18	half-|a-dozen
25.24	poverty-|stricken	72.16	half-|an-hour
29.8	be-|ruffled	72.20	household-|fire
31.18	dingy-|framed	81.30	russet-|apples
34.2	time-|stricken	82.11	back-|yards
40.4	awe-|stricken	82.17	high-|strained
40.18	jingle-|jangle	83.4	door-|panels
42.1	elbow-|chair	84.13	well-|meaning
42.11	shop-|door	87.12	Summer-|squashes
48.6	self-|partialities	88.5	farm-|house
50.16	pocket-|money	93.27	country-|air
52.33	cotton-|thread	99.28	hiding-|places

103.7	above-|stairs	207.20	meanly-|dressed
110.2	dew-|drops	209.23	laboring-|man
110.33	ill-|tempered	209.30	south-|east
113.12	great-|grandfather	217.13	country-|hotel
116.19	gold-|headed	219.21	clover-|fields
119.3	country-|girl	220.27	dew-|drop
120.22	steel-|hilted	223.14	shingle-|roof
121.9	weather-beaten	226.1	faint-|heartedness
131.24	limit-|loving	230.3	water-|puddle
137.12	wrought-|lace	231.21	looking-|glass
137.22	pear-|tree	240.17	chimney-|corner
142.1	half-|torpid	246.27	summer-|house
142.2	long-|silent	253.20	self-|guidance
145.7	summer-|house	258.16	Pyncheon-|street
147.6	household-|maiden	259.8	gimlet-|eyed
148.22	bean-|poles	265.18	cross-|beamed
152.12	mother-|hen	265.20	shirt-|bosom
155.1	frost-|bitten	266.17	three-|story
160.11	here-and-|there	270.5	five-and-|twenty
161.34,	scissor-|grinder's	270.6	Five-|and-twenty
162.11		270.16	leathern-|cushioned
164.4	shop-|door	273.6	dinner-|hour
165.19	shirt-|collar	275.18	feeding-|time
167.32	ascension-|robes	275.27	dinner-|table
174.24	flower-|fragrance	276.8	resurrection-|morn
176.15	district-|school	278.29	to-|night
176.18	twenty-|two	280.14	unlooked-|for
176.27	factory-|towns	280.19	silver-|headed
181.30	Pyncheon-|garden	281.35	world-|clock
182.18	garden-|fence	282.18	family-|physician
184.2	court-|houses	283.13	house-|flies
185.19	family-|existence	288.21	summer-|warmth
189.30	stage-|manager	291.6	women-|folks
190.7	church-| communicant	307.24	street-|door
		310.30	hand-|print
191.34	back-|door	315.12	model-|conservative
197.10	foreign-|bred	317.6	yellowish-|brown
207.6	middle-|age	318.11	mansion-|house

2. *End-of-the-Line Hyphenation in the Manuscript*

(NOTE: The following compounds, or possible compounds, are hyphenated at the end of the line in the manuscript copy-text. The form in which they have been transcribed in the Centenary Edition, as listed below, represents the practice of the manuscript as ascertained by other appearances or by parallels within the manuscript. Other Hawthorne manuscripts of the period have been consulted when evidence was not available in *The House of the Seven Gables* manuscript.)

2.3	by-gone	72.31	bed-chamber
5.5	Pynchen-street	79.17	self-love
6.31	cottage-door	83.4	sword-hilt
20.35	looking-glass	83.22	shop-bell
29.3	shop-door	86.16	seed-vessels
35.26	tallow-candles	94.13	fruit-trees
36.3	world-renowned	103.15	standstill
36.24	tiptoe	105.10	cross-beamed
46.11	sea-water	110.30	breakfast-table
49.4	shop-window	111.19	self-communing
50.33	cannibal-feast	112.35	shop-bell
52.5	copper-coin	116.35	ill-natured
52.34	near-sighted	120.19	ready-made
53.11	cotton-frock	143.22	wild-flower
65.34	copper-tokens	146.7	touch-stone
68.16	shop-door	151.13	crack-brained
69.11	country-cousin	152.8	arch-enemy
71.20	grand-aunt	155.26	town-pump

158.5	summer-afternoons	265.14	world-hunt
163.13	milk-maid	269.3	wide-open
167.30	well-brushed	269.25	spring-seated
167.34	sunshade	270.24	money-bags
169.6	age-stricken	275.12	lukewarm
171.3	fountain-head	275.28	shirt-bosom
174.32	seven-mile	275.33	beef-steak
176.21	country-store	277.24	above-stairs
176.22	political-editor	279.10	Ghost-stories
176.29	packet-ship	279.11	family-party
184.3	city-halls	280.18	gaiter-boots
193.19	cross-beam	285.6	elm-tree
201.15	fellow-being	285.19	sunlight
207.7	leather-breeches	289.10	north-gable
224.17	kitchen-fireplace	297.32	night-long
229.30	plate-glass	310.14	touch-stone
244.33	heart-sinking	314.10	garden-scenes

3. Special Cases

(a)

(NOTE: In the following list the compound, or possible compound, is hyphenated at the end of the line in the manuscript and in the Centenary Edition.)

6.5	Pyncheon-	house (i.e. Pyncheon-house)
32.32	fire-	board (i.e. fire-board)
39.31	bloody-	minded (i.e. bloody-minded)
46.12	half-a-	dozen (i.e. half-a-dozen)
81.3	tapestry-	stitch (i.e. tapestry-stitch)
84.21	come-	outers (i.e. come-outers)
165.21	vantage-	point (i.e. vantage-point)
263.13	dark-	chambered (i.e. dark-chambered)
279.13	steeple-	hat (i.e. steeple-hat)
289.25	half-	hour (i.e. half-hour)
307.31	street-	door (i.e. street-door)

(b)

(NOTE: In the following cases the hyphenated compound appears at the end of the line in the Centenary Edition but the hyphen is an editorial emendation not present in the manuscript.)

48.18   half-a-|lifetime (i.e. half-a-lifetime *for* MS half-a life time)
118.28   half-a-|dozen (i.e. half-a-dozen *for* MS half a dozen)
154.1   mosaic-|work (i.e. mosaic-work *for* MS mosaic work)
231.2   Pyncheon-|bull (i.e. Pyncheon-bull *for* MS Pyncheon bull)
293.17   door-|step (i.e. door-step *for* MS doorstep)

HISTORICAL COLLATION

This Historical Collation records substantive variants between editions as well as all plate changes in the first edition. Typographical errors not forming accepted words are not listed for editions after the first unless they involve revision of the plates. The basis of record is the reading to the left of the bracket, which is that of the Centenary Text; any unlisted edition is to be presumed to agree with Centenary.

The following editions were collated, and their substantive variants recorded: I, 1851 first edition; II, 1876 Little Classics Edition; III, 1883 Riverside Edition; IV, 1899 illustrated edition; and V, 1900 Autograph Edition. The plates of I were used for the 1865 untitled collected edition, 1876 Illustrated Library, 1879 Fireside, 1880 Globe, 1884 Globe (Crowell), and 1886 New Fireside editions; the plates of II, for the 1891 Popular, 1894 Salem, and 1899 Concord editions; and the plates of III for the 1884 Wayside, 1884–85 Complete Works (London), 1891 Standard Library, 1902 New Wayside, and 1909 Fireside editions.

Since the first-edition plates were the only ones that could have been revised during Hawthorne's lifetime, the intermediate printings of I have been spot-checked to locate the initial appearance of each variant. Machine collations of the plates of II and III record variants between the first and last printings of these plates, but the provenience of intermediate variants is not further specified in this listing. No attempt has been made to check the plates of IV and V after the first printing of each.

In this list the superior letter a indicates first printing, z last printing; b indicates the second 1851 printing of I. See the Textual Introduction for discussion of the concealed 1851 printings of the first edition.

5.9	fail] failed II–V
7.24	far] infinitely MS
9.5	the] the the III[a]
12.3	shadow] shadowy II–V
16.30	farther] further I
22.2	odder] older V
22.16	doubt] doubts V
24.16–17	horticulturist] horticulturalist MS, I
24.23	years'] years MS, I
24.31	The] In fine, the MS
26.23	them, of] them: of I; them: that of II; them, —that of III–V
26.28	psychology] pyschology I–III[a]
29.18, 35.31	shopkeeper] shokeeper MS
30.22	farthest] furthest I
31.33	the] a I–V
32.4	should] shall I–V
37.30	term] throe I–V
43.1	bartering] batering MS
43.28	apparent] apparen I[b-1864]
44.7	an] a I–V
45.14	have I] have I have I MS
45.33	the] an I–V
48.29	dry-goods] dry-good MS
48.32	farther] further I
52.4	That] The I–V
55.3	complacence] complaisance MS, I–V
57.3	mark, influence] marked influence II–V
57.30	complaisancy] complacency MS, I–V
58.21	up] up up MS
59.2	complaisancy] complacency MS, I–V
62.26	but] *omit* I–V
63.31	neither] either II–V
64.10	have never] never have I–V
64.25	projecting] perfecting I–V
65.8	become] became I–V
65.24	chambers] chamber's MS
68.7	farthest] furthest I
69.6	bolt] door I–V
69.13	be] he II
71.12	luxurious] luxuriant II[a]–V

75.17	jealousy] jealously V
79.19	choose] chose I–II
80.16	remembrancers] remembrances IV
80.31	farther] further I
80.32	old maid] Hepzibah MS
81.17	Higgins] Wiggins I
82.19	subtle] subtile II–V
84.1	sounded] had sounded I–V
88.15	-work] -word MS
88.20	welling] swelling I–V
88.24	farther] further I
89.34	cried] said I–V
90.27	barn-door] barn-yard I–V
93.33	-vegetables] -vegetable MS
94.34–95.1	department] apartment II–V
95.7	sideway] sideways V
102.8	gust] gush III–V
102.24	dearest] dear MS
103.15	involuntarily] involuntary II[a]
103.23	step] stop I
104.24	courtesy] curtsy V
105.27	that] that that MS
106.26	murmur] manner I
106.31	this] the I–V
108.10	towards] toward I–V
110.9	farther] further I
111.16	I'm] I am MS
112.25	subtle] subtile II–V
113.4	no resource] no other resource I–V
116.16	advantage of a] advantage a III
116.21	a white neckcloth] a neckcloth III–V
116.34	genuine] general III–V
118.3	courtesied] curtsied V
125.32	shown] shewn MS
127.11	fellow] fellows I–V
127.14	sturdy] steady I–V
127.32	a] omit I–V
129.14	your] you I
133.9	despairingly] de-|sparingly III[a]
135.14, 135.20	harpsichord] harpischord III[a]
137.2	Death] death I–III, V

137.10	attar] ottar I–V
137.23	such depth] such a depth I–V
138.17	with] ith I[a-1864]
142.11	he had lacked] he lacked V
143.7	grace] graces II–V
144.20	drowsyhead] drowsy head I; drowsihead II–V
147.34–35	about him with] about with IV
148.13	was] were III–V
149.25	chaos] class I–V
149.33	at] by II–V
151.16	Queerly] Queer II–V
151.26	excellencies] excellences I–V
152.16–17	two of body] two body III[a]
152.25	clues] clews I[1865-z]
152.31	sideway] side-way MS, I; sideways V
154.12	water] waters III–V
155.24	and at other] and other III–V
155.32	always talking] talking always III[a]
161.30	mothers'] mother's MS
168.23	in delightful] in a delightful IV
169.13	further] farther II–V
169.31	one's self] one's own self MS
170.9	its] his I–V
170.23	torture of] torture of of MS
171.2	come] were I–V
171.3	subtle] subtile II–III, V
171.22	on] or I
173.3	precincts] precints III[a]
174.19	subtle] subtile II–V
174.34	enjoyed] employed I–V
179.19	believed in what] believed what I–V
181.2–3	well as other] well other MS
181.8	in his] in his his MS
182.10	farther] further I
182.26	her] he MS
184.3	city-halls] city-hall III–IV; city hall V
185.5	home] house I–V
186.24	laughingly] laughing MS
187.21	quit] quiet II[z]–V
189.8	amends] amendment II–V

190.30	criticize] criticise I[1865-z]
192.24	trilled] thrilled I–V
196.35	were] where MS
200.8	crave] have IV
204.31	farther] further I–V
206.8	an'] an MS
208.29–30	inordinate] mordinate I[1865-z]
209.15	sorrow] sorrows I–V
214.14	is] are I–V
214.27–28	ruddy light of a cheerful fire] light of a ruddy, cheerful fire MS
221.33	him her] him at her MS
224.8	where] when I–V
225.35	capacious] capacions III[a]
226.4	visitor] visiter I[a-1864]
227.4	the] the the III[a]
228.12	spurn at you] spurn you I–V
228.18	unreasoning] unreasonable I–V
230.8	visitors] visiters I[a-1864]
231.12–13	roomy fashion] roomy-fashion III[a]
231.17	sundry his] sundry of his II–V
232.7	to] do II–V
234.3	fell far] fell very far MS
242.16	there been] there had been MS
242.20	be] he III
244.12	swayed her] swayed to her MS
246.5	subtle] subtile II–V
250.32–33	even if it] even it III[a]
254.5	her] his I–V
254.20	concentred] concentrated V
255.31	were] was I–V
259.15	clue] clew I[1865-z]
260.4	or] o I[b-1864]; of I[1865]–V
261.23	elder] older II–V
262.12	farther] further I
266.15–16	Farther] Further I
266.17	the three-story] a three-story MS
266.27–28	bubbling up-gush] bubbling-up gush I–V
267.3	looking down from] looking from III–V
269.33	pretty little utmost] pretty utmost V

271.15	demesne] demense III[a]
272.9	political] poliitcal I[1865-z]
275.3	attain] obtain I–V
276.8	morrow] tomorrow MS
278.30	in yonder chair] in yonder in chair MS; in yonder arm-chair I–III; in yonder arm-|chair IV; in yonder armchair V
280.8	leather] leathern V
280.26	this] the I–V
281.25	could] could could MS
282.1	keeps] keep MS
283.2	may have piled] may piled MS
283.6, 283.8	subtile] subtle II[z]–V
284.23	sweetly tempered] sweetly-tempered I; sweet-tempered II–V
287.31	with] by MS
288.14	visitor] visiter I[a-1864]
291.31	I have] I've MS
294.17–18	play as long as he] play as he V
295.10	trill] thrill II–V
299.22	within] inside MS
299.26	widely] wide II–V
300.8	undefinable] indefinable I–V
300.16	subtle] subtile II–V
303.20	not you] you not I–V
304.11	of] omit I–V
304.29	with] by III–V
305.29	so soon.] so. III–V
306.35	impulse] impulses I–V
307.11	replied] said I–V
307.12	droop] drop I–V
307.33–34	farther] further I
308.27	only] had I–V
309.2	social world] social and political world MS
310.3	county-newspapers] county ∧ newspapers I–IV; country newspapers V
310.24	that a murder] that a a murder MS
310.26	indicating] showing MS
311.33	ignominious] ignomnious III[a]
316.30	much of a] much a III–V
318.15	and—as] and—and, as MS

ALTERATIONS IN THE MANUSCRIPT

(NOTE: Only the alterations—whether corrections or revisions—that can be read are listed here; the numerous words where nothing can be made out of the deletion are omitted. Simple mendings of letters or words for clarity are ignored when no change is being made. Spaces between square brackets indicate illegible letters; letters enclosed in square brackets are doubtful.)

1.6	is pre-|] *written over erased* ', w'.
1.6	a very minute] *interlined with a caret above deleted* 'the minutest'.
1.7	possible] *written over wiped-out* 'probable'.
1.10	so far as] *written over wiped-out* 'if it swerves'.
1.14	or mellow] *interlined with a caret.*
1.15	and enrich] *interlined with a caret.*
2.1	keep] 'ke' *written over wiped-out* '[co]'.
2.8	almost] *written over wiped-out* 'lightly'.
2.11	humble] *interlined with a caret above deleted* 'mean'.
2.22	ill-gotten] *interlined above deleted* 'accumulated'.
2.24	accumulated] *interlined with a caret.*
2.26	the] *written over wiped-out* 'hopes'.
2.31–32	—or . . . butterfly—] *interlined with a caret;* **the** original semicolon and dash after 'rod' were not deleted.
2.35	crowning] *first* 'n' *interlined with a caret.*
3.17	had] 'd' *mended over original* 's'.
6.1	amplitude] *interlined above deleted* 'fulness'.
6.30	original] 'or' *written over wiped-out* 'fo'.

7.11	right;] *semicolon mended from original comma.*
7.12	acre] *this word not being clearly written, another hand has interlined* 'acre' *very legibly inscribed.*
7.18	appears] 'app' *written over wiped-out* 'seem'.
7.19	were] *written over wiped-out* 'had'.
7.31	area] *interlined in another hand above badly written* 'area'.
7.34	Old] *written over some wiped-out letters, perhaps* 'Matthew'.
8.12	their] *preceded by deleted* 'poor and rich'.
8.23	his] *written over wiped-out* 'th'.
9.16	would] *preceded by deleted* 'would,'.
9.24	he] *interlined with a caret.*
9.28	by] *written over wiped-out* 'with'.
10.2	very] *interlined above deleted* 'very'.
10.6	lurk at] 'k at' *written over wiped-out* 'at the'.
11.16	-smoke,] *followed by deleted* 'had'.
11.30	lime] *written over wiped-out* 'pebb'.
12.8	still] *written over wiped-out* 'already'.
13.12	was one] *written over wiped-out* 'had been'.
13.24	he] *interlined with a caret.*
13.28	courtesy] *written over some wiped-out word that may be* 'etiquette'.
14.26	awakening] 'awak' *written over wiped-out* 'effect'.
14.33	our host] *written over wiped-out* 'the Colonel'.
15.4	apartments] *interlined above deleted* 'chambers'.
15.32	stare] 's' *written over wiped-out* 'f'.
16.3	that] 'that' | *followed at start of next line by deleted* 'that'.
16.14	were] *interlined with a caret.*
16.17	fiercely] *interlined above deleted* 'forcibly'.
16.19	only a] *written over wiped-out* 'the figure'.
16.32–33	One—John] *the dash is written over a comma, and* 'John' *mended to the right over original* 'John'.
17.9	a] *interlined above deleted* 'any'.
17.9	murder] *interlined in another hand above badly written* 'murder'.
18.9	reigning] *written over wiped-out* 'prince's'.
18.17	necessary] 'neces-sary' *written over wiped-out* 'requir-ed'.
18.34	re-granted] 're-' *written over wiped-out* 'reg'.
19.5	wrested] *written over wiped-out* '[ted] from'.

19.32	Colonel] *interlined with a caret.*
20.3	Seven Gables will] *written over wiped-out* 'House of the Seven'.
20.15	it—] *the dash written over a comma.*
20.19	than the] *each word seems written over wiped-out* 'that'.
21.26	of a] 'a' *interlined with a caret.*
22.1	sympathies] *followed by deleted* 'and the seldom varying [ ] of its intelligence'.
22.6	at] *written over original* 'in'.
22.6	point] *interlined above deleted* 'nick'.
23.4	nostrils—] *the dash written over a comma.*
23.14	the old gentleman's] *written over wiped-out* 'his purpose awakened'.
23.22	even] *interlined with a caret.*
23.34	was reckoned] 'was rec' *written over wiped-out* 'had been'.
24.2	won] *interlined above deleted* 'attained'.
24.11	Judge Pyncheon] *written over wiped-out* 'He was unquestio'.
24.33	or] *interlined above deleted* 'and'.
25.14	massive] 'massi' *written over wiped-out* '[stron]g'.
25.26	on] *interlined above deleted* 'at'.
26.12	indefinable] *written over wiped-out* 'pecu'.
26.25–26	in the noonday streets] *written over wiped-out* 'during the [ ]'.
27.7	boards,] *interlined above deleted* 'boards,'.
27.8	in the midst,] *interlined with a caret deleting a comma.*
27.12	with] *written over wiped-out* 'the'.
27.31	an] *interlined above deleted* 'and'.
28.8–9	They . . . Posies.] *interlined with a caret and also written with* 'Inset' *on verso of the preceding fol.* 15.
28.33–34	(gentleman . . . himself)] *the parentheses written over dashes.*
29.1	royal Governor] *written over* 'King's [Governor]' *and then interlined for clarity.*
29.22	-book.] *followed by deleted* 'It appeared to be his doom to spend eternity'.
29.24–25	in a vain . . . balance.] *at the foot of folio 18 verso is the false start of folio 17,* 'in an ineffectual attempt to make his accounts balance.' *in which* 'ineffectual' *is written over wiped-out* 'effectual'.

31.9	maiden lady's] *interlined above deleted* 'Old Maid's'.
31.10	Not] *written over wiped-out* 'First'.
31.22	elderly person] *interlined above deleted* 'Old Maid'.
32.1	tender] 'tend' *written over wiped-out* 'lips'.
32.3	emotion] 'em' *written over wiped-out* 'se'.
32.18	darkened] *interlined above deleted* 'blackened'.
32.18	tall] *written over wiped-out* 'fig[ ]'.
32.19	feeling] *preceded by deleted* 'and'.
32.21	The sun] *written over wiped-out* 'Meanwhile'.
32.26	which—] *the dash written over a comma.*
33.5	slender] 'sl' *written over wiped-out* 'leg'.
33.8	contrived] 'trived' *written over wiped-out* 'structed'.
33.17	ornamental] 'ental' *written over wiped-out* '[entary]'.
34.8	brow] *written over wiped-out* 'face' *and then interlined with a caret.*
34.21	weaknesses] *interlined above deleted* 'attributes'.
34.26	In] *written over wiped-out* 'We'.
35.2	weighed.—It treasured] *the period is added;* 'It treasur' *written over wiped-out* 'and treas'.
35.6	old Hepzibah's] *written above deleted* 'the Old Maid's'.
36.5	equipments] 'equip' *written over wiped-out* 'uniforms'.
36.21	elderly maiden] *interlined above deleted* 'Old Maid'.
36.22	Colonel's] 'Co' *written over wiped-out* 'por'.
36.23	heaved] 'h' *written over wiped-out* 's'.
36.28	upper] 'u' *written over wiped-out* 's'.
37.16	dismemberment] *first* 'm' *interlined with a caret.*
37.18	has] *interlined with a caret.*
38.5	instant] *interlined above deleted* 'nick'.
38.28	cent-] 'cent' *interlined in ink for clarity in another hand.*
38.31	recluse] *interlined with a caret above deleted* 'Old Maid'.
39.29	maiden lady] *interlined above deleted* 'Old Maid'.
39.31	cautiously] 'c' *written over wiped-out* '[f]'.
39.32	villain] *interlined with a caret.*

39.35	in] *written over wiped-out* 'into'.
40.35	old Hepzibah] *interlined above deleted* 'Old Maid'.
41.4	which] *written over wiped-out* 'that'.
41.5	example] *interlined above deleted* 'instance'.
42.8	maiden lady] *interlined with a caret above deleted* 'Old Maid'.
42.17	responsive] 'respon' *written over some wiped-out letters, probably* 'tumult'.
43.9–10	door-way. Coming] *MS* 'doorway. Coming' *mended from* 'doorway, coming'.
43.23	material] *interlined above deleted* 'texture'.
43.28	old Hepzibah] *interlined with a caret above deleted* 'the Old Maid'.
43.28	alarm] *interlined above deleted* 'alarm'.
44.12–13	Yes;—] *the dash appears to be squeezed in.*
44.26	Hepzibah] *interlined with a caret above deleted* 'the Old Maid'.
45.17	though] 'tho' *written over wiped-out* 'alth'.
45.27	last] 'la' *written over wiped-out* 'f[i]'.
46.6	shopkeeper!"] *the quotation mark may be intended to delete the downstroke of the exclamation.*
46.20	her] *interlined above deleted* 'the Old Maid'.
46.20	moment] 'mo' *written over wiped-out* 'present'.
46.29	have] *written over wiped-out* 'gaze'.
48.1	very] 've' *written over wiped-out* '[so]'.
48.3	Hepzibah's] *interlined above deleted* 'the Old Maid's'.
48.5	hold up] *interlined with a caret above deleted* 'present'.
48.30	vast] *written over wiped-out* 'perfect'.
49.7	thrust] *interlined with a caret above deleted* 'presented'.
49.7	forward] *interlined with a caret.*
49.15	old gentlewoman's] *interlined above deleted* 'Old Maid's'.
49.34	Hepzibah] *interlined with a caret above deleted* 'the Old Maid'.
50.2	she] *interlined above deleted* 'Hepzibah'.
50.23	was!] *the exclamation mark written over a wiped-out parenthesis and then the new parenthesis added.*

50.35	maiden lady] *interlined above deleted* 'Old Maid'.
51.10	coin] 'co' *written over wiped-out* 'ce'.
51.11	hand] *an original partly formed plural 's' seems to have been currently mended to form the tail of final singular 'd'.*
51.12	new shopkeeper] *interlined with a caret above deleted* 'Old Maid'.
51.21	and] *written over deleted* 'with and' *and the preceding comma added.*
52.4	That] 'at' *mended over original* 'e'.
52.5	the] *mended from wiped-out* 'that'.
52.11	subtile operation] 'ile op' *written over wiped-out* 'le op'.
52.21	old gentlewoman] *interlined with a caret above deleted* 'Old Maid'.
52.34–35	old lady] *interlined above deleted* 'Old Maid'.
52.35	extremely] *interlined above deleted* 'very'.
53.8	money,] *followed by deleted* 'for it,'.
53.15	Hepzibah's] *interlined above deleted* 'the Old Maid's'.
53.17	she] *interlined above deleted* 'Hepzibah'.
53.31	poor gentlewoman] *interlined with a caret above deleted* 'Old Maid'.
53.33	housewife] *interlined above deleted* 'woman'.
55.15–16	old Hepzibah's] *interlined with a caret above deleted* 'the Old Maid's'.
55.19–20	in presence of] *interlined above* 'in presence of' *written over wiped-out* 'before the rich'.
55.21	live!] *the exclamation mark mended from a query.*
55.26	her. But] *mended from* 'her, but'.
56.18	gold] *interlined above deleted* 'ivory'.
56.20	had it chosen] 'had it ch' *written over wiped-out* 'would have'.
57.7	Midas-like] *mended from* 'Midaslike', *with* 'like' *wiped out.*
57.14	look] *written over some wiped-out word that may be* 'face'.
57.26	While] *written over wiped-out* 'Hepzib'.
57.27	Hepzibah] *interlined with a caret above deleted* 'the Old Maid'.
57.30	bowed] *followed by deleted* 'to Hepzibah' *with a comma then intended to succeed* 'bowed'.
58.12	whet before] *written over wiped-out* '[to dinner]'.

58.15–16	the maiden lady] *interlined above deleted* 'the Old Maid'.
58.25	portrait of the] *interlined with a caret.*
58.28	but] *interlined with a caret.*
58.33	time,] *interlined with a caret.*
59.20	Jaffrey] *interlined with a caret.*
59.29	spell] *interlined above deleted* 'force'.
60.9	Hepzibah,] *interlined with a caret above deleted* 'the Old Maid'.
60.14	far] *interlined above deleted* 'deeply'.
60.23	Venner] *interlined for clarity in another hand above original* 'Venner'.
60.25–26	pavement. But] *mended from* 'pavement; but'.
61.14	virtually] *interlined with a caret.*
61.24	it was the] *interlined with a caret above deleted* 'the'.
61.25	and gave] *interlined above deleted* 'giving'.
61.29	him] *interlined with a caret.*
62.13	neither] 'nei' *written over some wiped-out letters that may be* 'ei'.
62.14	It] *written over wiped-out* 'T'.
62.20	your work,] 'work,' *interlined with a caret; a final* 's' *after* 'your' *has been partly erased.*
62.29	now— . . . ago—] *the dashes written over commas.*
62.31	quite] *written over wiped-out* 'a little'.
62.33	you—] *the dash written over a wiped-out comma.*
63.3	gentlemen,] *written over wiped-out* 'people, that'.
63.12	Hepzibah] *interlined above deleted* 'the Old Maid'.
63.20	step] *interlined above deleted* 'come'.
63.31	that farm of mine] *interlined above deleted* 'that farm of mine' *written over* 'the great brick house'.
63.35	will be my case] *interlined with a caret above deleted* 'I shall'.
64.3	with no company but] *interlined above deleted* 'by the side of'.
64.7	as old as] *interlined with a caret above same written over wiped-out* 'who [ ]'.
64.16	Hepzibah] *interlined with a caret above deleted* 'The Old Maid'.
64.28	uncle—] *the dash written over a comma.*
64.33	now] *written over wiped-out* 'at the'.

65.27	her] *interlined above deleted* 'the Old Maid's'.
65.32	Never] *written over some wiped-out word, probably* 'Look'.
65.34	such] *written over wiped-out* 'which'.
66.12	poor Hepzibah] *interlined above deleted* 'our Old Maid'.
66.13	rustled] *written over wiped-out* '[blasted]'.
66.35	or into] 'into' *interlined with a caret.*
67.6–7	old gentlewoman] *interlined with a caret above deleted* 'Old Maid'.
67.17–18	After all] *written over wiped-out* 'The whole'.
67.28	devourer] *interlined above deleted* 'destroyer'.
67.30	In her] *interlined with a caret above deleted* 'In her' *written over wiped-out* 'She offered'.
68.2	Hepzibah's] *interlined with a caret above deleted* 'The Old Maid's'.
69.4–5	maiden lady] *interlined with a caret above deleted* 'Old Maid'.
70.6	in] *written over wiped-out* 'f[ ]'.
70.14	a gentle] 'a' *interlined with a caret.*
70.15	moves] 'm' *written over wiped-out* '[st]'.
70.16	brow] *written over wiped-out* 'cheek'.
71.15	the girl] *written over wiped-out* 'Phoebe'.
71.20	great-great-] *first* 'great-' *interlined with a caret.*
72.21	ghosts, and] *interlined with a caret.*
72.21	ghosts, and] *interlined with a caret.*
72.29	But—] *the dash written over a comma.*
72.35	now] *interlined with a caret.*
73.5	(as] *the parenthesis written over a comma.*
73.13	old gentlewoman] *interlined with a caret above deleted* 'Old Maid'.
73.16	been] *interlined with a caret.*
73.19	days] *preceded by deleted* 'maiden'.
73.32	the girl's] 'girl's' *interlined with a caret;* 'the' *is written over some wiped-out letters, perhaps* 'her'.
74.1	her] *interlined with a caret above deleted* 'the girl'.
74.4	kindred] 'kin' *written over wiped-out* '[rela]'.
74.14	Hepzibah] *interlined above deleted* 'the Old Maid'.
75.6	exclaimed] 'excl' *written over wiped-out* '[cried]'.
75.15	already described,] *interlined with a caret placed to the left of the original comma after* 'miniature'.

75.21   beautiful!] *the exclamation mark mended from a comma.*

75.27   her cousin] *interlined with a caret above deleted* 'the Old Maid'.

76.11   mistress of the house] *interlined with a caret above deleted* 'Old Maid'.

76.16   offices] *interlined above deleted* 'spheres'.

76.23   Whatever] *written over wiped-out* 'She [   ]'.

76.26   shadowy] *interlined above deleted* 'darksome'.

76.28   warbles] *written above deleted* 'does'.

77.6   great] *interlined with a caret before* 'grandmother'.

77.26   maiden lady] *interlined above deleted* 'Old Maid'.

77.34   and] *written over wiped-out* 'as'.

78.5   Hepzibah] *interlined above deleted* 'the Old Maid'.

78.17   Do] *written over wiped-out* 'Stop'.

78.28   old gentlewoman] *interlined with a caret above deleted* 'Old Maid'.

78.31   and] *interlined with a caret.*

79.17   assuming] 'assu' *written over wiped-out* '[   ]ing'.

79.31   aristocratic hucksteress] *interlined with a caret above deleted* 'Old Maid'.

80.7   if compatible,] *interlined with a caret.*

80.10   sure—] *the dash written over wiped-out* 'so'. *The original comma after* 'sure' *is not deleted, in error.*

80.14–15   the clear] 'the' *interlined with a caret.*

80.23   among] *interlined above deleted* 'with'.

80.32   old maid] 'old maid' *is the reading of the first edition; in the manuscript* 'Hepzibah' *is interlined above deleted* 'Old Maid'.

81.18   omnivorous] *interlined in pencil for clarity in another hand above* 'omniverous'.

81.21   Hepzibah] *interlined with a caret above deleted* 'Old Maid'.

82.20–21   day—] *the dash is written over a comma.*

82.36   old gentlewoman] *interlined with a caret above deleted* 'Old Maid'.

83.33   faded] *followed by deleted* 'out' *at end of line, and* 'out' *at start of the next.*

84.12   old lady] *interlined with a caret above deleted* 'Old Maid'.

84.12–13   began to talk about] *interlined above deleted* 'took up the subject of'.

84.20   temperance] *written over a wiped-out word that may be* 'alcohol[t   ]'.

84.23   but] *interlined above deleted* 'who'.

86.3   now] *interlined with a caret.*

86.7   just] *written over wiped-out* 'enou'.

86.15   such as] *interlined with a caret.*

87.1   rosebush] *mended from* 'rose bush'.

87.3–4   except . . . -bushes,] *interlined with a caret.*

87.7   flourishing] 'ing' *written over wiped-out* 'ly'.

87.12   praiseworthy] 'praise' *written over wiped-out* 'excellent'.

87.16   about] *interlined with a caret.*

88.9   depths] 'd' *written over wiped-out* '[g]'; *less likely, over* '[f]'.

88.10   golden] *interlined above deleted* 'sweet'.

88.16   colored] *interlined above deleted* 'cololored'.

88.20   welling] *the first stroke of the* 'w' *has been mended, but the word is definitely* 'welling'.

88.30   on] *written over deleted* 'f'.

89.3   degenerated,] *followed by deleted* 'in consequence of too strict a watchfulness to keep it pur'.

89.16   forlorn] *interlined with a caret.*

89.19   as were] *interlined with a caret.*

90.3   miniature] 'minia' *written over wiped-out* 'little—'.

90.3   mustered] *interlined above deleted* 'musterd'.

90.10   hand, and, while] *written over wiped-out* 'holding while'; *then* 'hand' *deleted and interlined with a caret for clarity.*

91.4   reaped] 'r' *written over wiped-out* '[g]'.

91.12   daguerreotype] 'd' *written over wiped-out* 'D'.

91.17   I suppose,] *interlined with a caret.*

91.33   on] *interlined above deleted* 'of'.

93.14–15   or one . . . competent.] *interlined with a caret.*

93.20   offensive] *written over wiped-out* 'positive'.

94.19   seize] *written over wiped-out* '[take]'.

94.34   department] 'de' *written over wiped-out* 'pa'.

95.4   old gentlewoman] *interlined with a caret above deleted* 'Old Maid'.

95.8   she] *written over wiped-out* 'asked'.

95.17   her cousin] *interlined with a caret above deleted* 'the Old Maid'.

95.22   It was] *written over wiped-out* 'strangely', *and the preceding comma mended to a period.*

95.24   such] 'su' *written over wiped-out* 'th'.

95.26   its] *interlined with a caret above deleted* 'mingled'.

95.26   echo] *followed by deleted* 'of it,'.

96.2   Hepzibah] *follows deleted* 'Old Maid', *at a later time.*

96.23   maiden lady] *interlined with a caret above deleted* 'Old Maid'.

96.34–35   Hepzibah] *interlined with a caret above deleted* 'the Old Maid'.

98.9   certainly] 'cert' *written over wiped-out* 'have'.

98.14   Cookery] 'C' *written over a* 'B'.

98.22   tidbit] 'd' *mended over* 't'.

99.12   Mocha] 'M' *mended from* 'v'.

99.13   maiden lady] *interlined with a caret above deleted* 'Old Maid'.

99.21   gladly] *interlined with a caret.*

99.32   fairly] *interlined with a caret.*

99.34   ictation] *written above wiped-out and deleted* 'turning'.

100.16   meal] *interlined with a caret.*

100.18   department] 'd' *written over what may be a* 'p'.

100.22   Hepzibah's] *interlined above deleted* 'The Old Maid's'.

101.1   it to] *written over wiped-out* 'to old'.

101.5–6   (Hepzibah's . . . porringer)] *the parentheses written over dashes.*

101.13   arranged] 'ar-|' *written over wiped-out* 'put them'.

101.20–21   her cousin] *interlined with a caret above deleted* 'the Old Maid'.

101.26   parlor-floor.] *followed by deleted* 'Sometimes, it seemed an ecstasy of delight and happiness'.

102.1   it were] 'it' *interlined with a caret*

102.4   imprisoned] *interlined with a caret.*

102.8   the] *interlined with a caret.*

102.13   except for] *interlined with a caret above deleted* 'except in'.

102.32   little,] *a slip of the pen makes the comma somewhat resemble a semicolon.*

103.4   old gentlewoman] *interlined with a caret above deleted* 'Old Maid'.

103.16	his] *interlined above deleted* 'their'.
103.22	her cousin's] *interlined with a caret above deleted* 'the Old Maid's'.
104.2–3	which— . . . floor—] *the dashes written over commas.*
104.7	countenance—] *the dash deletes a comma.*
104.17	Hepzibah's] *interlined above deleted* 'the Old Maid's'.
104.21	the parlor] *interlined with a caret.*
104.21	around] *interlined for clarity above* 'around' *in which* 'ar' *is written over wiped-out* 'ab'.
105.24	At one] *wiped out after* 'inhabitant.' *and rewritten to begin a new paragraph.*
106.3	countenance] *interlined above deleted* 'face'.
106.6	wrong] *interlined with a caret above deleted* 'harm'.
106.10	which] *interlined above deleted* 'that'.
106.16	Hepzibah] 'Hepzi' *written over wiped-out* '[Clifford]'.
106.35	of] *interlined with a caret.*
107.7	was] *interlined with a caret.*
107.23	the guest] 'the' *written over wiped-out* 'Cliffo'.
107.27	was] *interlined above deleted* 'might be'.
107.30	anxious] *interlined above deleted* 'trying'.
108.2	present] *written over wiped-out* '[show] itself'.
108.16	richest] *written over wiped-out* 'highest'.
109.3	Beautiful] 'B' *mended from* 'b'.
109.4	his hostess] *interlined with a caret above deleted* 'the Old Maid'.
109.6	Hepzibah's misfortune] *written over wiped-out letters that might be* 'her misfor|tune'.
109.23	never] *interlined with a caret.*
110.8	-window—] *the dash written over a comma.*
110.32	out] 'o' *written over wiped-out* 'f'.
111.15	in a trunk] *interlined for clarity with a caret above* 'in a trunk' *written over wiped-out* 'above-stairs'.
111.24	Hepzibah.] *added later after deleted* 'the Old Maid.'
112.3	with] 'wi' *written over wiped-out* 'wh'.
113.2	emotion] 'emo' *written above wiped-out* 'feel'.
113.13	need!] *followed by wiped-out quotation marks.*
113.20	befall] 'b' *mended over* 'f'.

113.32–34	breath— . . . character)—] *the first dash written over a comma; another comma, after* 'character', *is partly deleted by an extension of the parenthesis, these parentheses apparently being additions, not substitutions for the dashes.*
115.5	on the two] *written over wiped-out* 'on the day before'.
115.12	—reversing] *written over wiped-out* 'immediately'.
116.19	gold-] *interlined above deleted* 'ivory-' *and preceding* 'An' *erased to* 'A'.
116.20	cane] 'ca' *written over wiped-out* 'of'.
116.35	if the observer] *written over wiped-out* 'had the observer'.
117.1	would] *written over wiped-out* 'might'.
117.11	(besides] *the parenthesis written over a comma.*
118.7	(without] '(with' *written over wiped-out* 'without'.
118.17	Judge] *written over wiped-out* 'the Jud'.
118.24	entirely] 'en' *written over wiped-out* 'qu'.
120.17	barber's] *above this, interlined with a caret, is wiped-out* 'shop'.
120.20	with] *written over wiped-out* 'fo'.
120.23	gold-] *interlined above deleted* 'ivory-'.
120.24	steps forward as] *interlined with a caret above deleted* 'is'.
120.27–28	Possibly] 'oss' *written over wiped-out* 'rob'.
121.2	substance] *interlined above deleted* 'developement'.
122.5–6	courage and] *written over wiped-out* 'zeal and faithf'.
122.6–7	political] *interlined with a caret.*
122.9	eye] *interlined for clarity above* 'eye' *written over wiped-out* 'and for' *in which the* 'and' *is written over a dash.*
122.9	and for] 'an' *written over wiped-out* 'fo'.
123.11	Judge] 'Ju' *written over wiped-out* 'the'.
123.12	the lady] *written over wiped-out* 'she got her'.
124.3	posterity—] *the dash written over a comma.*
125.14	(but] *the parenthesis written over a wiped-out dash.*
126.1	one] *interlined with a caret.*
126.6	hardly knowing] *written over wiped-out* 'who was [ ]'.
126.20	likewise!—] *the dash written over wiped-out* 'I'.

126.31	old gentlewoman] *interlined with a caret above deleted* 'Old Maid'.
126.34	amazingly] *interlined above deleted* 'uncommonly'.
127.3–4	inadequately] 'ina' *written over wiped-out* 'little'.
127.4	of] *written over wiped-out* 'that'.
127.15	his cousin] *interlined above deleted* 'the Old Maid'.
128.21	Judge] 'Ju' *written over wiped-out* 'the'.
128.21–23	Pyncheon— . . . appealed—] *the dashes written over commas.*
130.1	deeds] *written over wiped-out* 'w[k]'.
130.8	gives] *written over a wiped-out word that may be* 'bathes'.
130.13	it] *written over wiped-out* 'you'.
130.17	I] *interlined with a caret.*
132.1	her cousin's] *interlined above deleted* 'the Old Maid's'.
133.2	our poor old Hepzibah!] *interlined with a caret above deleted* 'the Old Maid!', *the caret being wrongly positioned before* 'of'.
134.5	afternoon] 'after' *written above deleted* 'fore'.
134.6	up in] *followed by deleted* 'the great warm mantle of her love'.
134.23	Rasselas] 'las' *written over wiped-out* 'llas'.
134.32	His sister's] *interlined with a caret above deleted* 'The Old Maid's'.
135.8	whence they] *interlined with a caret.*
135.8	.hue.] *the period added, and following* 'from it.' *deleted.*
135.17	devoted sister] *interlined with a caret above deleted* 'Old Maid'.
135.18	on] *interlined with a caret.*
135.31	poor gentlewoman's] *interlined with a caret above deleted* 'Old Maid's'.
136.6	on her] *written over wiped-out* 'in h'.
136.6	turban] *interlined above deleted* 'ribbons'.
136.14	antiquated virgin] *interlined with a caret above deleted* 'Old Maid'.
137.5	scattered] *interlined above deleted* 'diffused'.
137.29	having] *interlined above* 'having' *written over wiped-out* 'the y[ ]'.

137.31	mistress of the house] *interlined with a caret above deleted* 'Old Maid'.
138.3	to Hepzibah's] *interlined with a caret above deleted* 'the Old Maid's'.
139.15	gleams of cheerful] *written over wiped-out* 'particles of light' *and then interlined for clarity.*
139.26	as with] *written over wiped-out* 'with'.
139.35–140.1	all;— . . . him;—] *the dashes are additions.*
140.12	Clifford's] *preceded by deleted* 'Cousin'.
140.18	shaped] *written over wiped-out* 'clumsy'.
140.24	therefore,] *the comma written over a wiped-out dash.*
141.6	its] *followed by deleted* 'its'.
141.11	of an] 'an' *interlined with a caret above deleted* 'the'; *an earlier interlined* 'an' *is deleted.*
141.15	probably] *written over wiped-out letters, perhaps* 'at h[ ]'.
141.18	There was something] *written over wiped-out* '[it] his feelings'.
141.22	liveliest] *interlined above deleted* 'deepest'.
141.23	had] *interlined with a caret.*
142.12	that] *interlined with a caret.*
142.12	symbol] *interlined with a caret above a deleted word, probably* 'picture'.
142.22	flung] *interlined above deleted* 'tost'.
143.2, 27	Clifford] *preceded by deleted* 'Cousin'.
144.5	result of] *interlined with a caret above deleted* 'effect on'.
144.6–7	involuntary] *preceded by deleted* 'own'.
144.8	gradually] *written over wiped-out* 'taught'.
144.20–21	old gentlewoman's] *interlined with a caret above deleted* 'Old Maid's'.
145.1, 14	Clifford] *preceded by deleted* 'Cousin'.
145.20	her elderly cousin's] *interlined with a caret above deleted* 'the Old Maid's'.
145.23	pebbly and] *written over wiped-out* 'brook-like'.
146.3	auditor] *followed by deleted* 'an'.
146.9	read] *preceded by deleted* 'would'.
146.12	drept] 'd' *written over wiped-out* 'f'.
146.31	them] *interlined with a caret above deleted* 'it'.
147.1	Clifford] *preceded by deleted* 'Cousin'.

147.2   feeling] 'fe' *written over wiped-out* '[t   ]'.
147.8   beautiful] 'beau' *written over wiped-out* 'g[   ]'.
147.23   often—] *the dash written over a comma.*
147.27   Thither] 'Thi' *written over wiped-out* 'Hi'.
147.33   Clifford] *preceded by deleted* 'Cousin'.
148.15   a] *written over wiped-out* 'this'.
148.20   hundred] *interlined above deleted* 'thousand'.
148.23   with] *interlined with a caret.*
148.24   Clifford] *preceded by deleted* 'Cousin'.
148.30   Hepzibah] *interlined with a caret above deleted* 'The Old Maid'.
149.17   had] *written over wiped-out* 'annihil'.
149.20   symptoms] *written over wiped-out* '[p   ] lay'.
150.17   original] 'o' *written over wiped-out* 'f'.
150.21   whom] *written over some wiped-out word that may be* 'which'.
150.28   abundant leisure] *interlined with a caret above deleted* 'time'.
150.29–30   evidently] *preceded by deleted* 'that was'.
150.30   tidbit] 'd' *written over* 't'.
151.8   odd] *written over wiped-out* 'queer'.
151.18   an] *interlined with a caret.*
151.22   founder] *written above deleted* 'forefather'.
151.26   fore-mothers] *the hyphen written over wiped-out* 'mo' *and then* 'mothers' *inscribed.*
151.26   excellencies] *mended from* 'excellences'.
152.17   While] 'W' *written over wiped-out* 'As'.
152.17–19   marks— . . . legs—] *the dashes written over commas.*
152.20   Daguerreotypist] 'Da' *written over wiped-out* 'artist'.
152.24   although] *followed by deleted* ', as such clues invariably are, an unintelligible one'.
152.24   an] *interlined with a caret.*
152.24   one,] *interlined with a caret.*
152.28   second] 's' *written over wiped-out* 'f'.
153.14   old gentlewoman] *interlined with a caret above deleted* 'Old Maid'.
153.19–20   Clifford] *preceded by deleted* 'Cousin'.
154.4   momentary] *interlined with a caret.*
154.5   at] *interlined with a caret.*

154.12	them. And] *mended after erasure from* 'them; and'.
154.27	his other] 'his' *interlined with a caret.*
154.31	wear] *interlined with a caret.*
155.2	up] *interlined with a caret.*
155.28	all] *interlined with a caret after a wiped-out similar interlineation before* 'had'.
155.34	man] *written over wiped-out* 'patches'.
156.3	wonderful] 'wonder' *written over wiped-out* 'great [ ]'.
156.17	Come,] *written over wiped-out* 'And then,'.
157.1	one] *interlined with a caret above wiped-out* 'a'.
157.10	banquet] 'banq' *written over wiped-out* 'feast'.
157.14	made] *interlined with a caret.*
158.1	is—] *a comma after* 'is' *has been deleted.*
159.23	Clifford] *preceded by deleted* 'Cousin'.
160.5	even] *interlined with a caret.*
160.15–16	raised by] *interlined with a caret above deleted* 'of' *and a preceding comma added.*
160.20	along] *written over wiped-out* 'by'.
160.21	Pyncheon-] *written over wiped-out* 'House of'.
160.24–25	commonest] *written over wiped-out* 'routine'.
160.28	lost] *written over wiped-out* 'forgot'.
161.6	and to keep . . . moment.] *interlined with a caret.*
161.14	his fastidious senses] *original* 'him' *mended to* 'his'; *and* 'fastidious senses' *interlined with a caret.*
161.18	was] 'w' *written over wiped-out* 'f'.
161.23	green] *written over wiped-out* 'and green'.
161.27	set] *written over wiped-out* 'just'.
161.35	wore away] *written over wiped-out* 'grinding'.
162.17	a plough-] 'a' *written over wiped-out* 'p'.
162.27	With] *written over wiped-out* 'T[ ]'.
162.30	melodies] *interlined above deleted* 'harmonies'.
163.15	and moved] *written over wiped-out* 'and at the self'.
163.24	torpor. Neither] *mended from* 'torpor; neither'.
163.25	there] *interlined with a caret.*
164.5	-door] *written over wiped-out* 'window'.
164.6	Clifford] *preceded by deleted* 'Cousin'.
164.16	which] *written over wiped-out* 'that'.

164.24   Doubtless] 'Doubt' *written over wiped-out*
          '[   ]y'.

164.32   spiritual] *interlined above deleted* 'moral'.

165.11   marched all] *interlined above* 'marched all' *writ-
          ten over wiped-out* 'passed through'.

165.13   As a] *interlined for clarity above* 'As a' *written
          over wiped-out* 'Nothing'.

166.6   in] *a stubbing of the pen would make the reading*
          'on' *possible, but the* 'i' *is clearly dotted and there
          appears to be no evidence of alteration of* 'i' *to* 'o'.

167.20   one] *written over wiped-out* 'bell'.

167.24   for mankind to breathe] *written over wiped-out*
          'to be [   ] [   ] prayer f[   ]'.

168.24   emotion] 'emo' *written over wiped-out* 'feel'.

170.1   griefless] 'grief' *written over wiped-out*
          'thoughtless'.

170.3   and contingencies] *interlined for clarity above* 'and
          contingencies' *written over wiped-out* 'to be settled
          whic'.

170.23   out of] *interlined above deleted* 'from'.

171.2   a] *written over wiped-out* 'the'.

171.4   them] *interlined above deleted* 'small people'.

171.15   an earthen] *written over wiped-out* 'a pipe'.

173.3   Clifford's] *preceded by deleted* 'Cousin'.

173.18   void] *interlined above deleted* 'calm'.

173.21   had] *interlined with a caret.*

173.23   Be the] *wiped out after continuing the text of the
          preceding paragraph.*

174.1   sunbeams] *interlined above same written over*
          'setting [   ]'.

174.11   Hepzibah] *interlined above deleted* 'The Old
          Maid'.

174.15   but] *interlined with a caret.*

174.15   Clifford] *preceded by deleted* 'Cousin'.

174.21   life] *interlined above deleted* 'beings'.

175.34   together] *a following comma has been partly
          wiped out as part of the revision.*

175.34   a kind] 'a' *interlined with a caret.*

175.35   friendly, and] *interlined for clarity above* 'friendly,
          and' *written over wiped-out* 'and friendly'.

175.35   be a] 'a' *interlined with a caret.*

175.35   way] *interlined for clarity above* 'way' *written
          over a wiped-out word that may be* 'terms'.

176.4	been] *preceded by deleted* 'already'.
176.10	may] *written over wiped-out* 'might'.
176.14	possible] *interlined with a caret.*
176.19	two] *interlined above deleted* 'three'.
176.21	either at the] *interlined for clarity above* 'either at the' *written over wiped-out* 'afterwards'.
177.30	Hepzibah and her brother] *interlined above deleted* 'the Old Maid, and Cousin Clifford' *in which* 'Cousin' *had earlier been deleted.*
178.10	but—] *the dash written over a comma.*
178.20–21	cheerful—] *the dash written over a comma.*
179.6	subtile] *mended currently from* 'subtle'.
179.19	what he said] *interlined with a caret above deleted* 'it'.
179.22	capable] 'capa' *written over wiped-out* 'wh[ ]'.
179.22	improved] *interlined above deleted* 'moulded'.
179.23	that] *interlined with a caret after being interlined and following* 'into' *with a caret.*
179.23	it ought] 'it o' *written over erased-out* 'that'.
180.3	supposing] *interlined above deleted* 'applying'.
180.4	is] *interlined with a caret above deleted* 'was'.
180.5	Antiquity] 'a' *mended to* 'A'.
180.15	him] *interlined with a caret.*
180.21	far] *written over wiped-out* 'humbler'.
180.28	might have] *interlined with a caret above deleted* 'had'.
180.32	deep] *interlined above deleted* 'strong'.
180.35	scarcely] *written over wiped-out* 'hardly'.
181.34	too] *written over wiped-out* 'by'.
181.35	kindly] *interlined above deleted* 'familiar'.
182.4	House] *written over wiped-out* 'old hou'.
182.9–10	of the fountain] *interlined with a caret.*
182.11	judge] *interlined above deleted* 'think'.
182.19	the] *written over wiped-out* 'you [ ]'.
182.35	only] *written over wiped-out* 'ought'.
183.10	repeat] *interlined above deleted* 'record'.
183.33	each] *interlined above deleted* 'every'.
184.8	old!] *exclamation mark altered from a comma.*
184.28	indeed!] *exclamation mark altered from a comma.*
184.28	Phoebe.] *period altered from a comma.*
185.8	perpetual] *interlined with a caret above deleted* 'constant'.

185.18	an] *interlined with a caret.*
185.32	prospect] *interlined with a caret.*
185.34	daguerreotype] 'd' *written over wiped-out* 'D'.
186.17	Godey,] *the comma written over a dash.*
186.19	bead-roll] *interlined above deleted* 'names'.
187.10	seven] *written over wiped-out* 'thirty'.
187.21	be] *interlined with a caret.*
189.6	as often] 'as' *interlined with a caret.*
189.6	living people] *interlined above deleted* 'the latter'.
189.11–12	appears—] *the dash written over a comma.*
189.34	people's minds] *written over wiped-out* '[ ] people's'.
190.17	to the house] 'to the' *interlined with a caret.*
190.25	had been] *interlined with a caret above deleted* 'was'.
190.30	eye] *preceded by deleted* 'his'.
190.34	been] *interlined with a caret above deleted* 'was'.
191.7	turkeys] 'turkeys' *is the original reading, deleted in favor of interlined* 'turkies'.
191.15	a] *interlined with a caret above deleted* 'the'.
191.18	jolly] *interlined above deleted* 'hearty'.
191.21	one] *written over wiped-out* 'the'.
191.23	kept them] *interlined with a caret above deleted* 'warmed the'.
192.8	felled] *preceded by deleted* 'built a cottage'.
192.23	into] *written over wiped-out* 'across'.
193.4	in] *mended from* 'of'.
193.22	its] *written over wiped-out* 'itself'.
194.15	pleased] 'p' *written over wiped-out* 'ex'.
194.31	incidental] *interlined with a caret above* 'incidental' *written over wiped-out* '[e ef]'.
195.22	conclude] 'conc' *written over wiped-out* 'cl'.
195.30	Maule] *interlined with a caret.*
196.24	discovered] *interlined above deleted* 'found'.
196.33	had some] *interlined for clarity above* 'had some' *written over wiped-out* 'had [ ] to f[ ]'.
197.1	Certain] *written over wiped-out* 'He'.
197.5	he said—but] *written over wiped-out* 'said he, was'.
197.15	may] *written over wiped-out* 'could com'.
197.18	made] *written over wiped-out* 'prof'.
197.22	time] *written over wiped-out* 'while'.

197.28   chimney-] 'ch' *written over wiped-out* 'le'.

198.1   conversation] 'convers' *written over wiped-out* 'scene be'.

199.2   more] *written over wiped-out* 'f[   ]'.

199.19   Maule!] *the exclamation mark written over a comma.*

199.19   cried] 'cr' *written over wiped-out* 'se'.

199.25   Matthew Maule] *interlined with a caret above deleted* 'he'.

199.31   persisted] *followed by a wiped-out comma.*

199.33   emptied] 'emp' *written over wiped-out* 'glass'.

200.10   Maule!] *the exclamation mark written over a comma.*

201.19   end] *written above deleted and partly wiped-out* 'handle'.

201.23–24   admiration— . . . conceal—] *the dashes written over commas.*

202.8   "Yes.] *followed by wiped-out double quotation marks.*

202.12   parchment] 'p' *written over wiped-out* 'm'.

203.6–7   power— . . . womanhood—] *the dashes written over commas.*

203.8   treachery] *preceded by deleted* 'some'.

203.33–34   this influence] *interlined with a caret above deleted* 'it'; *the caret was first placed in error after* 'it' *and then excised when moved.*

204.5   Maule!] *the exclamation mark written over a comma.*

204.5   Mr. Pyncheon] *interlined above deleted* 'the father'.

204.10   turned] *interlined above deleted* 'directed'.

204.20   power] *interlined with a caret.*

204.26–27   too undefined a purport] *interlined above deleted* 'make them audible'; 'audible' *was then wiped out and* 'a purport' *written over it and then interlined for clarity after* 'too undefined'.

205.13   which] *written over wiped-out* 'that had'.

205.20   axe] *written over wiped-out* 'the a'.

206.4   Maule.] *the period mended from a comma.*

206.26   (if . . . called)] *the parentheses have been added, the second deleting a comma.*

207.3–5   band;— . . . neck;—] *the dashes are later additions.*

207.28   It is too dear] *written over wiped-out* 'This, [   ]'.

209.10   court-like] *interlined above deleted* 'lofty'.

209.20   marry] *interlined above deleted* 'wed'.

209.25   that night] *interlined with a caret placed before a comma.*

211   GOOD BYE] *added after deleted* 'FAREWELL'.

211.7   auditress] 'tress' *written over wiped-out* 'for'.

211.9   perception] *interlined with a caret above deleted* 'eyes'.

211.11, 16   an] *interlined with a caret.*

213.2   has] 's' *mended over* 'd'.

213.7   oval] *interlined above deleted* 'round'.

214.8   in a grave-yard] *interlined above* 'in a grave-yard' *written currently over wiped-out* 'among **graves**'.

214.13   to] *interlined with a caret.*

215.12–13   regained—] *the dash written over a comma.*

215.18   smiling] *interlined with a caret.*

215.26   a] *interlined above deleted* 'the'.

216.4   exists] *mended from* 'exist'.

216.6   leave] *interlined above deleted* 'cross'.

216.16   what] *interlined above deleted* 'the'.

216.27   gentleman—] *the dash deletes a comma.*

216.28   Beautiful] 'B' *mended from* 'b'.

217.14   exclusively] *interlined above deleted* 'entirely'.

217.20   conviction] 'convic' *interlined for clarity in pencil by a different hand.*

217.23   Phoebe!] *the exclamation mark written over a comma.*

217.28   me] *interlined with a caret.*

217.28   I] *interlined with a caret.*

217.35   ruin he had} 'ruin' *interlined for clarity above* 'ruin he had' *written over wiped-out* 'calamity he had so'.

218.8   branded] 'bra' *written over wiped-out* 'half'.

218.15   (hark . . . murmuring!)] *the parentheses are later additions.*

218.29   good bye] *an original hyphen is wiped out.*

218.33   a] *written over wiped-out* 'her'.

219.8, 220.3   her] *interlined with a caret.*

220.29   cast] *preceded by deleted* 'so'.

221.5   together;] *the semicolon mended from a comma.*

221.11   to a man] *written over wiped-out* 'to a man's'.

221.24   never!] *the exclamation mark added later.*

223.5   the task of making] *interlined above* 'the task of making' *written over wiped-out* 'making [   ]'.

223.8   Clifford] *preceded by deleted* 'Cousin'.

223.18   seemed not] *written over wiped-out* 'appeared to be.

223.19   only] *interlined above deleted* 'merely'.

224.6–7   old gentlewoman.] *interlined above deleted* 'Old Maid,' *which is followed by deleted* 'in order that'.

224.7   could] *interlined with a caret.*

224.18   though] *interlined with a caret.*

224.26   chair.] *the period mended from a wiped-out semicolon.*

225.20   after] *interlined with a caret.*

225.26–27   or Clifford's] *written over wiped-out* 'if hers [   ]'; *the parentheses are an addition.*

225.27   were] *followed by deleted* 'were'.

226.1   her] *interlined with a caret.*

226.31   Hepzibah] *interlined in ink above deleted* 'the Old Maid' *in another hand.*

227.20   public] *interlined with a caret.*

228.2   power] *interlined above deleted* 'existence'.

228.12   spurn] *interlined above heavily deleted* 'spit'.

228.15   integrity] *interlined above deleted* 'character'.

228.18   unreasoning] *interlined with a caret.*

228.23   whether] *preceded by deleted* 'there was not an individual'.

228.24   capacities] *written over wiped-out* 'abilities'.

229.6   mankind] 'man' *written over wiped-out* 'himself'.

230.6–7   will not be conscious of it] *interlined with a caret.*

230.8   Neither will] *written over wiped-out* 'the visitors'.

230.33   of] *interlined with a caret.*

231.10   five] *interlined above deleted* 'two'.

231.23   he] *interlined above deleted* 'Judge Pyncheon'.

232.4   what] *written over wiped-out* 'his image'.

232.9   But our affair] 'But our' *written over wiped-out* 'Our bus', *and* 'affair' *interlined above deleted* 'business'.

232.12   given] *interlined with a caret.*

232.14   the Judge's] 'the Ju' *written over wiped-out* 'the coun'.

232.15   his cousin's] *first* 'Old Maid's' *was interlined with a caret after* 'the' *and then deleted, with* 'his cousin's' *substituted and* 'the' *deleted.*

232.18   look] 'lo' *written over wiped-out* 'fa'.

232.29   of] *written over wiped-out* 'the'.

232.29   lineage] *interlined above deleted* 'descent'.

232.34   she] *interlined above deleted* 'the Old Maid'.

233.7 | merely] *the line before ends with a wiped-out* 'merely'.

234.5–6   day. It] *written over wiped-out* ', alth'.

234.17   ceasing] 'ceas' *written over wiped-out* 'seeking'.

234.30–31   old gentlewoman] *interlined with a caret above deleted* 'Old Maid'.

235.13   to find] *written over wiped-out* 'the schedule'.

236.13   will] *written over wiped-out* 'depend'.

236.28   Hepzibah] *interlined above deleted* 'the Old Maid'.

236.29   passionately—] *the dash deletes a comma.*

236.33   man] *interlined above deleted* 'to man'.

237.24   secret!] *exclamation mark deletes a comma.*

237.28   business] *written over wiped-out* 'interview'.

238.6   his cousin] *interlined above deleted* 'the Old Maid'.

240   CLIFFORD'S] 'CLI' *written over wiped-out* 'THE'.

240.7   beside] *written over wiped-out* 'before'.

240.16–17   heretofore] 'eto' *written over wiped-out* 'fo'.

240.17   warm] *preceded by deleted* 'in'.

241.33   appalled] *interlined above deleted* 'apalled'.

242.11   Hepzibah] *interlined with a caret above* **deleted** 'The Old Maid'.

242.13   so shattered] *preceded by deleted* 'already'.

242.28   supposed] *written over wiped-out* 'fa[nci]e[d] Cli'.

242.33   required] *written over wiped-out* 'demanded'.

243.2   stubborn] *a following comma is wiped out.*

243.18   her brother's] *preceded by deleted* 'all'.

243.19   pictures] *interlined above deleted* 'projects'.

243.27   hastening] *interlined above deleted* 'rushing'.

243.27   rescue] 're' *written over* '[sho]'.

243.33   combined] *interlined with a caret.*

244.1	Congress] 'con' *written over wiped-out* 'the'.
244.5	hollow] *interlined with a caret.*
244.7	by-word] *the hyphen written over wiped-out* 'w'.
244.17	she] 's' *written over wiped-out* 'S'.
244.22	where] *written over wiped-out* 'which'.
244.23	now] *interlined with a caret.*
244.30	she] *interlined above deleted* 'the Old Maid'.
245.8	herself] 'her' *written over wiped-out* 'she'.
245.21	in a] *written over wiped-out* 'a b'.
245.22	sunlike] *preceded by deleted* 'warm,'.
245.24	warm] *interlined with a caret.*
245.27	that] *interlined above deleted* 'which'.
245.34	reply!] *followed by wiped-out* 'How'.
246.14	Hepzibah] *interlined above deleted* 'the Old Maid'.
246.30	concealment] 'concea' *written over wiped-out* 'shelter'.
247.1	Grimalkin] 'G' *written over wiped-out* 'g'.
247.7	old gentlewoman] *interlined above deleted* 'Old Maid'.
247.14	Hepzibah] *interlined with a caret above deleted* 'The Old Maid'.
247.21	the] *interlined above deleted* 'such'.
247.21	which] *interlined with a caret above deleted* 'as'.
249.1	stirred] *written over wiped-out* 'hardly'.
249.3	accident] 'a' *written over wiped-out* 'cha'.
250.1	his sister] *interlined above deleted* 'the Old Maid'.
250.3	What] *written over wiped-out* 'we can'.
250.12	She] *interlined with a caret above deleted* 'The Old Maid'.
250.23	Hepzibah] *written over wiped-out* 'Clifford'.
250.32	befall] *final* 'l' *written over wiped-out* '[ ]y'.
251.12	you] *written over wiped-out* 'to'.
251.19	actually] *interlined above deleted* 'really'.
251.23	she] *interlined in another hand above deleted* 'the Old Maid'.
251.30	before] *interlined with a caret above deleted* 'as'.
251.32	room.] *the period is mended from a comma and followed by wiped-out* 'at the time whispering'.
252.4	something] 'some' *written over wiped-out* 'a place'.
252.8	Pyncheon] *a following comma is wiped out.*

252.13	might!] *the exclamation mark written after a wiped-out period.*
253.1	as it] *written over wiped-out* 'thoug'.
253.5	although] 'al' *written over wiped-out* 'th'.
253.13–14	Clifford— . . . inexperience—] *the dashes delete commas;* 'in' *of* 'inexperience' *written over wiped-out* 'ex'.
254.4	that] *written over wiped-out* 'which'.
254.10	jarred loudest] *interlined above the same written over wiped-out* 'vibrated loudest'.
254.23	which] *interlined above deleted* 'as if it'.
256.5	its] *written over wiped-out* 'the'.
256.8	recklessness,] *the comma written over a wiped-out dash.*
256.20	recluse of the seven gables] *interlined with a caret above deleted* 'Old Maid'.
256.30	away.] *the period mended from a wiped-out semicolon.*
256.30	rest] *interlined above deleted* 'foundation'.
256.35	this pair of] *written over wiped-out* 'these two str'.
257.21	her] *interlined with a caret above deleted* 'the'.
258.19	angles]'a' *written over wiped-out* 'g'.
259.29	are] *interlined with a caret.*
260.3	temporary] *interlined with a caret.*
260.8	rear] *interlined above* 'rear' *written over wiped-out* 'build'.
260.19	made musical, and the] *interlined above the same written over wiped-out* 'got rid of, and the rumble and'.
260.25	can] *interlined with a caret.*
261.13	men] *written over wiped-out* 'painful'.
262.30	his sister] *interlined above deleted* 'the Old Maid'.
263.18	remotest] *interlined above deleted* 'immeasurably'.
264.17	eye] *a concluding* 's' *wiped out.*
264.17	rail-] *written over wiped-out* 'track'.
264.19	thing] *a following comma wiped out.*
264.23	-robber—] *the dash deletes a comma.*
265.10	deed] *a final* 's' *wiped out.*
265.21	us] *interlined with a caret.*
265.21	add to] *written over wiped-out* 'further' *or* 'farther'.
266.34	She] *interlined above deleted* 'The Old Maid'.

267.6	—our Father—] *the dashes written over original commas.*
267.6	are] *interlined above* 'are' *written over wiped-out* 'we'.
269.6	apprehensions] 'appr' *written over wiped-out* 'fears'.
269.8	man] *interlined with a caret.*
269.27	tame an] *interlined with a caret above deleted* 'much'.
271.10	in the street] *interlined above the same written over wiped-out* 'there was to be'.
271.21	proximate] *interlined above deleted* 'next'.
271.25	a] *interlined with a caret.*
271.32	take measures] *interlined above deleted* 'give orders for'.
271.33	marble] *written over wiped-out* 'face'.
272.11	towards carrying on the] *interlined above the same written over wiped-out* 'carrying on the fall campaign'.
272.28	it] *followed by deleted* 'it'.
273.6	ten] 'te' *written over wiped-out* 'fi'.
273.29	veteran] *a dash is partly formed after this word but left incomplete.*
273.31	substitutes] *interlined above deleted* 'leaves'.
273.33	—(for] *written over wiped-out* 'has ma'.
274.3	the] *written over wiped-out* 'your'.
274.25	descent] *interlined above deleted* 'descendant'.
275.9	it is absolutely] *written over wiped-out* 'we must [ ]'.
275.15	ogre—] *interlined above same written over wiped-out* 'huge'.
275.21	guests] *interlined with a caret; preceding* 'The' *is mended from* 'They'.
275.30	closely] *written over wiped-out* 'tightly'.
275.34	some] *interlined above same written over wiped-out* 'any'.
276.30	only] *written over wiped-out* 'the'.
277.5	in] 'i' *written over wiped-out* 'h'.
278.23	the] *interlined with a caret.*
279.26	his] *written over wiped-out* 'the'.
279.35	Pyncheon] 'Py' *written over wiped-out* 'gen'.
280.20	this] *written over wiped-out* 'his'.

281.12	that] *interlined above deleted* 'yonder'.
281.16–17	the better] 'the be' *written over wiped-out* 'perchance'.
281.28	nor] 'n' *written over wiped-out* 'o'.
281.33	neglected to wind] *interlined with a caret **above** deleted* 'should have wound'.
281.33	as usual] *interlined with a caret.*
282.2	us!] *the exclamation mark is an addition.*
282.20	utmost] 'utm' *written over wiped-out* 'last'.
282.23	festive] 'fe' *written over wiped-out* 'din'.
282.32	do] *interlined with a caret.*
282.34	loathsome] *interlined above deleted* 'sickening'.
283.14	as] *written over wiped-out* 'are'.
283.23	rings.] *the period added before a wiped-out exclamation mark; possibly the exclamation mark after 'hark' has been mended from a comma.*
284.5	lane] *interlined above deleted* 'street'.
284.6	dwellings] *interlined above* 'dwellings' *written over wiped-out* 'fences'.
284.16	and] *interlined with a caret.*
284.18	seen] 's' *written over wiped-out* 'th'.
285.23	virtue] 'vi' *written over wiped-out* 'the'.
286.1	religion] *written over wiped-out* 'honest'.
286.6	—the] *the dash and* 'the' *written over wiped-out* 'flow'.
286.9	fair] 'f' *written over* 'A'.
286.22	patched] *interlined above* 'patched' *written over wiped-out* 'good old'.
286.22	before] *interlined above deleted* 'on'.
286.26	house-] 'house' *written over* 'share' *and then* 'house-' *with a hyphen interlined for clarity.*
287.2	she's] ''s' *written over wiped-out* 'is'.
287.14	soul!] *exclamation mark mended from a comma.*
287.25	answered] 'answ' *written over wiped-out* 'said'.
288.5	Good] 'Go' *written over wiped-out* 'And'.
288.10	Well] 'W' *mended from* 'w'.
288.13	nothing] *originally* 'no thi' *but then wiped out and mended to* 'nothing'.
288.17	awhile] *originally* 'a while' *but the* 'a' *wiped out and mended to* 'awhile'.
288.18	as] *followed by deleted* 'as'.
288.28–29	ladyship] *interlined with a caret.*

288.29	break] *a final 'e' after 'k' wiped out.*
289.2	a] *written over wiped-out* 'half'.
289.24	brimming over with] *interlined above deleted* 'venting a great deal o'.
289.28	made] *written over wiped-out* '[ ]ing'.
289.35	our] 'ou' *written over wiped-out doubtful* 'lit'.
290.2	get] *interlined above* 'get' *written over doubtful* 'go'.
290.23	he] *written over wiped-out* 'as'.
290.27	scamp] *written over wiped-out* 'rogue'.
291.8–9	"Poor business! . . . business!"] *interlined.*
291.16	tidbit] 'd' *altered from* 't'.
291.36	curtain] *a following comma has been wiped out.*
292.14	Old] 'O' *mended from* 'o'.
292.15	I've] 've' *written over wiped-out* 'm'.
292.20	tidbit] 'd' *altered from* 't'.
293.29	no] *written over wiped-out* 'only'.
293.31–32	little enchantments] 'little enc' *written over wiped-out doubtful* 'fables, wh'.
294.21	observer—] *dash written over an original comma.*
294.24	-performer] *written over wiped-out* 'music'.
294.29	tossing] 'toss' *written over wiped-out* 'drop'.
294.33	It would] *written over wiped-out* 'the grinding' *and the preceding period altered from a semicolon.*
294.34–295.1	(who . . . mood)] *the parentheses written over commas.*
294.35	have] *interlined with a caret.*
295.13	young] *written over wiped-out* 'little'.
295.24	perceiving] 'per' *written over wiped-out* 'see'.
295.30	not] *interlined with a caret.*
295.32	the Judge's] *interlined above deleted* 'his'.
296.5	has] 's' *perhaps written over a wiped-out* 'd'.
296.7	tricks.] *the period was added after the deletion of following* 'again.'
296.8	having got] 'ing' *is an addition;* 'got' *is interlined above deleted* 'running'.
296.15	Well!] *the exclamation mark is added.*
296.26–27	diffused about] *interlined above* 'diffused about' *written over wiped-out* '[ ]ding ab'.
296.27	no] *interlined with a caret.*
296.32	the unreal] 'the un' *written over wiped-out* 'th[ ] s[ ]' *and finally* 'unreal' *interlined for clarity.*

297.4	race] *interlined above deleted* 'run'.
297.4	the mansion] *interlined with a caret above deleted* 'it'.
297.16	suspect] *interlined above deleted* 'know'.
298.9	movement] 'm' *written over wiped-out* 'ga'.
298.15	Phoebe] 'Pho' *written over wiped-out* 'she'.
298.18	mouth-] 'mo' *written over wiped-out* 'full'.
298.19	Phoebe!] *exclamation mark mended from a comma.*
298.33	her] *interlined with a caret.*
299.7	Well] 'W' *written over wiped-out* 'w'.
299.8	made] 'm' *written over wiped-out* 'f'.
299.22	within] 'within' *seems to have been written over some wiped-out word and then* 'inside' *interlined but then wiped out.*
300.2	bedimmed] *interlined with a caret.*
300.5	hand] *written over wiped-out* 'grasping'.
300.7	imparting] 'im' *mended from* 'em'.
300.14–15	warm hand with] *interlined above deleted* 'two warm hands—' *which had been preceded by wiped-out* 'their' *over which* 'a' *was written.*
300.21	conscious] *interlined with a caret.*
301.2	the] *written over wiped-out* 'his'.
301.3	by] *written over wiped-out* 'wh'.
301.13	Phoebe!] *the exclamation mark mended from a comma.*
301.26	undoubtingly] *interlined above deleted* 'stedfastly'.
302.7	-balancing] 'balanc' *written over wiped-out* 's[ ]'.
302.9	yesterday] 'y' *written over wiped-out* 'th'.
302.25	miniature.] *interlined with a caret.*
303.7	part] *written over wiped-out* 'region'.
304.6	the matter] 'th' *written over wiped-out* 'f'.
304.9	has been] *interlined with a caret above deleted* 'is'.
304.16	similarity] *interlined above* 'similarity' *written over wiped-out* 'coincidence'.
304.19	unnecessary] 'unnec' *written over wiped-out* 'not nec'.
304.30	seems] *followed by deleted* 'like'.
304.30	upon] *followed by deleted* 'upon'.
304.34	Judge's] *interlined above deleted* 'cousin's'; *the preceding* 'the' *is written over original* 'his'.

305.13   in the wind] *interlined with a caret.*

305.18   so long] *written over wiped-out* 'while it'.

305.22   widely sundered] *interlined with a caret above deleted* 'severed'.

305.24   two children] 'two child' *written over wiped-out* 'children'.

306.3   replied] 'rep' *written over wiped-out* 'said'.

307.17   were conscious] 'were' *interlined above* 'were con' *written over wiped-out* 'transfigur'.

307.21   in its] *interlined above deleted* 'like a'.

308.3   the gait] *interlined with a caret above deleted* 'those'.

308.29   Ah!] *the exclamation point written over a dash.*

311.1   so to account] *interlined above* 'so to account' *written over wiped-out* 'to account for'.

311.17–18   old bachelor's] *interlined above deleted* 'uncle's'.

311.27   old bachelor] *interlined with a caret.*

312.6   of the] *written over wiped-out* 'that'.

312.30   aside] *interlined with a caret above deleted* 'away'.

312.33   We leave] *preceding is deleted* 'It was now far too late'.

312.33   styled] *written over wiped-out doubtful* 'called'.

313.16   the calm of] 'the' *and* 'of' *interlined with carets.*

314.4   recovered] *written over wiped-out* 'retrieved'; *less certainly, the excised word may be* 'retained'.

314.6   was] *interlined above* 'was' *written over wiped-out* 'had'.

314.30   have] *interlined with a caret; the preceding* 'not' *is mended.*

315.33   picture] *interlined above deleted* 'portrait'.

317.3   patched] *interlined above* 'patched' *written over wiped-out* 'old [   ]'.

317.14   good] 'goo' *written over wiped-out* 'Unc'.

318.3   russet—] *the dash written over a comma.*

318.4   that] *written over wiped-out* 'which'.

318.35   will] *written over wiped-out* 'course'.

319.10   wise] *written over wiped-out* 'good'.

COMPOSITORIAL STINTS
IN THE FIRST EDITION OF 1851

(NOTE: This table gives the facts about the compositorial stints from the start of one signed paragraph to the next paragraph marked by a compositorial signature. The items are, in order: (a) name, (b) Centenary page-line references, (c) within square brackets the first and last words of the stint, (d) the manuscript folio references (the take will usually be one less), (e) the page-line references of the first edition, and (f) within parentheses the number of lines of type in the stint.)

Emery	1.1–3.30	[When . . . 1851.] MS π1–3. I, iii–vi (83)
Emery	5.1–6.12	[Half-way . . . shall] MS 1. I, 9.1–10.14 (34)
Letts	6.12–10.11	[commence . . . there.] MS 1–4. I, 10.15–14.20 (142)
Fox	10.12–12.34	[The . . . build.] MS 4–6. I, 14.21–17.13 (96)
Whittle	12.35–16.6	[One . . . drink!"] MS 6–8. I, 17.14–20.25 (113)
Willis	16.7–19.26	[Thus . . . themselves.] MS 8–10. I, 20.26–24.19 (130)
Fox	19.27–23.31	[In . . . representative.] MS 10–13. I, 24.20–28.33 (150)
Letts	23.32–26.30	[This . . . fabulous.] MS 13–15. I, 28.34–32.6 (109)
Willis	26.31–29.27	[A . . . narrative.] MS 15–17. I, 32.7–35.9 (105)

King	30.1–33.16	[It . . . chair.] MS 17–19. I, 36.1–39.20 (115)
Whittle	33.17–36.12	[As . . . Tophet.] MS 19–21. I, 39.21–42.22 (104)
King	36.13–38.28	[In . . . cent-shop!] MS 21–23. I, 42.23–45.7 (87)
Letts	38.29–41.27	[This . . . sordid.] MS 23–25. I, 45.8–48.15 (110)
Willis	42.1–45.6	[Miss . . . with!"] MS 25–27. I, 49.1–52.8 (103)
Whittle	45.7–48.24	["It . . . hallucination.] MS 27–29. I, 52.9–55.33 (127)
Fox	48.25–51.2	[Some . . . Crow!"] MS 29–31. I, 55.34–58.19 (87)
Loring	51.3–53.34	["Well . . . rebuke.] MS 31–33. I, 58.20–61.24 (106)
Fox	53.35–57.7	["A . . . gold.] MS 33–35. I, 61.25–65.5 (99)
King	57.8–59.28	[In . . . sane.] MS 35–36. I, 65.6–67.31 (93)
Letts	59.29–62.26	[By . . . up."] MS 37–39. I, 67.32–71.2 (106)
Loring	62.27–65.30	["Oh . . . capacity.] MS 39–41. I, 71.3–74.13 (111)
Jackman	65.31–71.30	["Give . . . chamber.] MS 41–45. I, 74.14–80.26 (200)
Letts	71.31–74.13	[Little . . . suppose."] MS 45–46. I, 80.27–83.14 (90)
Fox	74.14–77.12	["You . . . breaking!"] MS 47–49. I, 83.15–86.20 (108)
King	77.13–79.33	[The . . . affection:—] MS 49–51. I, 86.21–89.13 (95)
Fox	79.34–82.27	["What . . . Phoebe.] MS 51–53. I, 89.14–92.14 (103)
Loring	82.28–85.7	[The . . . do."] MS 53–55. I, 92.15–95.3 (91)
Letts	85.8–88.22	["But . . . channel.] MS 55–57. I, 95.4–98.21 (89)
Jackman	88.23–91.11	[Nor . . . productions?"] MS 57–59. I, 98.22–101.15 (96)
King	91.12–93.35	["A . . . -system."] MS 59–60. I, 101.16–104.11 (98)
Letts	93.36–96.29	[Silently . . . glad!"] MS 61–62. I, 104.12–107.12 (103)

Fox	96.30–101.10	[She . . . appetite.] MS 63–65. I, 107.13–111.11 (115)
King	101.11–103.20	[By . . . entrance.] MS 65–67. I, 111.12–113.25 (82)
Fox	103.21–106.15	["Dear . . . it.] MS 67–69. I, 113.26–116.26 (102)
Jackman	106.16–109.24	[Hepzibah . . . it.] MS 69–71. I, 116.27–120.10 (120)
King	109.25–114.8	[The . . . there.] MS 71–75. I, 120.11–125.12 (170)
Fox	115.1–119.25	[Phoebe . . . posterity.] MS 75–79. I, 126.1–130.31 (160)
Henderson	119.26–123.15	[But . . . master.] MS 79–82. I, 130.32–134.28 (133)
Jackman	123.16–126.10	[But . . . notice!"] MS 82–84. I, 134.29–137.30 (104)
Willis	126.11–128.31	[But . . . command."] MS 84–86. I, 137.31–140.26 (97)
Henderson	128.32–132.5	["It . . . poison.] MS 86–88. I, 140.27–144.5 (113)
Jackman	133.1–136.9	[Truly . . . anxiety.] MS 88–91. I, 145.1–148.10 (105)
King	136.10–138.33	[To . . . knee.] MS 91–93. I, 148.11–151.4 (96)
Loring	138.34–141.9	[It . . . delusion.] MS 93–95. I, 151.5–153.18 (82)
Fox	141.10–143.28	[By . . . her.] MS 95–97. I, 153.19–156.7 (91)
Willis	143.29–146.17	[Yet . . . -sorrows?] MS 97–99. I, 156.8–159.14 (80)
Fox	146.18–149.7	[With . . . return.] MS 99–101. I, 159.15–162.10 (98)
Willis	149.8–152.13	[Then . . . did.] MS 101–3. I, 162.11–165.22 (114)
Letts	152.14–154.19	[Phoebe . . . fate.] MS 103–5. I, 165.23–167.32 (78)
Loring	154.20–157.9	[On . . . studio.] MS 105–7. I, 167.33–170.28 (98)
King	157.10–160.4	[Clifford . . . girl!] MS 107–9. I, 170.29–172.28 (67)
Jackman	160.5–162.21	[If . . . -lanes.] MS 109–11. I, 173.1–175.20 (89)
Letts	162.22–165.34	[But . . . sympathies.] MS 111–13. I, 175.21–179.8 (124)

Henderson	165.35–167.25	[So . . . prayer.] MS 113–15. I, 179.9–181.4 (64)
King	167.26–170.34	[Clifford . . . then.] MS 115–17. I, 181.5–184.23 (121)
Loring	170.35–174.6	[Thus . . . evening.] MS 117–19. I, 184.24–188.3 (85)
Henderson	174.7–175.35	[This . . . way.] MS 119–21. I, 188.4–190.2 (66)
Fox	176.1–178.13	[The . . . within?"] MS 121–22. I, 190.3–192.20 (86)
Jackman	178.14–181.13	["I . . . land.] MS 123–25. I, 192.21–195.28 (109)
Willis	181.14–183.24	[His . . . gables!"] MS 125–27. I, 195.29–198.9 (83)
Fox	183.25–186.8	["And . . . method of] MS 127–29. I, 198.10–200.34 (93)
Henderson	186.8–189.23	[throwing . . . been!] MS 129–31. I, 201.1–204.24 (104)
Willis	189.24–191.24	[Now . . . ones.] MS 131–32. I, 204.25–206.29 (73)
Letts	191.25–194.12	[There . . . other.] MS 133–35. I, 206.30–209.22 (95)
King	194.13–197.3	[The . . . table.] MS 135–37. I, 209.23–212.20 (100)
Loring	197.4–199.21	[Matthew . . . own!"] MS 137–39. I, 212.21–215.8 (89)
Letts	199.22–202.22	[According . . . off."] MS 139–41. I, 215.9–218.13 (107)
Jackman	202.23–204.31	["Mistress . . . spoke.] MS 141–42. I, 218.14–220.28 (83)
Fox	204.32–207.22	["Behold . . . stain!] MS 143–45. I, 220.29–223.27 (101)
King	207.23–210.4	[At . . . more!] MS 145–47. I, 223.28–226.16 (90)
Loring	210.5–213.24	[The . . . glimmer.] MS 147–49. I, 226.17–229.26 (95)
Jackman	213.25–216.2	[So . . . here."] MS 149–50. I, 229.27–232.9 (85)
Fox	216.3–218.20	["You . . . ever!"] MS 151–53. I, 232.10–235.2 (95)
Letts	218.21–221.8	["Then . . . him.] MS 153–55. I, 235.3–237.32 (97)
Henderson	221.9–226.8	["We . . . excited.] MS 155–58. I, 237.33–242.11 (137)

Jackman	226.9–228.12	[Hepzibah's . . . you!"] MS 158–60. I, 242.12–244.22 (77)
Fox	228.13–231.25	[For . . . there"?] MS 160–62. I, 244.23–248.11 (121)
King	231.26–234.14	[And . . . it."] MS 162–65. I, 248.12–251.8 (96)
Letts	234.15–236.27	["And . . . it."] MS 165–66. I, 251.9–253.30 (88)
Loring	236.28–239.6	["Oh . . . Clifford.] MS 167–68. I, 253.31–256.18 (87)
Henderson	240.1–243.5	[Never . . . so!] MS 169–71. I, 257.1–260.8 (100)
Fox	243.6–245.9	[For . . . enemy.] MS 171–73. I, 260.9–262.19 (77)
Jackman	245.10–247.14	[Returning . . . window.] MS 173–75. I, 262.20–264.33 (80)
Henderson	247.15–249.35	[But . . . mind.] MS 175–77. I, 265.1–267.29 (95)
Fox	250.1–251.32	["Be . . . room.] MS 177–79. I, 267.30–270.2 (72)
Jackman	251.33–255.14	["What . . . gone.] MS 179–81. I, 270.3–273.15 (90)
Henderson	255.15–257.29	[Poor . . . itself!] MS 181–83. I, 273.16–276.6 (90)
Letts	257.30–259.20	[Clifford's . . . better."] MS 183–85. I, 276.7–278.5 (65)
King	259.21–261.34	["In . . . enjoy!"] MS 185–87. I, 278.6–280.28 (89)
Fox	262.1–263.32	[His . . . gentleman.] MS 187–88. I, 280.29–282.30 (68)
Willis	263.33–266.3	["These . . . next!"] MS 189–91. I, 282.31–285.12 (80)
Fox	266.4–269.11	[Just . . . asleep.] MS 191–92. I, 285.13–288.9 (76)
Loring	269.12–271.21	[It . . . occasion?] MS 193–94. I, 288.10–290.26 (83)
Letts	271.22–274.1	[The . . . Pyncheon?] MS 195–97. I, 290.27–293.16 (89)
Jackman	274.2–276.3	[Alas . . . veins.] MS 197–99. I, 293.17–295.26 (76)
Henderson	276.4–278.21	[Up . . . midnight.] MS 199–201. I, 295.27–298.15 (88)
King	278.22–280.12	[A . . . laughter.] MS 201–3. I, 298.16–300.14 (65)

Willis	280.13–283.3	[Indulging . . . being.] MS 203–5. I, 300.15–303.17 (102)
Jackman	283.4–286.3	[Rise . . . day.] MS 205–7. I, 303.18–307.4 (89)
Henderson	286.4–287.24	[One . . . night?"] MS 207–8. I, 307.5–308.30 (59)
Fox	287.25–290.14	["It . . . closed.] MS 209–11. I, 308.31–311.31 (99)
King	290.15–292.13	["Miss . . . withdraw.] MS 211–13. I, 311.32–314.6 (74)
Letts	292.14–294.30	["So . . . up?] MS 213–15. I, 314.7–316.28 (88)
Loring	294.31–297.4	[But . . . speed.] MS 215–17. I, 316.29–319.12 (83)
Henderson	297.5–299.15	[It . . . there.] MS 217–18. I, 319.13–321.29 (83)
King	299.16–301.35	[The . . . happened!"] MS 219–21. I, 321.30–325.2 (79)
Willis	301.36–304.22	["You . . . hands."] MS 221–23. I, 325.3–327.31 (95)
Fox	304.23–306.23	["Whence . . . happy."] MS 223–25. I, 327.32–330.8 (75)
Henderson	306.24–308.28	["You . . . two.] MS 225–27. I, 330.9–332.23 (80)
Letts	308.29–311.7	["It . . . shut.] MS 227–29. I, 332.24–335.9 (75)
Fox	311.8–313.7	[According . . . Holgrave!] MS 229–31. I, 335.10–337.15 (72)
King	313.8–315.14	[It . . . race."] MS 231–33. I, 337.16–339.28 (79)
Letts	315.15–317.28	["That . . . which!"] MS 233–35. I, 339.29–342.16 (87)
Willis	317.29–319.17	["Oh . . . End.] MS 235–37. I, 342.17–344.13 (62)

THE CENTENARY TEXTS:
EDITORIAL PRINCIPLES

T HE CENTENARY EDITION of Hawthorne provides for the first time established texts of the romances, tales, and associated shorter works. The general procedures governing this establishment are outlined here, whereas the specific problems for each text are treated in the separate Textual Introductions.

The text itself is a critical unmodernized reconstruction. It is critical in that it is not necessarily an exact reprint of any individual document: the print or manuscript chosen as copy-text (i.e., as the basis for this edition) may be emended by reference to other authorities or by editorial decision. The Centenary text, in short, has been established by the application of bibliographical and analytical criticism to the evidence of the various early documentary forms in which the text has appeared.[1] It is unmodernized in that every effort has been made to present the text in as close a form to Hawthorne's own inscription as the surviving documents for each work permit of such reconstruction, subject to normal editorial procedure.

The first step in the establishment of a critical text is the determination of the exact forms of the texts in the early docu-

---

[1] Various terms used here are discussed at length in Fredson Bowers, "Established Texts and Definitive Editions," *Philological Quarterly*, XLI (1962), 1-17.

ments and of the facts about their relationship to one another. When manuscripts are extant, the establishment of the texts of these documents involves the checking of the written form of all words and the determination of the texture of their spelling, capitalization, word-division, and punctuation, i.e., the "accidentals" of a text as distinguished from its "substantives," or the forms of the words as distinguished from the words themselves. Any manuscript alteration of the initial inscription is noticed, and whenever possible the author's rejected forms are reconstructed from the available evidence and recorded.

Since the first editions printed from Hawthorne's preserved manuscripts have a supplementary authority, the duty is placed on an editor to identify and analyze any variation in the readings of the printed texts that have primary or supplementary authority. To this end a number of copies of the first—and of any other edition possessing authority—have been mechanically compared for variation on the Hinman Collating Machine. Previously unknown differences that developed in the text during the course of printing have been discovered by this process, as well as such major variation within editions as the duplicate typesetting of the last gathering of the first and of the preliminary gathering of the second edition of *The Scarlet Letter*. Although it is too much to hope that every minor variant in an impression has been discovered by the extensive multiple collation, one can state with some confidence that the majority have probably been noticed; unknown major variation, at least, is not likely to exist in unseen copies of the editions examined by this method. Hence, the readings of the text in the authoritative documents, even in relatively minor respects of form, have been substantially established from the evidence of the machine comparison by superimposition of a number of exemplars, letter for letter and word for word.

The forms of other editions chosen for examination have

also been established by multiple collation of copies on the Hinman Machine. Technically, an edition comprises a particular typesetting, without regard for the number of different printings made at various times from this typesetting or its plates.[2] Since most Hawthorne book editions after the first (and often the first, too) were printed from stereotype plates, the history of the usual edition is the history of the textual variation in its set of plates throughout the various printings. Plates were occasionally altered between impressions, at times to correct errors in the edition-typesetting, at times to incorporate editorial normalizations and fancied improvements, and at times to repair plate damage caused by handling accidents and normal wear on the press. Therefore, in order to establish the exact forms of the editions (in respect to the history of their plates), the first impression from the plates of any edition-typesetting has been compared on the Hinman Machine against the last ascertained impression (in the Boston line of publication), and those variants affecting substantives have been recorded as between the early and late states of the plates. However, only when changes in plates were made before 1865 (Hawthorne died in 1864) have the individual variants been tracked down through the intermediate impressions in order to establish the dates of their first appearances. Finally, no attempt has been made to record variation in the plates in respect to non-verbal alteration. In punctuation readings, for instance, actual alterations are often impossible to distinguish from anomalies caused by plate wear and damage; moreover, for the purposes of the present edition non-verbal variants in unauthoritative prints have no textual significance, interesting as they might prove to a historian of printing practice.

Following the establishment of the variant documentary

[2] In the Centenary Edition the use of the bibliographical terms "edition," "impression" (or "printing"), "issue," and "state" follows that recommended in Fredson Bowers, *Principles of Bibliographical Description* (Princeton, 1949), pp. 379-426.

forms of all editions chosen as significant in the history of Hawthorne's text, these different edition-typesettings have been individually hand-collated against the first edition; and all substantive, or word, variants recorded, as well as such occasional variants among the accidentals as might bear on the question of the authority of any of the documents by which the texts were transmitted. From this evidence, printed in the Historical Collation appended to each edited work, the line of textual transmission can be traced from document to document and the general authority of each edition can thus be determined. This evidence, also, determines in large part the specific authority of any document, since bibliographical and critical analysis of the textual variants has demonstrated which are mere reprint editions—that is, editions in which the cumulative transmitted error was never corrected systematically but, instead, largely by chance. Evidence of this nature indicates that no comparison of the printer's copy had been made against any authoritative document, and thus that the various alterations observed (when not mechanical corrections) were in their turn corruptions and could not represent, in some manner, an editorial return to a purer version of the text.

On internal evidence like this, combined sometimes with external evidence, one can determine, usually with precision, the printed texts that have Hawthorne's immediate authority as against the number that are simply derived reprints without authority. In this connection, authority is defined as resident in any document printed directly from a Hawthorne manuscript or from some other document, such as another edition, that had been corrected or revised by Hawthorne or by some other person utilizing a Hawthorne manuscript. Such authoritative texts are called substantive, as contrasted with derived. Only substantive texts have been used as documentary sources of revisory emendation, although occasional correction may be drawn, for convenience, from derived editions.

After the derived reprints have been isolated, the next step in the editorial process is the selection of the copy-text from among the established substantive texts. In practice, the selection may differ from literary work to literary work according to the distinctive conditions, but the theory is firm: whenever practicable the copy-text selected is that form of the text, no matter how it may subsequently have been revised, that is nearest to the primary authority of Hawthorne's manuscript.

Obviously, when the manuscript is no longer in existence, the copy-text must be the first printed edition that was set directly from such a manuscript, since only this edition can preserve in any authoritative form such characteristics of the manuscript as have escaped the normalization of printing-house style imposed on the copy. If Hawthorne never intervened to revise or correct this text in any subsequent edition, the first edition remains the sole authority. However, if—as happened in *The Marble Faun*—Hawthorne did introduce corrections and revisions to a later edition (the first American edition, typeset from corrected sheets of the first English edition), the claims of more than the single, or copy-text authority must be considered.

The editorial procedure in such cases follows the principles laid down by Sir Walter Greg.[8] That is, a double authority is recognized. The copy-text remains the supreme authority for the accidentals, since it alone was set directly from Hawthorne's manuscript. On the other hand, the substantive variants in other texts not thought to be printer's errors must be taken to represent Hawthorne's revisions, and to these must be added such alterations in the accidentals as appear to derive from the author, although this last is a much more difficult matter to determine. Hence the resulting critical Centenary text will incorporate in the first-edition copy-text such variants

[8] "The Rationale of Copy-Text," *Studies in Bibliography*, III (1950-51), 19-36. See also Fredson Bowers, "Current Theories of Copy-Text," *Modern Philology*, XLVIII (1950), 12-20.

from later demonstrably authoritative editions as pass the editorial tests for authorial alterations. In effect this procedure attempts to reproduce the lost marked-up printer's copy that Hawthorne furnished for the revised text, and in this reconstruction to filter out the unauthorized printing-house variants that creep into any reprint and are thus found in the printed form even of a revised edition. Despite the fact that he "accepted" them (provided he read the proof for a revised edition), Hawthorne did not authorize these printing-house variants; hence they can have no place in the pure text that the Centenary Edition endeavors to establish.

Correspondingly, when Hawthorne's manuscript of a work has been preserved, this manuscript becomes the copy-text. In each case this manuscript has been collated against the first printed edition and all details of substantive variance have been recorded. However, the printing-house style imposed on the authoritative manuscript has been rejected except for necessary corrections,[4] and only those variants from the manuscript in substantives or in accidentals that appear to have been inserted by Hawthorne in the proof have been accepted and incorporated in the critical text. Thereafter, the determination of the history of the text and of the authority of all variants in editions after the first follows the regular procedures outlined above.

Hawthorne's shorter works that might have been published in periodical and gift-book form several times before collection present a special problem. In general, the Greg theory of copy-text holds, and an attempt has been made to separate the authority of the substantives from that of the accidentals in the different versions of the text and thus to establish the

[4] When in such a text as *The House of the Seven Gables* the printer of the first edition made on an average about fifteen alterations per page in conformity with house style, the cumulative effect on Hawthorne's own modes of expression as seen in the manuscript is very serious indeed. Only the manuscript contains the full record of the subtleties of Hawthorne's parenthetical expression and emphasis.

most authoritative form of each in a critical text that may fairly be said to synthesize the most authoritative versions. Only when one can determine that a later edition was set from an independent manuscript (not from marked-up copy of an earlier print) or was so thoroughly revised from printed sheets as to make distinction impossible between Hawthorne's and the printer's alterations, has the copy-text been shifted from the earliest printing from manuscript to a later substantive edition.

To repeat, the purpose of the Centenary Edition is to establish the text in as close a form, in all details, to Hawthorne's final intentions as the preserved documents of each separate work permit. This aim compels the editors to treat each work as a unit, with its own separate textual problems. That is, no attempt is made between texts to secure a uniformity of style that is not authorized from those documents for the texts in question that establish their most authoritative preserved forms. It follows that the texture of accidentals in a work like *The House of the Seven Gables,* established from authorial manuscript, will differ from that in a work like *The Scarlet Letter,* established from the first printed edition.

In the latter, the printing-house style imposed on the text removes it in various respects from conformity with Hawthorne's known practices in spelling, punctuation, capitalization, and word-division as seen in his manuscripts of about the same date. One might be able to alter some of these forms in *The Scarlet Letter* to bring the critical text, in theory, into a closer relationship with what one may reasonably suppose to have been certain of the details of the lost manuscript. But interesting as such an experiment might be, the result could never be wholly consistent and could not lead to any demonstrably established form of the text. Hence, each work in the Centenary Edition rests as a separate unit on the evidence of its own preserved documents, and represents a faithfulness to Hawthorne's full intentions in varying degrees of exactitude according to the authority of this evidence.

Editorial treatment of the text, then, is primarily concerned with synthesizing the evidence of all manuscripts and authoritative printed editions in order to arrive at Hawthorne's detailed final intentions as nearly as may be determined from the documents. In this situation any alteration believed to be Hawthorne's must be adopted, regardless of critical estimate of its literary worth, although, of course, an editor's literary judgment is one of the various criteria that operate to establish any alteration as a Hawthorne variant instead of the printer's. On the other hand, not all Hawthorne revisions are literary in their nature. When Hawthorne softened his original satire, or excised sections for personal reasons as with the passage on saloons in *The Blithedale Romance* revised in the print, presumably in deference to his wife's prejudices, the unrevised version has been retained in the established text as more faithfully representing Hawthorne's true intentions than the results of censorship even though self-imposed.

Revision of the copy-text, therefore, can be admitted only from the evidence of authoritative documents. On the other hand, correction may be drawn from any source, whether a substantive or reprint edition, or from independent editorial judgment. Indeed, no correction from an unauthoritative document can have any more validity than editorial correction; hence reprint editions are noted as sources for emendation only as a convenience and not because there is any secondary value in the fact that the chosen emendation first originated in them.

Editorial correction is of five kinds. First, since Hawthorne appears to have been a rapid and far from accurate proofreader,[5] he did not catch in proof all of the printer's errors

---

[5] For some information on this and other matters affecting the text, see Fredson Bowers, "Hawthorne's Text," in *Hawthorne Centenary Essays*, ed. Roy Harvey Pearce (Columbus, O., 1964), pp. 401-25.

that manifestly need setting right; hence some substantive emendation has proved necessary.

Second, inconsistencies may be present in the manuscripts in respect to spelling, capitalization, and division of words that were regularized in the prints. Such regularization of a manuscript has generally been accepted when the printer's version appears to coincide with Hawthorne's usual practice; however, if the print regularizes anomalies in opposition to Hawthorne's more habitual practice, or else fails to normalize an irregularity, independent emendation has been admitted.

Third, if Hawthorne's own usual practice cannot be determined (as in his frequent undifferentiated use of "subtle" and "subtile" and sometimes of "farther" and "further"), the variant forms are retained in the established text unless normalization seems justified on the authority of the dictionary that Hawthorne used—*A New Critical Pronouncing Dictionary of the English Language . . . By an American Gentleman* (Burlington, N. J.: Allinson, 1813).[6]

Fourth, whereas all characteristic spellings are followed in our unmodernized text when they are acceptable variants of more common forms and are regular in the literary text in question, misspellings, like Hawthorne's habitual manuscript "cieling", are always corrected.

Fifth, word-division is regularized according to the practice in the most authoritative documents for each text. If the matter is in doubt within a given text, the form has been adopted that agrees with parallels within the text or that is most characteristic of manuscripts closest in date to the print. When in the original documents a possible compound is hyphenated at the break between two lines, the editorial decision whether to establish the word in the Centenary Edition as a hyphenated compound or as a single word conforms to the same principle.

[6] This Hawthorne family dictionary was identified and described in Carroll A. Wilson, *Thirteen Author Collections of the Nineteenth Century and Five Centuries of Familiar Quotations,* ed. Jean C. S. Wilson and David A. Randall (New York, 1950), I, 154.

No attempt has been made in the Centenary Edition to reproduce the typographical details of the original documents such as the lineation, the number of lines of indentation for display capitals and the number of capitalized text-letters following them, or the capitals or lower-case in running-titles and chapter headings. For instance, the customary periods after running-titles, and chapter numbers and headings, have been omitted, and old-fashioned wide spacing like "I 'll" or "that 's" (not always uniform in Hawthorne's manuscripts) has been ignored. Although the text has been scrupulously treated, its appurtenances have been modernized.

In every other respect, however, the Centenary Edition reproduces the features of the copy-text or else notes an alteration. No variation of any kind from the copy-text (other than those enumerated above) has gone unreported; hence, the interested reader at any point can reconstruct the copy-text from the Centenary print in tandem with its records of emendation. These records are contained in an appendix to each literary work, where specialists may consult the details at leisure. The basis for the record is the page and line number in the Centenary text; *viz.*, 42.15 means page 42, line 15.

The usual textual appendix contains the following sections:

Textual Notes: Whenever an emendation of the copy-text, or a refusal to emend, seems to require special notice, a brief comment upon the reading is provided.

Editorial Emendations: All alterations to the copy-text made in the present edition are recorded, together with the immediate source of the approved reading, always the first appearance of the emendation in the editions consulted in the preparation of the particular text. Since the purpose of this emendations list is to present at a view only the departures from the copy-text, and the origin for each reading of the correction or revision, the history of the copy-text reading up to the point of emendation is provided, but not its subsequent history. For substantives, this last can be found in the Historical Collation.

The basic note provides, first, the precise form of the emended reading in the Centenary text. Following the square bracket appears the identification of the earliest source of the emendation in the editions collated. A semicolon succeeds this notation, and following this appears the rejected copy-text reading with the sigla of editions that provide its history up to the point of emendation. In these notations certain arbitrary symbols appear. When the variant to be noted is one of punctuation, a wavy dash ⁓ takes the place of the repeated word associated with the pointing. An inferior caret ∧ calls attention to the absence of punctuation either in the copy-text or in the early edition from which the alteration was drawn. Three dots indicate one or more omitted words in a series. The sigla for denoting the editions recorded are explained in the Textual Introduction for each work. In general, editions listed by their dates are those set from type, whereas roman numbers are used to identify the stereotype plates first put into use from a new typesetting in the listed edition. If a second edition were printed in the same year from a different setting of type, the two would be differentiated as in 1850^1 and 1850^2. All editions are American unless otherwise noted. English editions are identified as E. The notation (r) indicates reset type, and (s) standing type. Unless specifically excepted, the reading listed as originating in a plated edition comes from the original state of the plates and is constant in all recorded impressions made from these plates. An emendation assigned to CENTENARY is made for the first time in the present edition if by "the first time" is understood "the first time in respect to the listed editions chosen for collation."

The following examples are from *The Scarlet Letter*:

133.33   broad,] E, III; ⁓ ∧ $1850^{1-2(r)}$

Here the copy-text first edition in 1850 (1850[1]) places no punctuation after "broad", and the lack of punctuation is followed in the second edition of 1850, this reading occurring in one of the reset pages. The necessary comma, adopted in the Centenary text, was first inserted in the third American edition, printed from plates 1850; and it is also found in the first English edition of 1851. Since this English edition was set from a copy of 1850[2] independently, its sigla are placed for convenience before that of III in order not to interrupt the sequence of American plated editions beginning with III.

> *262.25   sombre-hued] CENTENARY; sobre-hued 1850[1-2(s)],
> E, L; sober-hued III–VII

In the above the Centenary original emendation of "sombre-" substitutes for the copy-text (1850[1]) misprint "sobre-" followed in the standing type of the second edition (1850[2]), by the first English edition, and by the Levin 1960 Riverside paperback, but sophisticated to "sober-" in the third edition (III) and repeated in this form by all subsequent texts collated, including the 1900 Autograph Edition (VII). The asterisk preceding the reference indicates that a Textual Note discusses this reading. Discussion of a reading that has not been emended is indicated in the emendations list as in the following, with the editions noted in which the unemended reading appears:

> *221.29   such personage] stet 1850[1]–III

Word-Division: Hyphenation of a possible compound at the end of a line in the Centenary Edition poses a problem for the reader as to the exact form in the copy-text. Moreover, end-of-the-line hyphenation in the copy-text itself requires editorial decision whether the reading should be reproduced in the Centenary text as one word or as a hyphenated compound. This double problem is faced in the appendix section on Word-Division, which is designed to record all the essential facts about the forms of possible compounds both in the Centenary and in the copy-text.

No hyphen at the end of a line in the Centenary text is present in the copy-text unless listed in this section of the apparatus, as in the form:

6.21   grizzly-|bearded

This notation indicates that "grizzly-", ending the line in the Centenary Edition, page 6, line 21, is printed as part of a hyphenated compound within the line in the copy-text.

Since many hyphens ending lines in the copy-text may actually break an original hyphenated compound, not just the syllables of a single word, the second part of this appendix section lists all occurrences of established hyphenated compounding and of possible compounding broken at the end of a line in the copy-text itself, except when the hyphen joins capitalized units and there can be no ambiguity. Here the reading is that of the Centenary Edition; whether the compound is hyphenated or unhyphenated in the listing is in accord with the determined practice of the copy-text or (failing this evidence) of the manuscripts closest in date. It is to be understood that each reading was broken in the copy-text at the point of the hyphen, or where one would normally have occurred if the compound had been hyphenated.

3.18   lifemates
7.21   slop-sellers

Here the copy-text readings were, respectively, "life-|mates" and "slop-|sellers".

The third section lists those rarer examples when, by chance, the same compound reading is broken at the hyphenation in both the copy-text and the Centenary Edition. Within parentheses, the established correct form is thereupon provided for the information of the reader.

These precautions being observed, anyone may transcribe a passage from the Centenary Edition with no ambiguity about word-division in the copy-text.

Historical Collation: A list is provided of all substantive variants from the Centenary text in the editions chosen for collation. Variant readings in the accidentals are ignored because of their copiousness and their basic lack of significance save when they affect the sense in a substantive manner and thus qualify for listing, or for some special reason in connection with the tracing of the family tree of textual derivation. Moreover, the various accidental forms in different editions of a recorded substantive reading are ignored.

The first reading, to the left of the bracket, is that of the Centenary Edition, which will not necessarily be that of the copy-text if emendation has taken place. To the right of the bracket is placed the variant and the sigla for the specific collated editions in which it appears. The reading is that of the Centenary text in any such edition not listed.

21.29   all of his] all his IV–VII

This example from *The Scarlet Letter* signifies that the first three American editions, the first English edition, and the Levin text read with the Centenary Edition "all of his" but that the variant "all his" appears first in the Little Classics Edition of 1875 (IV) and continues through the intervening collated editions, the Red-Line of 1878 (V), the Riverside of 1883 (VI), and the Autograph of 1900 (VII) and all their collated platings.

In this Historical Collation an attempt is made to distinguish the states of the plates of the various editions in respect to substantive readings. Thus in *The Scarlet Letter*, for example,

50.30   They] Thed III[a]

records the fact that the first impression made from the plates
of the third edition, in 1850, misprinted "They" as "Thed" at
page 50, line 30, of the present edition; but that the error was
corrected in the 1851 second impression of these plates.[7] For
each work the special sigla identifying the plates and their
printings are explained in a headnote preceding the Historical
Collation. The entry

26.12   make] made III[e-g]; have made IV–VII

indicates that as part of a repair of the third-edition plates
for the Illustrated Library Edition of 1871 (e), "make" was
inadvertently altered to "made", a reading that was reproduced in the 1876 Illustrated Library Edition state of the
plates (f) and the c. 1880 Globe Edition state (g) including
the last impression of this state to be collated, the undated
(c. 1886) New Fireside Edition. This error was sophisticated
to "have made" when type was set for the Little Classics Edition of 1875, a reading that persisted through the Autograph
typesetting (VII) but not in the Levin text (L).

An attempt is made in this Historical Collation to be complete and accurate in respect to this substantive plate variation in the several editions and their numerous impressions.
Additional plate variants, discovered after a Centenary volume
has gone to press, will be recorded in the Descriptive Bibliography of Hawthorne that will be appended to the Centenary Edition.

Variants in the First Edition: Any differences in the typesetting or plates that appear during the course of printing the
first edition, or any other substantive edition, are recorded
and identified in respect to the collated copies.

[7] If the error had appeared in all the impressions of the third-edition
plates, the notation would read simply: They] Thed III.

Special Lists: Whenever the textual situation warrants the addition of further information than that supplied in the standard sections of the textual appendix, special lists record the necessary data.

For example, in *The Scarlet Letter* the variants in the standing type of the second edition seem to have been ordered by the publisher and not by the author; thus, they have not been regularly incorporated as part of the establishment of the Centenary text. In addition, the variants in the reset pages of the second edition must represent a mixture of printer's divergences from copy and the publisher's markings for alteration similar to those made in standing type. Since a difficult and not wholly demonstrable decision about authority has had to be a matter of editorial judgment, the whole list is provided so that the reader may be in possession of all the evidence in the event that he wishes to make an independent study of the problem.

Also, when the manuscript of a Hawthorne text has been preserved, an appendix list details the facts of revision or alteration in the inscription of this manuscript insofar as recovery can be made from a close examination of the documents.

On the other hand, a full record of the differences between the manuscript and the first edition printed from it would usually run to quite extraordinary length: about five thousand items, for instance, for *The House of the Seven Gables*. As a consequence, the editors' early hope that every variant between the manuscript copy-texts and the initial prints could be recorded has had to be abandoned, regretfully, in respect to the accidentals. However, all substantive variation will be found recorded in the Historical Collation for such works, with the Editorial Emendations list indicating those readings in which the manuscript copy-text has been altered by reference to a variant in the prints.

In order to secure a common ground for collation of the different Hawthorne works, the following procedures have been adopted.

Multiple copies (usually eight or more) of the first appearances in print and of any later substantive editions[8] have been mechanically collated on the Hinman Machines at the Ohio State University and the University of Virginia where extensive collections of Hawthorne have been gathered in the Ohio State University Libraries Special Collections and in the University of Virginia's Alderman Library, including the Clifton Waller Barrett Collection.

The establishment of the text has then proceeded by the determination of the family tree and of the authority or non-authority of editions after the first. These facts are recorded in the Historical Collation appended to each work. The following collected editions have always been collated against the copy-text: Little Classics (1875), Riverside (1883), and Autograph (1900). These are the only collected editions in the Boston line of publishers to Houghton Mifflin Company that represent different typesettings.[9]

For each of these editions the latest identified impression

___

[8] Only substantive editions printed from type metal (and hence subject to change during impression) have been collated from multiple copies on the Hinman Machine, for the chances are infinitesimal that the plates of an edition would be altered during the course of an impression of a sheet. Nevertheless, since accidents will happen, the editors have taken certain precautions against such an occurrence, however remote the possibility. When hand collation of the copy-text edition is made against later editions for the record of the Historical Collation, different copies of the primary edition are used as the basis for the comparison of every subsequent edition. In this manner, plate variation if present in the copy-text should be reflected in variant readings of a kind that are automatically checked.

[9] The succession of the publishers is as follows: Allen and Ticknor (1832-34); William D. Ticknor (1834-43); William D. Ticknor and Company (1843-49); Ticknor, Reed, and Fields (1849-54); Ticknor and Fields (1854-68); Fields, Osgood and Company (1868-71); James R. Osgood and Company (1871-78); Houghton, Osgood and Company (1878-80); Houghton, Mifflin and Company (1880-1908); Houghton Mifflin Company (1908——).

made from the edition-plates has been collated on the Hinman Machine against the first impression in order to secure the maximum information about the changes made in the history of the plates. But only the blue-bound form of the Autograph Edition has been collated (not the form with the signed illustrations), and no further account of its plates has been provided beyond this one impression.

Within the limits of the information about impressions available at the time of editing each text, an attempt has been made to identify the exact printing in which each plate-variant originated up to 1865. Thereafter, only the last known impression has been collated against the first, the differences being recorded without specifying the impression in which they originated. *The Scarlet Letter* has been given fuller treatment than other texts, in that plate variation has been identified in specific impressions later than 1865.

As well as the collected editions issued by Hawthorne's Boston publishers and their successors to the present Houghton Mifflin Company, all separate editions representing different typesettings put out by these publishers before 1900, and a few later, have also been collated and their variants noted. For each work the first English edition has also been collated, in part to establish its derivation, and in part to determine whether authoritative alterations were made in the American sheets sent to England to serve as copy. When a work was first published in England, something of the English history of the text has been investigated by collation of later editions; the usual history of the American line of the text has, of course, also been established.

This extensive collation has been carried forward well beyond 1864, the year of Hawthorne's death, in order to insure against the possibility (however faint) that fresh authority has entered a text if it was compared with an authoritative manuscript by some conscientious editor; and partly to provide for its own sake the history of the text, in detail, in the standard editions up to the present.

The textual record is a sad one of pyramiding corruption, sometimes trivial but often serious. Yet occasionally a purpose may be served in this section by demonstrating in detail that the editions commonly used by scholars and critics for analysis and quotation are unreliable. More important, the Historical Collation provides for the reader the total substantive evidence for textual transmission available to the textual editor, who has been chiefly responsible for the establishment of the text. All the cards are on the table, face up.

To insure maximum accuracy, all hand collation of the different typesettings of later editions against the copy-text was duplicated by individual workers at the Ohio State University and the University of Virginia, the results conflated, differences checked, and every variant wherever noted was rechecked through the whole list of editions. This process should have produced exactness of fact unless the collators of an edition at both universities simultaneously passed over a variant unique to that edition, in which case no system of double checking could catch the error. All proofs have been read at least five times and by three or more editors.

F. B.

THE HOUSE OF THE
SEVEN GABLES

Volume II in the Centenary Edition of the Works of Nathaniel Hawthorne.

Published by the Ohio State University Press, Columbus.

The text of the novel is set in eleven-point Fairfield, with Caslon initial capitals. Chapter headings are set in fourteen-point Caledonia capitals.

Composition, presswork, and binding of the first printing by the Heer Printing Company Division of the National Graphics Corporation, Columbus, Ohio. Offset presswork and binding of the second printing by the Benson Printing Company, Inc., Nashville, Tennessee.

Paper for the second printing is seventy-pound Olde Style Antique Wove, manufactured by the S. D. Warren Company, Boston, Massachusetts.

Preliminary pages designed by Turck and Reinfeld, Inc., New York City.

APPENDIX TO THE SECOND PRINTING OF THE CENTENARY EDITION OF *THE HOUSE OF THE SEVEN GABLES*

The following changes in the typesetting of the Centenary Edition of *The House of the Seven Gables* have been made in the second printing (figures in the left-hand column refer to pages):

xxxiv.33	*For* death *read* Death.
xli	*For* ooo *read* xlv *in the last line of the note.*
l.27	*For* 214.27 *read* 214.27–28 (*the first-printing* the *has been dropped*).
liii	*For* Letts (1,742) *read* Letts (1,733) *in the second line of note 23.*
liv.3	*For* 581 *read* 578.
liv.14	*For* 1,742 *read* 1,733.
300.8	*For* indefinable *read* undefinable.
338	*For* half-a-dozen *read* Half-a-dozen *under* 33.7.
342	*For* 181.5 *read* 181.5–6.
344	*Insert* *261.3–4 no woman's eye . . . while it was beautiful!] *stet* MS.
344	*For* by-the-by *read* By-the-by *under* 275.28.
348	*Insert* 151.26 excellencies] excellences I *and* 300.8 undefinable] indefinable I.
349–50	*Add the following to section* 1:
	5.9 Pyncheon-|street
	67.18 half-|a-dozen
	72.16 half-|an-hour
	121.9 weather-|beaten

350   *Delete the two entries under 293.17 and 307.31.*

351   *Add to section 2:* 5.5 Pyncheon-street.

352   *Add the following to section 3(a):*
         6.5   Pyncheon-|house (i.e. Pyncheon-house)
         46.12   half-a-|dozen (i.e. half-a-dozen)

353   *Add the following to section 3(b):*
         48.18   half-a-|lifetime (i.e. half-a-lifetime *for*
                      MS half-a life time)
         231.2   Pyncheon-|bull (i.e. Pyncheon-bull *for*
                      MS Pyncheon bull)
         293.17   door-|step (i.e. door-step *for MS*
                      doorstep)

356   *Add the following:*
         29.18,   shopkeeper] shokeeper MS
         35.31
         43.1   bartering] batering MS
         65.24   chambers] chamber's MS

358   *Insert* 151.26 excellencies] excellences I–V.

360   *Insert* 300.8 undefinable] indefinable I–V.

365   *Under 43.9–10 read:* door-way. Coming] *MS*
         'doorway. Coming' *mended from* 'doorway,
         coming'.

371   *Under 102.1 read:* it were] 'it' *interlined with a caret.*

389   *For 296.26 read 296.26–27.*

390   *Under 304.6 read:* the matter] 'th' *written over
         wiped-out* 'f'.

397   *Under Letts 234.15–236.27 read:* ["And . . . it."]
         MS 165–66. I, 251.9–253.30 (88).

403   *For LXVIII read XLVIII in the last line of note 3.*